How's Life? 2015

MEASURING WELL-BEING

This work is published under the responsibility of the Secretary-General of the OECD. The opinions expressed and arguments employed herein do not necessarily reflect the official views of OECD member countries.

This document and any map included herein are without prejudice to the status of or sovereignty over any territory, to the delimitation of international frontiers and boundaries and to the name of any territory, city or area.

Please cite this publication as:
OECD (2015), *How's Life? 2015: Measuring Well-being*, OECD Publishing, Paris.
http://dx.doi.org/10.1787/how_life-2015-en

ISBN 978-92-64-21101-8 (print)
ISBN 978-92-64-23817-6 (PDF)

Annual:
ISSN 2308-9660 (print)
ISSN 2308-9679 (online)

The statistical data for Israel are supplied by and under the responsibility of the relevant Israeli authorities. The use of such data by the OECD is without prejudice to the status of the Golan Heights, East Jerusalem and Israeli settlements in the West Bank under the terms of international law.

Corrigenda to OECD publications may be found on line at: *www.oecd.org/publishing/corrigenda*.

Foreword

How's Life? is part of the OECD Better Life Initiative, which aims to promote "better policies for better lives", in line with the OECD's overarching mission. It is a statistical report released every two years that documents a wide range of well-being outcomes, and how they vary over time, between population groups, and across countries. This assessment is based on a multi-dimensional framework covering 11 dimensions of well-being, and four different types of resources that help to support well-being over time. Each issue also includes special chapters that provide an in-depth look at specific aspects of well-being. The 2015 edition features a focus on child well-being, the role of volunteering in well-being, and measuring well-being at the regional level.

The report was prepared by the Well-Being and Progress Unit of the OECD Statistics Directorate, with contributions from the Social Policy Division of the Directorate for Employment, Labour and Social Affairs (Chapter 4), and the Regional Development Policy Division of the Public Governance and Territorial Development Directorate (Chapter 6). Several other OECD Directorates also contributed to the data in this report; all are kindly acknowledged for their contributions and advice.

Lead authors for each of the chapters were: Carlotta Balestra (Chapter 5); Monica Brezzi and Paolo Veneri (Chapter 6); Carrie Exton (Chapters 1, 2 and 3); and Dominic Richardson and Clara Welteke (Chapter 4). Elena Tosetto is gratefully acknowledged for providing extensive statistical support and research assistance, particularly in relation to Chapters 2 and 3. Anne-Charlotte Boughalem and Eric Gonnard are also gratefully acknowledged for research and statistical assistance on Chapters 3 and 6 respectively. Carrie Exton led the project, which was supervised and edited by Romina Boarini, Marco Mira d'Ercole, and Martine Durand. Martine Zaïda is the communications coordinator for How's Life?, and has provided essential support throughout. Sophia Schneidewind is gratefully acknowledged for her work in preparing the country notes that accompany this publication. Willem Adema, Rolf Alter, Joaquim Oliveira Martins, Monika Quiesser, Paul Schreyer, Peter van de Ven and the OECD Health Division are kindly acknowledged for their comments on drafts of various chapters. Sue Kendall-Bilicki, Vincent Finat-Duclos and Patrick Hamm provided editorial support throughout. All are gratefully acknowledged for their valuable assistance, as well as many others who worked behind the scenes to help deliver the book.

Finally, the report has benefited from helpful comments on early drafts provided by national delegates to the OECD Committee on Statistics and Statistical Policy (all chapters), as well as the Working Party on Social Policy (Chapter 4) and the Working Party on Territorial Indicators (Chapter 6). Their contributions and advice are also kindly acknowledged.

Editorial: Better lives, today and tomorrow

Investing in tomorrow's well-being starts today

The final months of 2015 will be marked by two defining moments that will shape the well-being of generations to come: the agreement on the final set of Sustainable Development Goals at the UN General Assembly in New York, and the COP21 meeting in Paris – an opportunity for global leaders to take action to address the risks of climate change. These events bring into focus the importance of finding new ways to secure and improve well-being here and now, without placing at risk our children's chances to enjoy well-being later.

Good decisions about investments for the future rely, among other things, on having good data today. *How's Life?*, first launched in 2011, is a pioneering report that summarises an extensive range of well-being indicators, putting the latest information on the progress of OECD and partner countries at policy-makers' and citizens' fingertips. Besides documenting well-being today, this third edition of *How's Life?* also offers a first glimpse of future well-being prospects by looking at three key areas. First, it considers some of the stocks of natural, human, social and economic resources that can be measured now, and that will shape well-being outcomes in the future. Second, it documents well-being outcomes for children, whose future life chances will be affected by the living conditions they face today. And third, it offers a special focus on volunteering, which is a key form of investment in social capital, and one which pays dividends for volunteers themselves as well as for wider society now and in the future.

Every country has room to improve on well-being

The analysis of the relative well-being strengths and weaknesses among OECD countries featured in this report shows that while some countries do better than others across a wide range of well-being outcomes, no country has it all. Some aspects of well-being (such as household income, wealth, jobs and life satisfaction) are generally better in OECD countries with the highest levels of GDP per capita, but some high-GDP countries still face challenges in terms of work-life balance, unemployment risk, personal safety and low life expectancy. One striking finding shown in this report is just how different the well-being outcomes can be in countries with very similar levels of GDP per capita. This underlines the importance of giving more attention to the many factors *beyond GDP* that shape people's life experiences. It also implies that opportunities exist for countries with similar levels of economic development to learn from one another in terms of "what works" to deliver more inclusive growth and improved well-being.

Volunteer work can deliver "win-wins"

Volunteering makes an important "hidden contribution" to well-being, producing goods and services that are not captured by conventional economic statistics, and building social capital through fostering cooperation and trust. When you add up the value of the time people spend on volunteering in OECD countries, it amounts to roughly 2% of GDP per year, on average.

Not surprisingly, people who have more for themselves can afford to give more to others: volunteering rates tend to be higher among those who are better off, those who have higher levels of education, and those who have jobs (relative to the unemployed). Yet people who give time to their communities also get something back in return: volunteers benefit from the knowledge and skills fostered by volunteer work, and they feel more satisfied with their lives as a whole. This virtuous circle of volunteering offers win-wins for well-being. However, it also risks further excluding those who have less to start with. It should therefore be a priority to open up volunteering opportunities to a wider range of people, for instance through public initiatives such as the *Service Civique* in France.

Inequalities in well-being go well beyond income and wealth

Inequalities in income are now well-documented for OECD and emerging countries, but new data on *inequalities in household net wealth* are even more striking. On average in the 17 OECD countries for which data are available, households in the top 1% of the distribution own more wealth than households in the bottom 60% combined. In those same countries, wealth is much less equally distributed than income: while the top 10% earn only 25% of total income, they own 50% of the total wealth.

Inequalities in well-being go well beyond income and wealth, however. This report offers several different perspectives on well-being gaps. One is the large *differences in well-being between regions* within a single country – gaps that can be as large or larger than differences between OECD countries. For example, regional employment rates in Italy range from 40% in Campania to 73% in Bolzano, which is comparable to the gap between the national employment rate in Greece (49%) and Iceland (82%). Where people live has an impact on the quality of the air they breathe, the services they have access to, and the prevailing level of income inequality. With around 40% of public spending and two thirds of public investment carried out by sub-national governments in the OECD area, this regional dimension to well-being cannot be ignored.

Intergenerational inequalities in well-being take on many different forms. On average, people under 30 are more likely than those aged 50 or over to feel that they have friends or relatives that they can count on in troubled times. The younger generation of working-age adults are also much more likely than previous generations to have completed an upper secondary education. Yet these advantages are not necessarily coupled with better economic opportunities for younger people. In two-thirds of OECD countries, younger people (aged 15-24) are more likely than prime-aged workers (25-54 years old) to be unemployed for one year or more – and in the worst cases, the long-term unemployment rate is more than double among younger workers. In addition, the steep increase in long-term unemployment that has occurred since 2009 in several countries has often disproportionately affected younger workers. This presents an important risk factor for future well-being.

Not all children are getting the best possible start in life

Giving children a good start in life is important for well-being here and now, but it also improves a child's life chances later. The evidence reviewed in this report shows that some children are getting a much better start than others. Income poverty affects 1 child in 7 in the OECD area, and 10% of children live in jobless households. Around 1 in 10 children aged 11, 13 and 15 report having been bullied at least twice in the past two months, with this share rising to more than 15% in some countries.

Socio-economic background looms large in child well-being disparities. Higher family affluence is associated with better child health, as well as a happier school life. Conversely, children in less wealthy families feel more pressure in school, say that they like school less, find fewer of their classmates to be kind and helpful, and are more likely to be bullied in school. Life satisfaction, skills in reading and problem-solving, communication with parents and intentions to vote are all lower among children from families with poorer socio-economic backgrounds.

Countries that do better for children often do better for adults, but well-being outcomes for these two groups are not always well-aligned. In most OECD countries, the poverty rate for children is higher than for the population in general. Meanwhile, some countries that perform comparatively well in adult well-being do less well in child well-being. This implies that these countries need to do better for their children if they are to maintain the levels of well-being enjoyed by today's adults over time.

Putting the future in focus

Resources for future well-being need to be monitored today if they are to be managed effectively. This edition of *How's Life?* includes for the first time a set of illustrative indicators for elements of the natural, human, social and economic "capital stocks" that support well-being both now and in the future. It highlights some of the key risk factors in these areas – ranging from increasing concentrations of atmospheric greenhouse gases to rising obesity, and from recent falls in trust in governments, to low levels of investment in economic assets (such as buildings, infrastructure, machinery and equipment). While today's picture is only a partial one, bringing this information together in one place, and showing comparative trends over time and across countries, gives a new perspective on current well-being achievements and prospects for their maintenance over time.

Better data for better lives

OECD work on well-being highlights that new data sources (ranging from data on household wealth and its distribution, to job quality and subjective well-being) are instrumental to develop our understanding of progress in new ways. But in every well-being dimension there is still more to do to improve the quality and comparability of available data. The good news is that our ability to measure progress towards better lives is rapidly progressing. Integrating this diverse information can provide the basis for a more holistic approach to policy-making, as pursued in the OECD's *Inclusive Growth* project and *New Approaches to Economic Challenges* initiative. Globally, the new UN Sustainable Development Goals will give new impetus to better policies for better lives worldwide, policies that will need to be underpinned by better data even in areas that have traditionally fallen outside the remit of official statistics. The journey continues.

Martine Durand
OECD Chief Statistician
Director of the OECD Statistics Directorate

Table of contents

Follow OECD Publications on:

http://twitter.com/OECD_Pubs

http://www.facebook.com/OECDPublications

http://www.linkedin.com/groups/OECD-Publications-4645871

http://www.youtube.com/oecdilibrary

http://www.oecd.org/oecddirect/

This book has...

StatLinks

A service that delivers Excel® files from the printed page!

Look for the *StatLinks* at the bottom of the tables or graphs in this book. To download the matching Excel® spreadsheet, just type the link into your Internet browser, starting with the *http://dx.doi.org* prefix, or click on the link from the e-book edition.

Reader's guide

Conventions

- In each figure, data shown for OECD and OECD EU are simple mean averages of the OECD countries displayed in each figure, unless otherwise indicated. Where data are not available for all 34 OECD countries, the number of countries included in the calculation is specified in the figure (e.g., OECD 33). Where changes over time are shown in the figures, the OECD averages refer to only those countries with data available for all time points.

- When population-weighted OECD averages are used, this is specified in the figure notes. This refers to the mean average, weighted according to the size of the population in different countries as a proportion of the total OECD population. This procedure gives more weight to countries with a larger population, relative to those with a smaller population, and enables inferences to be made about the "average OECD citizen" (rather than focusing on the "average OECD country").

- Each figure specifies the time period covered, and figure notes provide further details when data refer to different years for different countries.

- Data for key partner countries, where available, are presented in a separate part of the figure to OECD countries.

- Several charts in Chapter 4 present 95% confidence intervals around point-estimates. Confidence intervals are interval estimates of plausible population parameters that in principle are unknown and are therefore estimated based on a sample of observations, such as available in surveys. The size of confidence intervals denotes the precision of the point-estimate.

For all figures, ISO codes for countries and world regions are used

AUS	Australia	GRC	Greece	NLD	Netherlands
AUT	Austria	FIN	Finland	NOR	Norway
BEL	Belgium	HUN	Hungary	NZL	New Zealand
BRA	Brazil	IDN	Indonesia	OECD	OECD average
CAN	Canada	IND	India	OECD EU	OECD Europe average
CHE	Switzerland	IRL	Ireland	POL	Poland
CHL	Chile	ISL	Iceland	PRT	Portugal
CZE	Czech Republic	ISR	Israel	RUS	Russian Federation
DEU	Germany	ITA	Italy	SVK	Slovak Republic
DNK	Denmark	JPN	Japan	SVN	Slovenia
ESP	Spain	KOR	Korea	SWE	Sweden
EST	Estonia	LUX	Luxembourg	TUR	Turkey
GBR	United Kingdom	MEX	Mexico	USA	United States

Executive summary

How's life, overall?

A better understanding of people's well-being is central to developing better policies for better lives. Well-being is multidimensional, covering aspects of life ranging from civic engagement to housing, from household income to work-life balance, and from skills to health status. A thorough assessment of whether life is getting better requires a wide range of metrics, captured on a human scale, and able to reflect the diverse experiences of people. That is what this report aims to supply.

The latest evidence on well-being in 11 different dimensions of life suggests that OECD countries have diverse patterns of strengths and weaknesses. Predictably, countries ranking in the top third of the OECD in gross domestic product (GDP) per capita terms tend to do well overall, especially in relation to material well-being outcomes such as household income and earnings. Nonetheless, countries can have comparative weaknesses in areas such as job security, air quality, housing affordability, and work-life balance at any level of GDP per capita. While we have known for a long time that there is more to life than GDP, this report shows where even the richest OECD countries still have room to improve the well-being of their citizens.

Inequalities in well-being

National averages only tell part of the well-being story: different groups within the population can have very different well-being experiences. These disparities often vary from country to country, and go well beyond differences in household income. For example, the bottom 60% of the distribution owns 20% or more of total net wealth in the Slovak Republic, Greece and Spain, but less than 8% in Germany, the Netherlands, Austria and the United States. Better-educated people tend to live longer, but at the age of 30, tertiary-educated men can expect to live anything from four to 18 years longer than their primary-educated neighbours, depending on the country. In several OECD countries (Italy, Belgium, Hungary, Australia, Luxembourg and the United Kingdom), the long-term unemployment rate among younger workers (aged 15-24) is at least twice the rate among those of prime working age. As well as having low levels of income inequality, Nordic countries tend to have much smaller differences in quality of life outcomes – including gender and age-related differences.

Are lives getting better?

In several respects, the average OECD citizen is doing better now than in 2009, but changes in well-being have been mixed – both across countries and across indicators. Household income has begun a slow recovery from crisis levels in most OECD countries, but progress in other areas (such as long-term unemployment, long working hours, and voter turnout) has failed to keep pace in several cases. Countries experiencing the most severe declines in household income since 2009 (such as Greece, Portugal, Italy and Spain) continue to feel the pain in other ways, ranging from high joblessness and reduced earnings, to less affordable housing. While almost all countries have experienced some gains in upper secondary educational attainment rates and life expectancy since 2009, these outcomes may evolve over different timeframes relative to material well-being outcomes.

Monitoring resources for the future

Monitoring the stocks of resources that exist today but that can help to maintain well-being over time provides a first step towards understanding the prospects for future well-being. This report considers a small set of measures to illustrate elements of the stocks of natural, human, social and economic capital that are likely to shape well-being opportunities in the future – as well as some of the investments, depletion and risk factors that affect those stocks. The trends considered range from rising concentrations of atmospheric greenhouse gases, to rising educational attainment in young adults, changes in household debt levels and recent falls in trust in government. This indicator set will be further developed over time, to complement the dashboard of current well-being outcomes used in *How's Life?* with indicators that take a longer-term view.

How's life for children?

Not all children are getting the best possible start in life. Across OECD countries, one child in seven lives in poverty, almost 10% of children live in jobless households, and one in 10 report being bullied in school. There are striking inequalities in child well-being associated with family socio-economic background: children from better-off families have better health, higher skills, higher civic engagement, and better relationships with parents and peers. Students from more advantaged families are also less likely to be bullied and more likely to feel a sense of belonging in school. These findings suggest that inequalities in well-being among adults translate into inequalities in opportunities for their children.

Volunteering and well-being

Volunteering comes in many different forms, from political participation to looking after an elderly neighbour. Current evidence suggests that one in three adults volunteers through an organisation at least once a year in OECD countries, and seven out of 10 Europeans report providing informal help to friends, neighbours and strangers. Volunteering can benefit volunteers themselves, bringing new skills and knowledge that may enhance career development or employment prospects. Volunteers also report higher life satisfaction than non-volunteers. This suggests a virtuous circle, where people do well by doing good. In the OECD area, the value of the time that people spend volunteering may be close to 2% of GDP. While only a rough estimate, this suggests that volunteering provides a large, but largely hidden, contribution to wider society.

Where people live can strongly affect their well-being

Many of the factors that shape people's lives – such as personal safety, air pollution, employment opportunities and access to services – are fundamentally influenced by where people live. Disparities in both quality of life and material conditions *within* countries can sometimes be as large as those between countries. For example, in 2014 the difference in the unemployment rate between the best- and worst-performing regions within Turkey, Spain, and Italy was close to 20 percentage points. This is almost as large as the national average difference in unemployment between Greece and Norway. In addition, regions differ in terms of how unequally income is distributed, with income inequality especially high in regions with large metropolitan areas. With evidence suggesting that some regional gaps in well-being are getting wider over time, the need for a regional perspective is all the more pressing.

Chapter 1

Well-being today and tomorrow: An overview

This chapter draws together the big picture on well-being, outlining the OECD framework for measuring well-being, and including an overview of the detailed findings in Chapters 2 and 3. An analysis of well-being strengths and weaknesses finds that every OECD country has room for improvement, and countries with similar levels of GDP per capita can have very different well-being profiles. There can also be large gaps in well-being within countries, for example between younger and older people, between men and women, and between people with different levels of education. Changes in well-being since 2009 suggest a mixed picture, with progress in some countries and on some indicators, but continuing challenges in others. Recent trends relating to natural, human, social and economic capital highlight resources and risks for future well-being. Data from www.oecdbetterlifeindex.org show which dimensions of well-being people prioritise when building their own Better Life Index. Finally, some of the latest advances in the measurement and use of well-being data are described.

The statistical data for Israel are supplied by and under the responsibility of the relevant Israeli authorities. The use of such data by the OECD is without prejudice to the status of the Golan Heights, East Jerusalem and Israeli settlements in the West Bank under the terms of international law.

Introduction

The OECD aims to promote "better policies for better lives". Doing this requires a good understanding of what it means to have a better life; an assessment of people's well-being today along with a sense of what improvements should be prioritised for the future. The statistics in this report provide a snapshot of people's lives in OECD countries and selected partners (Brazil and the Russian Federation). They include objective information about the conditions in which people live, and the opportunities they have in life, as well as data that reflect how people feel about different aspects of their lives. By building a broad picture of people's lives in different countries, this report aims to promote a deeper and more engaged discussion about the changes that are needed in order to make those lives better, including priorities for public policies.

While there is no single recipe for well-being, there is an increasing consensus around a common list of useful ingredients. The OECD framework for measuring individual well-being includes eleven different dimensions that are important for well-being today, grouped under the two broad headings: *material conditions* (income and wealth, jobs and earnings, housing), and *quality of life* (health status, work-life balance, education and skills, social connections, civic engagement and governance, environmental quality, personal security, and subjective well-being) (Figure 1.1). "Going beyond the average" is an important feature of the framework: it is important to look not just at whether life is getting better overall, but also *for whom*. This includes differences between men and women, between older and younger people, between high and low income groups, and between people with differing levels of education.

Yet the framework also goes beyond current well-being by considering the stocks of resources (or "capital") that can be measured today and that play a key role in shaping well-being outcomes over time, including natural capital, human capital, economic capital and social capital.

The goal of this chapter is to draw together the *big picture* on well-being, summarising findings in Chapters 2 and 3, which offer a more detailed account of well-being outcomes today (Chapter 2) and the resources that can help to support well-being over time (Chapter 3). The first section provides a snapshot of life in the OECD, and then a brief analysis of well-being strengths and weaknesses among OECD countries. Next, disparities in well-being between different groups of the population are considered, followed by a section that describes changes in well-being over time. This chapter also examines and summarises recent trends in the evolution of key capital stocks that will be important for maintaining well-being over time. Some data on user responses from the OECD's Better Life Index web-tool (*www.oecdbetterlifeindex.org*) are then described, offering some insights into what people say matters the most for their well-being. The final section describes some of the latest developments in the measurement and use of well-being data.

Figure 1.1. **The OECD framework for measuring well-being**

INDIVIDUAL WELL-BEING
[Populations averages and differences across groups]

Quality of Life

- Health status
- Work-life balance
- Education and skills
- Social connections
- Civic engagement and governance
- Environmental quality
- Personal security
- Subjective well-being

Material Conditions

- Income and wealth
- Jobs and earnings
- Housing

SUSTAINABILITY OF WELL-BEING OVER TIME
Requires preserving different types of capital:

Natural capital   Human capital
Economic capital   Social capital

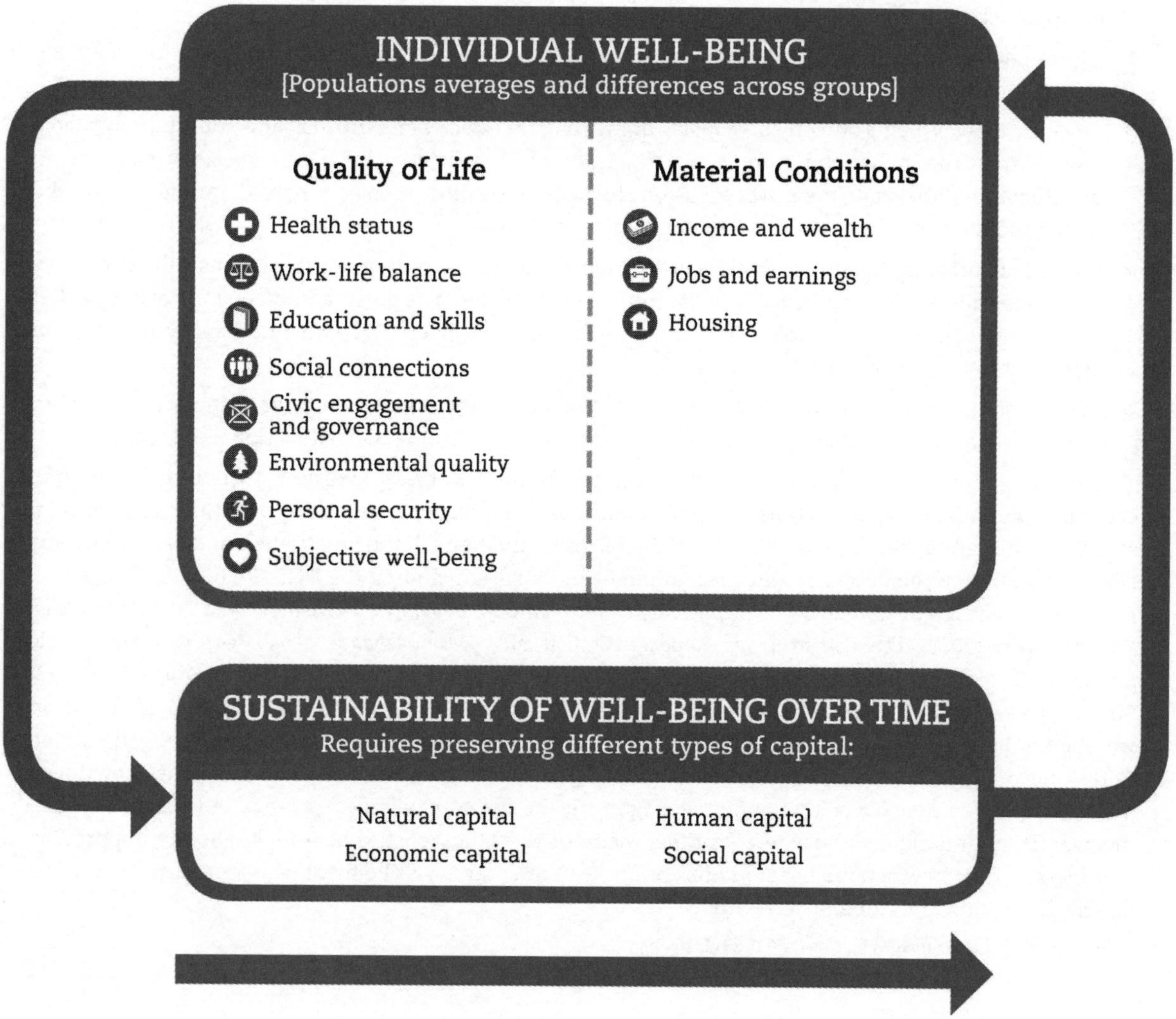

Source: OECD (2011), *How's Life?: Measuring Well-Being*, OECD Publishing, Paris, *http://dx.doi.org/10.1787/9789264121164-en.*

Box 1.1. **The OECD approach to measuring well-being**

The OECD framework for measuring well-being was first introduced in *How's Life? 2011*. It builds on a variety of national and international initiatives for measuring the progress of societies using a broad set of metrics, as well as on the recommendations of the Stiglitz, Sen and Fitoussi Report (2009) and the input provided by the National Statistical Offices (NSOs) represented in the OECD Committee on Statistics and Statistical Policy. Conceptually, the framework reflects elements of the *capabilities approach* (Sen, 1985; Alkire and Sarwar, 2009; Anand, Durand and Heckman, 2011), with many dimensions addressing the factors that can expand people's choices and opportunities to live the lives that they value – including health, education, and income (see OECD, 2013a).

Box 1.1. **The OECD approach to measuring well-being** (*cont.*)

The approach to measuring current well-being has several important features:

● It puts **people** (individuals and households) at the centre of the assessment, focusing on their life circumstances, and their experiences of well-being.

● It focuses on well-being **outcomes** – aspects of life that are directly and intrinsically important to people – rather than the inputs and outputs that might be used to deliver those outcomes. For example, in the education dimension, measures focus on the skills and competencies achieved, rather than on the money spent on schools or the number of teachers trained.

● It includes outcomes that are both **objective** (i.e. observable by a third party) and intrinsically **subjective** (i.e. where only the person concerned can report on their inner feelings and states), recognising that objective evidence about people's life circumstances can be usefully complemented by information about how people experience their lives.

● It considers the **distribution** of well-being outcomes across the population as an important feature to reflect in measurement, including disparities associated with age, gender, education and income.

The OECD approach to assessing the resources for future well-being focuses on the broader natural, economic, human and social *systems* that embed and sustain individual well-being over time. The focus on stocks of "capital" or resources is in line with the recommendations of the Stiglitz, Sen and Fitoussi Report (2009) as well as several other recent measurement initiatives, including the UNECE-Eurostat-OECD Task Force on Measuring Sustainable Development (United Nations, 2009), the UNU-IDHP and UNEP's *Inclusive Wealth Report* (2012), the *Conference of European Statisticians' Recommendations on Measuring Sustainable Development* (UNECE, 2014), and several country initiatives (e.g. the Swiss Federal Statistical Office, FSO, 2013; Statistics New Zealand, 2011). A key feature in several of these frameworks is the distinction made between well-being "here and now" and the stocks of resources that can affect the well-being of future generations "later". Several of these approaches go beyond simply measuring levels of stocks to consider how these are managed, maintained or threatened. Recognising the global challenges and shared responsibilities involved in maintaining well-being over time, many of these approaches also highlight the importance of understanding how actions taken in one country can affect the well-being of people in other countries, i.e. the dimension of well-being "elsewhere".

Source: How's Life? Measuring Well-Being (OECD, 2011; 2013a).

Current well-being: How's life in OECD countries?

According to the latest available data, the average OECD resident lives on an annual household income of around 27 000 USD (per capita, after taxes and transfers),[1] and their average household net financial wealth is more than double that (per capita). Around two thirds of people aged 15-64 have jobs, though 1 in 38 people in the OECD labour force have been unemployed for a year or more. Average annual gross earnings in the OECD area amount to 40 600 USD per full-time employee, and long working hours are not unusual: 1 in every 8 employees routinely works for 50 hours or more per week. People in full-time employment spend just under 15 hours per day on leisure and personal care, on average, including time spent sleeping. Paying for their home costs the average OECD household 20% of their gross adjusted disposable income each year. The average home has more rooms than residents (around 1.7 per person), though in ten OECD countries more than 2% of people still do not have access to an indoor flushing toilet for the sole use of their household. Around 80% of people in OECD countries say that they are satisfied with the water quality in their local area, but only 40% of OECD residents live in areas where annual exposure to fine particulate matter ($PM_{2.5}$) air pollution is lower than the World Health Organisation recommended threshold of 10 micrograms per cubic metre.

In more than two-thirds of OECD countries, a child born today can expect to live until they are 80 years old or more. Among adults, 69% of people describe their health as "good" or better. Each year, one in every 25 adults reports being the victim of an assault, and 1 in 25 000 people in the OECD area die from assault. Only two-thirds of people say that they feel safe walking alone at night in the area where they live. Not everyone uses their right to vote: around 68% of people registered to vote cast a ballot in the most recent election. Across the OECD, just over three-quarters of people aged 25-64 have attained at least an upper secondary education. Though the majority of people feel that they have a friend or relative that they could count on in times of trouble, around 1 in every 8 people do not. Every day in the OECD, nearly 25% of people report experiencing more anger, worry and sadness than enjoyment, well-restedness and smiling or laughter. When asked to evaluate their satisfaction with life as a whole, the average OECD resident reports a score just above 7 out of 10.

The "average OECD resident" is, of course, a statistical construction: a summary of the entire population's experiences, but one that may not resonate with the majority of individuals. In reality, there are large differences in people's life circumstances and experiences, both within and between countries. The remaining part of this section focuses on well-being differences at the country level, while the following section looks in further detail at patterns *within* countries.

Well-being is inherently multidimensional, and therefore difficult to summarise succinctly. It is not straightforward to identify who "has" well-being and who "lacks" it, both at the individual and at the national level. Chapter 2 details more than 30 indicators for measuring current well-being, spanning the eleven dimensions included in Figure 1.1, for 36 countries. This section highlights some of the general patterns observed across a smaller number of "headline" indicators. It suggests that different countries have different well-being strengths and weaknesses, and that every country has areas where it performs well or poorly. One striking finding is just how different the well-being outcomes in different dimensions can be for countries with very similar levels of GDP per capita – underlining the importance of giving more attention to the many factors *beyond GDP* that shape a country's well-being experiences.

The analysis that follows focuses on the latest available data for the core set of "headline" measures also reported in previous editions of *How's Life?* (OECD, 2011 and 2013a; see Table 1.1). These indicators have been selected on the basis of several criteria related both to their relevance to assessing well-being (e.g. face validity; focusing on individuals or households; referring to summary outcomes rather than inputs or outputs) and to their quality and availability (e.g. being based on agreed definitions and comparable methods of data collection; being produced with reasonable frequency and timeliness; and being available for the large majority of OECD countries; see OECD 2011a and 2013a for further details). While most of the headline measures meet most of these criteria, the development of better indicators is a continuing endeavour (see below and Chapter 2). When official statistics that meet these criteria are not available for all countries, placeholders taken from non-official data sources are used; this applies to data on social support, water quality, self-reported victimisation and subjective well-being. The availability of OECD-wide data remains an important constraint in the selection of indicators, which will be improved further as more suitable and more comparable statistics become available.

Table 1.1. **Headline indicators of current well-being**

Well-being domain	Concept	Indicator	Year[1]	Unit of measurement
Income and wealth	Household income	Household net adjusted disposable income	2013	USD at 2010 PPPs, per capita
	Financial wealth	Net household financial wealth	2013	USD at current PPPs, per capita
Jobs and earnings	Employment	Employment rate	2014	Employed aged 15-64, as a percentage of the population aged 15-64
	Earnings	Average annual gross earnings per full-time employee	2013	USD at 2013 PPPs
	Job security	Probability of becoming unemployed	2014	The annual inflow into unemployment (percentage points)
	Long-term unemployment	Long-term unemployment rate	2014	Percentage of the labour force unemployed for one year or more
Work-life balance	Working hours	Employees working very long hours	2013	Percentage of employees routinely working 50 hours or more per week
	Time off	Time devoted to leisure and personal care	Various	Hours per day, persons in full-time employment only
Housing	Rooms per person	Rooms per person	2013	Average number of rooms per person (excluding bathroom, toilet, kitchenette, scullery/utility rooms and garages)
	Housing affordability	Housing expenditure	2012	Percentage of household gross adjusted disposable income spent on housing and house maintenance
	Basic sanitation	Dwellings without basic sanitary facilities	2013	Percentage of people without an indoor flushing toilet for the sole use of their household
Environmental quality	Water quality	Satisfaction with water quality	2014	Percentage of satisfied people in the overall population
	Air quality ($PM_{2.5}$)	Annual exposure to fine particulate matter ($PM_{2.5}$) air pollution	2010-2012 average	Population-weighted exposure to $PM_{2.5}$ concentrations, micrograms per cubic metre
Health status	Life expectancy	Life expectancy at birth	2013	Number of years a newborn can expect to live
	Perceived health	Perceived health status	2013	Percentage of adults reporting that their health is "good" or better than good
Education and skills	Educational attainment	Educational attainment of the adult population	2013	Percentage of people aged 25-64 with at least an upper secondary education
	Cognitive skills	Cognitive skills of 15 year old students	2012	The OECD Programme on International Students Assessment (PISA) mean score for reading, mathematics and science
	Adult skills	Competencies of the adult population aged 16-65	2012	The OECD Programme for the International Assessment of Adult Competencies (PIAAC) mean proficiency scores on literacy and numeracy
Social connections	Social support	Perceived social network support	2014	Percentage of people who have friends or relatives that they can count on in times of trouble
Civic engagement and governance	Voter turnout	Voter turnout	2014	Percentage of votes cast among the population registered to vote
Personal security	Deaths due to assault	Deaths due to assault	2012	Age-standardised rate, per 100 000 population
	Self-reported victimisation	Self-reported assault	2010	Percentage of people declaring that they have been assaulted in the previous 12 months
Subjective well-being	Life evaluation	Life satisfaction	2014	Mean values reported using the "Cantril ladder" 0-10 scale, ranging from best possible to worst possible life.

1. In a limited number of countries, the latest available year will be earlier than shown.

Strengths and weaknesses in well-being at different levels of GDP per capita

To provide a truly multidimensional picture of well-being it is important to go beyond a simple summary approach and look at *which countries* do well in *which dimensions* of well-being. Annex 1.A (Figure 1.A.1) provides a detailed analysis of relative strengths and weaknesses on a country-by-country and indicator-by-indicator basis. It shows that while some countries do better than others in the various dimensions of well-being, no country has it all: when a very wide range of outcomes are considered, every country has areas of relative strength and areas of relative weakness. Annex 1.A presents a well-being summary for countries grouped in very broad geographical terms, but to provide a high-level picture, the section that follows looks at the relative well-being levels among countries with similar levels of economic development, i.e. those in the top third, middle third and bottom third of the OECD in terms of GDP per capita in 2013 (see Box 1.2).

Box 1.2. **Assessing comparative strengths and weaknesses in well-being at different levels of GDP per capita**

The analyses shown in Figures 1.2 to 1.4 (below) focus on the *relative* well-being performance of different countries within the OECD area. The indicators considered are the "headline" indicators detailed in Table 1.1. As a first step, country scores on each well-being indicator have been ranked from best to worst. An outcome is regarded as a relative "strength" if a country falls within the top third of all OECD countries; "mid-ranking" means that the country falls within the middle-third of all OECD countries; and an outcome is regarded as a relative "weakness" if the country falls within the bottom third of all OECD countries. Several countries have gaps due to missing data: adult skills (PIAAC) and time off (time devoted to leisure and personal care) are two outcomes particularly affected by this limited country coverage. In these instances, strengths and weaknesses are determined with reference to *only to those countries with available data*. Thus, if only 21 countries are covered, the top third refers to the top 7 of those countries.

Figures 1.2 to 1.4 summarise these strengths and weaknesses for three clusters of countries, grouped according to their level of GDP per capita in 2013 (expressed in US dollars at current PPPs; data are sourced from OECD, 2015a). Figure 1.2 shows well-being strengths and weaknesses for the 12 countries within the top third of the OECD area in terms of GDP per capita (ranging from USD 91 000 in Luxembourg to 43 000 in Canada). Figure 1.3 focuses on strengths and weaknesses for 11 countries with an intermediate GDP per capita (ranging from USD 42 000 in Iceland, to 32 500 in Israel). Finally, Figure 1.4 describes strengths and weaknesses for the 11 countries within the bottom third in the OECD area in terms of GDP per capita (ranging from USD 28 900 in Slovenia, to 16 900 in Mexico).

Although countries with a higher GDP per capita tend to do better in many well-being outcomes, Figures 1.2 to 1.4 also demonstrate that a high GDP is no guarantee of high level of well-being in every aspect of life. Countries with very similar levels of economic resources can also have strongly differing levels of performance on a number of well-being outcomes. This implies that a variety of factors *beyond GDP* can shape average levels of well-being in a given country. It also suggests that there are clear opportunities for countries with similar levels of economic development to learn from one another in terms of "what works" to deliver better well-being outcomes.

A country's position relative to other OECD countries is, of course, only one aspect of its well-being performance overall. While it can be informative to look at elements of relative strength and weakness, this type of analysis has some obvious limitations. The classification of both GDP and well-being outcomes into "top third", "middle third" and "bottom third" is essentially arbitrary; there is no empirical basis for the use of these particular thresholds. This type of analysis also cannot highlight areas of well-being in which all countries might be struggling (albeit with some countries struggling more than others) or areas of well-being where all OECD countries are generally performing well, relative to people's expectations, or to more specific policy targets. In the future, it could also be valuable to extend this analysis to consider inequalities in well-being, as well as changes in well-being over time.

Well-being strengths and weaknesses among OECD countries with the highest GDP per capita

Among the OECD countries with the highest GDP per capita (i.e. with a level of GDP per capita within the top third of OECD countries: Luxembourg, Norway, Switzerland, the United States, the Netherlands, Ireland, Austria, Australia, Sweden, Denmark, Germany and Canada), average well-being performance tends to be high. Figure 1.2 shows that the outcomes for these countries tend to be particularly strong in terms of earnings, water quality, household net adjusted disposable income, and rooms per person – which are strengths in at least two thirds of cases (and no high-GDP countries have significant weaknesses in these areas). More than half of all high-GDP countries also have strengths in perceived health, basic sanitation, net financial wealth, employment, life satisfaction, and working hours.

A high GDP per capita does not, however, guarantee a high performance across all well-being indicators. Only 4 out of the 12 top-GDP countries have strengths in job security (measured as the probability of becoming unemployed) and self-reported victimisation. Among the high-GDP countries where data are available, only one third have strengths in adult skills and time off (time devoted to leisure and personal care). Indeed, time off, job security and life expectancy are common areas of weakness for high-GDP countries – with at least 3 high-GDP countries falling in the bottom third of the OECD on these measures. At least 2 high-GDP countries also have weaknesses in relation to working hours, housing affordability, deaths due to assault, self-reported victimisation, and voter turnout.

Figure 1.2. **Well-being strengths and weaknesses in OECD countries with the highest GDP per capita**

Number of countries with strengths, weaknesses and mid-ranking outcomes, latest available year

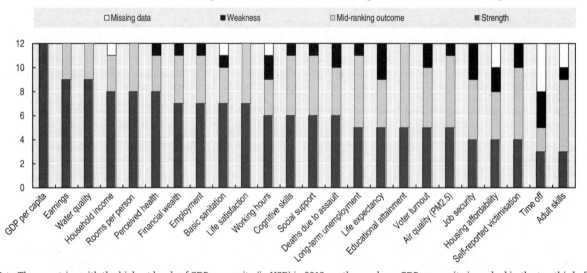

Note: The countries with the highest levels of GDP per capita (in USD) in 2013 are those whose GDP per capita is ranked in the top third of the OECD area (i.e., Luxembourg, Norway, Switzerland, the United States, the Netherlands, Ireland, Austria, Australia, Sweden, Denmark, Germany and Canada). For the well-being indicators shown along the x-axis, "strengths" refer to outcomes ranked in the top third of the OECD area as a whole (34 countries); "weaknesses" refer to outcomes ranked in the bottom third of the OECD area as a whole.

StatLink ⟲⟳ *http://dx.doi.org/10.1787/888933258838*

Well-being among OECD countries with intermediate GDP per capita

A mid-ranking level of GDP is not always associated with mid-ranking well-being outcomes: countries in the middle third of the OECD in terms of GDP per capita (Iceland, Belgium, Finland, the United Kingdom, France, Japan, New Zealand, Italy, Spain, Korea and Israel) show a very mixed performance across the headline indicators. More than half of all intermediate-GDP countries (6 out of 11) have strengths in relation to life expectancy and self-reported victimisation, and 5 out of 11 have strengths in net financial wealth, voter turnout, deaths due to assault, rooms per person, social support, and long-term unemployment.

Challenges for intermediate-GDP countries include educational attainment and adult skills, which are weaknesses for around 60% of the countries in this group. Working hours and housing affordability are also weaknesses for around half the countries in this group. Over one third also have challenges in relation to self-reported victimisation, long-term unemployment, job security, basic sanitation, air quality and water quality. By contrast, none of the intermediate-GDP countries have relative weaknesses in household income, net financial wealth, or life expectancy.

Figure 1.3. **Well-being strengths and weaknesses in OECD countries with intermediate GDP per capita**

Number of countries with strengths, weaknesses and mid-ranking outcomes, latest available year

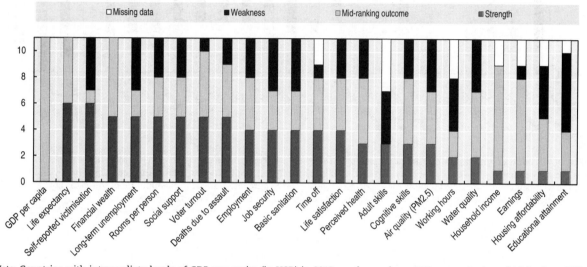

Note: Countries with intermediate levels of GDP per capita (in USD) in 2013 are those whose GDP per capita is ranked in the middle third of the OECD area (i.e., Iceland, Belgium, Finland, the United Kingdom, France, Japan, New Zealand, Italy, Spain, Korea and Israel). For the well-being indicators shown along the x-axis, "strengths" refer to outcomes ranked in the top third of the OECD area as a whole (34 countries); "weaknesses" refer to outcomes ranked in the bottom third of the OECD area as a whole.

StatLink ᴍˢ꒱ http://dx.doi.org/10.1787/888933258845

Well-being among OECD countries with the lowest GDP per capita

Countries whose GDP per capita falls within the lowest third of the OECD area (Slovenia, the Czech Republic, Portugal, the Slovak Republic, Estonia, Greece, Poland, Hungary, Chile, Turkey and Mexico) generally have lower well-being across most of the headline indicators (Figure 1.4), but there are exceptions. Nearly half of all countries with available data in this group have strengths in relation to educational attainment and housing affordability; and around one quarter have strengths in relation to job security and air quality. Two out of the 11 countries in this group also have strengths in relation to working hours and cognitive skills among 15 year olds.

Countries in this group share some common well-being challenges. As would be expected, all lower-GDP countries have weaknesses in relation to household income and earnings. More than two-thirds also have weaknesses in relation to net financial wealth, voter turnout, life satisfaction, life expectancy, and rooms per person. By contrast, housing affordability and job security were weaknesses for only around one third of low-income countries. There are very significant data gaps for lower-GDP countries in relation to both adult skills and time off.

Figure 1.4. **Well-being strengths and weaknesses in OECD countries
with the lowest GDP per capita**

Number of countries with strengths, weaknesses and mid-ranking outcomes, latest available year

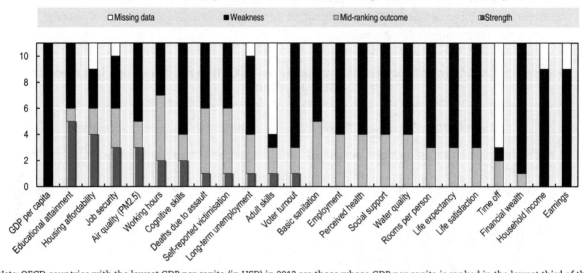

Note: OECD countries with the lowest GDP per capita (in USD) in 2013 are those whose GDP per capita is ranked in the lowest third of the OECD area (i.e. Slovenia, the Czech Republic, Portugal, the Slovak Republic, Estonia, Greece, Poland, Hungary, Chile, Turkey and Mexico). For the well-being indicators shown along the x-axis, "strengths" refer to outcomes ranked in the top third of the OECD area as a whole (34 countries); "weaknesses" refer to outcomes ranked in the bottom third of the OECD area as a whole.

StatLink ⟐⟐ *http://dx.doi.org/10.1787/888933258857*

Going beyond the average: How are well-being outcomes distributed?

Although detailed analysis of the distribution of well-being is often constrained by data availability, a number of disparities in outcomes are described in Chapter 2 – including those associated with education, income, gender and age. *How's Life?* 2013 (OECD, 2013a) included a special focus on gender disparities, while this edition addresses age-related differences in well-being in particular, complementing the evidence child well-being in Chapter 4. In considering these findings, no distinction is made between differences associated with age itself (e.g. differences due to the ageing process, or life-course changes) as opposed to cohort effects (e.g. those associated with the life experiences of people born in a particular time). In addition, people at different stages in life can often have different life circumstances, such as levels of income, social relationships and health status. Thus, age-related differences are not necessarily always caused by age itself *per se*, and should be understood with reference to a variety of other factors that co-vary with age.

The labour market outcomes of young people were particularly affected during the first few years of the financial crisis (OECD, 2013b; 2014a), and this is a trend that has continued in more recent years. In two thirds of OECD countries, younger people (aged 15-24) are currently more likely than prime-age (25-54) workers to be long-time unemployed, and in several countries (e.g. Belgium, Hungary, Australia, Luxembourg, the United Kingdom and Italy) the rates of long-term unemployment among younger workers are more than double those of prime-age workers. The steep increase in long-term unemployment that has occurred between 2009 and 2014 in several countries (e.g. Portugal, the Slovak Republic, Italy, Spain and Greece) has also disproportionately affected 15-24 year olds, relative to prime-age workers.

The younger generation of working-age adults in OECD countries are much more likely than the older generation to have completed an upper secondary education. In almost every OECD country younger people are also more likely than older age groups to feel that they have friends or relatives that they can count on in a time of need. On average, 93% of people aged 15-29 in OECD countries report having someone they can count on, while only 87% of people over 50 say the same. Age-related disparities in perceived social support are particularly large in Turkey, Korea, Chile, Greece and Portugal, but very small in Canada, Australia, New Zealand, the United Kingdom, Denmark, Iceland and Ireland. People aged 50 and over are also less likely than other adults to feel safe when walking alone at night in the area where they live: while around 75% of people aged 15-29 and 30-49 say that they feel safe, only 68% of those aged over 50 do.

In terms of subjective well-being outcomes, age-related differences vary substantially between countries. For several Southern and Eastern European countries, both life satisfaction and daily emotions and feelings[2] tend to be lower among older age groups. By contrast, in many Northern European and English-speaking countries, subjective well-being outcomes are lowest in middle age (30-49), with the over-50s enjoying levels of subjective well-being similar to those of 15-29 year olds. Some OECD countries exhibit very few differences in subjective well-being at different ages, however, and this is especially true for life satisfaction in many Nordic countries.

Other well-being disparities explored in Chapter 2 include differences between men and women in relation to long-term unemployment, work-life balance and personal security. Across countries, gender differences vary both in relation to the size of the gender gaps, but also sometimes the direction of the difference (i.e. whether men or women do better on a given outcome). For the OECD as a whole, men and women are now equally likely to be long-term unemployed; men are more likely than women to work 50 hours or more per week on a routine basis; but women typically spend less time than men do on leisure and personal care (implying a much higher burden on women of total work, i.e. both paid and unpaid). Men's full-time, full-year earnings are higher than women's in every OECD country, with women on average earning around 85 cents for every dollar earned by men.[3] In every OECD country, women are also less likely than men to feel safe walking alone at night in the area where they live, while men experience higher rates of death due to assault.

The benefits of education are often framed in terms of jobs and earnings, but people with a higher level of education also enjoy better health, are more likely to be civically engaged (see Chapter 5), they report higher levels of social support from friends and relatives, and they are more likely to be satisfied with their lives overall. As with other forms of inequalities in well-being, the size of education-related gaps varies from country to country. For example, in the 15 OECD countries where data are available, a 30 year old man with a tertiary education can expect to live 8 years longer, on average, than a man without an upper secondary education – but the size of this gap ranges from 18 years to just 4 years, depending on the country.

Finally, income inequalities, as measured through the Gini index and the inter-decile income share ratio (S90/S10),[4] also suggest wide differences between OECD countries. For example, the ratio of the income share earned by the top 10% (relative to the bottom 10%) in the United States, Chile and Mexico is over three times higher than the one observed in Denmark, the Czech Republic, Slovenia, Finland and Iceland, suggesting a much higher concentration of income in the former set of countries relative to the latter. New OECD data on the distribution of household net wealth (including non-financial assets) suggest that wealth is much more unevenly distributed than income: among the 18 countries for which net wealth data are available, the top decile of the distribution accounts for 25% of all household income, but around 50% of all household wealth.

How's life changed in the past few years?

Material well-being has been getting better for some, but worse for others

For the average OECD resident, material well-being has recovered only slowly since the early years of the financial crisis. While average household net financial wealth has increased throughout OECD countries since the depths of the crisis, average household adjusted disposable incomes in 2013 were only 1.9% higher in real terms than in 2009. Similarly, in 2013, average annual gross earnings in the OECD were only 2.3% higher than in 2009, while the average employment rate in 2014 was around 1 percentage point higher than in 2009. For more than two thirds of OECD countries, the long-term unemployment rate in 2014 remained higher than in 2009. The probability of becoming unemployed in 2013 was 1.8 percentage points lower than in 2009.

In practice, however, the OECD average masks strongly divergent trends in material well-being across countries. Incomes, employment and earnings have fallen relative to their 2009 levels in Italy, Spain, Portugal and Greece in particular, and these countries have also experienced sharp increases in the long-term unemployment rate, housing expenditure as a proportion of overall income, and the probability that workers will become unemployed (with the exception of Spain, where the probability of becoming unemployed was already over twice the OECD average level in 2009). Ireland, the Netherlands, Denmark and Slovenia have also faced worsening material conditions since 2009 across several indicators, such as long-term unemployment, the employment rate and earnings, and (with the exception of Denmark) household income. In more than one quarter of OECD countries both the long-term unemployment rate *and* the probability of becoming unemployed remained higher in 2014 than in 2009. Net household adjusted disposable income fell in one third of countries in real terms between 2009 and 2013, as did average annual gross earnings. In the meantime, housing became less affordable in half of all OECD countries. Between 2011 and the latest available year (usually 2012), the inter-decile income share ratio increased in the United States, the United Kingdom, Italy, Luxembourg, Mexico and Israel – indicating that a larger proportion of the total income is going to the top 10% than previously. Over the same time period, the Gini index of income inequality also increased in the United States, New Zealand and Luxembourg, but decreased in the Slovak Republic and Israel.

Korea and Germany have experienced improvements in almost all aspects of material well-being since 2009, with an increase in household income, financial wealth, employment and earnings, coupled with a reduction in long-term unemployment, in the probability of becoming unemployed and in the number of households lacking basic sanitation. Mexico experienced strong growth in household income per capita and higher employment, and falls in long-term unemployment, housing expenditure as a proportion of income and households lacking basic sanitation; however, average earnings also decreased slightly. Estonia, Japan, Canada and Sweden experienced growth in household income, an increase in employment, earnings and financial wealth, and a decrease in the probability of becoming unemployed, but (like the majority of OECD countries) Sweden and Canada experienced an increase in long-term unemployment between 2009 and 2014. Norway, Switzerland and

Australia experienced over 3% (cumulative) growth in household incomes and earnings from 2009 to 2013. Hungary and Turkey experienced strong growth in employment and reductions in both long-term unemployment and the probability of becoming unemployed, but Hungary saw little improvement in average household income and a small drop in average earnings (data for Turkey are not available on these indicators).

Changes in quality of life since 2009 have been mixed

Data availability is more limited for assessing change over time in quality of life terms, and the data that are available paint a mixed picture. In terms of health, average life expectancy in the OECD increased by 9 months between 2009 and 2013, while perceived health remained reasonably stable in most countries. The proportion of adults (aged 25-64) having attained at least an upper secondary education has increased by more than three percentage points across the OECD area as a whole. However, voter turnout has dropped by more than five percentage points, on average, since 2007, and the proportion of people routinely working more than 50 hours per week has gone up by more than half a percentage point since 2009.

Looking beyond the OECD average reveals that:

● Although life expectancy was generally stable or improving between 2009 and 2013, some countries experienced much stronger improvements than others over this period. Gains in life expectancy since 2009 ranged from just a few months in Iceland, Japan, and Germany (countries where life expectancy was already high in 2009) to over two years in Turkey and Estonia (where life expectancy was among the lowest in the OECD).

● Between 2009 and 2013, increases in the proportion of adults with at least an upper secondary education were largest (more than 5 percentage points) in Portugal, Greece, Iceland, Ireland and the United Kingdom – countries either around or below the OECD average on this outcome. Gains in attainment were smallest (less than 1 percentage point) in the United States, the Slovak Republic, Germany and Switzerland, all of which began with levels well above the OECD average in 2009.

● The share of people routinely working 50 hours or more per week rose in several countries but fell in others between 2009 and 2013. Increases of around 1 percentage point occurred in the United Kingdom, Ireland and the Slovak Republic, and increases of more than 4 percentage points were recorded in Portugal and Chile. By contrast, the incidence of working very long hours declined by more than 2 percentage points in Brazil, the Czech Republic, Israel and Turkey.

● Voter turnout has declined between 2007 and 2014 in around two-thirds of OECD countries, with some of the most significant reductions occurring in the United States, Japan, Greece, Slovenia, Italy, Portugal and Spain. Voter numbers have proved more stable in Korea, Poland, the United Kingdom, Israel and Turkey.

● The number of deaths due to assault increased in Mexico between 2009 and 2012, but fell in several other countries over the same period, including the Russian Federation, Estonia and Chile.

No country has seen strong "across-the-board" improvements in well-being since 2009 – though different well-being outcomes are likely to evolve at different speeds. Korea saw a strong improvement in material conditions in the last five years, but experienced reductions in self-reported health and perceived social support, as well as an increase in negative emotions and feelings relative to positive ones. Mexico experienced improvements in several aspects of material well-being, but recorded a small decrease in average earnings and perceived social support, while the rate of deaths by assault has climbed significantly. Germany experienced strong improvements in many aspects of material conditions, but recorded relatively small changes in most quality of life outcomes that could be assessed, and saw a decrease in voter turnout since the 2005 parliamentary election.

The countries most affected by the crisis (Greece, Portugal, Italy and Spain) have experienced the most severe declines across multiple well-being outcomes since 2009. More so than any other country, Greece experienced very strong declines in all material well-being outcomes, but also in terms of subjective well-being (life satisfaction and positive affect balance) and voter turnout. Greece has experienced a rise in adult upper secondary educational attainment, and a decrease in the proportion of homes lacking basic sanitation. Portugal shares a similar profile of well-being changes with Greece, though with less severe declines on most indicators. However, the proportion of people working 50 or more hours per week nearly doubled in Portugal between 2009 and 2013 (up by 4.4 percentage points), but increased less dramatically in Greece (up by around 1 percentage point).

Resources for well-being in the future

For the first time, this edition of *How's Life?* presents a small set of indicators focused on some of the factors likely to affect people's future well-being prospects (Chapter 3). The indicators shown refer to resources that can be measured today but that will shape the well-being opportunities available to people over time. The selected indicators relate to four different types of capital: stocks of natural, human, social and economic resources that can act as stores of well-being "wealth". Investments in – or depletions of – these resources, and some of the risk factors that can influence the stability and value of these stocks are also considered. This set of provisional indicators implements elements of the measurement framework for sustainable development recommended by the Conference of European Statisticians (UNECE, 2014) and discussed in *How's Life? 2013* (Chapter 6, OECD, 2013a).

The limited set of indicators shown in Chapter 3 cannot tell a complete story about the maintenance of well-being over time, particularly not at the level of individual countries. Data gaps are also considerable in many cases – especially for the assessment of changes in capital stocks over time, and across a wide range of countries. Nonetheless, some broad patterns do emerge from the data currently available:

● For *natural capital*, the risk of climate change continues to present a major threat to future well-being. Concentrations of greenhouse gases in the atmosphere have been growing rapidly in the last four decades, and the reductions in per capita greenhouse gas emissions achieved in several OECD countries in the past decade have not been sufficient to offset the climbing global concentrations. Although considered under current well-being (in Chapter 2) chronic exposure fine particulate matter ($PM_{2.5}$) air pollution also poses threats to future health. An estimated 40% of OECD residents live in areas where annual exposure to fine particulate matter ($PM_{2.5}$) air pollution is well within recommended levels, but around 42 million people in the OECD area are estimated to be exposed at annual levels of $PM_{2.5}$ between 25 and 35 micrograms per cubic metre, significantly higher than both WHO and EU air quality guidelines. Forests provide many different services that benefit human well-being, and countries in the OECD area account for around 25% of the world's forest area. There has been a 7% decline in the average forest area per 1 000 inhabitants across the OECD as a whole since 2000, due to a small decrease in forest cover as a percentage of total land area, and increasing population levels. Net world losses in forest area were estimated to be around 5.2 million hectares per year (an area roughly the size of Costa Rica) between 2000 and 2010 (FAO, 2010). Biodiversity loss is also a concern for most of the OECD, with significant proportions of mammals, birds and vascular plants considered to be threatened species.

- Several elements in the stock of *human capital* have been increasing in recent years, with growing proportions of working-age people attaining at least an upper secondary education in the majority of OECD countries, and rising life expectancy throughout the OECD. Nonetheless, the rise in the educational attainment of people aged 25-34 has begun to level off, or even decline, in some countries, making it more difficult for them to replace the skills of the current labour force in future. Long-term unemployment can also deplete human capital. Following the crisis, long-term unemployment increased sharply in several countries, and in 2014 it remained higher than in 2009 in two thirds of all OECD countries. Although life expectancy continues to increase throughout the OECD, some risk factors could affect the quality of health that people experience later. While the prevalence of smoking has declined in most OECD countries since 2000, growing rates of obesity in almost all OECD countries may present a new set of future challenges for health.

- *Social capital* is the most difficult area to illustrate with high-quality data sets. Some of the most interesting recent data on social trust is limited to European countries only. This suggests that in Europe, people's trust in the legal system is higher than trust in police, which in turn is higher than trust in the political system. Both trust in other people and trust in institutions are higher among higher-income groups, and among people with higher educational attainment, while unemployed people have notably lower levels of trust than people who are employed, retired, or in education or training (Eurostat, 2015a). Civic engagement, a measure of current well-being, can also be viewed as a form of investment in social capital. When considering voter turnout, people have been investing less since 2007: voter turnout rates declined in 21 out of 34 OECD countries, with an average decline of 5 percentage points. Volunteering also plays an important role in building the social capital stock. Around 1 in 3 adults in OECD countries volunteer through an organisation at least once a year, and evidence suggests that this has significant economic as well as social impacts (see Chapter 5 for further details).

- Levels of *economic capital* vary widely across OECD countries. At the household level, net financial wealth (excluding non-financial assets) in most OECD countries was higher in 2013 than in 2009. When household debts are considered separately (as a proportion of net disposable income), the OECD average household debt level in 2013 was slightly lower than in 2007, but this masks divergent trends across countries. At the economy-wide level, the stock of net fixed assets per capita increased between 2005 and 2010 in the 15 OECD countries for which comparable data are available. However, OECD-wide rates of investment in fixed capital went sharply negative in 2008 and 2009. They returned to positive growth in 2010, but have remained weak in the years since. The economy-wide per capita financial position has also shown divergent trends across the OECD in the last decade, as have the leverage of the banking sector and the financial net worth of the general government sector.

Which aspects of well-being matter the most, and to whom?

The OECD's Better Life Index website enables users to explore some of the well-being statistics described in Chapter 2 through a set of interactive data visualisations (Box 1.3). Now available in seven languages (English, French, German, Italian, Portuguese, Russian and Spanish), the website has been visited over 7 million times since it was first launched in May 2011. A key feature of the site is that users are invited to build their own customised index of overall well-being, by rating the different domains of well-being according to their perceived importance. Users can then see how countries rank in terms of overall performance based on their own customised index.

Box 1.3. **The Better Life Index: How it works**

What does a better life mean to you? Which dimensions of well-being matter most? The Better Life Index (BLI) is an interactive website for exploring well-being statistics in the OECD, the Russian Federation and Brazil. The tool draws on a set of 24 headline well-being indicators, as detailed in Chapter 2, which are aggregated together into 11 composite and normalised measures, reflecting the 11 dimensions in the OECD's framework for measuring well-being. Website users can then build their own summary index, based on these 11 dimensions, using the toolbar shown on the right hand side of Figure 1.5. This enables users to set the weights assigned to the different dimensions, according to how important they feel each dimension is for them.

Figure 1.5. **The Better Life Index**

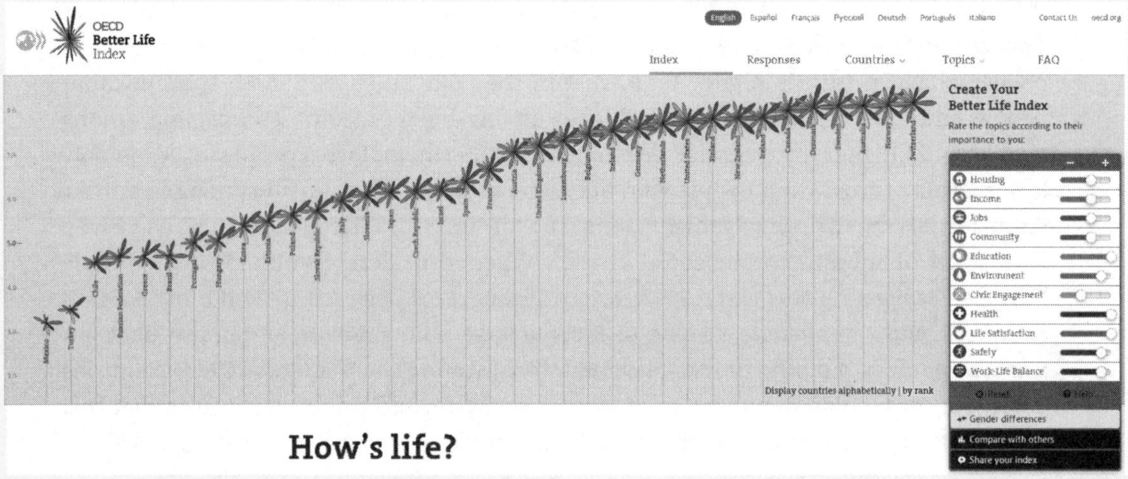

Source: www.oecdbetterlifeindex.org.

The website also enables users to examine gender differences in well-being and to explore disaggregated well-being statistics by topic and by country. Users can share the information on the importance that they have assigned to the different life dimensions with their social networks and with the OECD.

At the time of writing, around 74 000 BLI visitors living within the OECD area have shared their ratings of the different well-being dimensions through the website. These ratings suggest that all dimensions of well-being are generally considered to be important, but health, life satisfaction and education are ranked particularly highly. Conversely, civic engagement and community tend to attract a lower rating on average (Figure 1.6).[5] As people sharing their BLI ratings tend to differ from the wider population in terms of both gender and age (for example, younger and older women tend to be under-represented in most countries), the data have been adjusted to correct for these biases.[6] Even after these adjustments, however, interpreting the data requires much caution: the sample of users is self-selected rather than random; the website is likely to attract only people who know about and are interested in the OECD's work; and the user base is restricted to speakers of the languages provided.[7] Despite these limitations, the results shed some light on which dimensions resonate most strongly with users' views about what matters for well-being. Box 1.4 describes other recent research in this area.

Figure 1.6. **Well-being priorities among Better Life Index users in OECD countries**
Percentage of the total ratings

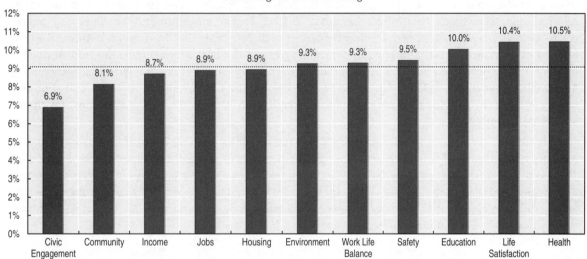

Notes: Responses have been weighted ex post to correct for biases in the age and gender composition of the sample of users, using the information on age and gender that they provided. The website uses a 0-5 rating scale. Ratings are expressed here as a percentage of the total ratings assigned; this implies that if users gave equal weights to all eleven dimensions, each would attract 9.09% of the total (this level is shown as the dotted horizontal line in the Figure). Thus, if a user rates health as "5" and all other outcomes as "4", the sum of all weights will be 45, and the health rating as a percentage of the total will be 11.1%.

Source: OECD calculations, based on 73,761 BLI user ratings shared by OECD residents.

StatLink ᐧ᠊ᓵᓬ *http://dx.doi.org/10.1787/888933258861*

There are some small differences in the ratings assigned to the different dimensions by men and women on average in OECD countries – particularly in the cases of income (rated 8.4% by women, and 9% by men), environmental quality (rated 9.4% by women, and 9.1% by men), and community ties (rated 8.3% by women, and 8.0% by men). There are also some differences in the ratings assigned by people of different ages (see Annex 1.B, Figures 1.B.1 and 1.B.2). For example, while people of all age groups rate education relatively highly, this is especially true for people aged under 25. By contrast, the importance attributed to income is slightly lower among higher age groups. On average, younger and working-aged people place slightly more importance on education, income, jobs and life satisfaction; while older people place slightly more importance on the environment, health and civic engagement. The importance attributed to work-life balance is also highest among people aged 25-34, and lowest among people aged 55 and over, while safety and housing are seen as slightly less important among 25-34 year olds. While these differences between age groups are interesting, they tend to be smaller than the overall differences in the ratings given to different dimensions: this suggests more agreement than disagreement among people of different ages on the outcomes that matter most.

Box 1.4. **Measuring what matters to people**

The importance of better measuring what matters to people is reflected in recent research to elicit information on people's preferences about different dimensions of well-being using more detailed questions and more representative samples (e.g. Benjamin, Heffetz, Kimball and Szembrot, 2014; Benjamin, Heffetz, Kimball and Rees-Jones, 2014; Becchetti, Corrado and Fiaschetti, 2013; Kettner, Köberl, Mayrhuber and Karmasin Steiniger, 2012). Many initiatives to measure well-being undertaken by national statistical offices have also involved extensive public consultations, in a bid to understand what well-being means to people, and what people value the most (e.g. in Australia, Austria, Italy, Mexico and the United Kingdom). In 2015, France and Germany launched new public consultations, building on previous commissions in both countries that focused on better reflecting notions of economic, social and environmental progress in the indicator sets used to inform policy-making (France Stratégie and CESE, 2015; Bundesregierung, 2015). In connection with the forthcoming Sustainable Development Goals (SDGs, see Box 1.7 below), the UN has also launched a global online survey ("My World"), inviting people to vote for 6 issues, from a list of 17, that matter most for them: *http://vote.myworld2015.org/*.

A key reason for collecting information about people's views on well-being is to ensure that the measurement effort in this field reflects what people themselves feel is most important for a good life. There is also a policy interest in better understanding people's well-being priorities in different contexts. This might include informing target-setting for policy, or understanding people's views on the trade-offs among different objectives (e.g. between material well-being outcomes and work-life balance) – and how these views might differ among different groups.

Measuring and using well-being data: an update on OECD and partner activities

The OECD has been heavily engaged in international work to advance the statistical agenda on measuring well-being. While the other chapters in this edition outline some of the main measurement challenges and priorities in some specific areas, this section provides an update on some of the key initiatives undertaken by the OECD and partners to fill some of these gaps. Some steps that have already been taken to introduce well-being indicators into the OECD's policy work are also discussed. Finally, this section describes the implications that the UN Sustainable Development Goals, agreed by the UN General Assembly in September 2015, will have for the future statistical agenda in this field.

Ongoing OECD projects to develop and refine measures of current well-being include:

● The further development of OECD databases on the distribution of household economic resources, including the launch of a new database providing comparable information on the distribution of household wealth across 18 OECD countries *(http://stats.oecd.org/ Index.aspx?DataSetCode=WEALTH)*. A new online tool has also been developed to enable visitors to compare their perceptions and ideals about income inequalities to the realities prevailing in their home country *(www.oecd.org/statistics/compare-your-income.htm)*. In an effort to reconcile micro and macro-types of household data, the OECD is also pursuing work to measure disparities among households within a national accounting framework (e.g. Fesseau and Mattonetti, 2013a; Fesseau, Wolff and Mattonetti, 2013b).

- Work to define, measure and assess job quality (Box 1.5).

- The OECD's Gender Data Portal, which continues to provide updated statistics that illustrate how men and women differ in terms of education, employment and entrepreneurship outcomes (*www.oecd.org/gender/data*).

- A new project on measuring health inequalities, which will aim to gather more comparable measures of disparities in the ages of death by gender, education and cause of death.

Box 1.5. **The OECD Job Quality Framework**

Job quality is a key determinant of workers' well-being. The OECD has developed a framework for measuring job quality, as well as a set of three high-level indicators for assessing it: i) a synthetic index of earnings quality, taking into account both the *level* of earnings and their *distribution* across the workforce; ii) an indicator of labour market (in)security that combines the risk of unemployment, the expected duration of unemployment and the level of unemployment insurance, both in terms of coverage and generosity; and iii) a measure of the quality of the working environment, focusing on the incidence of job strain – which reflects a combination of high job demands (e.g. time pressure; exposure to physical health risks) and low job resources (e.g. work autonomy; good relations at work).

Other outputs from the OECD's work on job quality include an **Inventory of Survey Questions on the Quality of Working Environment**, which maps out existing international data sources for OECD and non-OECD countries. A new OECD database on **Job Quality** will be available by the end of 2015 through www.OECD.stat.org, and this will enable users to download the OECD's job quality indicators. This dataset will also feature disaggregated data, enabling users to compare job quality in relation to workers' characteristics. As a next step, the OECD aims to develop a set of measurement guidelines on the "quality of the working environment" that data producers could use to fill data gaps and enhance the comparability of measures in the future.

Source: OECD (2014b), "How good is your job? Measuring and assessing job quality", in OECD, *OECD Employment Outlook 2014*, OECD Publishing, Paris, *http://dx.doi.org/10.1787/empl_outlook-2014-6-en; Cazes*, Hijzen and Saint-Martin (2015), forthcoming.

Several measurement initiatives are expected to improve the quality and comprehensiveness of the indicators used to reflect the natural, human, social, and economic resources that help to maintain well-being over time. These include:

- New methodological work to create better and more policy-relevant indicators of trust, both in other people and in public institutions, as part of the OECD's Trust Strategy. This activity will contribute to the work of the recently established UN City Group of Governance Statistics (the Praia Group; UNECE, 2015). Other developments in governance statistics include the forthcoming *Regulatory Policy Outlook* (OECD, 2015b), which will feature a new composite indicator on government stakeholder engagement, based on the 2014 OECD Regulatory Indicators Survey.

- Ongoing work in the OECD to implement the new System of Environmental-Economic Accounting (SEEA) core framework, which sets out internationally agreed concepts, definitions, classifications and accounting rules for collecting comparable information about interactions between the economy and the environment, adopting a structure that is compatible with the System of National Accounts framework (UNSC, 2012).

- The Green Growth Indicators initiative (OECD, 2014c), which continues to develop improved measures of the natural asset base and its management, as well as aspects of the environmental quality of life. Recent innovations include new estimates of exposure to fine particulate matter ($PM_{2.5}$) air pollution from satellite-based observations (Brezzi and Sanchez-Serra, 2014; OECD 2014d). In the future, geospatial and geo-referenced data may provide a valuable source of national and sub-national information about both the natural asset base (e.g. land use and land cover) as well aspects of the environmental quality of life (e.g. access to green space).

In 2013, a High Level Expert Group on the Measurement of Economic Performance and Social Progress (HLEG), hosted by the OECD, was established to follow up on the recommendations of the Commission on the Measurement of Economic Performance and Social Progress (Stiglitz, Sen and Fitoussi, 2009). The HLEG is focusing its work in four measurement areas: income and wealth inequality; multidimensional and global inequalities; subjective well-being; and sustainability (see *www.oecd.org/statistics/measuring-economic-social-progress for further details*).

Since 2013, the *How's Life?* series has also been expanding. *How's Life in Your Region?* (OECD, 2014d) examines well-being outcomes at the sub-national level across 362 different OECD regions. This work is complemented by an online data visualisation tool *(www.oecdregionalwellbeing.org/)*, which includes eight of the *How's Life?* well-being dimensions. Key findings on regional differences in well-being, and the statistical work underpinning the regional well-being initiative are discussed in Chapter 6 of this report. A recent partnership between the OECD and the Clio Infra research project also led to the publication in 2014 of *How Was Life? Global Well-Being since 1820*, which provides a historical perspective on well-being and its development around the world (van Zanden et al., 2014).

Well-being indicators are already being introduced in a variety of new and existing OECD policy activities (Box 1.6). Through a variety of events and platforms, the OECD is also continuing to engage with policy-makers, statisticians, civil society and the research community on well-being. These include the 5th OECD World Forum on Statistics, Knowledge and Policy, taking place in Guadalajara, Mexico, in October 2015, themed "Transforming Policy, Changing Lives". These events aim to deepen on-going reflection about how to measure well-being and social progress, and how to integrate these new measures into policy-making. The OECD-hosted website Wikiprogress.org provides a global platform for sharing information about well-being and progress and is building an online community for researchers, policy-makers and civil society groups interested in this. As a follow-up to the release of its *Guidelines on Measuring Subjective Well-Being* (OECD, 2013c), the OECD has also been running a series of regional workshops on the measurement and policy use of subjective well-being data, engaging both data producers and data users drawn from the world of policy, statistics, civil society and academia. The outcomes of these discussions will be reflected in a forthcoming stocktake of the OECD *Guidelines*.

Box 1.6. **Bringing well-being statistics into OECD policy advice**

Well-being indicators are being introduced in a variety of new and existing activities at the OECD, for example:

● *Economic country surveys*, which provide an in-depth review of OECD economies every 18 months, focusing on policies that have the potential to improve countries' long-run economic performance. These surveys typically cover a wide range of policy areas – from labour markets and human capital through to taxation and public spending. Recent reviews for Austria (OECD, 2013d), the United States (OECD, 2014e), Italy (OECD, 2015c) and Mexico (OECD, 2015d) have each included a special focus on aspects of well-being and its distribution.

● *Multi-dimensional country reviews* (MDCRs), which offer a new approach to advice on development policy, tailoring OECD frameworks to a non-member country context. The MDCRs, conducted by the OECD Development Centre, consider multiple development objectives and are grounded in a well-being framework that is adapted from the one used for OECD countries (Boarini, Kolev and McGregor, 2014). It benchmarks a country's progress across the different domains of well-being against the progress that could be expected given its level of economic development. The MDCRs aim to help countries to identify constraints that limit progress towards a more equitable and sustainable development. Initial assessment reviews have so far been published for Myanmar (OECD, 2013e) and Uruguay (OECD/ECLAC, 2014), with further reviews underway for the Philippines, Ivory Coast, Peru and Kazakhstan.

● The OECD's *Inclusive Growth* project is a central component of the New Approaches to Economic Challenges (NAEC) initiative*, and aims to shed light on the policy options and trade-offs that need to be balanced in order to deliver growth that is inclusive. Statistical work includes the development of a measurement framework to examine whether economic growth has translated into higher living standards for various groups of the population. This tool makes it possible to evaluate the impact of policies on a subset of well-being dimensions (income, employment and health) across the whole population.

● *Skills for Social Progress* is examining the role of social and emotional skills (e.g. perseverance, sociability and self-esteem) in shaping a wide range of both material and non-material well-being outcomes, including income, employment, health and subjective well-being. In 2015, a report synthesising analytical work conducted on datasets from 9 OECD countries was published (OECD, 2015e); this will be followed by an OECD-led longitudinal study in major cities around the world from 2019 onwards.

* The NAEC initiative has been promoting a more multidimensional approach to policies, developing tools for more integrated policy analysis, and bringing in expertise from the experimental and behavioural sciences. The 2015 *NAEC Synthesis Report* "calls for a greater focus on well-being and its distribution to ensure that growth delivers progress for all", and states that "Policy choices should be informed by an assessment of their impact on different dimensions of well-being as well as their distributional consequences" (OECD, 2015f).

Within Europe, Eurostat is continuing to develop a set of Quality of Life (QoL) indicators for the European Union (Eurostat, 2015b). An online publication (*http://ec.europa.eu/eurostat/statistics-explained/index.php/Quality_of_life_indicators*) details the available statistics and features information about trends over time and differences between countries and between demographic groups. Recent developments include the fielding of an ad hoc module on well-being as part of the EU Statistics on Income and Living Conditions data collection in 2013, which has provided high-quality estimates of several aspects of subjective well-being (Eurostat, 2015c), and statistics on social trust (Eurostat, 2015a), described in Chapters 2 and 3 of this report respectively. A variety of initiatives related to measuring well-being and its maintenance over time are also underway in individual countries, including work by the National Statistical Offices of Australia (ABS, 2014), Austria (Statistik Austria, 2014), France (INSEE, 2015), Germany (DESTATIS, 2014), Italy (ISTAT, 2015), Mexico (INEGI, 2014), the Netherlands (Statistics Netherlands, 2015), Spain (INE, 2015), Switzerland (FSO, 2014), Portugal (Statistics Portugal, 2014; 2015) and the United Kingdom (ONS, 2015).

The UN Sustainable Development Goals (SDGs, Box 1.7) will provide a major focus for worldwide statistical capacity-building over the next 15 years. The SDGs are concerned with the *implementation* of sustainable development practices; they represent a politically-negotiated set of aspirational goals and targets, highlighting global sustainable development priorities. While the SDG process is a policy-driven exercise, it will have major implications for the statistical agenda on "measuring performance beyond GDP", as many of the goals, targets and indicators featured in the SDGs bear some relation to the well-being outcomes described in this report. Indeed, the Conference of European Statisticians' recommendations on measuring sustainable development (UNECE, 2014) frame the issue in terms of meeting the well-being needs of people "here and now", "later" and in other countries (i.e. "elsewhere"). In some cases, the emphasis will be on building the statistical infrastructure to meet the demands of SDG monitoring. In other cases, measurement initiatives on specific topics, such as on governance (e.g. the Praia Group on Governance Statistics) or on new methodologies (such as the use of Big Data, and geospatial and geo-referenced data) will also contribute to advancing the well-being measurement agenda.

Box 1.7. **Sustainable Development Goals and the post-2015 development agenda**

The UN Sustainable Development Goals (SDGs) will play a critical role in shaping the measurement agenda on well-being and sustainable development over the next 15 years to 2030. Intended as universal, global objectives for people-centred, sustainable development in all countries, the SDGs are an ambitious successor framework to the Millennium Development Goals.

Proposals for the SDGs have been developed through an unprecedented and wide-ranging multi-stakeholder consultation process. In July 2014, an intergovernmental Open Working Group, under the mandate of the UN General Assembly, set out a proposal for 17 SDGs and 169 targets (OWG, 2014). Following the expected adoption of the SDGs by the UN General Assembly in the autumn of 2015, work will continue to develop the indicator set for monitoring progress against the goals, led by the UN Statistical Commission. At the time of writing, it is expected that an indicator framework will be endorsed by the UN Statistical Commission at its March 2016 meeting.

Source: The UN Sustainable Development Knowledge Platform, https://sustainabledevelopment.un.org/topics/sustainabledevelopmentgoals

---

Notes

1. Reported at 2010 prices; see Chapter 2, Box 2.1, for a full definition.

2. Daily emotions are measured as the share of people with a positive affect balance, i.e. when a person's positive feelings and emotions outnumber the negative feelings and emotions that they report (Chapter 2, Box 2.11).

3. The OECD average gender wage gap, calculated as the difference between the median wage of men and women, divided by the median wage of men, is 15.5%.

4. The share of income received by the top 10%, divided by the share of income received by the bottom 10% (S90/S10).

5. Readers interested in seeing country differences in how BLI users ranked the various domains can find further information on *www.oecdbetterlifeindex.org*. Average user ratings at the country level can also be downloaded directly from the site, although these data are not adjusted for sample biases.

6. The data have been corrected *ex post* to be representative of countries' population in terms of age and gender, by using the information on age and gender provided by users. The design weights are computed as the inverse of the inclusion probabilities and then rescaled so that they sum up to the sample size. However, no data are available on other key characteristics, such as respondents' education levels.

7. It is also not possible to know whether visitors to the website are expressing deeply-held views; nor is it possible to be sure that all users have a common understanding of what each of the dimensions is intended to represent, though the website does explain this in detail for those who want to learn more.

References

ABS (Australian Bureau of Statistics) (2014), *Measures of Australia's Progress, 2013*, *www.abs.gov.au/AUSSTATS/abs@.nsf/mf/1370.0* (accessed on 22 May 2015).

Alkire, S. and M.B. Sarwar (2009), *Multidimensional Measures of Poverty and Well-being*, Oxford Poverty and Human Development Initiative, Oxford Department of International Development, University of Oxford.

Anand, P., M. Durand and J. Heckman (2011), "Editorial: The Measurement of Progress – some achievements and challenges", *Journal of the Royal Statistical Society*, Vol. 174, pp. 851-855.

Becchetti, L., L. Corrado and M. Fiaschetti (2013), "The heterogeneity of wellbeing 'expenditure' preferences: evidence from a simulated allocation choice on the BES indicators", *CEIS Research Paper 297*, Tor Vergata University, *http://papers.ssrn.com/sol3/papers.cfm?abstract_id=2344695*.

Benjamin, D.J., O. Heffetz, M.S. Kimball, and A. Rees-Jones (2014), "Can Marginal Rates of Substitution Be Inferred From Happiness Data? Evidence from Residency Choices", *American Economic Review*, Vol. 104, No. 11, pp. 3498-3528.

Benjamin, D.J., O. Heffetz, M.S. Kimball, and N. Szembrot (2014), "Beyond Happiness and Satisfaction: Toward Well-Being Indices Based on Stated Preference", *American Economic Review*, Vol. 104, No. 9, pp. 2698-2735.

Boarini, R., A. Kolev and A. McGregor (2014), "Measuring Well-being and Progress in Countries at Different Stages of Development: Towards a More Universal Conceptual Framework", *OECD Development Centre Working Papers*, No. 325, OECD Publishing, Paris, *http://dx.doi.org/10.1787/5jxss4hv2d8n-en*.

Brezzi, M. and D. Sanchez-Serra (2014), "Breathing the Same Air? Measuring Air Pollution in Cities and Regions", *OECD Regional Development Working Papers*, No. 2014/11, OECD Publishing, Paris, *http://dx.doi.org/10.1787/5jxrb7rkxf21-en*.

Bundesregierung (2015) website, *www.gut-leben-in-deutschland.de/DE/Home/home_node* (accessed on 5 May 2015).

Cazes, S., Hijzen, A. and A. Saint-Martin (2015), "How good is your job? The new OECD framework for measuring and assessing job quality", *OECD Working Paper*, forthcoming.

Destatis (2014), *Sustainable Development in Germany Indicator Report 2014*, Statistisches Bundesamt (Federal Statistical Office), Wiesbaden, *www.destatis.de/EN/Publications/Specialized/EnvironmentalEconomicAccounting/Indicators2014.pdf?__blob=publicationFile* (accessed on 29 May 2015).

Eurostat (2015a), "Quality of life in Europe – facts and views – governance", in *Quality of Life*, an online publication, *http://ec.europa.eu/eurostat/statistics-explained/index.php/Quality_of_life_indicators* (accessed on 4 July 2015).

Eurostat (2015b), *Quality of life indicators*. Online publication, Eurostat, Luxembourg, *http://ec.europa.eu/eurostat/statistics-explained/index.php/Quality_of_life_indicators* (accessed on 25 May 2015).

Eurostat (2015c), *Quality of life in Europe – facts and views – overall life satisfaction*, *http://ec.europa.eu/eurostat/statistics-explained/index.php/Quality_of_life_in_Europe_-_facts_and_views_-_overall_life_satisfaction* (accessed on 25 May 2015).

Fesseau, M. and M.L. Mattonetti (2013a), "Distributional Measures Across Household Groups in a National Accounts Framework: Results from an Experimental Cross-country Exercise on Household Income, Consumption and Saving", *OECD Statistics Working Papers*, No. 2013/04, OECD Publishing, Paris, *http://dx.doi.org/10.1787/5k3wdjqr775f-en*.

Fesseau, M., F. Wolff and M.L. Mattonetti (2013b), "A Cross-country Comparison of Household Income, Consumption and Wealth between Micro Sources and National Accounts Aggregates", *OECD Statistics Working Papers*, No. 2013/03, OECD Publishing, Paris, *http://dx.doi.org/10.1787/5k3wdjrnh7mv-en*.

FAO (2010), *Global Forest Resources Assessment 2010*, Main Report, *FAO Forestry Paper 163*, the Food and Agricultural Organisation of the United Nations, Rome, *www.fao.org/docrep/013/i1757e/i1757e.pdf*.

France Stratégie and CESE (2015), website, *www.strategie.gouv.fr/actualites/indicateurs-evaluer-situation-pays* (accessed on 5 May 2015).

FSO (2014), *Indicator system for the measurement of well-being 2014*, Swiss Federal Statistical Office, Neuchâtel, *www.bfs.admin.ch/bfs/portal/en/index/news/medienmitteilungen.html?pressID=9882* (accessed on 29 May 2015).

FSO (2013), *Sustainable Development – A Brief Guide 2013: 17 key indicators to measure progress*. Swiss Federal Statistical Office, Neuchâtel, *www.bfs.admin.ch/bfs/portal/en/index/themen/21/01/new.html?gnpID=2013-267* (accessed on 29 May 2015).

INE (2015), *Quality of Life Indicators*, *www.ine.es/ss/Satellite?param1=PYSDetalleGratuitas&c=INEPublicacion_C&p=1254735110672&param4=Ocultar&pagename=ProductosYServicios%2FPYSLayout&cid=1259937499084&L=1* (accessed on 25 May 2015).

INEGI (2014), *Niveles de bienestar en México*, Instituto Nacional de Estadística Geografía e Informática, INEGI, Aguascalientes, *www3.inegi.org.mx/sistemas/biblioteca/ficha.aspx?upc=702825450557* (accessed on 29 May 2015).

INSEE (2015), *Economic performance and social progress – Following up on the Stiglitz Report*, *www.insee.fr/en/publications-et-services/default.asp?page=dossiers_web/stiglitz/performance_eco.htm#deux* (accessed on 25 May 2015).

ISTAT (2015), "The BES project to measure equitable and sustainable well-being", *www.misuredelbenessere.it/index.php?id=documents* (accessed on 25 May 2015).

Kettner, C., K. Köberl, C. Mayrhuber, S. Karmasin and N. Steiniger (2012), "Mehr als Wachstum. Messung von Wohlstand und Lebensqualität in ausgewählten Ländern mit dem OECD Better Life Index auf Basis der österreichischen Präferenzen", *Austrian Institute of Economic Research (WIFO) monograph*, Vienna: WIFO, *www.wifo.ac.at/publikationen?detail-view=yes&publikation_id=45900* (accessed on 5 May 2015).

OECD (2015a), "Aggregate National Accounts, SNA 2008: Gross domestic product", *OECD National Accounts Statistics* (database), *http://dx.doi.org/10.1787/data-00001-en* (accessed on 24 May 2015).

OECD (2015b), *Regulatory Policy Outlook*, OECD Publishing, Paris (forthcoming).

OECD (2015c), *OECD Economic Surveys: Italy 2015*, OECD Publishing, Paris, *http://dx.doi.org/10.1787/eco_surveys-ita-2015-en*.

OECD (2015d), *OECD Economic Surveys: Mexico 2015*, OECD Publishing, Paris, *http://dx.doi.org/10.1787/eco_surveys-mex-2015-en*.

OECD (2015e), *Skills for Social Progress: The Power of Social and Emotional Skills*, OECD Skills Studies, OECD Publishing, Paris, *http://dx.doi.org/10.1787/9789264226159-en*.

OECD (2015f), *Final NAEC Synthesis: New Approaches to Economic Challenges*, a report presented at the Meeting of the OECD Council at Ministerial Level, Paris, 3-4 June 2015, *www.oecd.org/mcm/documents/Final-NAEC-Synthesis-Report-CMIN2015-2.pdf*.

OECD (2014a), *OECD Employment Outlook 2014*, OECD Publishing, Paris, *http://dx.doi.org/10.1787/empl_outlook-2014-6-en*.

OECD (2014b), "How good is your job? Measuring and assessing job quality", in OECD, *OECD Employment Outlook 2014*, OECD Publishing, Paris, *http://dx.doi.org/10.1787/empl_outlook-2014-6-en*.

OECD (2014c), *Green Growth Indicators 2014*, OECD Green Growth Studies, OECD Publishing, Paris, *http://dx.doi.org/10.1787/9789264202030-en*.

OECD (2014d), *How's Life in Your Region? Measuring Regional and Local Well-being for Policy Making*, OECD Publishing, Paris, *http://dx.doi.org/10.1787/9789264217416-en*.

OECD (2014e), *OECD Economic Surveys: United States 2014*, OECD Publishing, Paris, *http://dx.doi.org/10.1787/eco_surveys-usa-2014-en*.

OECD (2013a), *How's Life? 2013: Measuring Well-being*, OECD Publishing, Paris, *http://dx.doi.org/10.1787/9789264201392-en*.

OECD (2013b), *OECD Action Plan for Youth: Giving Youth a Better Start in the Labour Market*, Meeting of the OECD Council at Ministerial Level, Paris, 29-30 May 2013, *www.oecd.org/newsroom/Action-plan-youth. pdf* (accessed on 7 May 2015).

OECD (2013c), *OECD Guidelines on Measuring Subjective Well-being*, OECD Publishing, Paris, *http://dx.doi. org/10.1787/9789264191655-en*.

OECD (2013d), *OECD Economic Surveys: Austria 2013*, OECD Publishing, Paris, *http://dx.doi.org/10.1787/ eco_surveys-aut-2013-en*.

OECD (2013e), *Multi-dimensional Review of Myanmar: Volume 1. Initial Assessment*, OECD Development Pathways, OECD Publishing, Paris, *http://dx.doi.org/10.1787/9789264202085-en*.

OECD (2011), *How's Life?: Measuring Well-being*, OECD Publishing, Paris, *http://dx.doi. org/10.1787/9789264121164-en*.

OECD/ECLAC (2014), *Multi-dimensional Review of Uruguay: Volume 1: Initial Assessment*, OECD Development Pathways, OECD Publishing, Paris, *http://dx.doi.org/10.1787/9789264209459-en*.

ONS (2015), Measuring National Well-Being website, *www.ons.gov.uk/ons/guide-method/user-guidance/ well-being/index.html* (accessed on 25 May 2015).

OWG (2014), "Open Working Group Proposal for Sustainable Development Goals", *Full report of the Open Working Group of the General Assembly on Sustainable Development Goals*, Document A/68/970, *http:// undocs.org/A/68/970* (accessed on 29 May 2015).

Sen, A. (1985), *Commodities and Capabilities*, North-Holland Publishing, Amsterdam.

Statistics Netherlands (2015), *Sustainability Monitor of the Netherlands 2014*, Statistics Netherlands, the Hague, *www.cbs.nl/en-GB/menu/themas/dossiers/duurzaamheid/publicaties/publicaties/archief/2015/ monitor-duurzaam-nederland-2014.htm* (accessed on 29 May 2015).

Statistics New Zealand (2011), *Key findings on New Zealand's progress using a sustainable development approach: 2010*, Statistics New Zealand, Wellington, *www.stats.govt.nz/browse_for_stats/ snapshots-of-nz/Measuring-NZ-progress-sustainable-dev-%20approach/key-findings-2010.aspx* (accessed on 29 May 2015).

Statistics Portugal (2014), "The Portuguese Index of Wellbeing", Statistics Portugal, Lisbon, *https://www. ine.pt/xportal/xmain?xpid=INE&xpgid=ine_indbemestar&xlang=en* (accessed on 12 July 2015).

Statistics Portugal (2015), "Sustainable Development Indicators", Statistics Portugal, Lisbon, *https://www. ine.pt/xportal/xmain?xpid=INE&xpgid=ine_dossie_idsustentavel&xlang=en* (accessed on 12 July 2015).

Statistik Austria (2014), *How's Austria? www.statistik.at/web_en/statistics/------/hows_austria/index.html* (accessed on 11 July 2015).

Stiglitz, J.E., A. Sen and J.-P. Fitoussi (2009), *Report by the Commission on the Measurement of Economic Performance and Social Progress*, *www.stiglitz-sen-fitoussi.fr/documents/rapport_anglais.pdf* (accessed on 12 May 2015).

UNECE (2014), *Conference of European Statisticians Recommendations on Measuring Sustainable Development*, United Nations, New York and Geneva, *www.unece.org/fileadmin/DAM/stats/publications/2013/CES_ SD_web.pdf* (accessed on 10 April 2015).

UNECE (2015), Report of Cabo Verde on Governance, Peace and Security Statistics, Note by the Secretary-General for the forty-sixth session of UN Statistical Commission on 3-6 March 2015, *https://unstats.un.org/unsd/statcom/doc15/2015-17-CaboVerde.pdf* (accessed on 29 May 2015).

United Nations (2009), *Measuring Sustainable Development*, United Nations, prepared in cooperation with the OECD and the Statistical Office for European Communities (Eurostat), New York and Geneva.

UNSC (2012), *System of Environmental-Economic Accounting Central Framework*, UN Statistical Commission, white cover publication, pre-edited text subject to official editing, *http://unstats.un.org/unsd/ envaccounting/White_cover.pdf*.

UNU-IHDP and UNEP (2012) *Inclusive Wealth Report 2012. Measuring progress towards sustainability*. Cambridge: Cambridge University Press.

van Zanden, J., et al. (eds.) (2014), *How Was Life?: Global Well-being since 1820*, OECD Publishing, Paris, *http://dx.doi.org/10.1787/9789264214262-en*.

ANNEX 1.A

Well-being strengths and weaknesses at the country level

The well-being outcomes summarised in this chapter, and described in detail in Chapter 2, have very different units of measurement – ranging from employee earnings in US dollars to life expectancy per person expressed in years. In order to show these diverse measures on a similar scale, Figure 1.A.1 uses standardised scores (also known as "z scores") where, for each indicator, the OECD average is set to zero and values reflect standard deviations above and below the OECD average.*

When a country has a score above the OECD average on a given indicator, the standard score takes on a positive value, while scores below the OECD average take on a negative value. For most indicators, roughly two-thirds of countries have outcomes that range between +1 and -1 standard deviations from the mean. A value greater than +1 on an indicator means that the country has a score that is much higher than the average: typically only around 5 out of 34 countries will have a value like this. Meanwhile, a value of -1 means that the country has a score that is much lower than the OECD average, and typically only around 5 countries will have a score like this. The limits of the scale are set at -2 to +2 for ease of presentation; standardised values for some countries exceed these boundaries in extreme cases.

These standardised scores provide a snapshot of countries' relative strengths and weaknesses across the headline well-being indicators. In Figure 1.A.1, countries are grouped into broad geographic clusters.

* The simple mean average value for all OECD countries is used here for benchmarking purposes; this sometimes differs slightly from the OECD averages shown in Chapter 2, which are usually weighted by population size to provide an estimate that is representative of the average OECD *resident* (rather than focusing on the average OECD *country*).

Figure 1.A.1. **Relative well-being strengths and weaknesses, by country**

Standardised scores, latest available year

Panel A: Northern European countries

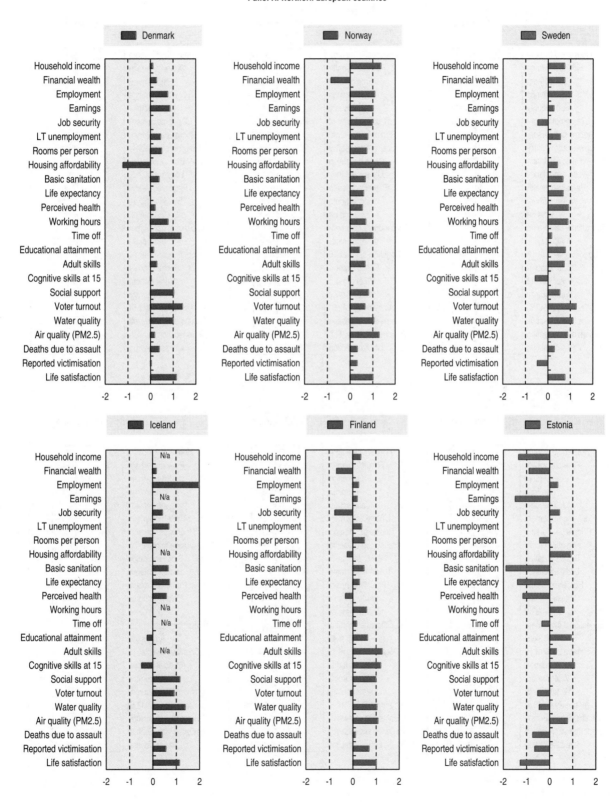

Figure 1.A.1. **Relative well-being strengths and weaknesses, by country** (*cont.*)

Panel B: Continental European countries, the United Kingdom and Ireland

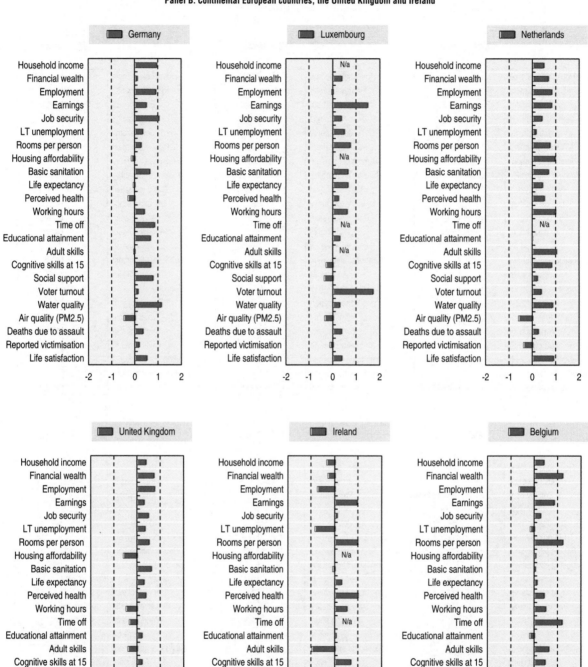

Figure 1.A.1. **Relative well-being strengths and weaknesses, by country** (cont.)

Panel C: Southern and Eastern European countries

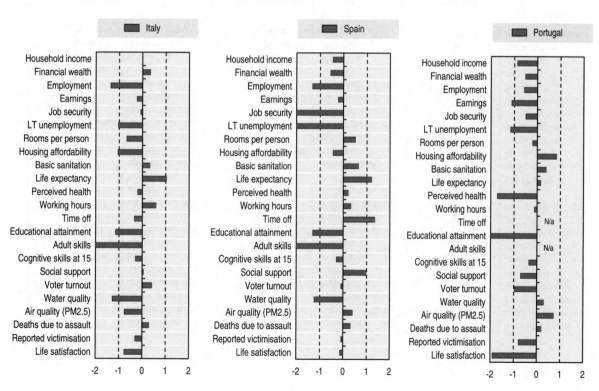

Figure 1.A.1. **Relative well-being strengths and weaknesses, by country** (cont.)

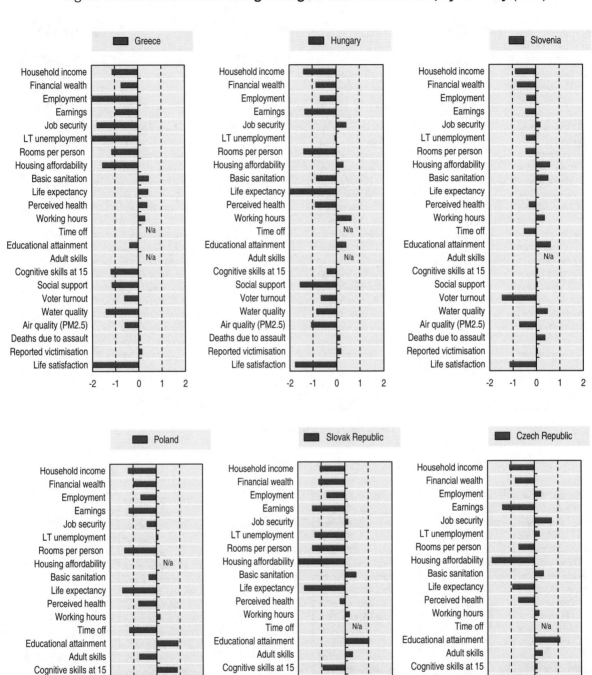

Figure 1.A.1. **Relative well-being strengths and weaknesses, by country** (*cont.*)

Panel D: The United States, Canada and Asia-Pacific countries

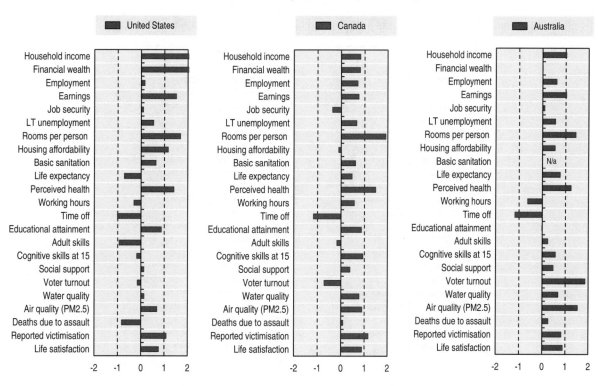

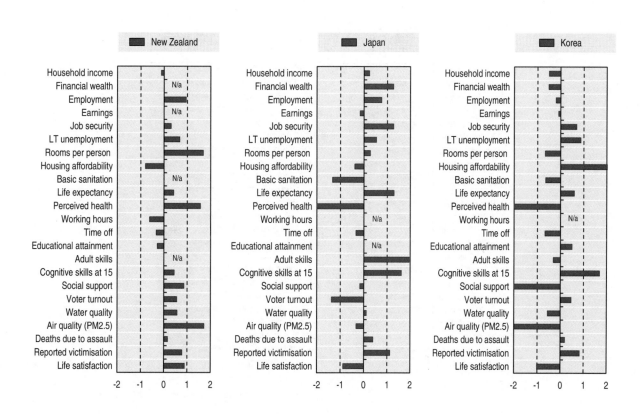

Figure 1.A.1. **Relative well-being strengths and weaknesses, by country** (cont.)

Panel E: Other countries

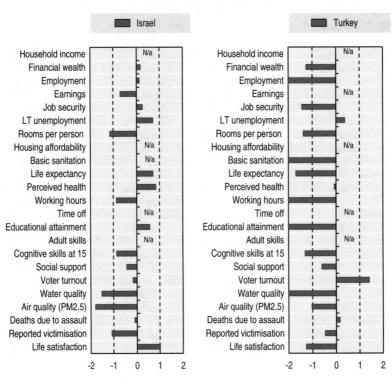

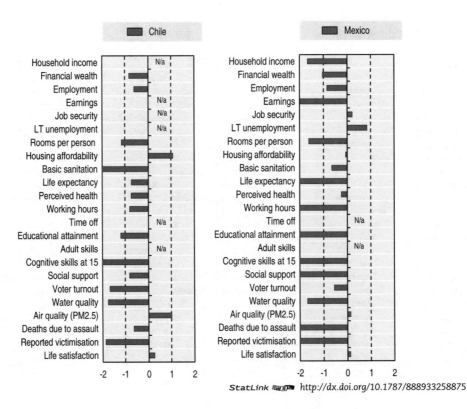

StatLink ᵃᵐˢᵖ http://dx.doi.org/10.1787/888933258875

ANNEX 1.B

Better Life Index user ratings, by age

Figure 1.B.1. **Better Life Index user ratings of education, income, life satisfaction and work-life balance, at different ages**

Average ratings, expressed as a percentage; equal weights would be equal to 9.09% (the dotted line)

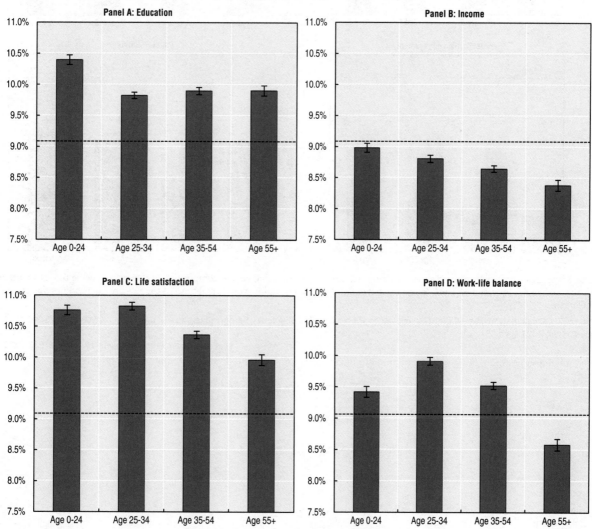

Note: Responses have been weighted *ex post* to correct for biases in the age and gender composition of the sample, using the information on age and gender provided by users. Blue bars show the mean average rating; whiskers represent the 95% confidence intervals around the mean.

Source: OECD calculations, based on BLI user ratings shared by OECD residents. Sample sizes: 20 457 aged 0-24; 22 908 aged 25-34; 23 242 aged 35-54; 7 124 aged 55+.

StatLink ᐧᒥᔅᒫ *http://dx.doi.org/10.1787/888933258882*

Figure 1.B.2. **Better Life Index user ratings of environment, health, civic engagement and safety, at different ages**

Average ratings, expressed as a percentage; equal weights would be equal to 9.09% (the dotted line)

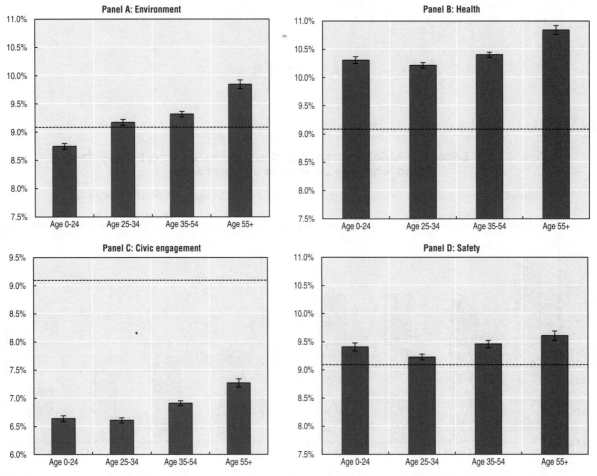

Note: Responses have been weighted *ex post* to correct for biases in the age and gender composition of the sample, using the information on age and gender provided by users. Blue bars show the mean average rating; whiskers represent the 95% confidence intervals around the mean.

Source: OECD calculations, based on BLI user ratings shared by OECD residents. Sample sizes: 20 457 aged 0-24; 22 908 aged 25-34; 23 242 aged 35-54; 7 124 aged 55+.

StatLink ⟪ᵐˢ⟫ *http://dx.doi.org/10.1787/888933258893*

Chapter 2

How's life? in figures

Measuring what matters for people's well-being requires wide range of indicators, captured on a human scale, and able to reflect the diverse experiences of different population groups. This chapter documents the latest evidence on current well-being in OECD and partner countries, providing key statistics on 11 different dimensions of life, ranging from people's material living conditions (such as their income and wealth, jobs and earnings, and housing), through to the factors that affect their quality of life (from their health status, to work-life balance, education and skills, social connections, civic engagement and governance, environment quality, personal security and subjective well-being). Besides providing a snapshot of people's current levels of well-being, this chapter also examines whether life has been getting better lately. It focuses on the five years since 2009 and reports a very mixed performance – both across indicators and among countries. Differences in the levels of people's well-being by age, gender, education and income are also described, highlighting how inequalities in well-being outcomes can differ substantially across OECD countries.

The statistical data for Israel are supplied by and under the responsibility of the relevant Israeli authorities. The use of such data by the OECD is without prejudice to the status of the Golan Heights, East Jerusalem and Israeli settlements in the West Bank under the terms of international law.

This chapter provides the latest evidence on cross-country differences, changes over time and inequalities in well-being across OECD and partner countries. It builds on and updates the headline indicators from the 2011 and 2013 editions of *How's Life?* (OECD 2011a; 2013a), spanning the eleven dimensions of current well-being included the OECD framework (see Chapter 1), and documenting how life has changed in the five years since 2009.

Income and wealth

While money is not all that matters for well-being, income is important for meeting people's basic needs, ranging from adequate housing to good nutrition. Having a store of wealth to draw on cushions people from economic shocks and can help to provide security for the future. Beyond this, income and wealth enhance people's freedom to make choices about their lives, whether that means spending more time with friends and family or investing in securing a comfortable retirement.

In 2013, the OECD average *household net adjusted disposable income* (HADI) – i.e. the income available to people after taxes have been paid, and including both cash and in-kind transfers received (see Box 2.1 for the exact definition) – was around 27 630 USD per capita. Cross-country variations are large, however: the average HADI in the United States was around three times larger than that in Mexico and Hungary, while incomes in Estonia and the Slovak Republic were around half the size of those in Australia, Canada and Switzerland (Figure 2.1).

Figure 2.1. **Household net adjusted disposable income**
USD at 2010 PPPs, per capita

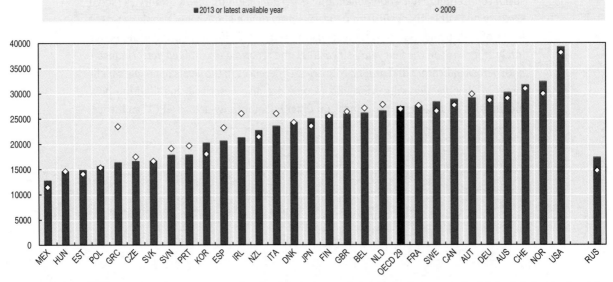

Note: The latest available year for Italy, Norway, Portugal and Sweden is 2014; and 2012 for Mexico, New Zealand, Poland, Switzerland and the Russian Federation. The first year shown for Korea is 2010. The OECD average is population-weighted.

Source: OECD calculations based on *OECD National Accounts Statistics* (database), *http://dx.doi.org/10.1787/na-data-en*; data for Norway are drawn from Statistics Norway's Statbank (database), *https://www.ssb.no/en/statistikkbanken*.

StatLink ⟨⟨⟨ *http://dx.doi.org/10.1787/888933258909*

Between 2009 and 2013, the OECD average HADI per capita grew by 1.9% cumulatively. However, one-third of OECD countries experienced a fall in household incomes over this period. The largest cumulative falls occurred in the countries most affected by the financial and economic crisis, i.e. Greece (-30%), Ireland (-18%), Spain (-11%), Portugal and Italy (both -9%). By contrast, the largest gains were recorded in Norway (8%), Mexico and Korea (both 12%) and the Russian Federation (18%).

In 2013, *household net financial wealth* (see Box 2.1 for the definition) was higher than in 2009 in all OECD countries with available data, and the average cumulative increase was around 30% (Figure 2.2). In 2013, it ranged from over 160 000 USD per capita in the United States to less than 10 000 USD in the Slovak Republic and Turkey. This measure, however, excludes non-financial assets such as land and dwellings, which represent the largest share of households' overall net wealth in most OECD countries.

Figure 2.2. **Household net financial wealth**

USD at current PPPs, per capita

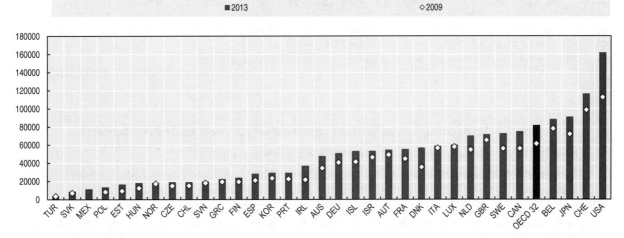

Note: The latest available year for Korea is 2012, and 2009 for Mexico. Data refer to SNA 2008, except for Chile, Japan, Korea and Mexico, which refer to SNA 1993. Purchasing Power Parities (PPPs) are those for private consumption of households. The OECD average is population-weighted.

Source: OECD calculations based on *OECD National Accounts Statistics* (database), *http://dx.doi.org/10.1787/na-data-en.*

StatLink ᐃᔑ᠍ᑊ *http://dx.doi.org/10.1787/888933258917*

Estimates of households' total *net wealth* (i.e. including non-financial assets; see Box 2.1) are available from a new OECD data collection covering 18 OECD countries. In around 2010, mean levels of net wealth per household were highest in Luxembourg and the United States, and lowest in the Slovak Republic and Finland (Figure 2.3). The median value is much lower than the mean for the United States, Austria and Germany and the Netherlands in particular, suggesting a very unequal distribution of net wealth.

Figure 2.3. **Mean and median net wealth per household, including non-financial assets**

2010 or latest available year, values in 2005 USD

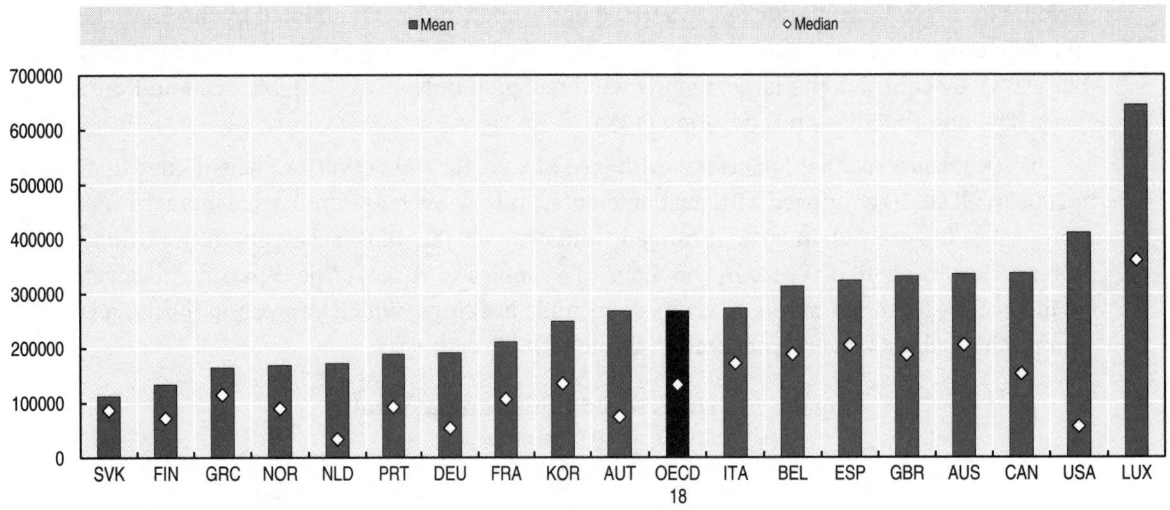

Note: The latest available year ranges between 2010 and 2013. Purchasing Power Parities (PPPs) are those for private consumption of households. Data for the United Kingdom are limited to Great Britain only.

Source: OECD Wealth Distribution (database), *http://stats.oecd.org/Index.aspx?DataSetCode=WEALTH*.

StatLink 🔗 *http://dx.doi.org/10.1787/888933258927*

Box 2.1. **Measuring household income and wealth and their distribution**

The indicators used to capture income and wealth are defined as follows:

- **Household net adjusted disposable income** (HADI) per capita is obtained by adding to people's gross income (earnings, self-employment and capital income, as well as current monetary transfers received from other sectors) the social transfers in-kind that households receive from government (such as education and health care services), and then subtracting taxes on income and wealth as well as the social security contributions paid by households. The measure used here, which is drawn from the OECD National Accounts, also takes into account the depreciation of capital goods consumed by households. HADI is shown in per capita terms, and expressed in United States dollars (USD) at 2010 prices, adjusted using purchasing power parities (PPPs) for actual individual consumption.

- **Household net financial wealth** per capita consists of currency and deposits, securities other than shares, loans, shares and other equity (including shares issued by investment funds), insurance technical reserves, and other accounts receivable or payable, net of household financial liabilities, as defined by the System of National Accounts (SNA). In most cases, unfunded pension entitlements are not included. Household net financial wealth is shown here in per capita terms, expressed in USD at current prices, adjusted using purchasing power parities (PPPs) for household private consumption. The data shown here are drawn from the OECD National Accounts Statistics Database.

- **Household net wealth** refers to both the real and financial assets and liabilities held by private households resident in the country, as measured in microdata. Values are expressed in USD at 2005 prices, adjusted using purchasing power parities (PPPs) for household private consumption. The concept of wealth corresponds to the recommendations of the *OECD Guidelines for Micro Statistics on Household Wealth* (OECD, 2013b) and data are shown per household (rather than per person or per adult), with no adjustment made to reflect differences in household size. Data are drawn from the OECD Wealth Distribution Database, which includes data supplied by National Statistical Offices and other producers

Box 2.1. **Measuring household income and wealth and their distribution** (*cont.*)

of official statistics (based on household surveys or tax and administrative records), and public use data from the European Central Bank (for 11 countries participating in the Euro-System Household Finance and Consumption Survey). These data exclude pension wealth, the size and distribution of which differs markedly across OECD countries, depending on the characteristics of retirement systems. There are some country differences in the degree to which rich households are oversampled (ranging from no oversampling in Australia, to large oversampling for the United States and Spain).

● The **Gini Index** is a summary measure of income inequality in the population. It is computed based on microdata (collected from household surveys and administrative records) for household income after taxes and transfers, where household income is adjusted to reflect the differences in the needs of households of different sizes. The Gini index, which is more sensitive to changes in the middle of the distribution, ranges between zero (where everybody has the same mean level of income) and one (where all the income goes to the richest individual only). A change of one "Gini point" means a change of 0.01, on this 0-1 scale. The estimates presented here are based on household income data from the OECD Income Distribution Database.

● The **inter-decile income share ratio (S90/S10)** is a measure of income inequality that is more sensitive to changes in the extremes of the distribution; it refers to the share of all income received by the richest 10% of the population, divided by the share of all income received by the poorest 10%. It is computed based on measures of equivalised household disposable income (i.e. adjusted for differences in household size), after taxes and transfers. Estimates shown here come from the OECD Income Distribution Database.

For the first two (National Account-based) indicators, data refer to the aggregate of households, including unincorporated enterprises and non-profit institutions serving households. The indicators shown here are consistent with economy-wide indicators, such as GDP and productivity. The income concept used is the broadest measure of households' consumption possibilities available within the national accounts system. The net financial wealth measure, however, excludes a range of assets that are critical for households' material well-being, such as dwellings and land. Data on these non-financial assets are currently only available in the National Accounts for a small number of OECD and partner countries. The measure of household net wealth shown above does include non-financial assets for 18 OECD countries, but is based on micro data.

The data shown here have limitations. First, only a few national accounts systems provide data that exclude non-profit institutions serving households: this means that the coverage of the first two indicators shown here is somewhat broader than the one used in household surveys. Second, to better reflect differences in household needs, data should ideally be "equivalised", i.e. expressed in terms of consumption units, while the SNA data are per capita. More generally, national accounts data at the macro-economic level do not provide information on the distribution of economic resources. To reconcile micro and macro-data on households, the OECD is pursuing work to measure disparities among households within a national accounting framework (e.g. Fesseau and Mattonetti, 2013a; Fesseau, Wolff and Mattonetti, 2013b). The OECD has also recently published guidelines for the measurement of the distribution of household wealth (OECD, 2013b), as well as a framework for the integrated analysis of income, consumption and wealth (OECD, 2013c).

Further reading:

● Murtin, F. and M. Mira d'Ercole (2015), "Household wealth inequality across OECD countries: New OECD evidence", *OECD Statistics Brief*, No. 21, *www.oecd.org/social/household-wealth-inequality-across-OECD-countries-OECDSB21.pdf*.

● OECD (2015a), *In It Together: Why Less Inequality Benefits All*. OECD Publishing, Paris, *http://dx.doi.org/10.1787/9789264235120-en*.

● OECD (2013b), OECD Guidelines for Micro Statistics on Household Wealth, OECD Publishing, Paris, *http://dx.doi.org/10.1787/9789264194878-en*.

The distribution of income and wealth

In most OECD countries the gap between rich and poor households is now at its highest level in 30 years (OECD, 2015a). The *Gini index* of income inequality (see Box 2.1 for a definition) in around 2012 was highest in Mexico, Turkey, the United States and Israel, and lowest in Denmark, Slovenia, the Slovak Republic, Norway and the Czech Republic (Figure 2.4). Since 2011, which is the earliest available year for strictly comparable data,[1] the OECD average Gini index has remained broadly stable. However, the level of income inequality decreased by 1 Gini point in the Slovak Republic and Israel, while it increased by 1 point or more in the United States, New Zealand, and Luxembourg.

Figure 2.4. **Gini index of income inequality**

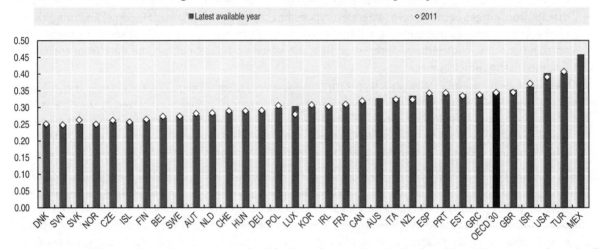

Note: The latest available year is 2014 for Hungary; 2013 for Finland, Israel, Korea, the Netherlands and the United States; and 2012 for all other countries. The first year shown refers to 2010 for Canada; and 2012 for Hungary, Korea and the United States. The OECD average is population-weighted.

Source: "Income Distribution", *OECD Social and Welfare Statistics* (database), *http://dx.doi.org/10.1787/data-00654-en.*

StatLink ⟨⟩ *http://dx.doi.org/10.1787/888933258936*

An alternative perspective on income distribution is provided by the **inter-decile income share ratio** S90/S10 (Figure 2.5; see Box 2.1 for the definition). In around 2012, this ratio was lowest in Denmark, the Czech Republic, Slovenia and Finland, where the share of income received by the top 10% was just over five times that received by the bottom 10%. By contrast, in Israel, people in the top decile received 15 times the income of people in the bottom decile, in United States this was close to 19 times, and in Mexico it was 25 times. Since 2011, the inter-decile income share ratio has increased by around 1 point in the United States, the United Kingdom, Italy and Luxembourg, and by around 2 points in Israel.

Household net wealth in OECD countries is heavily concentrated towards the top of the distribution. Figure 2.6 shows that in the majority of countries, the top 1% of the distribution usually own more wealth than the bottom 60% combined. On average, the bottom 60% own around 13% of household net wealth in the OECD, while the top 1% owns 18%. Wealth is more unequally distributed than income: in the countries shown here, the top 10% of the distribution accounts for 50% of all household wealth, but only around 25% of all household income (OECD, 2015a). These data, however, exclude pension wealth – the

Figure 2.5. **Inter-decile income share ratio (S90/S10)**

The share of income received by the top 10% divided by the share of income received by the bottom 10%

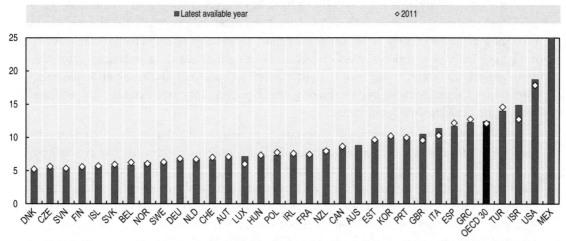

Note: The latest available year is 2014 for Hungary; and 2013 for Finland, Israel, Korea, the Netherlands and the United States. The first year shown refers to 2010 for Canada; and 2012 for Hungary, Korea and the United States. The OECD average is population-weighted.

Source: "Income Distribution", *OECD Social and Welfare Statistics* (database), *http://dx.doi.org/10.1787/data-00654-en*.

StatLink http://dx.doi.org/10.1787/888933258949

Figure 2.6. **The distribution of household net wealth**

2010 or latest available year

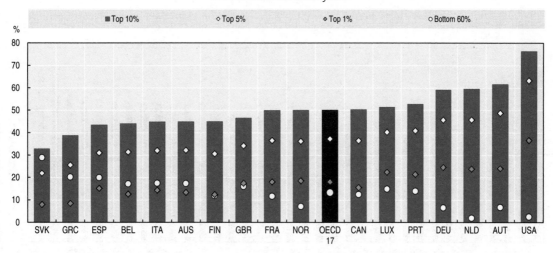

Note: The latest available year ranges between 2010 and 2013. Data for the United Kingdom are limited to Great Britain only.

Source: OECD Wealth Distribution (database), *http://stats.oecd.org/Index.aspx?DataSetCode=WEALTH*.

StatLink http://dx.doi.org/10.1787/888933258958

size and distribution of which differs markedly across OECD countries depending on the characteristics of retirement systems.

As discussed in more depth in OECD (2015a), household wealth is generally higher when the head of the household is better educated and aged between 55 and 64. The principal residence is the most important asset for most households, and non-financial assets are more equally distributed than financial assets. Levels of debt increase with rising income, but over-indebtedness is highest among middle-income groups and among households headed by young adults.

Jobs and earnings

Jobs play a central role in many people's lives. Beyond providing a source of income, good jobs can bring many other well-being benefits, from extending people's social networks to providing people with new skills. Unemployment affects a household's financial security, but it can also have a negative effect on physical and mental health as well as on subjective well-being. Both quantity and quality matter when it comes to jobs, however: while being unemployed is bad for well-being on many levels, poor quality jobs can also put workers' health and broader well-being at risk.

The *employment rate* provides important information about the availability of jobs (see Box 2.2 for definitions). In general, employment rates are relatively low in Southern and (some) Eastern European countries, and high among Nordic and Northern European countries, as well as Switzerland, New Zealand and Japan. The employment rate has risen by around 1 percentage point between 2009 and 2014 on average in the OECD (Figure 2.7).[2] However, large reductions have been recorded over the same time period in countries most affected by the crisis: in Greece, the employment rate in 2014 was still 11.4 percentage points lower than in 2009, and large reductions have also been recorded over the same time period in Spain (-4.0 percentage points), Slovenia (-3.6 points), Portugal (-3.5 points), Denmark (-2.5 points), and the Netherlands (-2.5 points).

Figure 2.7. **Employment rate**
Employed people aged 15-64, as a percentage of the population of the same age

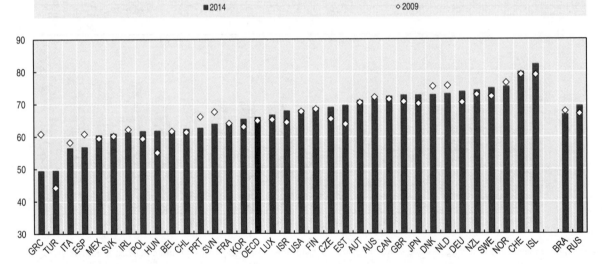

Note: The latest available year is 2013 for Chile and Brazil. The first year shown for Chile is 2011 due to a break in the series. Comparisons over time for Germany and Portugal need to be interpreted with caution, due to a redesign of the labour force survey that occurred in 2010. The OECD average is population-weighted.

Source: "Labour Force Statistics", OECD Employment and Labour Market Statistics (database), http://dx.doi.org/10.1787/lfs-lfs-data-en.

StatLink ⟶ http://dx.doi.org/10.1787/888933258961

Long-term unemployment places people at risk of poverty, deprivation, social exclusion and stigmatisation, and can involve psychological costs such as lower self-esteem and discouragement. In 2014, the proportion of the labour force unemployed for one year or more ranged from below 1% in Korea, Mexico, Norway, Israel, Iceland,

New Zealand and Canada, to more than 7% in Italy, Portugal and the Slovak Republic, 12.9% in Spain, and 19.5% in Greece (Figure 2.8). Since 2009, long-term unemployment has risen in over two thirds of OECD countries, and the OECD average has increased by 0.7 percentage points (cumulatively). In Greece, long-term unemployment in 2014 was over five times higher than in 2009; it tripled over the same period in the Netherlands, Spain, Slovenia and Denmark; and doubled in Italy, New Zealand, Portugal and Ireland. By contrast, long-term unemployment fell by more than one percentage point in Turkey, Germany and Israel.

Figure 2.8. **Long-term unemployment rate**

Percentage of the labour force unemployed for one year or more

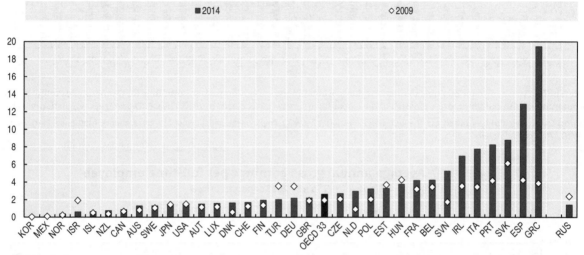

Note: The latest available year is 2013 for Korea. The first year shown for Belgium is 2011 due to a break in the series. Comparisons over time for Germany and Portugal need to be interpreted with caution, due to a redesign of the labour force survey that occurred in 2010. The OECD average is population-weighted.

Source: "Labour Force Statistics", OECD Employment and Labour Market Statistics (database), http://dx.doi.org/10.1787/lfs-lfs-data-en.

StatLink ⟡ http://dx.doi.org/10.1787/888933258975

In 2014, the **probability of becoming unemployed** (see Box 2.2 for the definition) was lowest in Japan, Germany, Switzerland and Norway, where it affected fewer than 1 in every 33 workers (Figure 2.9). By contrast, it affected around 1 in every 15 workers in Portugal and Finland, more than 1 in 11 workers in Turkey, nearly 1 in 10 workers in Greece, and more than 1 in 7 workers in Spain. Across the OECD as a whole, the probability of becoming unemployed in 2014 was 1.8 percentage points lower than in 2009. However, the risk of unemployment increased in around one quarter of OECD countries, including in Portugal, Italy, the Netherlands and Greece.

Average gross annual *earnings* of full-time employees in 2013 (see Box 2.2 for the definition) ranged from USD 56 000 in the United States and Luxembourg, to below USD 20 000 in Estonia and Mexico (Figure 2.10). Gross earnings decreased between 2009 and 2013 in one-third of countries, dropping by 22% in Greece, 6% in Ireland and Spain, 4% in the United Kingdom and 3% in Mexico. By contrast, average earnings grew by 5% or more in Norway, Korea, Canada and Poland.

Figure 2.9. **Probability of becoming unemployed**

Annual inflows into unemployment, as a percentage of employed people in the preceding year

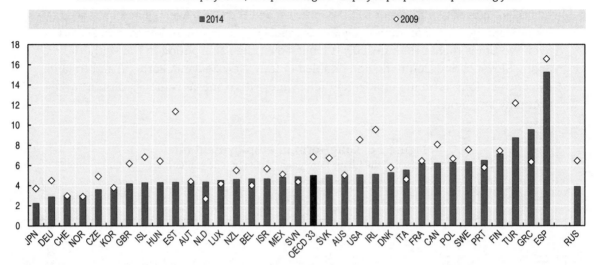

Note: The first year shown for Belgium refers to 2011 due to a break in the series. Comparisons over time for Germany and Portugal need to be interpreted with caution, due to a redesign of the labour force survey that occurred in 2010. The OECD average is population-weighted.

Source: OECD calculations based on "Labour Force Statistics", OECD Employment and Labour Market Statistics (database), http://dx.doi. org/10.1787/lfs-lfs-data-en.

StatLink ⬛⬛⬛ http://dx.doi.org/10.1787/888933258986

Figure 2.10. **Average annual gross earnings per full-time employee**

USD at 2013 PPPs and 2013 constant prices

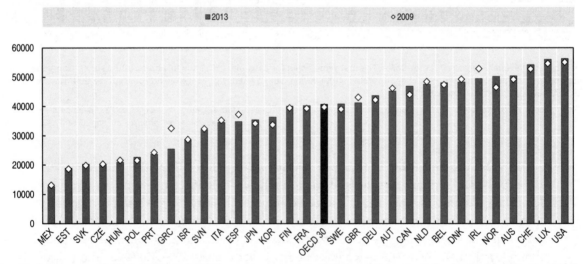

Note: The latest year available for Mexico is 2011. Wages are expressed on a full-time, full-year basis. Purchasing Power Parities (PPPs) are those for private consumption of households. The OECD average is population-weighted.

Source: OECD calculations combining data from the OECD Earnings Distribution Database and the OECD Average Annual Earnings per Full-time and Full-year Equivalent Dependent Employee Database.

StatLink ⬛⬛⬛ http://dx.doi.org/10.1787/888933258996

Measuring job quality: The OECD Job Quality Framework

The well-being of workers is also affected by the *quality of jobs* available, not just their quantity. In line with the *How's Life?* approach, and building on the International Labour Office (2012) and United Nations Economic Commission for Europe (2015) work in this area, the OECD has developed a framework for measuring and assessing job quality that focuses on outcomes at the individual level, as well as their distribution. It has three distinct dimensions:

- **Earnings quality**, a measure that considers both hourly wages and their distribution across the workforce.[3]

- **Labour market (in)security**, which captures the expected earnings loss associated with unemployment, combining the probability of becoming unemployed, the average expected duration of completed unemployment spells and the unemployment insurance available.

- **Quality of the working environment**, measured as the incidence of job strain among employees. This is defined as a combination of high job demands (e.g. time pressure, and exposure to physical health risks) and low job resources (e.g. work autonomy, opportunities for learning, and good workplace relationships), and is measured through self-reports.

Detailed findings for these three dimensions are reported in the OECD *Employment Outlook 2014* for OECD countries, and in the *OECD Employment Outlook 2015* for twelve emerging economies. As shown in Figure 2.11, some countries perform well across all dimensions of job quality (e.g. Norway, Switzerland, Denmark), while others have more clearly defined areas of relative strength and weakness.

Figure 2.11. **Job quality in OECD countries**
Normalised score between 0 and 1[4]

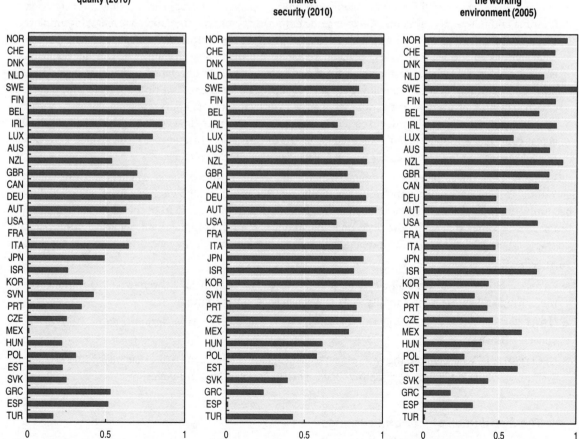

Note: Data refer to 2010 for earnings quality and labour market security; and 2005 for the quality of the working environment.

Source: OECD calculations based on "Job Quality", *OECD Employment and Labour Market Statistics* (database), *http://dx.doi.org/10.1787/lfs-data-en*.

StatLink ᵃᵐˢᵖ *http://dx.doi.org/10.1787/888933259006*

Box 2.2. **Measuring jobs and earnings**

The four headline indicators used to measure jobs and earnings are defined as follows:

- The **employment rate** is the share of the working-age population (people aged 15 to 64 in most OECD countries) who declare having worked in gainful employment for at least one hour in the previous week. This also includes persons who, having already worked in their present job, were temporarily absent from work during the reference period while having retained a formal attachment to their job (e.g. due to parental leave, sickness, annual leave). The data on employment rates come from national Labour Force Surveys (LFSs) as compiled in the *OECD Annual Labour Force Statistics (ALFS) Database*, and are consistent with International Labour Office (ILO) recommendations.

- The **long-term unemployment rate** is the number of persons who have been unemployed for one year or more, as a percentage of the labour force (the sum of employed and unemployed persons). Unemployed persons are defined as those who are currently not working but are willing to do so and actively searching for work. The data are drawn from national Labour Force Surveys as available in the *OECD Employment Outlook Database*.

- The **probability of becoming unemployed** is calculated as the annual inflow into unemployment – i.e. the number of people who have been unemployed for less than one year, as a proportion of the number of employed persons the year before. The indicator is calculated based on the OECD's Labour Force Statistics Database and is expressed as an annual figure. While the unemployment rate measures the "stock" of people who cannot find a job, the probability of becoming unemployed measures how many people are at risk of not having a job tomorrow even though they have one today.

- **Average gross annual earnings of full-time employees** refer to the average annual wages of employees working in all sectors of the economy and in all types of dependent employment; they are expressed as full-time and full-year equivalents. Wages include employees' gross remuneration, i.e. including employers' social contributions and before any deductions are made by the employer in respect of taxes, workers' contributions to social security and pension schemes, life insurance premiums, union dues and other employee obligations. The indicator is computed as the total wage bill from National Accounts, divided by the number of full-time equivalent employees in the economy. The number of full-time equivalent employees is obtained by multiplying data on the number of employees by the ratio of hours worked by all employees and by those working full-time, in order to correct for the prevalence of part-time work, which varies considerably across countries. The indicator combines data from the *OECD Earnings Distribution Database* and *OECD Average Annual Earnings per Full-time* and *Full-year Equivalent Dependent Employee Database*.

Generally, data on employment, unemployment and earnings are of good quality, and are collected according to internationally standardised definitions. The measure shown here for the probability of becoming unemployed relies on cross-sectional data (rather than panel data from the same individuals over time). This assumes that all inflows into unemployment come from employment, while all outflows from unemployment go to employment, and means that flows into and out of the labour force are not captured.

Further reading:

- Cazes, S., Hijzen, A. and A. Saint-Martin, (2015), "How good is your job? the new OECD framework for measuring and assessing job quality", *OECD Working Paper*, forthcoming.

- OECD (2015b), *OECD Employment Outlook 2015*, OECD Publishing, Paris, *http://dx.doi.org/10.1787/empl_outlook-2015-en*.

- OECD (2013d), "Well-being in the workplace: Measuring job quality", in OECD, *How's Life? 2013: Measuring Well-being*, OECD Publishing, Paris, *http://dx.doi.org/10.1787/how_life-2013-9-en*.

The distribution of jobs and earnings

In two thirds of all OECD countries, young people are more likely to suffer long-term unemployment than prime-aged workers (Figure 2.12). In Belgium, Hungary, Australia, Luxembourg, and the United Kingdom, long-term unemployment among younger workers is at least double that of prime-aged workers. In Italy, 1 in every 14 prime-age workers is long-term unemployed, but for young people the rate increases to 1 in every 4. In Greece, 1 in 3 workers aged 15-24 is long-term unemployed.

Increases in the long-term unemployment rate between 2009 and 2014 have also hit younger workers particularly hard, for example in the Slovak Republic, Portugal, Spain, Italy and Greece (Figure 2.13). Younger workers generally also face challenges in terms of non-regular employment, with a high incidence of temporary work, often coupled with low transition rates from temporary to permanent jobs (OECD, 2014a).[5]

Figure 2.12. **Differences in long-term unemployment rates for young and prime-aged workers**
Percentage of the labour force unemployed for one year or more, 2014

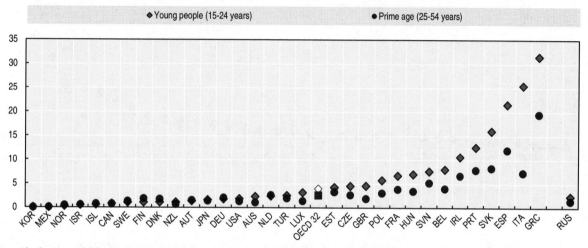

Note: The latest available year is 2013 for Korea. The OECD average is population-weighted.

Source: "Labour Force Statistics", *OECD Employment and Labour Market Statistics* (database), *http://dx.doi.org/10.1787/lfs-lfs-data-en.*

StatLink ⬛️🖳 *http://dx.doi.org/10.1787/888933259013*

Figure 2.13. **Changes in long-term unemployment from 2009 to 2014, by age**
Percentage point increase or decrease in the proportion of the labour force unemployed for one year or more

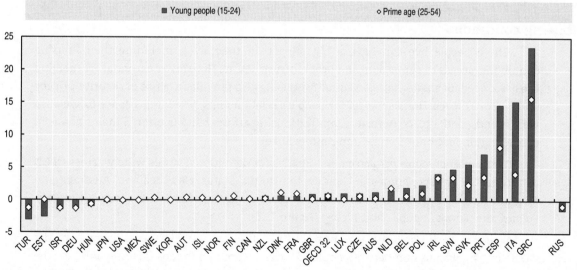

Note: The latest available year is 2013 for Korea. Changes for Belgium are calculated over the period 2011-2014 due to a break in the series. The OECD average is population-weighted.

Source: "Labour Force Statistics", *OECD Employment and Labour Market Statistics* (database), *http://dx.doi.org/10.1787/lfs-lfs-data-en.*

StatLink ⬛️🖳 *http://dx.doi.org/10.1787/888933259023*

Across the OECD area as a whole, men and women are equally likely to be long-term unemployed (at a rate of 1 in every 38 people in the labour force). However, there are large gender differences in Ireland, where long-term unemployment rates among men are almost double those among women, and in Turkey, Greece and the Czech Republic, where rates are higher among women.

Figure 2.14. **Gender differences in long-term unemployment rates**
Percentage of the labour force unemployed for one year or more, 2014

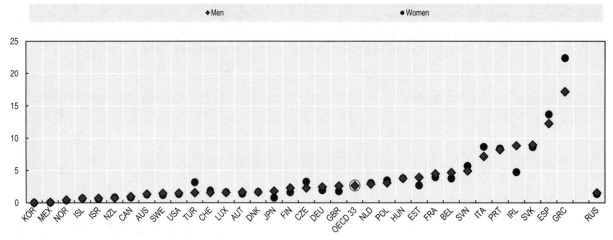

Note: The OECD average is population-weighted.

Source: "Labour Force Statistics", OECD Employment and Labour Market Statistics (database), http://dx.doi.org/10.1787/lfs-lfs-data-en.
StatLink ᴹˢᴾ http://dx.doi.org/10.1787/888933259039

Men's (full-time, full-year) earnings are higher than women's in every OECD country, and the average gender wage gap[6] now stands at 15.5% (OECD, 2015c). In other words, women earn just under 85 cents for every dollar earned by men. The difference in earnings between men and women is largest in Korea, Estonia, Japan and Israel (with wage gaps well above 20%), and smallest in Greece, Luxembourg, Belgium and New Zealand (where the wage gap is less than 7%).

Housing conditions

Where people live can have a big impact on their lives, including their housing conditions, access to sanitation, and other infrastructure. Housing is essential for meeting the basic need for shelter, but good quality housing also provides a sense of security, privacy and personal space. Homes matter for people's relationships, providing a space to socialise with friends, and a place to raise a family. Housing affordability is often a major financial consideration for home-owners and renters alike.

The *number of rooms per person* (see Box 2.3 for definitions) varies widely across OECD countries. On average, homes in Canada, the United States, New Zealand, Australia and Belgium have twice as many rooms per person, relative to homes in Mexico, Hungary, Poland, the Slovak Republic and Turkey (Figure 2.15).

Access to *basic sanitation* (see Box 2.3 for definition) is widespread throughout the OECD, but significant numbers of people still live without an indoor flushing toilet for the sole use of their household – including over 5% of people in Japan, Estonia, Chile, Turkey, Brazil and the Russian Federation (Figure 2.16). In most countries, the proportion of people living in housing that lacks basic sanitation has generally declined since 2009.

Figure 2.15. **Rooms per person**
Average number, 2013 or latest available year

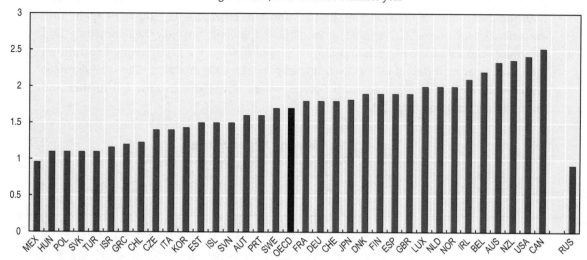

Notes: OECD estimates for Australia, Canada, Israel, New Zealand, the United States, Chile and the Russian Federation are based on national data. The latest available year is 2012 for Ireland and Israel; 2011 for Australia, the Russian Federation, Turkey and Canada; 2010 for Korea and Mexico; 2008 for Japan; and 2002 for Chile. The OECD average is population-weighted.

Sources: European Union Statistics on Income and Living Conditions (EU-SILC) for EU countries and Norway; 2011 ABS Census of Population and Housing for Australia; Canadian National Household Survey for Canada; INE Censo 2002 for Chile; Israeli Household Expenditure Survey for Israel; Housing and Land Survey of Japan for Japan; Population and Housing Census of Korea for Korea; INEGI Censo de Población y Vivienda 2010 for Mexico; Census of New Zealand for New Zealand; Population and Housing census of Turkey for Turkey; American Community Survey for the United States; and ROSSTAT Income, Expenditure and Consumption of Households statistical report for the Russian Federation.

StatLink http://dx.doi.org/10.1787/888933259048

Figure 2.16. **People living in dwellings without basic sanitary facilities**
Percentage of people living in dwellings without an indoor flushing toilet for the sole use of their household

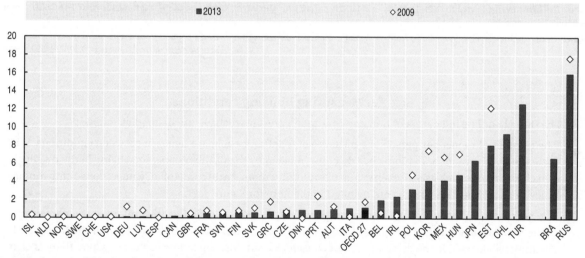

Notes: The latest available data for Ireland refer to 2012; and to 2010 for Korea and Mexico. The first year shown refers to 2006 Mexico, and to 2005 for Korea. The only available observation refers to 2010 for Brazil and Turkey; to 2008 for Japan; to 2001 for Chile; and to 1997 for Canada. The OECD average is population-weighted.

Sources: European Union Statistics on Income and Living Conditions (EU-SILC) *http://epp.eurostat.ec.europa.eu/portal/page/portal/microdata/ eu_silc* for EU countries and Norway; Canadian Household Facilities and Equipment Survey for Canada; INE Censo 2002 for Chile; Housing and Land Survey of Japan for Japan; Population and Housing Census of Korea for Korea; INEGI Censo de Población y Vivienda 2010 for Mexico; Turkish Income and Living Conditions survey for Turkey; American Housing Survey for the United States; Universo do Censo Demográfico 2010 of Brazil for Brazil; and ROSSTAT Income, Expenditure and Consumption of Households statistical report for the Russian Federation.

StatLink http://dx.doi.org/10.1787/888933259057

Housing costs typically take up a sizeable proportion of household budgets. On average, people in OECD countries spend just over 20% of their annual gross adjusted disposable household income on housing (see Box 2.3 for a full definition). Housing expenditure exceeds 23% of household annual gross adjusted income in New Zealand, Italy and Denmark, and 25% in the Czech and Slovak Republics (Figure 2.17). Housing expenditure increased in around half of all OECD countries between 2009 and 2012. The steepest rises occurred in Portugal, Italy, Spain and Greece, where household income fell further and more rapidly than housing costs.

Figure 2.17. **Housing expenditure**
As a percentage of household gross adjusted disposable income

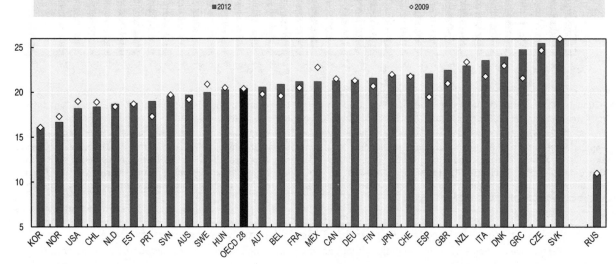

Notes: The latest available year for New Zealand is 2011. The earlier year shown for Korea and the Netherlands is 2010. The OECD average is population-weighted.

Source: OECD calculations based on OECD National Accounts Statistics (database), http://dx.doi.org/10.1787/na-data-en.

StatLink ⟪═⟫ http://dx.doi.org/10.1787/888933259064

Box 2.3. **Measuring housing conditions**

The three headline indicators of housing conditions presented above are defined as follows:

● The **number of rooms per person** is a measure of whether people are living in crowded conditions. It is measured as the number of rooms in a dwelling, divided by the number of persons living in the dwelling. It excludes rooms such as a kitchenette, scullery/utility room, bathroom, toilet, garage, consulting rooms, office or shop. The data sources are detailed in the note for Figure 2.15.

● The **percentage of people living in dwellings without access to basic facilities** refers to the percentage of the population living in a dwelling without an indoor flushing toilet for the sole use of the household. Flushing toilets outside the dwelling are not considered, but flushing toilets in a room where there is also a shower unit or a bath are included. Data sources are detailed in the note for Figure 2.16.

● The **share of household gross adjusted disposable income spent on housing and maintenance of the house**, as defined in the System of National Accounts (SNA), includes actual and imputed rentals for housing, expenditure on maintenance and repair of the dwelling (including miscellaneous services), on water supply, electricity, gas and other fuels, as well as the expenditure on furniture, furnishings,

---

Box 2.3. **Measuring housing conditions** (*cont.*)

household equipment and goods and services for routine home maintenance, expressed as a percentage of the household gross adjusted disposable income. This measure of housing costs excludes household payments for interest and principal on housing mortgages. The data refer to the sum of households and non-profit institutions serving households and are sourced from the *OECD National Accounts Database*.

The indicator on household crowding suffers from a number of limitations. First, it does not take into account the possible trade-off between the size of the dwelling and its location: some households may choose to live in smaller dwellings located in better serviced areas than in larger homes in less desirable locations. Second, an ideal indicator of the available space per person should refer not only to the number of rooms available, but also to their overall size (e.g. number of square metres per person). For instance, the size of accommodation is generally smaller in urban areas than in rural ones, which may hamper international comparisons. Indicators of housing overcrowding should ideally be complemented with data on the perceived lack of space, as reported in household surveys.

The second indicator, which focuses on access to indoor flushing toilets, provides a proxy measure of the notion of "decent housing". However, an ideal indicator set would also include other basic aspects of housing conditions such as adequate electrical and plumbing installations, the quality of floors and doors, structural damage and adequate heating. An ideal set of housing indicators would also inform about the tenure status of households, people's subjective perceptions of the pressure of housing costs on household budgets, and other types of housing expenditures (e.g. those related to mortgages) that are not covered by the indicator used here. It would also include measures of the environmental characteristics of the areas where dwellings are located (e.g. outdoor pollution, exposure to noise and the proximity to public services). In practice, it is difficult to measure housing conditions, as there are very few internationally comparable indicators and no harmonised housing surveys across countries. The OECD is currently developing an internationally comparable database focusing on House Price Indices (HPIs) – also called Residential Property Prices Indices (RPPIs) – and other associated indicators to provide a more complete picture of the residential real estate market. This work includes the release of a new OECD "House prices and related indicators" database in summer 2015.

Further reading:

● Balestra, C. and J. Sultan (2013), "Home Sweet Home: The Determinants of Residential Satisfaction and its Relation with Well-being", *OECD Statistics Working Papers*, No. 2013/05, OECD Publishing, Paris, *http://dx.doi.org/10.1787/5jzbcx0czc0x-en*.

● OECD (2011b), "Housing conditions", in OECD, *How's Life? Measuring Well-being*, OECD Publishing, Paris, *http://dx.doi.org/10.1787/9789264121164-6-en*.

Health Status

Health and well-being go hand-in-hand. Being healthy enough to participate in the activities that people value, and to pursue the lives that they want to live, is a crucial element of well-being for people of all ages. Poor health is consistently associated with lower satisfaction with life as a whole and with worse daily emotions and experiences. Health also affects people's ability to work, study and make the most of their leisure time.

In more than two-thirds of OECD countries, *life expectancy* at birth now exceeds 80 years (Figure 2.18, see Box 2.4 for definitions). The lowest level of life expectancy is observed in Mexico, Hungary, the Slovak Republic and Turkey, where it is below 77 years. Cumulative gains in life expectancy between 2009 and 2013 vary from around 4 months in Iceland, Germany, the United States and Japan, to more than two years in Turkey and Estonia.

Figure 2.18. **Life expectancy at birth**

Years

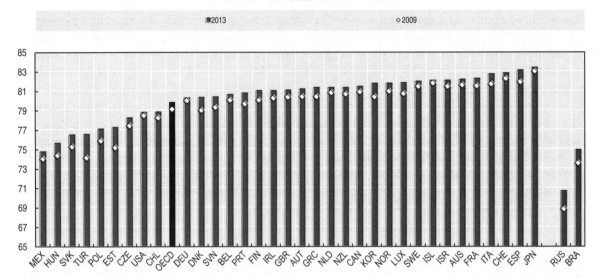

Notes: The latest available year is 2014 for Mexico and 2011 for Canada. Values for Germany are provided by Destatis, and refer to 2007-09 and 2010-12. The OECD average is population-weighted.

Source: "Health status", OECD Health Statistics (database), *http://dx.doi.org/10.1787/data-00540-en*; and Destatis (2015), *www.destatis.de/DE/ ZahlenFakten/GesellschaftStaat/Bevoelkerung/Sterbefaelle/Tabellen/SterbetafelDeutschland.xlsx*.

StatLink 🔗 *http://dx.doi.org/10.1787/888933259075*

Longer lives are not necessarily *healthier* lives, and **percevied health** offers a complementary perspective on people's experiences. Just over two-thirds of people in the OECD area report that they are in "good" or "very good" health (Figure 2.19; see Box 2.4 for a definition). Between 2009 and 2013, the proportion remained fairly stable in most countries, though it declined by 3 percentage points or more in Korea, Finland, Iceland and the United Kingdom, and increased by 4 percentage points or more in Slovenia and the Slovak Republic.

Figure 2.19. **Perceived health status**

Percentage of adults reporting "good" or "very good" health

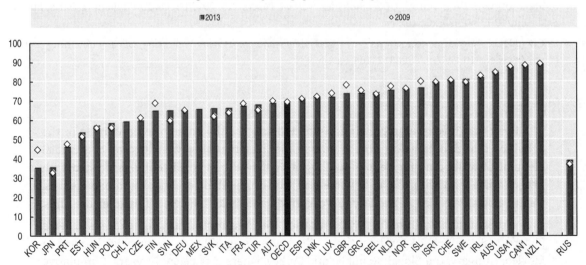

Notes: The latest available year is 2014 for the Russian Federation. 2009 values refer to 2007 for Australia, Japan and New Zealand; and to 2011 for the Russian Federation. The single data point for Mexico refers to 2006; and to 2011 for Chile. Adults are generally defined as people aged 15 years and over. Results for countries marked with a "1" are not directly comparable with those for other countries, due to differences in reporting scales, which may lead to an upward bias in the reported estimates. The OECD average is population-weighted.

Source: "Health status", OECD Health Statistics (database), *http://dx.doi.org/10.1787/data-00540-en*.

StatLink 🔗 *http://dx.doi.org/10.1787/888933259086*

Box 2.4. **Measuring health status**

The two headline indicators of health status presented above are defined as follows:

- **Life expectancy at birth** measures the average number of years that people born today could expect to live based on currently prevailing age-specific death rates. Life expectancy at birth for the population as a whole is computed as a weighted average of life expectancy for men and women. The data are based on official national statistics compiled by the OECD and available in the OECD Health Statistics Database.

- **Perceived health** refers to the percentage of the population aged 15 and over who report being in "good" or "very good" health. The indicator is based on the following question: "How is your health in general?" with, in most countries, response categories of the type, "very good/ good/ fair/ bad/ very bad". Some cross-country differences in the measurement methodology (for example, the use of different response scales) can limit comparability across countries; the note for Figure 2.19 provides more details. Data are compiled as part of the OECD Health Statistics Database, and are drawn from European Union Statistics on Income and Living Conditions (EU-SILC), general household surveys or more detailed Health Interviews undertaken as part of national official surveys in various countries.

Life expectancy at birth provides only an estimate of the expected life span of people born in a specific year, as the actual age-specific death rates of any particular birth cohort are not known in advance. Measures of life expectancy at birth are based on good quality data for all OECD countries, and can be broken down by gender. However, relatively few countries are able to provide routine information on life expectancy by educational attainment and income, as these measures require either linking mortality records to a population census, or information on the educational attainment of the deceased to be reported on the death certificate.

Measuring morbidity (i.e. the incidence of disease and illness) is more challenging. One approach is to focus on a person's *functioning* – i.e. whether they experience any limitations in domains such as vision, hearing, walking, cognition or affect (moods, emotions and feelings) – as well as pain and fatigue. The UNECE-WHO-Eurostat taskforce on measuring health status (or Budapest Initiative) and the Washington Group on disability statistics have proposed a set of questions to measure functioning, but comparable data are yet to emerge on an international level. A major gap also exists for internationally comparable statistics on mental health outcomes. The European Health Interview Survey 2014 should produce comparable data on a range of health status indicators in the near future for European countries.

Indicators of perceived health are among the few morbidity indicators that are available for all OECD countries. Such measures can summarise a broad range of dimensions of morbidity, since they address the overall health status of the respondent. However, indicators of perceived health focus on people's *experiences* of their health, rather than defining morbidity in objective terms. The use of different measurement methods, possible cultural biases and other contextual factors can potentially constrain data comparability across countries.

Further reading:

- OECD (2015d), *Health at a Glance 2015: OECD Indicators*, OECD Publishing, Paris, forthcoming.

- OECD (2014b), *Making Mental Health Count: The Social and Economic Costs of Neglecting Mental Health Care*, OECD Health Policy Studies, OECD Publishing, Paris, *http://dx.doi.org/10.1787/9789264208445-en*.

The distribution of health outcomes

Women live longer lives but generally feel less healthy than men: women's life expectancy is higher than men's in every OECD country but their self-reported health status is typically worse (OECD, 2013a). Evidence also suggests that health varies by education, with highly educated people enjoying a longer life expectancy relative to those with less education (OECD, 2012; OECD 2015d; EU, 2013). For instance, among the 15 OECD countries for which data are available,[7] a 30-year-old man with a tertiary education can expect to live, on average, 8 years longer than someone without upper secondary education; among women the average difference is 4 years (OECD, 2015d). These differences are largest in the Czech Republic, Estonia, Hungary and Poland, and smallest in Italy, Sweden, and Portugal. For example, in the Czech Republic, a 30-year-old man with a tertiary degree can expect to live 18 years longer than a man who has not attained an upper secondary education; in Estonia the difference is 15 years, while in Italy, Sweden and Portugal the difference is just 4 years.

A social gradient also exists for perceived health in OECD countries: while 78% of people with incomes in the highest quintile report being in good or better health, only 60% of those with income in the lowest quintile do so (Figure 2.20). Inequalities in self-reported health status are particularly large in Estonia, the Czech Republic, Finland, Belgium, Germany, the United Kingdom and Slovenia, where the gap in perceived health between the highest and lowest income quintile is 25 percentage points or greater. By contrast, the gap is less than 10 points in New Zealand, Greece and Iceland.[8]

Figure 2.20. **The gap in perceived health between high and low income groups**
Percentage of adults reporting "good" or "very good" health, 2013 or latest available year

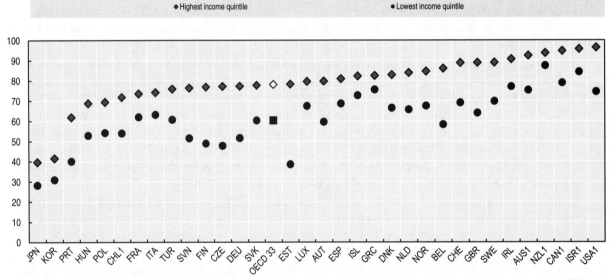

Notes: Data refer to 2014 for New Zealand; 2011 for Chile; and 2007 for Australia. Adults are generally defined as people aged 15 years and over. Results for countries marked with a "1" are not strictly comparable with those for other countries, due to differences in reporting scales, which may lead to an upward bias in the reported estimates. The OECD average is population-weighted.

Source: "Health status", OECD Health Statistics (database), *http://dx.doi.org/10.1787/data-00540-en.*

StatLink 🔗 *http://dx.doi.org/10.1787/888933259090*

Work-life balance

How people spend their time is a critical determinant of their broader well-being, and most workers dedicate a larger proportion of their waking hours to work than to any other type of activity. Getting the right balance between life and work matters for people's health and happiness, but also for the relationships that people have with their friends, families and the wider community. People's ability to balance work and life also has implications for the well-being of others: caring for children and other dependents is an important form of "unpaid work" that many people need to reconcile alongside a full-time job.

One in every eight employees across the OECD works 50 hours or more each week on a routine basis (Figure 2.21, see Box 2.5 for definitions). The proportion of employees **working very long hours** varies from just 1 in every 250 in the Netherlands to 1 in every 2.4 employees in Turkey. Since 2009, the average proportion of employees working very long hours increased by 0.7 percentage points across the OECD. In Portugal and Chile, the incidence of very long hours in 2013 was nearly double the level in 2009 – an increase of 6.9 percentage points in Chile, and 4.4 percentage points in Portugal. It also increased by around 1 percentage point in Slovak Republic, Ireland, the United Kingdom, the United States, Greece and New Zealand. By contrast, reductions of around 2 percentage points or more have been recorded in Turkey, Israel, the Czech Republic, Austria and Brazil.

Figure 2.21. **Employees working very long hours**
Percentage of all employees usually working 50 hours or more per week

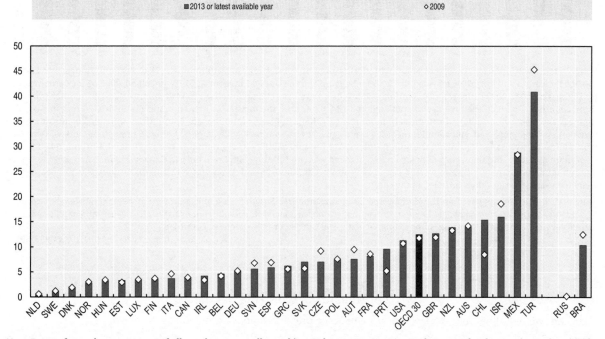

Note: Data refer to the percentage of all employees usually working 50 hours or more per week, except for the Russian Federation for which data refer to people who worked 51 hours or more. The jobs covered are the main job for Austria, Canada, the Czech Republic, Finland, Hungary, Mexico, Poland, the Slovak Republic, Sweden, Turkey and the United States, and all jobs for Australia, New Zealand and Norway. Starting from 2002, the number of usual hours worked excludes the main meal breaks for the Slovak Republic. Data refer to 2012 for Chile and Brazil. The OECD average is population-weighted.

Source: "Labour Force Statistics", *OECD Employment and Labour Market Statistics* (database), *http://dx.doi.org/10.1787/lfs-lfs-data-en.*

StatLink ᵃᵐˢᴾ *http://dx.doi.org/10.1787/888933259105*

Having sufficient time for *leisure and personal care* – which include activities such as sleep, eating, hygiene, exercise and time with friends and family – is important for people's sense of work-life balance and for their overall well-being. Among the 20 OECD countries where data are available, the average full-time worker spends just under

15 hours per day on leisure and personal care (Figure 2.22). There is some variation in how time is spent across countries: full-time employed people living in France, Spain, Denmark, Belgium, Norway and Germany spend more than 15½ hours per day on leisure and personal care. This drops to less than 14½ hours in the United States, Poland, Canada and Australia.

Figure 2.22. **Time devoted to leisure and personal care**

Hours per day, people in full-time employment, latest available year

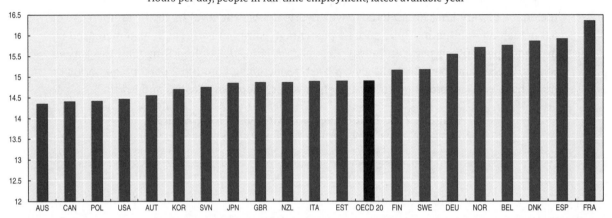

Notes: Data refer to 2013 for the United States; 2011 for Japan; 2010 for Canada; 2009-10 for Spain, New Zealand, France, and Estonia; 2008-09 for Austria and Italy; 2006 for Australia; 2005 for Belgium and the United Kingdom; 2003-04 for Poland; 2001-02 for Germany; 2001 for Denmark; and to 2000-01 for Norway, Slovenia and Sweden. Data have been normalised to 1440 minutes per day: in other words, for those countries for which the time use did not sum up to 1440 minutes, the missing or extra minutes (around 30-40 minutes usually) were equally distributed across all activities. Data for Hungary, Ireland, Portugal, Turkey and South Africa were excluded as they also include part-time employed. Full samples include people aged 12 or more in New Zealand; 15 or more in Austria, Canada, Denmark, Finland, France, Italy, Japan, Spain and the United States; 20 to 74 years old in Belgium, Germany, Norway, Poland, Slovenia, Sweden; and 20 or more in Korea – but in practice data are limited to those who are full-time employed only. In Canada, Japan, Korea and the United States a minimum number of hours worked per week is also set at 30, 35, 36 and 35 respectively. The OECD average is the population-weighted average of the values included in the chart.

Source: OECD calculations based on the Harmonised European Time Use Survey web application for European countries (*https://www. h2.scb.se/tus/tus/*); Eurostat database, *http://appsso.eurostat.ec.europa.eu/nui/show.do?dataset=tus_00selfstat&lang=en*; and public-use time use survey micro-data and tabulations from National Statistical Offices for non-European countries.

StatLink ᔛᔕᔐ *http://dx.doi.org/10.1787/888933259111*

Box 2.5. **Measuring work-life balance**

The two headline indicators of work-life balance presented above are defined as follows:

● Data on **employees who usually work for pay for 50 hours or more per week** are shown as a percentage of the total number of employees, of all ages. The indicator excludes self-employed workers. The threshold is set at 50 hours because, after commuting, unpaid work and basic needs (such as sleeping and eating) are taken into account, workers routinely working more than 50 hours per week are likely to be left with very few hours (one or two per day) for other activities. Moreover, in countries where there is a regulation on maximum working time, this is generally limited to 48 hours per week. Data come from National Labour Force Surveys and are broadly comparable across countries.

● Data on the **time devoted to leisure and personal care** are shown for a typical day and refer to full-time employed people only in order to improve comparability across countries where employment rates differ. The information is collected through national Time Use Surveys, which

---

Box 2.5. **Measuring work-life balance** (cont.)

involve respondents keeping a diary of their activities over one or several representative days for a given period. Activities considered under the definition of "time devoted to leisure and personal care" include sleep, eating, hygiene, exercise, time spent with friends and family, and travel time devoted to leisure and personal care. For some countries and some specific types of activities, the comparability of these surveys might be an issue. The data shown here have been harmonised *ex post* by the OECD. Data are sourced from the Harmonised European Time Use Survey; the Eurostat time use database, public-use time use survey micro-data, and tabulations from National Statistical Offices.

The headline indicators used here provide both an indirect and a direct measure of the time available for non-work activities that contribute to individual and family well-being. Yet measuring work-life *balance* is a more challenging task. First, the way people allocate their time is determined by necessity, individual preference and cultural, social and family contexts. This means that what feels "balanced" for one person might not feel balanced for someone else. People running their own business might have an extra incentive to work long hours – and as a consequence the self-employed are excluded from data on very long working hours, but this can have a bearing on the results when self-employed people form a significant proportion of the total workforce. Second, because the indicators used here focus only on the quantity of time allocated to different tasks, they do not shed light on the *quality* of the time spent outside work, and thus on people's personal enjoyment or perceived time stress. Third, Time Use Surveys are, in most OECD countries, undertaken on an ad hoc or infrequent basis (i.e. every 5 or 10 years), leading to estimates that are typically not very timely.

Further reading:

● OECD (2014c), "Improving well-being", in OECD, *OECD Economic Surveys: United States 2014*, OECD Publishing, Paris, *http://dx.doi.org/10.1787/eco_surveys-usa-2014-5-en*.

● OECD (2011c), *The Future of Families to 2030*, OECD Publishing, Paris, *http://dx.doi.org/10.1787/9789264168367-en*.

● OECD (2007), *Babies and Bosses – Reconciling Work and Family Life: A Synthesis of Findings for OECD Countries*, OECD Publishing, Paris, *http://dx.doi.org/10.1787/9789264032477-en*.

The distribution of work-life balance outcomes

Gender is a key factor when considering inequalities in work-life balance (OECD, 2013a). In all OECD countries, male employees are more likely than female employees to work for pay for 50 hours or more per week. However, while men spend longer hours in paid work, women have the longest hours when considering paid and unpaid work (such as domestic work) together (OECD, 2013a). Indeed, in two-thirds of the OECD countries for which data are available, women who work full-time devote less time to leisure and personal care than men who work full-time (Figure 2.23). The largest differences are found in Korea and Slovenia, where men spend over 1 hour more than women per day on leisure and personal care, and in Italy and Estonia where the gender gap is around 55 minutes. By contrast, women spend around 6 minutes more on leisure and personal care than men do in Sweden, New Zealand and Denmark, and around 18 minutes more than men in the United States.

Figure 2.23. **Time spent on leisure and personal care for men and women**

Hours per day, people in full-time employment, latest available year

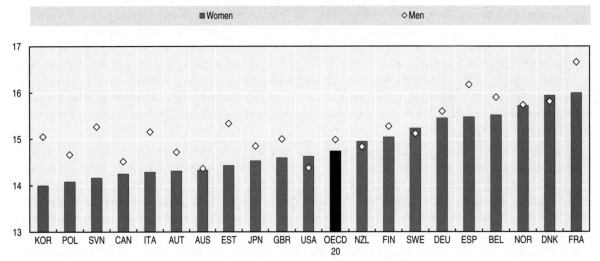

Note: Data refer to 2013 for the United States; 2011 for Japan; 2010 for Canada; 2009-10 for Spain, New Zealand, France, and Estonia 2008-09 for Austria and Italy; 2006 for Australia; 2005 for Belgium and the United Kingdom; 2003-04 for Poland; 2001-02 for Germany; 2001 for Denmark; and to 2000-01 for Norway, Slovenia and Sweden. Data have been normalised to 1440 minutes per day: in other words, for those countries for which the time use did not sum up to 1440 minutes, the missing or extra minutes (around 30-40 minutes usually) were equally distributed across all activities. Data for Hungary, Ireland, Portugal, Turkey and South Africa were excluded as they also include part-time employed. Full samples include people aged 12 or more in New Zealand; 15 or more in Austria, Canada, Denmark, Finland, France, Italy, Japan, Spain and the United States; 20 to 74 years old in Belgium, Germany, Norway, Poland, Slovenia, Sweden; and 20 or more in Korea – but in practice data are limited to those who are full-time employed only. In Canada, Japan, Korea and the United States a minimum number of hours worked per week is also set at 30, 35, 36 and 35 respectively. The OECD average is the population-weighted average of the values included in the chart.

Source: OECD calculations based on the Harmonised European Time Use Survey web application for European countries (*https://www.h2.scb.se/tus/tus/*), Eurostat database, *http://appsso.eurostat.ec.europa.eu/nui/show.do?dataset=tus_00selfstat&lang=en*, public-use time use survey micro-data and tabulations from National Statistical Offices for non-European countries.

StatLink ᴍᴤ☍ *http://dx.doi.org/10.1787/888933259124*

Education and skills

While having a good education makes it easier for people to get a good job, a good education is more than just a passport to work. The opportunity to learn new skills can be intrinsically rewarding, and education is generally valued by people as an outcome in its own right. Higher levels of education are also associated with better health status and greater civic engagement.

Across the OECD, just over three-quarters of the population aged 25-64 have completed *upper secondary education* (Figure 2.24, see Box 2.6 for definitions). The share rises to 90% or more in Poland, Estonia, the Slovak Republic, the Czech Republic and the Russian Federation. On the other hand, fewer than 60% of 25-64 year olds have completed upper-secondary education in Italy, Chile, Spain, Portugal, Mexico and Turkey. Between 2009 and 2013, educational attainment increased in almost every OECD country, and by 3.2 percentage points on average.

Cognitive skills in reading, mathematics and science at age 15 (Figure 2.25, see Box 2.6 for the definition) refer to what students know and can do, rather than the number of years spent at school or the qualifications attained. In 2012, the cognitive skills of students across OECD countries were highest in Korea, Japan, Finland and Estonia, and lowest in Mexico, Chile, Turkey and Greece.

Figure 2.24. **Educational attainment of the adult working-age population**

Percentage of people aged 25-64 with at least an upper secondary education

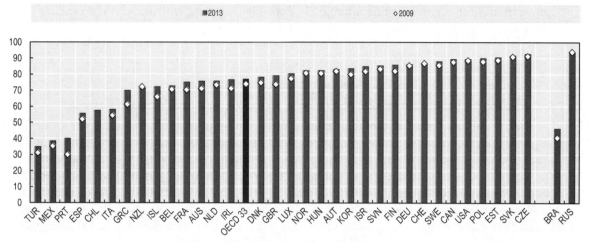

■ 2013   ◇ 2009

Note: Data for Chile refer to 2011 only. For the Russian Federation, the latest available year is 2012, and the first available year is 2011. The OECD average is population-weighted.

Source: OECD (2015e), *Education at a Glance Interim Report: Update of Employment and Educational Attainment Indicators*, OECD, Paris, *www.oecd.org/edu/EAG-Interim-report.pdf*.

StatLink 🖳 *http://dx.doi.org/10.1787/888933259133*

Figure 2.25. **Cognitive skills of 15-year-old students**

PISA mean scores in reading, mathematics and science, 2012

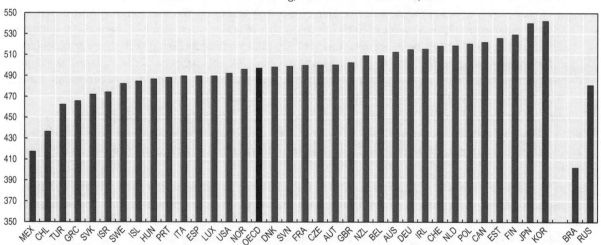

Note: The PISA scores on reading, mathematics and science are each measured on a scale which is normalised to be 500 for the OECD average.

Source: OECD (2014e), *PISA 2012 Results: What Students Know and Can Do* (Volume I, Revised edition): *Student Performance in Mathematics, Reading and Science*, PISA, OECD Publishing, Paris, *http://dx.doi.org/10.1787/9789264208780-en*.

StatLink 🖳 *http://dx.doi.org/10.1787/888933259140*

The OECD Survey of Adult Skills (PIAAC) assesses the proficiency of adults in the domains of literacy, numeracy and problem-solving in technology-rich environments (see Box 2.6 for the precise definition). According to this source, ***adults' competencies*** vary significantly across countries (Figure 2.26), especially in the case of numeracy. Japan and Finland have the highest levels of proficiency in both numeracy and literacy, while Italy and Spain perform poorly in both of these domains. Countries' relative rankings for adult skills tend to mirror the results for cognitive skills among 15-year-olds, although Sweden and Norway rank much more highly on the adult skills measure, and Korea's top-ranking for cognitive skills among 15-year-olds contrasts with its average ranking on adult skills.

Box 2.6. **Measuring education and skills**

The three headline indicators of education and skills presented above are defined as follows:

- The **educational attainment of the adult population** is the number of adults aged 25 to 64 having completed at least an upper secondary education, over the total population of the same age. The definition of "at least upper secondary education" corresponds to the International Standard Classification of Education (ISCED) levels 3 and above (excluding ISCED level 3C short programmes), and includes both i) programmes defined as "general" which are often designed for preparing students for further education, and ii) programmes geared towards vocational education and training (VET). The data underlying this indicator are collected through the annual OECD questionnaire on National Educational Attainment Categories (NEAC) and are based on national Labour Force Survey (LFS) data.

- **Students' average score in reading, mathematics and science** is based on data collected through the Programme on International Student Assessment (PISA) coordinated by the OECD, and refers to students aged 15. Skills in reading, mathematics and science are each assessed separately, and measured on a scale which is normalised such that a value of 500 represents the OECD average. The summary shown here represents the average score across the three assessments.

- The **mean proficiency in numeracy and literacy for the adult population** is based on data collected through the OECD Survey of Adult Skills, which is part of the Programme for the International Assessment of Adult Competencies (PIAAC) coordinated by the OECD. The indicator refers to adults aged 16-65. A major component of the PIAAC is the direct assessment of key information-processing skills: literacy, numeracy and problem-solving in the context of technology-rich environments. In each of the domains assessed, proficiency is considered as a continuum of ability involving the mastery of information-processing tasks of increasing complexity. The results are represented on a 500-point scale.

Educational attainment reflects the level of schooling or paper qualifications that people have achieved, while PIAAC aims to capture the net result of a person's lifetime learning experiences to date, both formal and informal. At present, however, PIAAC has limited country coverage, and is carried out on a 10 year cycle.

An ideal set of measures of people's education and skills would include both the cognitive and non-cognitive skills of the entire population, based on standardised achievement scores. The indicators presented here are proxies for this ideal. They have some limitations: first, they measure individuals' acquired abilities, without informing about how these abilities are actually used in life; and second, they do not capture non-cognitive (i.e. social and emotional) skills. The OECD project on Education and Social Progress (see OECD, 2015f) is developing a set of measures to capture this latter construct, which will be the subject of a longitudinal study, co-ordinated by the OECD, to be launched in 2019.

Further reading:

- OECD (2015f), *Skills for Social Progress: The Power of Social and Emotional Skills*, OECD Skills Studies, OECD Publishing, Paris, *http://dx.doi.org/10.1787/9789264226159-en*.

- OECD (2014d), *Education at a Glance 2014: OECD Indicators*, OECD Publishing, Paris, *http://dx.doi.org/10.1787/eag-2014-en*.

- OECD (2013e), *OECD Skills Outlook 2013: First Results from the Survey of Adult Skills*, OECD Publishing, Paris, *http://dx.doi.org/10.1787/9789264204256-en*.

Figure 2.26. **Competencies of the adult population**

Mean proficiency of adults aged 16-65, 2012

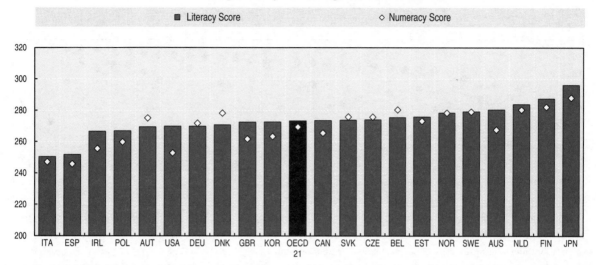

Note: Data for Belgium refer to Flanders; data for the United Kingdom refer to England and Northern Ireland. In each domain, the results are represented on a 500-point scale.

Source: OECD (2013e), *OECD Skills Outlook 2013: First Results from the Survey of Adult Skills*, OECD Publishing, Paris, *http://dx.doi. org/10.1787/9789264204256-en.*

StatLink ⟐ *http://dx.doi.org/10.1787/888933259156*

The distribution of education and skills

While in all OECD countries young women have generally closed the gap with young men in terms of educational attainment, this is not yet the case for competencies at age 25-64; according to the OECD Survey of Adult Skills (PIAAC), women's proficiency is generally lower than men's, particularly in numeracy (OECD, 2013e). Among 15-year-olds, gender gaps in education vary depending on the subject of study: boys perform worse than girls, on average, in reading but do better in mathematics (OECD, 2015g; OECD, 2015h).

15-year olds' educational outcomes are strongly related to parents' socio-economic background. Gaps in cognitive skills between students from the highest and lowest socio-economic backgrounds (defined as the top and bottom quintile of the PISA index of economic, social and cultural status) vary widely across countries – and are roughly equivalent to the skills acquired in more than two school years in countries with the widest gap (OECD, 2013a). Countries such as Belgium, New Zealand, Germany and France have average or above-average PISA scores, but suffer from large gaps between the performance of students with high and low socioeconomic status; by contrast, Korea, Japan, Finland, Estonia and Canada are characterised by high PISA scores overall and smaller gaps between students from different backgrounds.

The gap in educational attainment between younger and older working-age adults also varies across countries (Figure 2.27). The younger generation of working adults are much more likely than the older generation to have completed upper secondary education: on average across the OECD area, the attainment rate among 25–34 year olds is 16 percentage points higher than that among 55–64 year olds.

Figure 2.27. **Educational attainment among younger and older adults of working age**

Percentage of age groups 25-34 and 55-64 with at least upper secondary education, 2013

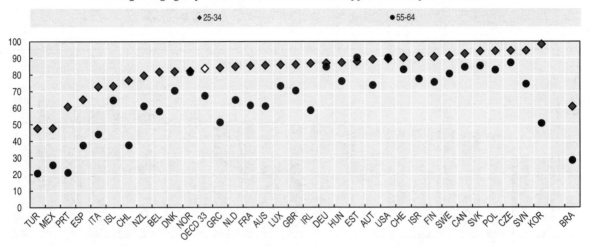

Note: Data for Chile refer to 2011. The OECD average is population-weighted.

Source: OECD (2015e), *Education at a Glance Interim Report: Update of Employment and Educational Attainment Indicators*, OECD, Paris, *www.oecd. org/edu/EAG-Interim-report.pdf.*

StatLink ᵃᵐˢ᷈ *http://dx.doi.org/10.1787/888933259168*

Social connections

Positive social relationships are a powerful source of well-being. Time-use surveys suggest that socialising is the highlight of most people's daily activities. Loneliness and a lack of *social support* are critical factors in low subjective well-being. People with strong social networks are also more likely to have a job and to be in better health.

In most OECD countries, at least 85% of people report having someone to count on in times of need (Figure 2.28). While the differences in social support among the top-performing OECD countries are small, there is a 20 percentage point gap between the

Figure 2.28. **Perceived social network support**

Percentage of people who report having relatives or friends they can count on, 2014

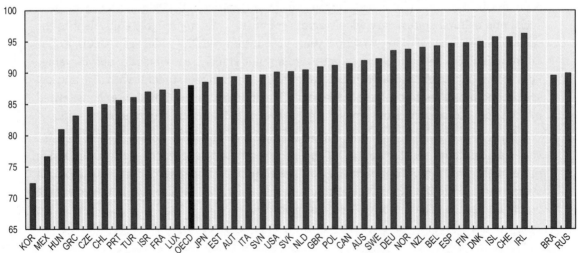

Note: The latest available year is 2013 for Iceland. The OECD average is population-weighted.

Source: Gallup World Poll, *www.gallup.com/services/170945/world-poll.aspx.*

StatLink ᵃᵐˢ᷈ *http://dx.doi.org/10.1787/888933259177*

support levels reported in Switzerland, Ireland and Iceland (where this share is around 95-97%) relative to those reported in Mexico and Korea (around 72-77%). Between 2009 and 2014, the levels of perceived support declined in Mexico (by 9 percentage points) and Korea (by 7 points), but rose in Turkey (by 10 points)(Gallup, 2015).

Box 2.7. **Measuring social connections**

The headline indicator for social connections presented above refers to:

- **Perceived social network support.** This is based on the survey question: "If you were in trouble, do you have relatives or friends you can count on to help you whenever you need them, or not?". The data shown here reflect the percentage of the sample responding "yes". The source for these data is the Gallup World Poll, which samples around 1 000 people per country, per year. The sample is *ex ante* designed to be nationally representative of the population aged 15 and over (including rural areas); to correct for non-random response patterns, the sample data are weighted to the population using weights supplied by Gallup.*

Social support can come from a variety of sources (e.g. a partner, a friend, a family member, a work colleague) and take many different forms: emotional support; practical support (e.g. caring for dependents); financial support; and career- or work-related support, to name just a few. The measure presented here focuses on help in times of trouble, but does not provide any information about the quality or nature of the support provided.

Ideally, a set of indicators of social connections would describe a range of different relationships – both in terms of quality and quantity. Some of the most common approaches to measuring social connections have relied on indirect indicators, such as statistics on membership in associations (e.g. sporting clubs, religious or professional organisations) or on the density of voluntary organisations in a given area (see also Chapter 5). However, such measures have been criticised because they are limited to participation in formal networks, and do not describe informal connections such as those that people maintain with friends and relatives. Moreover, formal membership in associations and its importance for people's well-being can differ over time and across countries, thus hampering international comparability. Time use diaries could prove to be a useful source of information about time spent with others – both in terms of quantity, but also quality.

Various official surveys collect information on social networks and personal relationships, e.g. the General Social Surveys in Australia, Canada and New Zealand. However, most official statistics on social connections are not internationally comparable (Scrivens and Smith, 2013).

Further reading:

- Scrivens, K. and C. Smith (2013), "Four Interpretations of Social Capital: An Agenda for Measurement", *OECD Statistics Working Papers*, No. 2013/06, OECD Publishing, Paris, *http://dx.doi.org/10.1787/5jzbcx010wmt-en*.

- Siegler, V. (2015), "Measuring National Well-Being – An Analysis of Social Capital in the UK", Office for National Statistics, *www.ons.gov.uk/ons/rel/wellbeing/measuring-national-well-being/analysis-of-social-well-being--social-capital--in-the-uk---2013-14/art-measuring-national-well-being---an-analysis-of-social-capital-in-the-uk.html*.

* The weighting procedure used for data in the Gallup World Poll has multiple stages: first, an adjustment is made for geographic disproportionalities (e.g. due to oversampling in major cities); second, an adjustment is applied for sample selection probabilities (number of adults in the household; landline and mobile dual users); and third, weights are adjusted to reflect the distribution of the population by age, gender and educational attainment.

The distribution of social connections

In most OECD countries, people with higher levels of education and income are more likely to report having someone to count on in times of need (OECD, 2013a). Younger people (aged 15-29) are also generally more likely than older people (aged 50 and over) to report having someone they can count on (Figure 2.29). Among OECD countries, age-related gaps are largest in Korea, Chile, Greece, Portugal and Turkey and smallest in English-speaking countries, Mexico, Denmark and Iceland. In two-thirds of OECD countries, the proportion of older people *without* social support is between two and three times higher than for younger people, and this holds true even in countries where the overall level of support is very high.

Figure 2.29. **Differences in social support among different age groups**

Percentage of people who report having relatives or friends they can count on, by age, pooled results 2006-2014

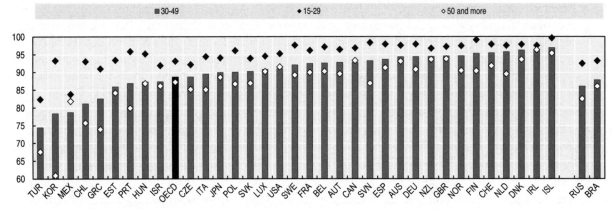

Note: Data are pooled across all available years, 2006-2014. The OECD average is population-weighted.

Source: Gallup World Poll, *www.gallup.com/services/170945/world-poll.aspx.*

StatLink ⬛️🖵 *http://dx.doi.org/10.1787/888933259181*

Civic engagement and governance

For a society to function well, people need to play their part in it: civic engagement and the right to express one's political voice are basic freedoms and essential components of effective democracies. There are large variations across OECD countries in **voter turnout** for national elections, expressed as a ratio of the population registered to vote (Figure 2.30, Panel A). These partly reflect differences in countries' electoral systems, and in particular the practice of compulsory voting in some OECD countries (e.g. Australia, Luxembourg, Belgium and Turkey, IDEA, 2015)[9] which consequently have very high levels of voter turnout (above 85% of the registered population). Switzerland has the lowest voter turnout rate for national elections in the OECD, but also practices a highly participatory form of direct democracy where voters are polled several times a year on issues at the community, regional or national level. Since 2007, voter turnout rates have declined in nearly two-thirds of the OECD countries, with the largest reductions occurring in Chile (which abandoned compulsory voting in 2012), the United States, Japan, Greece, Slovenia and Italy.[10]

When considering the percentage of votes cast among the voting-age population as a whole (rather than only those registered to vote) the cross-country pattern in levels of voter turnout is slightly different (Figure 2.30, Panel B), reflecting country differences in voter registration, how electoral registers are maintained, rules on non-resident voting and the number of residents who are not eligible to vote in national elections. Nonetheless, both Panel A and Panel B generally tell a consistent story of a downward trend in voting patterns in recent years across the OECD area as a whole.

Figure 2.30. **Voter turnout**

Panel A. Percentage of votes cast among the population registered to vote

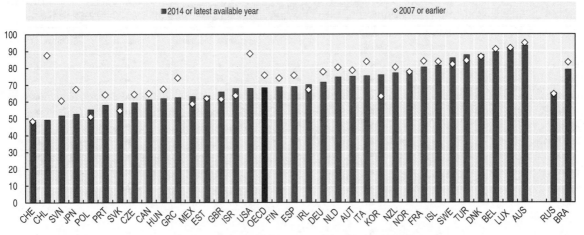

Panel B. Percentage of votes cast among the voting-age population

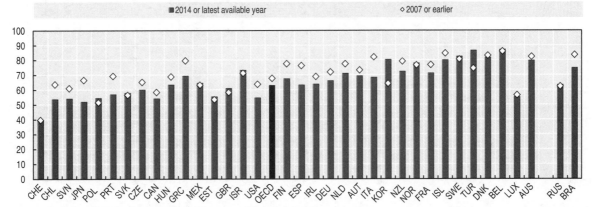

Note: National elections refer to parliamentary elections, with the exceptions of Finland, France, Korea, Mexico, Poland, the United States, Brazil and the Russian Federation, where Presidential elections are considered. The latest available year refers to 2014 for Slovenia, Japan, New Zealand, Hungary, Sweden, Brazil and Belgium; 2013 for Luxembourg, Chile, Germany, Norway, Austria, the Czech Republic, Italy, Australia and Iceland; 2012 for the United States, the Russian Federation, Israel, the Netherlands, the Slovak Republic, Finland, Mexico, Greece, France and Korea; 2011 for Spain, Portugal, Canada, Switzerland, Denmark, Estonia, Ireland and Turkey; and 2010 for the United Kingdom and Poland. The first year refers to 2007 for Australia, Belgium, Switzerland, Denmark, Estonia, Greece, Ireland, Iceland, Turkey, France and Korea; 2006 in Austria, Canada, the Czech Republic, Hungary, Israel, Italy, the Netherlands, the Slovak Republic, Sweden, Finland, Mexico and Brazil; 2005 for Chile, Germany, the United Kingdom, Japan, Norway, New Zealand, Portugal and Poland; and 2004 for Spain, Luxembourg, Slovenia, the United States and the Russian Federation. The OECD average is population-weighted in each panel.

Source: International Institute for Democracy and Electoral Assistance (IDEA) (2015), *www.idea.int.*

StatLink ᘯᑭ *http://dx.doi.org/10.1787/888933259196*

Institutional arrangements also influence *citizen's ability to engage in public policy making*. Engaging stakeholders in the development of laws and regulations improves the quality and inclusiveness of those acts, by gathering inputs from people affected by the proposals, enabling public scrutiny, safeguarding against corruption, and promoting citizens' trust in government. Nearly two thirds of OECD member countries have implemented a requirement to engage stakeholders when developing all primary laws, and just over half have a similar requirement when developing subordinate regulations (Table 2.1). However, much stakeholder engagement in rule-making tends to take place at a late stage in the process, when a legislative draft has already been prepared. Most OECD countries engage

2. HOW'S LIFE? IN FIGURES

Table 2.1. **Government stakeholder engagement when developing regulations**

	Requirement to conduct stakeholder engagement		Early-stage stakeholder engagement to inform officials about the problem and possible solutions		Later-stage: Consultation on draft regulations/ proposed rules	
	Primary laws	Subordinate regulations	Primary laws	Subordinate regulations	Primary laws	Subordinate regulations
Australia	▲	◠	▲	▲	■	▲
Austria	◠	◠	◠	◠	◠	◠
Belgium	■	■	▲	▲	▲	▲
Canada	■	■	▲	■	■	■
Chile	◠	◠	◠	◠	◠	◠
Czech Republic	▲	▲	◠	◠	■	■
Denmark	■	◠	◠	◠	■	◠
Estonia	■	▲	◠	◠	■	■
Finland	■	■	◠	◠	■	■
France	◠	▲	◠	◠	◠	▲
Germany	■	■	◠	◠	◠	◠
Greece	■	●	◠	●	■	▲
Hungary	■	■	●	●	■	■
Iceland	◠	●	◠	◠	■	■
Ireland	◠	◠	◠	●	■	●
Israel	●	◠	●	●	■	▲
Italy	■	■	◠	◠	◠	◠
Japan	●	▲	●	●	●	◠
Korea	▲	▲	◠	●	■	■
Luxembourg	■	■	◠	◠	■	■
Mexico	■	■	◠	◠	■	■
Netherlands	◠	●	●	●	◠	◠
New Zealand	■	■	■	■	■	■
Norway	■	■	◠	◠	■	■
Poland	■	■	◠	◠	■	■
Portugal	▲	▲	●	●	■	■
Slovak Republic	■	■	◠	◠	■	■
Slovenia	■	■	▲	▲	■	■
Spain	■	■	◠	◠	■	■
Sweden	■	■	◠	◠	■	▲
Switzerland	■	▲	◠	◠	■	▲
Turkey	■	■	◠	◠	▲	▲
United Kingdom	■	■	▲	◠	■	■
United States	×	■	×	◠	×	■
EU	▲	▲	▲	▲	●	■
OECD total						
■ For all regulations	21	18	1	2	24	18
▲ For major regulations	4	7	5	3	2	7
◠ For some regulations	6	6	22	21	6	8
● Never	2	3	5	8	1	1
× Not applicable	1	0	1	0	1	0

Note: Data only cover primary laws and subordinate regulations initiated by the executive. All questions on primary laws are not applicable in the United States.

Source: OECD (2015i), *Regulatory Policy Outlook 2015*, based on the 2014 OECD Regulatory Indicators Survey results.

HOW'S LIFE? 2015: MEASURING WELL-BEING © OECD 2015

in this type of later-stage consultation during the development of all primary laws, and around half of OECD countries also consult at a later stage for all subordinate regulations. Stakeholder engagement to inform officials about problems and possible solutions at an early stage in the policy-making process is more rare, and in most countries this applies only to some regulations.

Figure 2.31 shows the change over time in the number of OECD countries that have mandatory requirements to consult with stakeholders when developing new regulations. As of 2014, only two countries have no requirement to consult in relation to primary laws, and only three countries have no requirements in relation to subordinate regulations. This suggests an improvement since the OECD's previous data collection in 2008/09.

Figure 2.31. **Changes in government consultation on rule-making over time**
Number of countries in which mandatory consultation with parties affected by regulations is part of developing new draft regulations

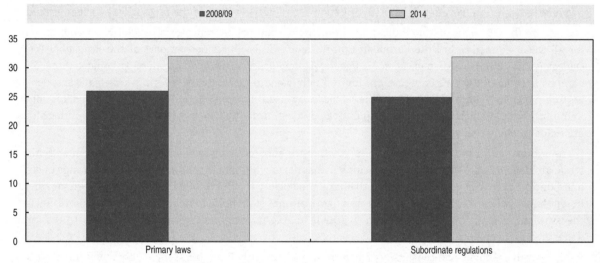

Note: Results shown here are based on the OECD Regulatory Management Systems' Indicators Survey 2008/09, and on the 2014 OECD Regulatory Indicators Survey.

Source: OECD (2015j) *Government at a Glance*, OECD Publishing, Paris, *http://dx.doi.org/10.1787/gov_glance-2015-en*.

StatLink 🔗 *http://dx.doi.org/10.1787/888933259208*

Box 2.8. **Measuring civic engagement and governance**

The headline indicators of civic engagement and governance presented above are defined as follows:

● **Voter turnout** concerns the extent of electoral participation in national elections. It is shown here using two different measures: i) the number of individuals who cast a ballot in a national election, as a percentage of the population registered to vote; and ii) the number of individuals who cast a ballot in a national election, as a percentage of the total voting-age population. As institutional features of voting systems vary across countries and by types of elections, the measures shown here refer to national elections (parliamentary or presidential), which attract the largest proportions of voters in each country. The registered population refers to the population listed on the electoral register. Data on voter turnout are gathered by National Statistical Offices and National Electoral Management Bodies, and are compiled by the International Institute for Democracy and Electoral Assistance (IDEA).

Box 2.8. **Measuring civic engagement and governance** (*cont.*)

● **Stakeholder engagement:** The indicators presented draw upon country responses to the 2014 OECD Regulatory Indicators Survey for all OECD countries and the European Commission. Responses were provided by central government officials to the OECD Regulatory Policy Committee. The indicators reflect country requirements and practices as of 31 December 2014 and follow up on previous Regulatory Management Surveys carried out in 1998, 2005, and 2008/09. Compared to previous indicators, those presented in Table 2.1 put a stronger focus on evidence and examples to support expert responses, as well as on insights into how different countries approach similar regulatory policy requirements. The data only cover primary laws and subordinate regulations initiated by the executive. Primary laws must be approved by the legislature, while subordinate regulations can be approved by the head of government, by an individual minister or by the cabinet. All questions on primary laws are not applicable to the United States, as the US executive does not initiate primary laws at all. Early-stage consultation refers to stakeholder engagement that occurs at an early stage to inform officials about the nature of the problem and possible solutions. Later-stage consultation refers to stakeholder engagement where the preferred solution has already been identified and/or a draft version of the regulation has been issued.

Based on the OECD Regulatory Indicators Survey, new a composite indicator on stakeholder engagement for all OECD countries and the European Commission will be published as part of the *Regulatory Policy Outlook* (OECD, 2015i; see also *www.oecd.org/gov/regulatory-policy/measuring-regulatory-performance.htm*). This composite indicator will be composed of four equally weighted categories covering: *systematic adoption* of requirements to engage stakeholders, the *methodology* used for consultation, *oversight and quality control*, and *transparency* (which relates to principles of open government, such as whether government decisions are made publicly available).

The indicators for civic engagement and governance shown here cover only a limited set of activities, while an ideal indicator set would also include measures of whether citizens are involved in a range of civic and political activities that enable them to shape the society in which they live. Stakeholder engagement in regulatory policy-making is only one form of government stakeholder engagement. Furthermore, having the systems in place for stakeholder engagement in rule-making may not necessarily lead to real and widespread citizen engagement in practice.

Comparative evidence on the *quality* of governance is currently limited in scope. The newly-initiated UN Praia Group on Governance Statistics will address the conceptualisation, methodology and instruments for producing governance statistics, with the aim of providing international recommendations in this area. The OECD is also undertaking new methodological work to create better and more policy-relevant indicators of trust, both in public institutions and in other people more generally, as part of the OECD's Trust Strategy.

Further reading:

● Boarini, R. and M. Díaz (2015), "Cast a Ballot or Protest in the Street – Did our Grandparents Do More of Both?: An Age-Period-Cohort Analysis in Political Participation", *OECD Statistics Working Papers*, 2015/02, OECD Publishing, Paris, *http://dx.doi.org/10.1787/5js636gn50jb-en*.

● OECD (2015j), *Government at a Glance 2015*, OECD Publishing, Paris, *http://dx.doi.org/10.1787/gov_glance-2015-en*.

● OECD (2015i), *Regulatory Policy Outlook 2015*, OECD Publishing, Paris, forthcoming.

The distribution of civic engagement

The limited comparative data available suggest that people under the age of 35 are less likely to vote, and turnout among the under 25s is, on average, 28 percentage points below that of people aged 65 and over (OECD, 2011a). Using data from the *European Social Survey*,

Boarini and Díaz (2015) also found less political participation among younger birth-cohorts in Europe, both for formal participation (such as voting) and less formal (such as protest) activities. People with lower incomes are also less likely to vote, although this varies across countries (OECD, 2011a).

Environment quality

The environment plays an important role in people's quality of life. Living in an environment that is free from dangerous pollutants, hazards and noise contributes to individual physical and mental health. The health of the environment also has intrinsic value to people, ranging from the quality of green space through to the preservation of natural environments for other species. More broadly, humans rely on the natural environment to provide a wide range of natural resources and services that are important for maintaining well-being over time. While these longer-term considerations are discussed in more depth in Chapter 3, this section concentrates on aspects of the quality of the environment that have an immediate bearing on current quality of life.

Exposure to air pollution is a public health concern. The greatest health risks are associated with long-term exposure to poor quality air: for example, chronic exposure to particulate matter (PM) contributes to the risk of developing cardiovascular and respiratory diseases as well as lung cancer (OECD, 2014f). Fine particulate matter ($PM_{2.5}$) from sources such as vehicle emissions, energy production, and the burning of agricultural biomass poses a particular threat to people's health. Air quality guidelines from the World Health Organisation (WHO) recommend a $PM_{2.5}$ concentration standard below 10 micrograms per cubic metre for average annual exposure (WHO, 2006). A European Union Air Quality Directive places an obligation on countries to limit the population's annual $PM_{2.5}$ concentration exposure to 20 micrograms per cubic metre, based on a three-year average period (European Commission, 2015).

Ground-level monitoring stations offer the most accurate information about air pollution in local areas, enabling a wide range of pollutants to be studied over short time periods and in specific locations. However, data from ground-level monitoring can be difficult to compare across countries due to the uneven coverage of monitoring stations across locations, as well as variations in measurement techniques and reporting methods (Brezzi and Sanchez-Serra, 2014). As a complement to local data collected through ground-level monitoring stations, new air pollution measures derived from satellite-based observations offer estimates that, although less precise (particularly for desert and snow-covered surfaces), are based on comparable methods across all countries, and consider the average exposure of the whole population rather than only those living in urban centres (see Box 2.9 for further details). These satellite-based data indicate that the average annual exposure to $PM_{2.5}$ exceeds the WHO recommended threshold in 21 out of 34 OECD countries (Figure 2.32). Annual exposure to $PM_{2.5}$ is lowest in New Zealand, Iceland, Australia and Norway and highest in Israel and Korea, where it exceeds both the WHO and EU air quality recommendations.

Figure 2.32. **Annual exposure to PM$_{2.5}$ air pollution**

Population-weighted exposure to PM$_{2.5}$ concentrations, micrograms per cubic metre, averaged over 2010-2012

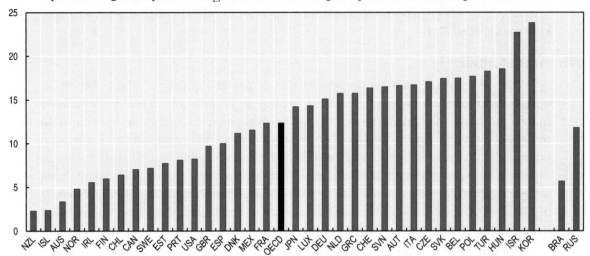

Note: Values are OECD estimates, averaged over three years (2010-2012), and based on satellite image data from van Donkelaar, A., R.V. Martin, M. Brauer and B.L. Boys (2015), "Use of Satellite Observations for Long-Term Exposure Assessment of Global Concentrations of Fine Particulate Matter", *Environmental Health Perspectives*, Vol. 123, Issue 2. A 50% relative humidity standard has been adopted for consistency with ground-level measurements. The values for each country represent the population weighted average of the annual concentration of PM$_{2.5}$. The OECD average is also population-weighted.

Source: OECD Regional Well-being Statistics (database), http://dx.doi.org/10.1787/data-00707-en.

StatLink ᴍᴤᴘ *http://dx.doi.org/10.1787/888933259218*

Because air pollution is particularly associated with urbanisation, industry and transport, there are substantial within-country differences in exposure to air pollution, both at the regional and city level (see Chapter 6; Brezzi and Sanchez-Serra, 2014; and OECD, 2014g). In 2010-12, around 40% of OECD residents had an average annual exposure below the WHO-recommended threshold of 10 micrograms per cubic metre (Figure 2.33). However, an estimated 42 million people across the OECD area were exposed to PM$_{2.5}$ levels of 25 micrograms per cubic metre or above in 2010-2012, in excess of both WHO and EU air quality guidelines. This includes more than 15% of the population in Korea, Israel, and Italy.

Other important forms of air pollution include ground-level ozone, sulphur dioxide (SO$_2$), nitrogen dioxide (NO$_2$), and (PM$_{10}$) particulate matter. World Bank PM$_{10}$ estimates previously reported in *How's Life?* (OECD, 2013a) show that, although urban exposure to PM$_{10}$ has been reduced over the last two decades, in 2009 nearly half of all OECD countries had annual urban PM$_{10}$ concentrations above the 20 micrograms per cubic metre level recommended by the WHO (WHO, 2006). European data from Eurostat meanwhile indicate that exposure to ambient ozone concentrations increased in the EU between 2000 and 2011 by 1.7% per year on average – though there is considerable variation in exposure both across cities and over time (OECD, 2014f).

Access to *clean, safe water* is another aspect of environmental quality. While comparable objective measures of water quality across all OECD countries are lacking, data are available that capture people's subjective satisfaction with the quality of local water (Figure 2.34, see Box 2.9 for a definition). In 2014, a large majority of respondents in OECD countries reported being satisfied with the quality of local water. However, in Turkey, Mexico, Israel and Greece, less than 70% of people were satisfied, and in the Russian Federation the share was around 50%.

Figure 2.33. **Population exposed to PM$_{2.5}$ air pollution, by different thresholds**
Percentage of the population, mean annual exposure, 2010-2012

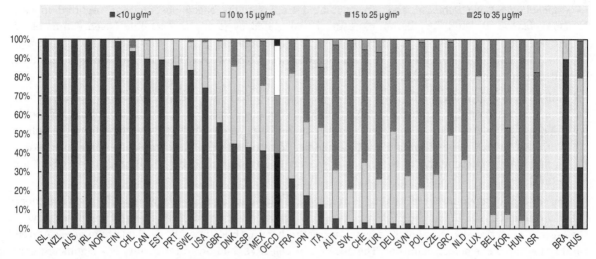

Note: Values are OECD estimates, averaged over three years. A 50% relative humidity standard has been adopted for consistency with ground-level measurements. The figure displays percentages of the population exposed according to four PM$_{2.5}$ concentration levels based on the WHO guidelines. Average annual exposures higher than 35 ug/m3 are not shown as this applies to less than 1% of the population in all countries shown. The OECD average is population-weighted.

Source: OECD (forthcoming) *Regions at a Glance 2016*, OECD Publishing, Paris.

StatLink 🔗 *http://dx.doi.org/10.1787/888933259225*

Figure 2.34. **Satisfaction with local water quality**
Percentage of satisfied people in the overall population, 2014 or latest available year

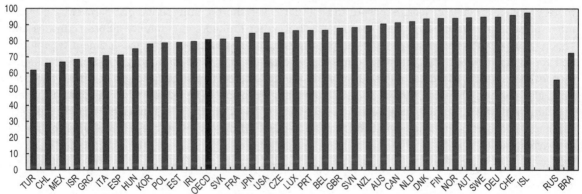

Note: Data refer to 2013 for Iceland. The OECD average is population-weighted.

Source: Gallup World Poll, *www.gallup.com/services/170945/world-poll.aspx.*

StatLink 🔗 *http://dx.doi.org/10.1787/888933259236*

Box 2.9. **Measuring environmental quality**

The two headline indicators of environmental quality presented above are defined as follows:

● **Annual exposure to air pollution** refers to the population-wide average exposure to fine particulate matter that is less than 2.5 microns in diameter ($PM_{2.5}$), as well as the share of the population exposed at different levels of $PM_{2.5}$. The major components of particulate matter are sulphate, nitrates, ammonia, sodium chloride, black carbon, mineral dust and water. The data shown here are drawn from the *OECD Regional Well-Being Database*, and are calculated from satellite-based observations reported in van Donkelaar et al. (2014). Population exposure is calculated by taking the satellite-based estimates of air pollution at a 1 km² resolution, multiplied by the population living in that area. National average exposure is then given by the sum of the population-weighted values of $PM_{2.5}$ in the 1 km² grid cells that fall within the country's borders.

● **Satisfaction with water quality** captures people's perceptions about the quality of water in their local area. It is based on the question: "In the city or area where you live, are you satisfied or dissatisfied with the quality of water?", and it considers people who declared being satisfied. Data come from the Gallup World Poll, which samples around 1 000 people per country, per year. The sample is *ex ante* designed to be nationally representative of the population aged 15 and over, including rural areas (see Box 2.7 for details).

The concept of "environmental quality" is broad, and an ideal set of indicators would inform on a number of environmental media (soil, water, air), on people's access to environmental services and amenities, as well as on the impact of environmental hazards on human health. Unfortunately, available data are scattered and not comparable across countries. The absence of objective data on water quality is a significant gap, and the perception-based measure shown may suffer from comparability problems (e.g. it is not clear whether the question refers to drinking water or all forms of water in the local area). Data on access to green space is another important omission that could potentially be addressed in the future through satellite-based data.

Developing summary measures of air pollution is also challenging, as air quality is the result of a complex mixture of pollutants that vary over time, space and form. Brezzi and Sanchez-Serra (2014) provide a detailed discussion of the advantages and disadvantages of satellite-based estimates of air pollution, as compared to data from ground-based monitoring stations. In brief, ground-level monitoring stations offer more precise estimates of local exposure to pollution, over shorter time periods, and covering a wider range of pollutants (such as ground-level ozone), but suffer limited comparability across countries and regions, due to the uneven coverage of monitoring stations and variations in measurement techniques and reporting methods. $PM_{2.5}$ concentrations are also rarely monitored through ground-based stations. By contrast, satellite-based estimates can provide methodological consistency across countries and over time, globally, and including rural areas – thus enabling exposure to be estimated for a country's whole population. However, satellite-based estimates rely on modelled data, are less precise for bright surfaces (e.g. snow or desert), and do not enable the evaluation of short time periods as they currently rely on multi-year averages.

Even within a single urban area, personal exposure to air pollution varies substantially, depending on where people live and work and on their occupations, lifestyles and behaviours. This means that the average population exposure can hide substantial variations and inequalities. The young, elderly and people who are already ill are particularly vulnerable to the damaging health effects of air pollution.

Further reading:

● Brezzi, M. and D. Sanchez-Serra (2014), "Breathing the Same Air? Measuring Air Pollution in Cities and Regions", *OECD Regional Development Working Papers*, No. 2014/11, OECD Publishing, Paris, *http://dx.doi. org/10.1787/5jxrb7rkxf21-en*.

Box 2.9. **Measuring environmental quality** (cont.)

- OECD (2014g), *How's Life in Your Region?: Measuring Regional and Local Well-being for Policy Making*, OECD Publishing, Paris, *http://dx.doi.org/10.1787/9789264217416-en*.

- OECD (2014h), "Environmental quality of life", in OECD, *Green Growth Indicators 2014*, OECD Publishing, Paris, *http://dx.doi.org/10.1787/9789264202030-9-en*.

Personal security

Personal security concerns people's vulnerability to a wide range of threats, as well as how safe they feel. Experiences of crime and violence can have a strong impact on victims' physical and mental health in both the short and long term. Both the risk of crime and violence, and people's perceptions about their own safety, have wider impacts on well-being either through increased anxiety and worry or by restricting people's behaviour.

In most OECD countries, *deaths due to assault* (see Box 2.10 for the definition) are relatively rare, with rates typically below 2 per 100 000 people per year (Figure 2.35). The highest rates of death by assault are recorded in Chile, Estonia, the United States and Mexico – with Mexico experiencing rates more than five times the OECD average. Between 2009 and 2012, deaths by assault decreased in over two-thirds of OECD countries, but increased in Mexico.

Figure 2.35. **Deaths due to assault**
Age-standardised rate, per 100 000 population

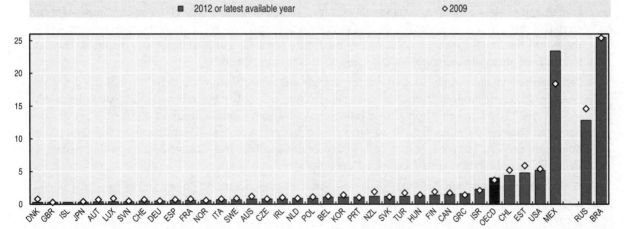

Note: The latest available year is 2011 for Australia, Canada, Chile, France, Greece, Israel, Luxembourg, Japan and Turkey; 2010 for Belgium, Ireland, Italy, New Zealand, the Slovak Republic, Slovenia, Switzerland, the United Kingdom and the United States, the Russian Federation and Brazil; and 2009 for Iceland. The OECD average is population-weighted.

Source: "OECD Health Data: Causes of Mortality", *OECD Health Statistics* (database), *http://dx.doi.org/10.1787/data-00540-en*.

StatLink ᴍ🖧 *http://dx.doi.org/10.1787/888933259242*

In 2010, 1 out of every 25 people in the OECD area *reported having been the victim of an assault* in the last 12 months (Figure 2.36). Several countries with higher rates of death by assault also have higher rates of self-reported victimisation: around 1 in every 8 people in Mexico, and around 1 in every 13 people in Chile and Brazil reported having been the victim of an assault in the last 12 months.

Figure 2.36. **Self-reported victimisation**

Percentage of people declaring that they have been assaulted in the previous 12 months, 2010

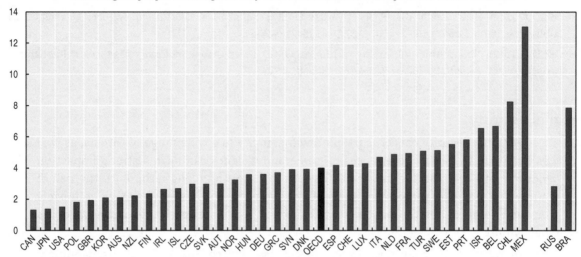

Note: Data refer to 2012 for Mexico; 2011 for Chile; 2009 for Estonia and Switzerland; and 2008 for Iceland and Norway. The OECD average is population-weighted.

Source: Gallup World Poll, *www.gallup.com/services/170945/world-poll.aspx.*

StatLink ᴍ∎ᔑ⊐ *http://dx.doi.org/10.1787/888933259259*

Box 2.10. **Measuring personal security**

The indicators used to measure personal security are defined as follows:

- **Deaths due to assault** refer to cases in which assault is registered as the cause of death in official death registers. It is shown as an age-standardised rate, and expressed per 100 000 people.* Cause-of-death statistics come from country civil registration systems, compiled by national authorities and collated by the World Health Organisation (WHO). Only medically certified causes of death are included. The data shown here are available in the OECD Causes of Mortality Database.

- **Self-reported victimisation** is based on the survey question: "Within the past 12 months, have you been assaulted or mugged?", and the data shown here reflect the percentage of all respondents who replied "yes". The data come from the Gallup World Poll, which samples around 1 000 people per country, per year. Latest data refer to 2010 because this question has been discontinued in the Gallup core questionnaire. The sample is *ex ante* designed to be nationally representative of the population aged 15 and over, including rural areas (see Box 2.7 for details).

- **Feeling safe when walking alone at night** is based on the survey question: "Do you feel safe walking alone at night in the city or area where you live?", and the data shown here reflect the percentage of all respondents who replied "yes". The source for these data is the Gallup World Poll (see above and Box 2.7 for details).

An ideal set of indicators of personal security would inform about the various crimes and offences experienced by individuals, weighting these crimes according to their seriousness. However, official crime records are not comparable across countries due to differences in what is counted as a crime and in both reporting and recording practices. The data shown here refer to deaths due to assault as recorded in country civil registration systems, rather than homicides as recorded by the police. A recent joint report by the National Institute of Statistics and Geography of Mexico (INEGI) and the United Nations Office on Drugs and Crime provides a roadmap to improve the availability and quality of crime statistics at national and international level (UNODC, 2013, see below).

Crime victimisation surveys are a critical tool for measuring people's experience of crime, and while these do exist in some countries, they are not based on common standards and methodologies. The indicator presented here refers to assaults only (rather than property and other crimes), and is based on data from the

Box 2.10. **Measuring personal security** (cont.)

Gallup World Poll, a non-official survey characterised by small sample sizes – a feature that can be particularly problematic when measuring events that typically affect only a small proportion of the entire population.

Survey data can bring into focus the crime problems that affect people most often and – if conducted at regular intervals and with a consistent methodology – can provide measures of changes in levels of crime over time. Unfortunately, few OECD countries regularly conduct such surveys, and the national data that exist are not comparable across countries. The available data provide only a proxy for the volume of illegal acts that occur in society. First, some crimes may be underestimated or overestimated due to respondents' subjective interpretation of what constitutes a crime. Second, some people may be reluctant to disclose information for incidents of a sensitive nature, such as sexual assaults or inter-partner violence. Third, the accuracy of victimisation surveys is influenced by people's ability to recall past crimes (the longer the elapsed period, the less likely it is that a victimisation will be recalled accurately). Finally, unconventional types of crime such as corruption may be difficult to capture through household surveys.

Risks to people's personal security can come from sources other than crime. Transport and road-traffic accidents, work-related hazards and the risk of natural disaster are among the factors that can affect personal security. Violent conflict and war also have a profound impact on security by putting people's lives and livelihoods in danger.

Further reading:

● OECD (2011d), "Personal security", in *OECD, How's Life?: Measuring Well-being*, OECD Publishing, Paris, *http://dx.doi.org/10.1787/9789264121164-13-en*.

● United Nations Office on Drugs and Crime (UNODC)(2013), *Report of the National Institute of Statistics and Geography of Mexico and the United Nations Office on Drugs and Crime*, *http://unstats.un.org/unsd/statcom/doc13/2013-11-CrimeStats-E.pdf*.

* Age-standardisation is used to ensure that the data are comparable across countries with different population age structures.

Feelings of safety (Figure 2.37; see Box 2.10 for a definition) are another important aspect of personal security. In the OECD area as a whole, only two-thirds of people report feeling safe when walking alone at night in the area where they live.

Figure 2.37. **Feelings of safety when walking alone at night**

Percentage of the population declaring feeling safe when walking alone at night in the city or area where they live, 2014

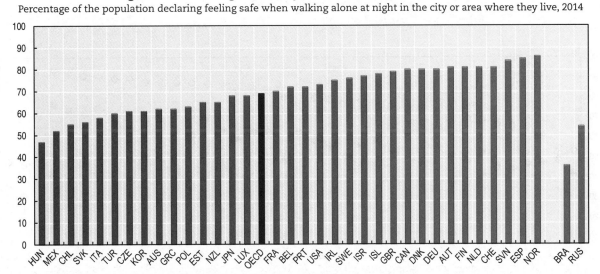

Note: The latest available year for Iceland is 2013. The OECD average is population-weighted.

Source: Gallup World Poll, *www.gallup.com/services/170945/world-poll.aspx*.

StatLink ⟐ *http://dx.doi.org/10.1787/888933259265*

The distribution of personal security

On average across the OECD, men are five times more likely than women to die from assault (Figure 2.38). Women in Mexico, Russia and Brazil run a much higher risk than women elsewhere, but their risks are still lower relative to men living in these countries. In all OECD countries, women report feeling less safe than men when walking alone at night in the area where they live (Figure 2.39), and in most countries, people aged 50 and over also feel less safe than younger people (Figure 2.40).

Figure 2.38. **Deaths due to assault among men and women**
Age-standardised annual rate, per 100 000 people, 2012 or latest available year

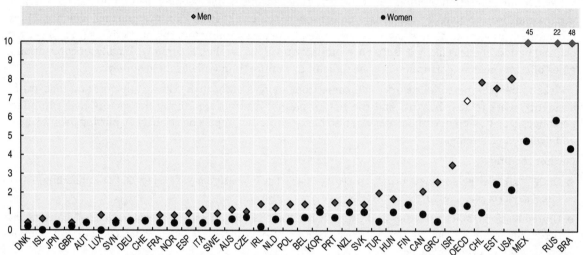

Notes: Death by assault rates for men in Mexico (44.5), Russia (21.8) and Brazil (48.1) exceed the upper boundary of the y-axis. The latest available year is 2011 for Australia, Canada, Chile, France, Greece, Israel, Japan and Turkey; 2010 for Belgium, Brazil, Ireland, Italy, New Zealand, the Russian Federation, the Slovak republic, Slovenia, Switzerland, the United kingdom and the United States; and 2009 for Iceland. The OECD average is population-weighted.

Source: "OECD Health Data: Causes of Mortality", OECD Health Statistics (database), *http://dx.doi.org/10.1787/data-00540-en.*

StatLink 🔗 *http://dx.doi.org/10.1787/888933259279*

Figure 2.39. **Feelings of safety among men and women**
Percentage of the population who declare feeling safe when walking alone at night in the area where they live, pooled results 2006-2014

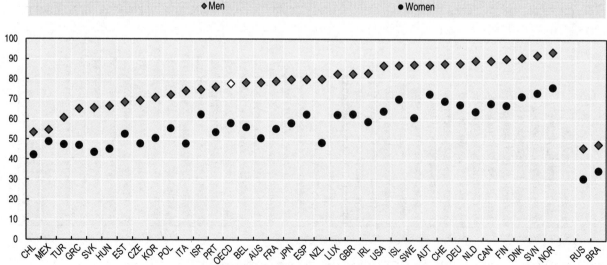

Note: The data are pooled across all available years 2006-2014. The OECD average is population-weighted.

Source: Gallup World Poll, *www.gallup.com/services/170945/world-poll.aspx.*

StatLink 🔗 *http://dx.doi.org/10.1787/888933259283*

Figure 2.40. **Feelings of safety among people of different ages**
Percentage of the population who feel safe when walking alone at night in the area where they live,
pooled results 2006-2014

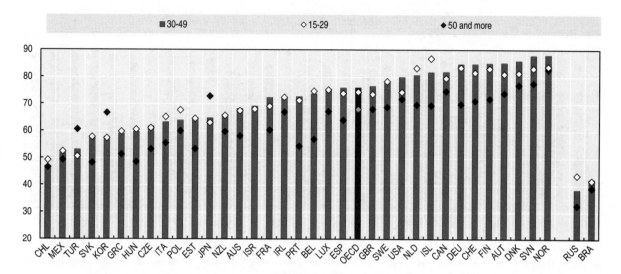

Note: The data are pooled across all available years 2006-2014. The OECD average is population-weighted.

Source: Gallup World Poll, *www.gallup.com/services/170945/world-poll.aspx*.

StatLink ᴹᴵˢᴾ *http://dx.doi.org/10.1787/888933259299*

Subjective well-being

No answer to the question "how's life?" would be complete without considering people's own views of their lives. Subjective well-being consists of people's evaluations, feelings and experiences of their lives. There are three distinct components of subjective well-being, each offering a different perspective: *life evaluations* focus on a person's overall assessment of their life as a whole (such as their life satisfaction); *eudaimonic* measures[11] concern a person's sense of meaning, purpose and worthwhileness in life; and *affect* measures (also known as *experienced well-being*) focus on moods, feelings and emotions, including experiences of both positive (enjoyment, well-rested) and negative (sadness, worry) states (OECD, 2013f).

In a large majority of OECD countries, data on **life satisfaction** are now available from official sources, based on comparable measures that are consistent with the recommendations of the *OECD Guidelines on Measuring Subjective Well-Being* (OECD, 2013f; see Box 2.11). Mean average life satisfaction ranges from just above 6 out of 10 in Portugal, Hungary and Greece to 8 out of 10 in Sweden, Canada, Denmark, Mexico, Finland and Switzerland (Figure 2.41).[12] Generally, people living in Southern and Eastern Europe report being less satisfied with their lives than those living in Northern and Western Europe, Australia, New Zealand, Canada and Mexico. For European countries, data about life feeling worthwhile are also shown in Figure 2.41. Country differences on this indicator are generally smaller than those for life satisfaction.

Figure 2.41. **Life satisfaction and feeling life is worthwhile**
Mean values on a 0-10 scale, 2013 or closest available year

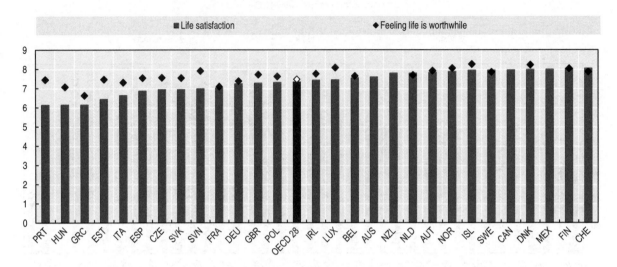

Note: Data refer to 2014 for New Zealand and Australia; and to the first quarter of 2012 for Mexico. Data on life feeling worthwhile include European countries only (OECD 24). The OECD average is population-weighted.

Source: Eurostat (2015), "European Union Statistics on Income and Living Conditions (EU-SILC), *http://ec.europa.eu/eurostat/web/income-and-living-conditions/overview* for EU countries; Australian Bureau of Statistics, 2014 General Social Survey, *www.abs.gov.au/ausstats/abs@.nsf/mf/4159.0#Anchor3* for Australia; Statistics Canada, Canadian Community Health Survey 2013, *http://www23.statcan.gc.ca/imdb/p2SV.pl?Function=getSurvey&SDDS=3226* for Canada; INEGI, the National Survey of Household Expenditure (BIARE-ENGASTO) 2012, *www.inegi.org.mx/inegi/contenidos/investigacion/Experimentales/Bienestar/default.aspx* for Mexico; and Statistics New Zealand, 2014 General Social Survey, *www.stats.govt.nz/browse_for_stats/people_and_communities/Households/nzgss_HOTP2014/Tables.aspx*, for New Zealand.

StatLink ⬛ᵐˢ⃫ *http://dx.doi.org/10.1787/888933259308*

In the near future, comparable official data are expected to cover additional OECD countries, including Korea and Israel. In the interim, an alternative life evaluation measure (Figure 2.42, see Box 2.11 for the definition) is shown. In 2014, life evaluations in Turkey, Korea, Japan and the Russian Federation were below the OECD average, while Chile, Brazil, the United States and Israel were slightly above the average. Between 2009 and 2014, life evaluations in Greece dropped by 1.3 scale points on a 0-10 scale (Gallup, 2015). Several of the countries most affected by the Great Recession also experienced declines in life evaluations during the first years of the crisis (OECD, 2013a).

People's everyday experiences and emotions also matter for their quality of life overall. In 2014, three-quarters of people in the OECD had a *positive affect balance* (i.e., they experienced more positive than negative emotions, see Box 2.11 for the full definition). In Mexico, Denmark, Finland, Luxembourg, Switzerland, the Netherlands and Iceland, the rate was more than 80%, while in Turkey, Greece, Italy and Portugal it was less than 65%. In 2014, the proportion of people with a positive affect balance was 8 percentage points lower than in 2009 in Greece, Italy, Korea and Portugal, but it was 9 percentage points higher than 2009 in France (OECD calculations, based on Gallup, 2015).

Figure 2.42. **People's evaluations of their lives as a whole**

Measured on a 0-10 scale from "best possible" to "worst possible", mean values, 2014

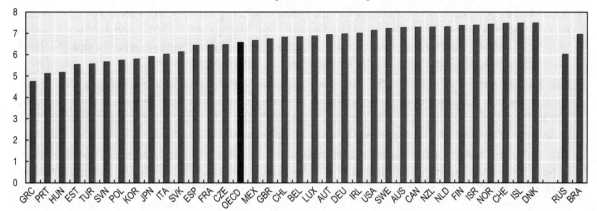

Note: The latest available data for Iceland refer to 2013. The OECD average is population-weighted.

Source: Gallup World Poll, *www.gallup.com/services/170945/world-poll.aspx.*

StatLink ᐧᒥᔆᐧ *http://dx.doi.org/10.1787/888933259317*

Figure 2.43. **Positive affect balance**

Percentage of people reporting more positive than negative feelings overall yesterday, 2014

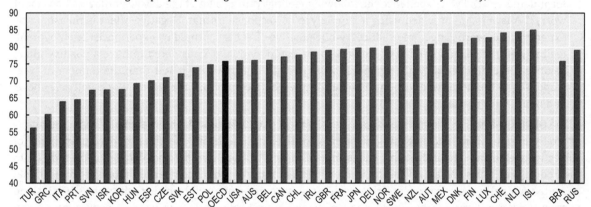

Note: The latest available year is 2013 for Iceland. Positive feelings assessed relate to enjoyment, feeling well-rested and laughing or smiling a lot; negative feelings were worry, anger and sadness. The OECD average is population-weighted.

Source: OECD calculations based on the Gallup World Poll, *www.gallup.com/services/170945/world-poll.aspx.*

StatLink ᐧᒥᔆᐧ *http://dx.doi.org/10.1787/888933259326*

Box 2.11. **Measuring subjective well-being**

This edition of *How's Life?* features a range of different measures of subjective well-being, reflecting the recent measurement advances that have been made in this area:

● **Life satisfaction**, which refers to the mean average score on an 11-point scale. It is based on survey questions that broadly follow the format recommended by the *OECD Guidelines* (OECD, 2013f): "Overall, how satisfied are you with life as a whole these days?", with responses ranging from 0 ("not at all satisfied") to 10 ("completely satisfied"). The European data come from the European Union Statistics on Income and Living Conditions (EU-SILC) ad hoc module on well-being, conducted in 2013, and are available for all EU countries. EU-SILC is a nationally representative survey with large samples (from around 4 000 individuals in the smallest member states, to around 16 000 in the largest) covering all members of private households aged 16 or older. Data for Australia are based on the Australian Bureau of Statistics' General

2. HOW'S LIFE? IN FIGURES

Box 2.11. **Measuring subjective well-being** (cont.)

Social Survey 2014; for Canada, Statistics Canada's Canadian Community Health Survey 2013; for Mexico, INEGI's National Survey of Household Expenditure for the first quarter of 2012; and for New Zealand, Statistics New Zealand's General Social Survey 2014. Data for Australia, Canada and New Zealand refer to the population aged 15 and over; data for Mexico refer to people aged 18-70 years old.

- **Life feeling worthwhile** refers to the mean average score on an 11-point scale, ranging from 0 (not worthwhile at all) to 10 (completely worthwhile). It is based on the question: "Overall, to what extent do you feel that the things you do in your life are worthwhile?" The data shown here come from the EU-SILC ad hoc module on well-being (see above) and are available for all EU countries.

- **Life evaluation based on the Cantril ladder measure** is expressed as the mean score on an 11-point scale. It is measured using the "Cantril Ladder" scale, a survey question in which respondents are asked to imagine a ladder with rungs from 0 to 10, where 10 is the best possible life for them and 0 the worst possible life. They are then asked to indicate whereabouts on the ladder they see themselves. The data shown here come from the Gallup World Poll, which samples around 1 000 people per country per year. The sample is *ex ante* designed to be nationally representative of the population aged 15 and over (see Box 2.7).

- **Positive affect balance** is defined here as the proportion of the population who reported experiencing more positive than negative emotions yesterday. It is based on responses to six different questions formulated as: "Did you experience the following feelings during a lot of the day yesterday? …how about worry?" Answers are provided using a simple yes/no response format. Negative affect is measured by experiences of worry, anger and sadness, while positive affect is captured by experiences of enjoyment, feeling well-rested, and smiling or laughing a lot. An individual is considered to have a positive affect balance if the number of "yes" responses to the positive questions is greater than the number of "yes" responses to the negative questions. The data shown here come from the Gallup World Poll (see above, and Box 2.7, for details).

The OECD *Guidelines on Measuring Subjective Well-Being* (OECD, 2013f) provide international recommendations on collecting, reporting and analysing subjective well-being data across the three major components of subjective well-being (life evaluations, eudaimonia and affect). The *Guidelines* give detailed consideration to methodological issues and survey design, and include a number of prototype question modules that national and international agencies can adopt if they wish to measure subjective well-being in their surveys. While there is much evidence that subjective well-being questions produce valid and meaningful responses even when used in different cultural contexts, it remains possible that differences introduced when translating items into different languages, or systematic country differences in how people use response scales, can introduce some degree of measurement error that affects the comparability of estimates between countries. As a result, small differences in the mean average estimates of subjective well-being between countries should not be given a strong interpretation (OECD, 2013f; Exton, Smith and Vandendriessche, forthcoming OECD *Statistics Working Paper*).

Further reading:

- Eurostat (2015), "Quality of life in Europe – facts and views – overall life satisfaction", *http://ec.europa.eu/ eurostat/statistics-explained/index.php/Quality_of_life_in_Europe_-_facts_and_views_-_overall_life_satisfaction*.

- OECD (2013f), *Guidelines on Measuring Subjective Well-Being*, *www.oecd.org/statistics/guidelines-on-measuring-subjective-well-being.htm*.

The distribution of subjective well-being

On average, men and women's experiences of life satisfaction are quite similar across the OECD area, but in most countries men are more likely to report a positive affect balance (OECD, 2013a). Higher levels of education are generally associated with higher life satisfaction, but the effect of education is stronger in some countries (most notably Portugal, Korea, Greece and Hungary) than in others (OECD, 2013a). Life satisfaction data collected for EU countries also show a similar pattern in relation to both gender and education (Eurostat, 2015).

For a majority of OECD countries, life evaluations are lowest among those aged 50 and over (Figure 2.44). However, among English-speaking countries in particular, the lowest life evaluations are reported in middle age (Figure 2.44). A small "retirement effect" (slightly higher life satisfaction among the 65-74 age group, relative to the 50-64 age group) has also been observed in many European countries (based on official European life satisfaction data, Eurostat, 2015).

Figure 2.44. **Life evaluations among people of different ages**

Measured on a 0-10 scale from "best possible" to "worst possible", mean values, pooled results 2006-14

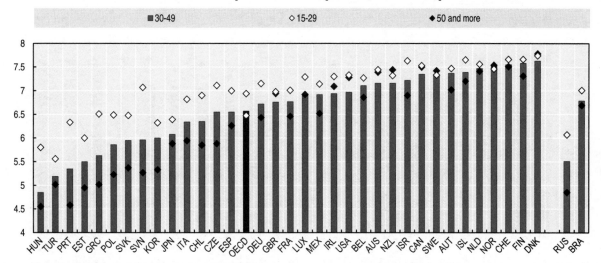

Note: Data are pooled across all available years 2006-2014. The OECD average is population-weighted.

Source: Gallup World Poll, *www.gallup.com/services/170945/world-poll.aspx*.

StatLink ⬛⬛⬛ *http://dx.doi.org/10.1787/888933259332*

In some OECD countries, there are also wide differences in experienced well-being at different ages. Young people (aged 15-29) tend to report the highest levels of positive affect balance in over half of all OECD countries (Figure 2.45, Panels A and B), but middle age is the emotional low-point for English-speaking countries, as well as most of Northern Europe, Turkey, Japan and Korea.

Figure 2.45. **Positive affect balance among people of different ages**

Percentage of the population reporting more positive than negative affect yesterday, pooled results 2006-2014

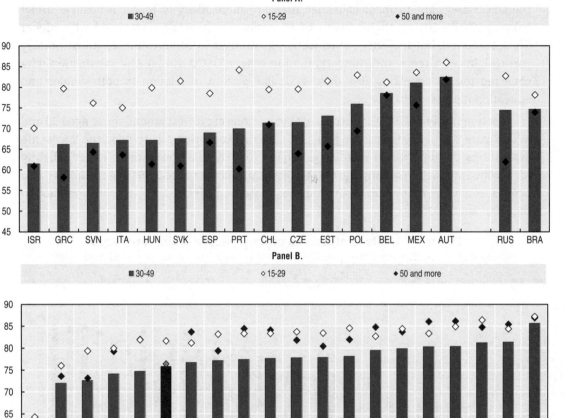

Note: Data are pooled across all available years from 2006-2014. Positive feelings assessed relate to enjoyment, feeling well-rested and laughing or smiling a lot; negative feelings were worry, anger and sadness. The OECD average is population-weighted.

Source: OECD calculations based on the Gallup World Poll, *www.gallup.com/services/170945/world-poll.aspx*.

StatLink ᵃˢᶫ *http://dx.doi.org/10.1787/888933259342*

Notes

1. The earliest available comparison year is usually 2011 for the Gini index and the inter-decile income share ratio, due to a recent methodological change in how these values are estimated. Changes in income inequality over longer time periods are documented in *In It Together* (OECD, 2015a).

2. The evolution of employment and unemployment rates between 2007 and 2014 has varied widely across the OECD. In Japan and the United States (and on average across the OECD as a whole), employment growth was lowest, and unemployment peaked, in 2009, before gradually recovering towards pre-crisis levels in 2014. By contrast, unemployment continued to increase in the Euro area after 2009, peaking in 2013. OECD (2015b) provides further detail.

3. The OECD Job Quality framework considers hourly earnings to abstract from differences in working time between workers – differences that relate more to job quantity than to job quality.

4. $x' = \dfrac{x - \min(x)}{\max(x) - \min(x)}$

5. For example, one-quarter or more of employees aged 15 to 24 had a fixed-term contract in almost all OECD countries in 2011-12, a rate often three times higher than that for prime-aged workers 25-54 years old (OECD, 2014a).

6. i.e., difference between the median wage of men and women, divided by the median wage of men.

7. The Czech Republic, Estonia, Hungary, Poland, Slovenia, the United States, Ireland, Norway, Finland, Denmark, Canada, Italy, the Netherlands, Sweden and Portugal. Reference years range from 2005 to 2010.

8. In interpreting these findings, consideration should be given to the interactions between age, income, and health, since both younger people and retirees may have lower incomes than prime-aged workers, but different susceptibilities to ill-health.

9. Several other OECD countries have non-enforced rules (e.g. Greece) or some history of compulsory voting in the past (e.g. Italy, France, Netherlands and Austria). Chile abandoned compulsory voting in 2012.

10. Changes in this indicator are considered over a longer time period than that used in other sections of this chapter, to ensure that all countries have experienced at least one election during the intervening years.

11. *Eudaimonic* measures are also sometimes referred to as "psychological well-being" or "flourishing"; they cover aspects of psychological functioning such as feelings of self-esteem and competence.

12. The indicator shown in Figure 2.41 is limited to EU Countries because it is sourced from European Statistics on Income and Living Conditions (EU-SILC).

References

Balestra, C. and J. Sultan (2013), "Home Sweet Home: The Determinants of Residential Satisfaction and its Relation with Well-being", *OECD Statistics Working Papers*, No. 2013/05, OECD Publishing, Paris, *http://dx.doi.org/10.1787/5jzbcx0czc0x-en*.

Boarini, R. and M. Díaz (2015), "Cast a Ballot or Protest in the Street – Did our Grandparents Do More of Both? An Age-Period-Cohort Analysis in Political Participation", *OECD Statistics Working Papers*, No. 2015/02, OECD Publishing, Paris, *http://dx.doi.org/10.1787/5js636gn50jb-en*.

Brezzi, M. and D. Sanchez-Serra (2014), "Breathing the Same Air? Measuring Air Pollution in Cities and Regions", *OECD Regional Development Working Papers*, No. 2014/11, OECD Publishing, Paris, *http://dx.doi.org/10.1787/5jxrb7rkxf21-en*.

Cazes, S., Hijzen, A. and A. Saint-Martin (2015), "How good is your job? the new OECD framework for measuring and assessing job quality", *OECD Working Paper*, forthcoming.

European Commission (2015), *Air Quality Standards*, *http://ec.europa.eu/environment/air/quality/standards.htm* (accessed on 5 July 2015).

European Union (2013), "Health inequalities in the EU" – Final report of a consortium, *http://ec.europa.eu/health/social_determinants/docs/healthinequalitiesineu_2013_en.pdf*.

Eurostat (2015), "Quality of life in Europe – facts and views – overall life satisfaction", *http://ec.europa.eu/eurostat/statistics-explained/index.php/Quality_of_life_in_Europe_-_facts_and_views_-_overall_life_satisfaction* (accessed on 3 July 2015).

Exton, C., Smith, C., and D. Vandendriessche (forthcoming), "Comparing happiness across countries: does culture matter?", *OECD Statistics Working Papers*.

Fesseau, M. and M.L. Mattonetti (2013a), "Distributional Measures Across Household Groups in a National Accounts Framework: Results from an Experimental Cross-country Exercise on Household Income, Consumption and Saving", *OECD Statistics Working Papers*, No. 2013/04, OECD Publishing, Paris, *http://dx.doi.org/10.1787/5k3wdjqr775f-en*.

Fesseau, M., F. Wolff and M.L. Mattonetti (2013b), "A Cross-country Comparison of Household Income, Consumption and Wealth between Micro Sources and National Accounts Aggregates", *OECD Statistics Working Papers*, No. 2013/03, OECD Publishing, Paris, *http://dx.doi.org/10.1787/5k3wdjrnh7mv-en*.

Gallup (2015), the *Gallup World Poll*, *www.gallup.com/services/170945/world-poll.aspx* (accessed on 5 July 2015).

International Institute for Democracy and Electoral Assistance (IDEA), *www.idea.int/* (accessed on 22 March 2015).

International Labour Office (ILO)(2012), *Decent Work Indicators: Concepts and definitions*, ILO Manual, First edition, Geneva.

Murtin, F. and M. Mira d'Ercole (2015), "Household wealth inequality across OECD countries: New OECD evidence", *OECD Statistics Brief*, No. 21, *www.oecd.org/social/household-wealth-inequality-across-OECD-countries-OECDSB21.pdf*.

OECD (forthcoming), *Regions at a Glance 2016*, OECD Publishing, Paris.

OECD (2015a), *In It Together: Why Less Inequality Benefits All*, OECD Publishing, Paris, *http://dx.doi.org/10.1787/9789264235120-en*.

OECD (2015b), *OECD Employment Outlook 2015*, OECD Publishing, Paris, *http://dx.doi.org/10.1787/empl_outlook-2015-en*.

OECD (2015c), *OECD Gender Portal*, *www.oecd.org/gender/data/* (accessed on 12 May 2015).

OECD (2015d), *Health at a Glance 2015: OECD Indicators*, OECD Publishing, Paris, forthcoming.

OECD (2015e), *Education at a Glance Interim Report: Update of Employment and Educational Attainment Indicators*, OECD Publishing, Paris, *www.oecd.org/edu/EAG-Interim-report.pdf*.

OECD (2015f), *Skills for Social Progress: The Power of Social and Emotional Skills*, OECD Skills Studies, OECD Publishing, Paris, *http://dx.doi.org/10.1787/9789264226159-en*.

OECD (2015g), "What Lies Behind Gender Inequality in Education?", *PISA in Focus*, No. 49, OECD Publishing, Paris, *http://dx.doi.org/10.1787/5js4xffhhc30-en*.

OECD (2015h), *The ABC of Gender Equality in Education: Aptitude, Behaviour, Confidence*, PISA, OECD Publishing, Paris, *http://dx.doi.org/10.1787/9789264229945-en*.

OECD (2015i), *Regulatory Policy Outlook*, OECD Publishing, Paris, forthcoming.

OECD (2015j), *Government at a Glance 2015*, OECD Publishing, Paris, *http://dx.doi.org/10.1787/gov_glance-2015-en* .

OECD (2014a), *OECD Employment Outlook 2014*, OECD Publishing, Paris, *http://dx.doi.org/10.1787/empl_outlook-2014-en*.

OECD (2014b), *Making Mental Health Count: The Social and Economic Costs of Neglecting Mental Health Care*, OECD Health Policy Studies, OECD Publishing, Paris, *http://dx.doi.org/10.1787/9789264208445-en*.

OECD (2014c), "Improving well-being", in OECD, *OECD Economic Surveys: United States 2014*, OECD Publishing, Paris, *http://dx.doi.org/10.1787/eco_surveys-usa-2014-5-en*.

OECD (2014d), *Education at a Glance 2014: OECD Indicators*, OECD Publishing, Paris, *http://dx.doi.org/10.1787/eag-2014-en*.

OECD (2014e), *PISA 2012 Results: What Students Know and Can Do* (Volume I, Revised edition, February 2014): *Student Performance in Mathematics, Reading and Science*, PISA, OECD Publishing, Paris, *http://dx.doi.org/10.1787/9789264208780-en*.

OECD (2014f), *Green Growth Indicators 2014*, OECD Green Growth Studies, OECD Publishing, Paris, *http://dx.doi.org/10.1787/9789264202030-en*.

OECD (2014g), *How's Life in Your Region?: Measuring Regional and Local Well-being for Policy Making*, OECD Publishing, Paris, *http://dx.doi.org/10.1787/9789264217416-en*.

OECD (2014h), "Environmental quality of life", in OECD, *Green Growth Indicators 2014*, OECD Publishing, Paris, *http://dx.doi.org/10.1787/9789264202030-9-en*.

OECD (2013a), *How's Life? 2013: Measuring Well-being*, OECD Publishing, Paris, *http://dx.doi.org/10.1787/9789264201392-en*.

OECD (2013b), *OECD Guidelines for Micro Statistics on Household Wealth*, OECD Publishing, Paris, *http://dx.doi.org/10.1787/9789264194878-en*.

OECD (2013c), *OECD Framework for Statistics on the Distribution of Household Income, Consumption and Wealth*, OECD Publishing, Paris, *http://dx.doi.org/10.1787/9789264194830-en*.

OECD (2013d), "Well-being in the workplace: Measuring job quality", in OECD, *How's Life? 2013: Measuring Well-being*, OECD Publishing, Paris, *http://dx.doi.org/10.1787/how_life-2013-9-en*.

OECD (2013e), *OECD Skills Outlook 2013: First Results from the Survey of Adult Skills*, OECD Publishing, Paris, *http://dx.doi.org/10.1787/9789264204256-en*.

OECD (2013f), *OECD Guidelines on Measuring Subjective Well-being*, OECD Publishing, Paris, *http://dx.doi.org/10.1787/9789264191655-en*.

OECD (2012), *Education at a glance 2012: OECD Indicators*, OECD Publishing, Paris, *http://dx.doi.org/10.1787/eag-2012-en*.

OECD (2011a), *How's Life? Measuring Well-Being*, OECD Publishing, Paris, *http://dx.doi.org/10.1787/9789264121164-en*.

OECD (2011b), "Housing conditions", in OECD, *How's Life? Measuring Well-being*, OECD Publishing, Paris, *http://dx.doi.org/10.1787/9789264121164-6-en*.

OECD (2011c), *The Future of Families to 2030*, OECD Publishing, Paris, *http://dx.doi.org/10.1787/9789264168367-en*.

OECD (2011d), "Personal security", in OECD, *How's Life? Measuring Well-Being*, OECD Publishing, Paris, *http://dx.doi.org/10.1787/9789264121164-13-en*.

OECD (2007), *Babies and Bosses - Reconciling Work and Family Life: A Synthesis of Findings for OECD Countries*, OECD Publishing, Paris, *http://dx.doi.org/10.1787/9789264032477-en*.

United Nations Economic Commission for Europe (UNECE)(2015), *Handbook on Measuring Quality of Employment: A Statistical Framework*, prepared by the Expert Group on Measuring the Quality of Employment, *www.unece.org/fileadmin/DAM/stats/documents/ece/ces/2015/4_Add.2_Rev1_Guidelines_on_QoEmployment.pdf* (accessed on 14 July 2015).

United Nations Office on Drugs and Crime (UNODC) (2013), Report of the National Institute of Statistics and Geography of Mexico and the United Nations Office on Drugs and Crime, *http://unstats.un.org/unsd/statcom/doc13/2013-11-CrimeStats-E.pdf*.

van Donkelaar, A., R.V. Martin, M.Brauer and B.L. Boys (2015), "Use of Satellite Observations for Long-Term Exposure Assessment of Global Concentrations of Fine Particulate Matter", *Environmental Health Perspectives*, Vol. 123, Issue 2.

World Health Organisation (WHO) (2006), *World Health Organization: Air Quality Guidelines for Particulate Matter, Ozone, Nitrogen Dioxide and Sulfur Dioxide*, Global Update 2005, *www.who.int/phe/health_topics/outdoorair/outdoorair_aqg/en/*.

Database references

Eurostat (2015) "European Union Statistics on Income and Living Conditions (EU-SILC)", *European Commission*, Brussels, *http://ec.europa.eu/eurostat/web/income-and-living-conditions/overview* (accessed on 28 June 2015).

Eurostat (2015) *Time Use Database*, *http://appsso.eurostat.ec.europa.eu/nui/show.do?dataset=tus_00selfstat&lang=en* (accessed on 5 July 2015).

Gallup World Poll, *www.gallup.com/services/170945/world-poll.aspx* (accessed on 5 July 2015).

Harmonised European Time Use Survey web application, *https://www.h2.scb.se/tus/tus/* (accessed on 1 July 2015).

International Institute for Democracy and Electoral Assistance (IDEA), *www.idea.int/* (accessed on 22 March 2015).

OECD *National Accounts Statistics* (database), *http://dx.doi.org/10.1787/data-00652-en* (accessed on 5 July 2015).

OECD *Wealth Distribution*, (database), *http://stats.oecd.org/Index.aspx?DataSetCode=WEALTH* (accessed on 5 July 2015).

OECD *Social and Welfare Statistics* (database), *http://dx.doi.org/10.1787/socwel-data-en* (accessed on 5 July 2015).

OECD *Employment and Labour* Market Statistics (database), *http://dx.doi.org/ 10.1787/lfs-data-en* (accessed on 5 July 2015).

OECD *Health Statistics* (database), *http://dx.doi.org/10.1787/health-data-en* (accessed on 5 July 2015).

Chapter 3

Resources for future well-being

Choices and decisions that are made today can have important consequences for well-being tomorrow. To provide a first glimpse of future well-being prospects, this chapter focuses on some of the key resources that are likely to shape well-being outcomes over time. It provides a small set of measures to illustrate elements of the natural, human, social and economic "capital stocks" that exist today, and that provide a store of wealth for later well-being. It also considers some of the risk factors that can have a bearing on those stocks. The indicators range from forest area through to trust in public institutions, and from educational attainment in young adults, to household debt. While there is considerable work to be done to further develop this indicator set, this chapter shows the wide range of evidence that is already available today, and highlights some of the gaps that need to be filled in order to have a more complete dashboard of measures in the future. In the longer term, the goal is to be able to evaluate current well-being outcomes in the context of the resources left for future generations.

The statistical data for Israel are supplied by and under the responsibility of the relevant Israeli authorities. The use of such data by the OECD is without prejudice to the status of the Golan Heights, East Jerusalem and Israeli settlements in the West Bank under the terms of international law.

What can be said today about future prospects for well-being? In all walks of life, people need to make decisions today that can affect well-being in the future. The *How's Life?* measurement framework includes both current well-being outcomes and the factors that can support well-being over time (Box 3.1). This chapter addresses this latter part of the framework, focusing on four types of resources (or "capital") that can be observed today, that are shaped by decisions taken here and now, and that are important for the well-being of both current and future generations.

The approach taken in this section follows the special chapter on *Measuring the sustainability of well-being over time* included in *How's Life? 2013* (OECD, 2013a), and implements several components of the recommendations of the Conference of European Statisticians on measuring sustainable development (UNECE, 2014). It introduces for the first time a small set of measures to reflect elements of natural, human, social and economic resources that are key to ensuring future well-being, alongside some of the factors that can cause these resources to increase or decrease over time. While the evidence described below is far from complete, the goal is to start evaluating today's well-being ("here and now") in the context of the resources available for supporting the well-being of future generations ("later"). Several of these resources are global public goods, and thus what happens "elsewhere" (beyond any single country's borders) is another important consideration – although one that can only be partially addressed through the evidence at hand (Box 3.1).

Box 3.1. Measuring the capital stocks that support well-being over time

Consistent with the recommendations of the Conference of European Statisticians on measuring sustainable development (UNECE, 2014) and the Stiglitz, Sen and Fitoussi Report (2009), the *How's Life?* framework for measuring well-being adopts a "capital-based approach" to understand whether current well-being is likely to be maintained over time (see Chapter 6 in OECD, 2013a). In particular, it focuses on four broad types of resources (Figure 3.1).

Figure 3.1. Capital stocks featured in the *How's Life?* framework for measuring well-being

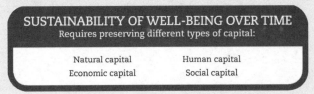

Source: OECD (2011), *How's Life? Measuring Well-Being*, OECD Publishing, Paris, *http://dx.doi.org/10.1787/9789264121164-en*.

These resources are referred to as forms of "capital", reflecting the notion of stocks that represent a store of value for well-being in the future. These different types of capital share a number of common characteristics: they each influence a broad range of well-being outcomes; they each have some degree of persistence over time; and they each require investment and careful management to be maintained. This approach suggests

---

> ## Box 3.1. **Measuring the capital stocks that support well-being over time** (cont.)
>
> that it is important to monitor the evolution of capital over time to properly inform the management of the underlying stocks. Wherever possible, therefore, the indicators included in this chapter are shown over a 10 to 15 year time period – although in practice the relevant time-spans are likely to depend on the nature of the capital stock in question.* Information is also presented about inflows (e.g. investments), outflows (e.g. depletion or degradation of resources) and other risk factors that can affect the value of these capital stocks and their resilience to shocks. These latter indicators suggest some of the levers through which decision-makers can take action today to improve prospects for well-being in the future.
>
> The approach used in this chapter has parallels with several other existing measurement initiatives, including the UNECE-Eurostat-OECD *Task Force on Measuring Sustainable Development* (United Nations, 2009; UNECE 2014), the UNU-IDHP and UNEP's *Inclusive Wealth Report* (2012; 2014), and the initiatives developed by several National Statistical Offices, such as the Swiss Federal Statistical Office (2013) and Statistics New Zealand (2011). A key feature of many of these frameworks is the distinction made between meeting well-being needs "here and now", and the stocks of resources that can affect the well-being of future generations "later". Several of these approaches go beyond simply measuring levels of stocks to also consider how they are managed, maintained or threatened.
>
> Recognising the global challenges involved in maintaining well-being over time, the UNECE (2014) approach highlights the importance of understanding how actions taken in one country can also affect the well-being of people in other countries, i.e. the well-being "elsewhere" dimension. These cross-boundary impacts can be either positive (e.g. well-designed poverty-reduction programmes in fragile states financed through Official Development Assistance) or negative (e.g. outflows of skilled workers that deplete the human capital of countries that invested in their education and training). They can affect elements of the capital stocks that are truly "global" (e.g. additions to the stocks of greenhouse gases in the atmosphere) or stocks that might be located in specific countries, but whose depletion can be a global concern and a global responsibility (e.g. depletion of tropical forests driven by global consumption patterns). While a detailed examination of these trans-boundary effects is beyond the scope of this chapter, it remains an important priority for future research and measurement.
>
> *The choice of the most appropriate timespan for the assessment of well-being over time depends on the type of capital considered. The focus of this chapter is on the resources that exist and can be measured today but that are also relevant for maintaining well-being in the future. Implicitly, the measures of human and social capital proposed in this section imply that "later" (i.e. future well-being) typically refers to the later life-span of people currently living (i.e. today's children or young adults). Conversely, in the case of non-renewable natural capital, the management of resources today can affect the well-being for all generations to come in the distant future. The appropriate timespan for economic capital is intermediate between these two: economic capital includes physical infrastructure (buildings, bridges, etc.) that can endure over many lifetimes but also financial capital, which can be subject to rapid fluctuations in times of crisis. There is, therefore, no "one size fits all" timeframe that can be applied to all the different forms of capital stocks.
>
> *Sources:* OECD (2013), *How's Life? 2013: Measuring Well-being*, OECD Publishing, Paris, *http://dx.doi.org/10.1787/9789264201392-en*; and United Nations Economic Commission for Europe (UNECE) (2014), *Conference of European Statisticians Recommendations on Measuring Sustainable Development*, United Nations, New York and Geneva, *www.unece.org/fileadmin/DAM/stats/publications/2013/CES_SD_web.pdf*.

The measurement of current well-being focuses very much on the experiences of individuals, households and communities. By contrast, threats to future well-being often involve disruptions to the wider systems in which individual well-being is embedded – for example, changes in the climate system, or a build-up of risks in the financial system that can lead to economic crises. It follows that a dashboard of indicators focused on the maintenance of well-being over time will need to look beyond people-centred measures to also consider society-wide and system-based characteristics. That said, many of the measures considered in this section are expressed on a per capita basis, as this can help both to relate systemic features back to the experiences of individuals, and to reflect the impact that population changes can have on resource availability.

In practice, the four types of "capital" (natural, human, social and economic) considered in this section are very heterogeneous, and their measurement is challenging. The illustrative set of indicators referred to in this chapter are presented in Table 3.1. In some areas, the same factors that are considered as well-being outcomes "here and now" also provide critical information about possibilities for well-being in the future. This means that several measures used to capture current well-being in Chapter 2 are also very relevant here. This is true for factors such as household wealth (a stock of economic capital); the skills and competencies of the adult population (which provide information about the stock of human capital); long-term unemployment (as a risk factor that can affect human capital); voter turnout and government stakeholder engagement (which can be seen as investments in social capital); and exposure to air pollution (an aspect of environmental quality that can have both short- and long-term well-being consequences). When the well-being benefits (or costs) stemming from these outcomes extend into the future, the same indicators that are used for monitoring current well-being will also inform about well-being over time. To avoid repetition of material from Chapter 2, trends in these aspects are not reviewed in what follows, but these indicators are highlighted in the first column of Table 3.1 below, and should be considered as part of the wider "dashboard" of indicators for assessing resources for future well-being.

Table 3.1. **Illustrative indicators to monitor resources for future well-being, as shown in Chapters 2 and 3**

Capital stock	Chapter 2 Indicators relevant to both current and future well-being	Chapter 3 Indicators of the "stock" of capital	Chapter 3 "Flow" indicators (investment in, and depletion of, capital stocks)	Chapter 3 Other risk factors
Natural capital	Annual exposure to air pollution (PM$_{2.5}$)	Concentration of greenhouse gases in the atmosphere Land assets: Forest cover per capita Freshwater resources per capita	Greenhouse gas emissions per capita Freshwater abstractions per capita	Threatened species
Human capital	Educational attainment Cognitive skills among 15 year-old students Competencies of the adult population Long-term unemployment Life expectancy at birth	Educational attainment of 25-34 year olds	Educational expectancy (at age 5 to age 39)	Smoking prevalence Obesity prevalence
Social capital	Voter turnout Government stakeholder engagement	Trust in others Trust in public institutions		
Economic capital	Net wealth of households Net financial wealth of households	Net fixed assets per capita Knowledge capital per capita Financial net worth of the total economy per capita	Gross fixed capital formation Investment in R&D	Indebtedness of the private (household) sector Financial net worth of general government Leverage of the banking sector

While the measures presented here are intended to provide some insights into the stocks of natural, human, social and economic capital available to current and future generations, they by no means offer a complete assessment. Important features of capital stocks are missing from the dashboard described in Table 3.1. These include indicators in the areas of social capital (where many measures remain under development) and several aspects of natural capital (for example, mineral, energy and land resources are important omissions). A much larger variety of "flow" indicators and risk factors could also be considered.[1] In addition, the well-being of the youngest generation today will be an essential input into the human, social and economic capital stocks of tomorrow, and will have important consequences for their well-being as adults. Thus, the measures of child well-being featured in Chapter 4 are also pertinent to the discussion of well-being over time.

Even among the indicators shown in Table 3.1, country coverage, comparability over time, and data quality are limited in several cases. In other words, the data described in this chapter represent a first collection of measures, rather than an "ideal" set of indicators. A fuller assessment of future well-being prospects will require a wider dashboard of indicators, as well as a more sophisticated understanding of the interactions between the different indicators. One important subject for research that will also enhance the interpretation of these data considerably is an assessment of non-linearities, such as critical thresholds and tipping points – where the threats to future well-being can increase substantially (and perhaps irreversibly). Yet despite the many further developments still needed, this chapter also shows that it is possible to begin monitoring a wide range of resources for future well-being, based on the data that are available today.

Natural capital

Natural capital refers to critical aspects of the natural environment. It can include individual assets such as minerals, energy resources, land, soil, water, trees, plants and wildlife. However, it also includes broader ecosystems – i.e. the joint functioning of, or interactions among, different environmental assets, as seen in forests, soil, aquatic environments and the atmosphere. Some of the well-being benefits of natural assets can be felt "here and now": for example, having clean air to breathe, safe water to drink, or green space for recreation, leisure and community events. Measures of air pollution and water quality are included in Chapter 2 as indicators of current well-being, though the cumulative effects of exposure to pollution in particular also has important consequences for health over time.

Many of the benefits of natural assets, however, come from their role in the production of other capitals which, in turn, contribute to people's material well-being and quality of life today and in the future. For example, natural assets often play a central role in economic production – providing the physical space, energy and raw materials for economic activities ranging from manufacturing to agriculture and tourism. Natural assets are also central to human capital, including through their role in the provision of water and food, fuel to heat homes and workspaces, and a healthy living environment for people. Ecosystems also provide important sink functions (e.g. by storing pollution, waste and carbon) as well as protection from natural hazards (such as ultra-violet rays or flooding). Similarly, competition for scarce natural resources or insecurity around the future provision of food, water, minerals or energy can threaten social capital and be a source of conflicts within and between countries. While these factors often go unnoticed in many people's daily lives, they have major implications for well-being in the longer run.

A wide variety of indicators exist for the stocks and flows of natural capital, but relatively few are routinely collected in a consistent manner across all OECD countries. Many of these indicators also pertain to types of resources (e.g. freshwater; forests) that may be naturally scarce in some countries, but relatively abundant in others. Continuous improvements to measurement methodologies also mean that comparisons over time are challenging for many of the relevant indicators. To illustrate the concept of natural capital, a small number of measures have been selected here (see Box 3.2), drawing on indicators for the "natural asset base" featured in the OECD *Green Growth Indicators* publication (OECD, 2014a) which, alongside the OECD's *Environment at a Glance* (2013b), includes a much richer set of measures.

Box 3.2. **Illustrative indicators for measuring natural capital**

The following indicators have been selected to illustrate the concept of natural capital:

- **Forest area per 1 000 inhabitants** refers to the stock of forest and wooded land, expressed in square kilometres. It includes forested land spanning more than 0.5 hectares, and with a canopy cover of more than 10%, or trees able to reach these thresholds *in situ*. It excludes woodland or forest predominantly under agricultural or urban land use, or used only for recreational purposes. The data shown here come from the *OECD Environment Statistics Database,* which features data reported by UNECE and the UN Food and Agriculture Organisation's *Global Forest Resources Assessment*. The FAO's assessment methodology relies on both country reports prepared by national correspondents and remote sensing.

- **Greenhouse gas emissions** concern man-made emissions of six different greenhouse gases – carbon dioxide (CO_2, including emissions from energy use and industrial processes, e.g. cement production); methane (CH_4, including methane emissions from solid waste, livestock, mining of hard coal and lignite, rice paddies, agriculture and leaks from natural gas pipelines); nitrous oxide (N_2O); hydrofluorocarbons (HFCs); perfluorocarbons (PFCs); and sulphur hexafluoride (SF_6) – weighted by their "warming potential". The data, which form part of the *OECD Environment Statistics Database,* are compiled on the basis of National Inventory Submissions 2014 to the *United Nations Framework Convention on Climate Change* (UNFCCC), and on replies to the OECD State of the Environment Questionnaire. The data refer to gross direct emissions excluding emissions or removals from land-use, land-use change and forestry.

- **Renewable freshwater resources** are expressed as the long-term annual average availability, in cubic metres per capita. They refer to internal flow (the total volume of river run-off and groundwater generated, in natural conditions, exclusively by precipitation into a territory), plus the external flow (the total volume of the flow of rivers and groundwater coming from neighbouring territories). The data shown here form part of the OECD's Green Growth Indicator set, and are drawn from the *OECD Environment Statistics Database*.

- **Freshwater abstractions** are expressed as gross abstraction from groundwater or surface water bodies, in cubic metres per capita. They include abstractions for agricultural (e.g. irrigation) and industrial use (e.g. cooling and industrial processes), as well as for public supply. For some countries, these data refer to water permits rather than to actual abstractions. The data shown here form part of the OECD's Green Growth Indicator set, and are drawn from the *OECD Environment Statistics Database*.

- **Threatened species** refers to the percentage of mammals, birds and vascular plants that are critically endangered, endangered or vulnerable – i.e. those plants and animals that are in danger of extinction or soon likely to be, based on the IUCN Red List categories and criteria. The data shown here do not include fish, reptiles, amphibians, invertebrates or fungi. Data refer to the latest year available, which corresponds to the late 2000s for most countries. The data source is the OECD's Green Growth Indicator set, part of the *OECD Environment Statistics Database*. Data for Israel were supplied by the Israel Nature and Parks Authority. The data on the state of threatened species build on country replies to the *Annual Quality Assurance (AQA)* of OECD environmental reference series. These data are harmonised through the work of the OECD Working Party on Environmental Information (WPEI).

Forest area per 1 000 inhabitants, together with measures of forest cover, provide information about the *quantity* of forest in a given area, but a more complete picture of forest stocks would also consider their *quality*, i.e. aspects such as species diversity (for both trees and other species) and forest degradation, and whether forest cover is highly fragmented. In addition, as in some countries forest is naturally scarce, other forms of natural vegetation should be considered. In this context, the fragmentation of contiguous natural areas would be another possible indicator for consideration.

> Box 3.2. **Illustrative indicators for measuring natural capital** (cont.)
>
> Water stress may vary substantially within countries and over time, as different regions within a country can have very different levels of freshwater resources, and seasonal variations can affect the level of pressure on those resources. Definitions and estimation methods for freshwater resources can vary both across countries and over time (OECD, 2014a).
>
> The data on threatened species suffer from a number of limitations: the standards and definitions of the International Union for Conservation of Nature (IUCN) are applied with varying degrees of rigour in countries, and the number of species known or assessed does not always accurately reflect the number of species in existence. Historical data are also generally not available or not comparable (OECD, 2014a).
>
> A comprehensive dashboard of natural capital stocks would include a much greater range of assets than the ones shown here (OECD 2013a; UNECE 2014). Further details of other critical natural assets, including a fuller account of land use changes, water extraction and species abundance is provided by the OECD *Green Growth Indicators* (OECD, 2014a).
>
> Over time, the OECD *Green Growth Indicators* will include measures of a wider range of natural assets, including: i) the availability and quality of renewable stocks of natural resources, such as freshwater, forest, and fish; ii) the availability and accessibility of stocks of non-renewable natural resources such as metals, industrial minerals and fossil energy carriers; and iii) biological diversity and ecosystems, including species and habitat diversity, and the productivity of land and soil resources.
>
> Work is also proceeding within the OECD to implement key aspects of the new international standard of economy-environment accounting (SEEA). This aims to provide estimates of natural capital that can complement the measures of economic capital in the system of national accounts.
>
> **Further reading:**
>
> - FAO (UN Food and Agriculture Organisation) (2010), *Global Forest Resources Assessment 2010 Main Report*, FAO Forestry Paper 163, www.fao.org/docrep/013/i1757e/i1757e.pdf.
> - IEA (2014), *Energy, Climate Change and Environment: 2014 Insights*, IEA, Paris, http://dx.doi.org/10.1787/9789264220744-en.
> - OECD (2014a), *Green Growth Indicators 2014*, OECD Green Growth Studies, OECD Publishing, Paris, http://dx.doi.org/10.1787/9789264202030-en.
> - OECD (2012), *OECD Environmental Outlook to 2050: The Consequences of Inaction*, OECD Publishing, Paris, http://dx.doi.org/10.1787/9789264122246-en.

Forests serve many different environmental, socio-economic and cultural roles. For example, they provide inputs to economic production, such as building timber, fuel, wood- and paper-based products; they protect land from soil erosion and flooding; they provide a habitat for plants and wildlife; and they provide space for recreation and leisure. Forests also play a crucial role in the global carbon cycle, by acting as a carbon sink.

Overall, OECD countries account for around 25% of the world's forest area, and on average around one-third of the land area in OECD countries is covered by forest. In Finland, Sweden and Japan, forests cover more than 65% of total land area, but this share drops to below 10% for Iceland and Israel (OECD, 2014a). Expressed relative to the size of the population (Figure 3.2), Norway, Sweden, Finland, Australia and Canada had forest stocks of over 20km² per 1 000 inhabitants in 2011, but the majority of OECD countries had less than 5km²; in Israel, the Netherlands and the United Kingdom, the value is below 1 km² per 1 000 inhabitants.

Between 2000 and 2012, the average forest area per 1 000 inhabitants in the OECD area fell by 7%, from 9.1 km² in 2000, to 8.4 km² in 2012. Large reductions occurred in Australia, Canada and also Brazil. In the cases of Australia and Brazil, this reflects decreases in forest cover as a percentage of total land area (from 20% to 19% in the case of Australia; and from 65% to 62% in Brazil), combined with increases in population size. In the case of Canada, forest cover as a percentage of total land area has remained stable but the population has increased substantially, resulting in a decline in forest area per capita.

Figure 3.2. **Forest area**

Forest area in square kilometres, per thousand people

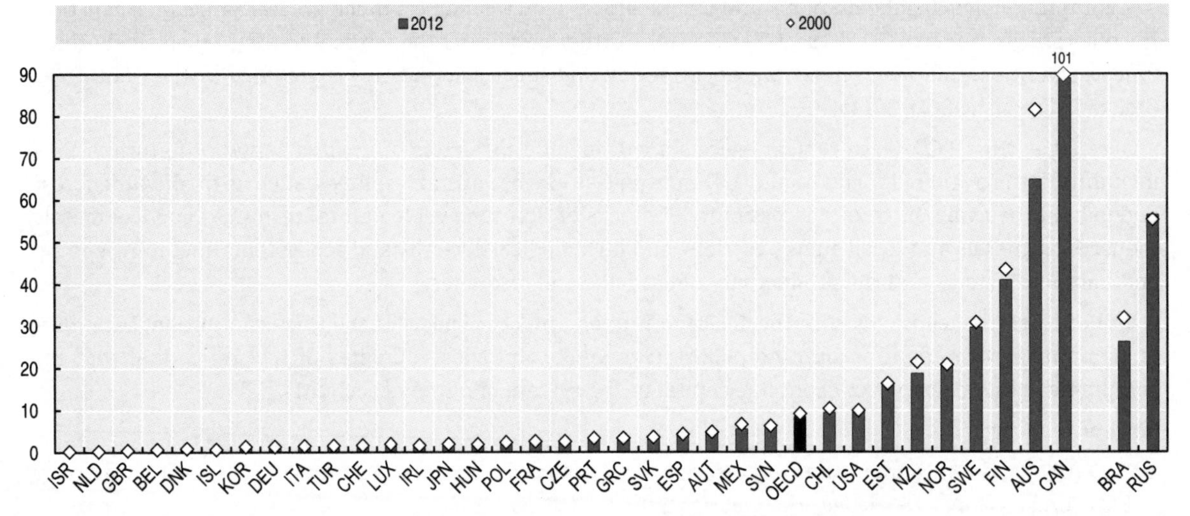

Notes: The first available year is 2009 for the United States. The OECD average is population-weighted.

Source: OECD calculations based on "Land Resources", OECD Environment Statistics (database), http://stats.oecd.org/Index.aspx?DataSetCode=LAND_USE.

StatLink ⬛⬛⬛ http://dx.doi.org/10.1787/888933259359

While forests have many local benefits, the total stock of forest resources is also important on a global scale. The decline in forest area per capita across the OECD since 2000 has occurred in the context of a wider global trend towards deforestation, with worldwide net losses estimated at around 5.2 million hectares per year – an area roughly the size of Costa Rica – between 2000 and 2010 (FAO, 2010).

In some countries, forests are naturally scarce, and thus forest cover should be considered alongside other measures of vegetation and natural habitats, as well as information about land use change (e.g. the amount of land area sealed by urban areas). Manmade fragmentation of natural vegetation and biodiversity-rich areas (for example, arising from built-up areas and transport infrastructure) can have important consequences for species habitats – and thus fragmentation of contiguous natural areas would also be a valuable indicator for future consideration.

The *atmosphere* is a globally shared natural asset that plays a central role in climate regulation. In particular, the concentration of greenhouse gases in the atmosphere is a critical risk factor for climate change that, if un-checked, will have profound consequences for human well-being in the future (OECD, 2012; OECD, 2015a). At their current levels, the concentrations of the six greenhouse gases included in the Kyoto Protocol[2] imply a 50% probability that the global temperature rise will not exceed 2 degrees Celsius above pre-industrial levels (European Environment Agency, 2015). Stabilising greenhouse gas concentrations in the atmosphere is therefore a key international policy challenge.

Atmospheric concentrations of CO_2 and of other greenhouse gases are reported by the World Meteorological Association (WMO), a specialised agency of the United Nations. The 2014 WMO *Greenhouse Gas Bulletin* (WMO, 2014) reported that global average estimates of atmospheric concentrations of carbon dioxide (CO_2), methane (CH_4) and nitrous oxide (N_2O) reached new highs in 2013, with global average values of CO_2 at 396.0+/-0.1 parts per million (ppm); CH_4 at 1 824+/-2 parts per billion (ppb); and N_2O at 325.9+/-0.1 ppb. This means that current concentrations of CO_2 are 42% higher than in pre-industrial times (i.e. before 1750), CH_4 concentrations are 153% higher and N_2O concentrations are 21% higher. Between 2012 and 2013, the largest year-to-year change in atmospheric CO_2 was recorded since 1984, at 2.9 ppm (WMO, 2014). Together, the six greenhouse gases included in the Kyoto Protocol reached 449 ppm CO_2 equivalent in 2012, an increase of 171 ppm (around +62 %) compared to pre-industrial levels (European Environment Agency, 2015).[3]

Greenhouse gas emissions into the air (Figure 3.3, see Box 3.2 for the definition) provide a "flow" indicator that complements information about the atmospheric stock of greenhouse gases. In the OECD area in 2012, annual greenhouse gas emissions from activities located in each country were highest in Canada, the United States, Luxembourg and Australia (at 20 000 kilograms per capita or greater), and lowest in Mexico, Sweden, Turkey and Chile (around 6 000 kilograms per capita). In most OECD countries, per capita greenhouse gas emissions from domestic economic production declined between 2000 and 2012. In Ireland, Denmark, Belgium, the United Kingdom, Spain, Sweden, Italy and Portugal, emissions fell by 20% or more. In a small number of countries – usually those starting from a much lower per capita base – greenhouse gas emissions per capita increased between 2000 and 2012, including in Korea (by nearly 30%), Estonia and Turkey (by over 15%), the Russian Federation and Mexico (by 10% or more).

Figure 3.3. **Greenhouse gas emissions from domestic production**
Kilograms per capita of CO_2 equivalent, in thousands

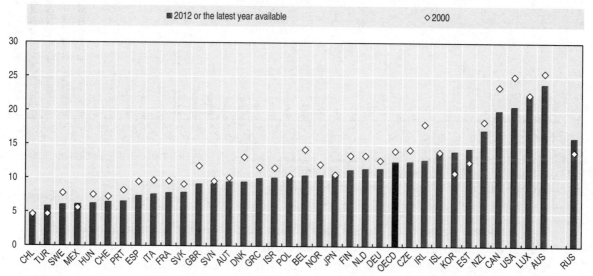

Note: The latest available year is 2011 for Israel and Korea; 2010 for Mexico; and 2006 for Chile. The OECD average is population-weighted.

Source: "Greenhouse gas emissions by source", *OECD Environment Statistics* (database), http://dx.doi.org/10.1787/data-00594-en.

StatLink ⛗ http://dx.doi.org/10.1787/888933259362

Expressing carbon emissions on a per capita basis can mean that if a country's population is increasing, its total emissions can increase even as per capita levels fall. Wherever emissions take place, their impacts are inherently trans-boundary: they contribute to higher concentrations of greenhouse gases in the atmosphere regardless of where they are emitted, and the effects of climate change are expected to be felt hardest in some of the countries that have contributed the least to global emissions. In addition, the emissions associated with one country's economic production do not necessarily reflect the emissions caused by that country's consumption patterns. Experimental measures of CO_2 emissions from consumption, as embodied in international trade (and based on global input-output tables) indicate that OECD countries are net importers of embedded carbon - i.e., for the OECD as a whole, emissions from consumption are higher than those from production (OECD, 2015b, *www.oecd.org/sti/inputoutput/co2*).

Freshwater resources are essential inputs to both agricultural and industrial production, as well as to the domestic water supply. The average availability of renewable freshwater resources varies considerably among OECD countries (Figure 3.4). The highest levels are found in Iceland, New Zealand, Canada, Norway and Chile, each with over 50 000 m³ of renewable freshwater resources per capita available annually. This contrasts with the majority of OECD countries, where fewer than 20 000 m³ per capita are typically available (and the OECD average value is 9 080 m³ per capita). Stocks of renewable freshwater resources are lowest in Israel, Korea, the Czech Republic, Poland, Belgium and Italy, each with fewer than 2 000 m³ available per capita on an annual basis.

Figure 3.4. **Total renewable freshwater resources**

1 000 m³ per capita, long-term annual average availability

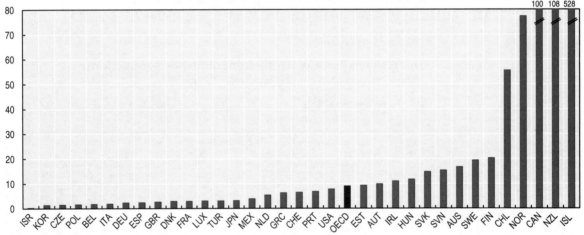

Note: Values for the United Kingdom refer to England and Wales only. Values for Canada (100), New Zealand (108), and Iceland (528) exceed the bounds of the figure. The OECD average is population-weighted.

Source: "Water: Freshwater resources", OECD Environment Statistics (database), *http://dx.doi.org/10.1787/env-data-en*.

StatLink ⟲ *http://dx.doi.org/10.1787/888933259375*

Freshwater abstractions provide some information about the intensity of water use. Among OECD countries for which data are available, gross freshwater abstractions are highest in the United States, Finland, Estonia, New Zealand and Canada (over 1 000 m³ per capita) and lowest in Luxembourg, Denmark, the United Kingdom, the Czech Republic, Ireland and Israel (less than 200 m³ per capita) (Figure 3.5). While some countries with high abstraction rates have relatively abundant freshwater resources (e.g. New Zealand, Finland, Canada), several OECD countries (e.g. the Netherlands, Belgium, Hungary and Israel) experience "water stress" in relation to their internal water resources (with abstractions at more than 40% of the available resources). After increasing in the 1970s, total freshwater abstraction for the OECD area as a whole has remained stable between 1990 and 2011 (OECD, 2014a). At the world level, however, it is estimated that the growth in water demand over the last century was more than twice the rate of population growth (OECD, 2014a; 2015c). Water stress is also expected to increase globally in the future, with over 40% of the global population projected to live under severe levels of water stress by 2050 (OECD, 2012; 2013c).

Figure 3.5. **Freshwater abstractions**

Cubic metres per capita, latest available year after 2006

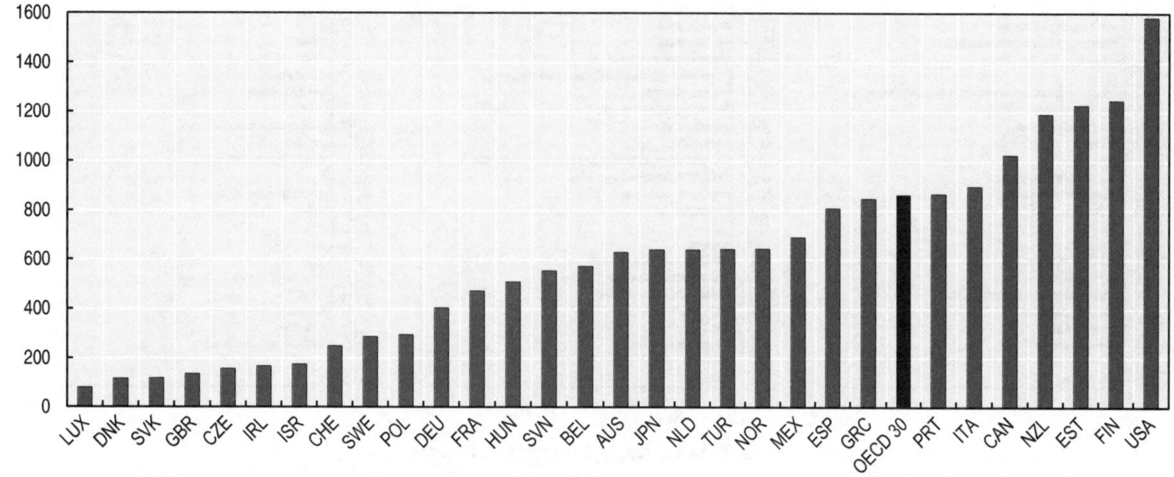

Note: The latest available year is 2013 for Luxembourg, the Slovak Republic, the Czech Republic, Poland, Slovenia, and Mexico; 2012 for Denmark, Switzerland, France, Hungary, the Netherlands, Spain and Estonia; 2011 for the United Kingdom, Australia and Canada; 2010 for Israel, Sweden, Germany, Turkey, New Zealand and the United States; 2009 for Ireland, Belgium and Japan; 2008 for Italy; 2007 for Norway, Greece and Portugal; and 2006 for Finland. Values for the United Kingdom refer to England and Wales only. The OECD average is population-weighted.

Source: "Water: Freshwater abstractions", *OECD Environment Statistics* (database), *http://dx.doi.org/10.1787/data-00602-en.*

StatLink ⟦⟧ *http://dx.doi.org/10.1787/888933259380*

Biodiversity is intrinsically valuable to people, and biological resources also provide important ecosystem services that support human well-being. Risks to biodiversity include changes in land use and land cover, chemical contamination and pollution, invasive alien species, and climate change (OECD, 2014a). Data on threatened species (i.e. those in danger of extinction or soon likely to be; see Box 3.2 for the definition) provide one indication of the pressure on biodiversity.

As shown in Figure 3.6, risks to biodiversity differ significantly across OECD countries, and vary according to whether mammals, birds or vascular plants are considered. More than 30% of known mammal species are threatened in Israel, Slovenia, Hungary, Germany and Switzerland; more than 30% of known bird species are threatened in the Czech Republic, Luxembourg, Iceland, Germany and Switzerland; and 30% or more of known vascular plant species are threatened in Austria, the Czech Republic and the Slovak Republic (Figure 3.6, Panel A). By contrast, fewer than 20% of each type of species is threatened in Canada, Denmark, Estonia, Korea, and Turkey. When the percentage of indigenous species are considered (rather than the percentage of known species), the proportions of species threatened are often higher (Figure 3.6, Panel B). In most OECD countries, the number of animal and plant species identified as endangered is increasing over time, and globally one in eight bird species is threatened with extinction (OECD, 2014a).

Figure 3.6. **Threatened species, latest available year**

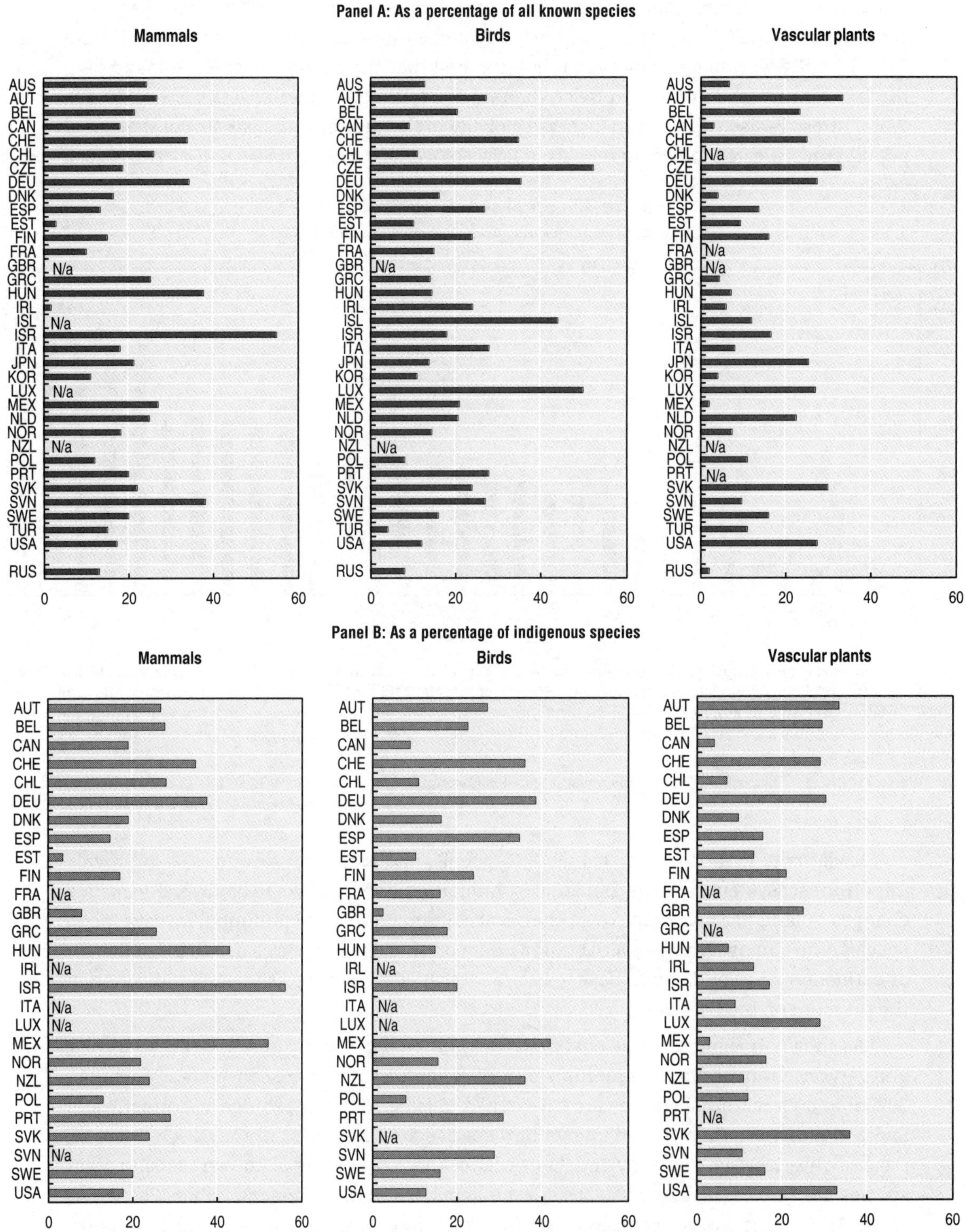

Panel A: As a percentage of all known species

Mammals — Birds — Vascular plants

Panel B: As a percentage of indigenous species

Mammals — Birds — Vascular plants

Note: "Threatened" refers to "endangered", "critically endangered" and "vulnerable" species, i.e. species in danger of extinction and species soon likely to be in danger of extinction. The data presented here refer to the latest year available, which corresponds to the late 2000s for most countries.

Source: "Threatened species", *OECD Environment Statistics* (database). *http://dx.doi.org/10.1787/data-00605-en*; data for Israel were supplied by the Israel Nature and Parks Authority.

StatLink ᴍᴎꜱᴘ *http://dx.doi.org/10.1787/888933259398*

Human capital

Human capital typically refers to the skills, competencies and health status of individuals. The concept of human capital was originally rooted in work on the importance of the "quality" of labour – which viewed human capital as an essential input to economic production and income generation. Beyond this economic role, however, there are considerable non-monetary benefits to high levels of human capital: good physical and mental health status enables participation in education, training and the labour market, as well as social relationships, and health is also strongly related to subjective well-being (OECD, 2011; 2013a). Similarly, higher skills and competencies have been associated with higher earnings and greater employability, better health status, greater civic awareness and political participation, and, at the societal level, with lower criminality, stronger social cohesion and greater political stability (UNECE, 2014; OECD, 2011).

Chapter 2 includes several indicators with strong relevance to the measurement of human capital: education and skills, long-term unemployment, and health status. These indicators are relevant to both current well-being "here and now", as well as to the stock of human capital that will help to maintain well-being "later". For example, long-term unemployment is a risk factor for human capital due to the potential for skills loss and long-term scarring, both economic and psychological. In this chapter, additional indicators that provide information about the *future stock* of skills are presented, alongside selected indicators of risk factors that could impact on people's health conditions in the future (see Box 3.3).

Box 3.3. **Illustrative indicators for measuring human capital**

Several indicators relevant to human capital are already described in Chapter 2 (under "jobs and earnings", "health status" and "education and skills"). Four further indicators presented here provide insights on the likely future supply of skills and health:

● The **educational attainment of the young adult population** is the proportion of adults aged 25 to 34 who have completed at least upper secondary education, as a share of the total population of the same age. The definition of "at least upper secondary education" corresponds to the International Standard Classification of Education (ISCED) levels 3 and above (excluding ISCED level 3C short programmes), and includes both i) programmes defined as "general" which are often designed for preparing students for further education, and ii) programmes geared towards vocational education and training (VET). The data underlying this indicator are collected through the annual OECD questionnaire on National Educational Attainment Categories (NEAC), which uses Labour Force Survey (LFS) data.

● **Education expectancy** is defined as the average duration of education that a 5-year-old child can expect to experience during his/her lifetime until reaching the age of 39. It is calculated based on current enrolment conditions by adding the net enrolment rates for each single year of age from the age of 5 onwards. Data for this indicator are collected through the annual OECD data collection on the school-work transitions, which rely on Labour Force Surveys as the main source of information.*

● **Smoking prevalence** is defined as the proportion of the population aged 15 and over who report that they are daily smokers. International comparability is limited due to the lack of standardisation in the measurement of smoking habits in health interview surveys across OECD countries. For example, there are variations in the question wording, in the response categories provided to interviewees, and in the methods used for data collection. Data collections within OECD countries are also periodic rather than annual. The data come from national health interviews, health surveys and other household survey sources, and are compiled as part of the *OECD's Health Statistics Database*.

Box 3.3. **Illustrative indicators for measuring human capital** (cont.)

● **Obesity** (either self-reported or measured) refers to the proportion of people aged 15 and over who meet the criteria for obesity, defined as a Body Mass Index of 30 or more. The Body Mass Index evaluates an individual's weight in relation to their height (weight/height², where weight is measured in kilograms and height in metres). The classification for obesity used here may not be suitable for all ethnic groups, which may have equivalent levels of risk at a lower or higher BMI. The data shown here refer to different sources in different countries (see the note to Figure 3.11): in some countries, the data are based on self-reported information drawn from health interview surveys (which use a variety of different question formats and response scales), while in others this is measured directly in health examinations (with varied methods of administration). The estimates from health examinations are generally higher and more reliable than those from health interviews (OECD, 2013d). The data are drawn from the *OECD's Health Statistics Database.*

Educational attainment and educational expectancy measures reflect the level of schooling or paper qualifications that people have achieved, but these measures cannot speak to the quality of education or to the competencies that people have developed or retained. Facets of people's knowledge, skills, and health can combine to influence the total stock of human capital, but each feature in isolation provides only a necessary rather than a sufficient condition for human capital.

Measures of human capital would therefore ideally consider the joint distribution of these different factors to capture the notion of a human capital *stock*. This has been the goal of techniques that have been developed to estimate the monetary value of human capital stocks, such as the lifetime income approach (see Boarini et al., 2012, for a review and Liu, 2011, for an example). Existing approaches, however, tend to focus only on the *economic value* of the total human capital stock, and they exclude the wide range of non-market well-being benefits that can flow from factors such as higher skills and better health.

Further reading:

● Boarini, R., M. Mira d'Ercole and G. Liu (2012), "Approaches to Measuring the Stock of Human Capital: A Review of Country Practices", *OECD Statistics Working Papers*, 2012/04, OECD Publishing, Paris, *http://dx.doi. org/10.1787/5k8zlm5bc3ns-en.*

● Liu, G. (2011), "Measuring the Stock of Human Capital for Comparative Analysis: An Application of the Lifetime Income Approach to Selected Countries", *OECD Statistics Working Paper No. 41*, 2011/06, OECD Publishing, Paris, *http://dx.doi.org/10.1787/5kg3h0jnn9r5-en.*

● OECD (2015d), *Education at a Glance Interim Report: Update of Employment and Educational Attainment Indicators,* OECD, Paris, *www.oecd.org/edu/EAG-Interim-report.pdf.*

● OECD (2013d), *Health at a Glance 2013: OECD Indicators,* OECD Publishing, Paris, *http://dx.doi.org/10.1787/ health_glance-2013-en.*

* This indicator was included as a measure of current well-being in OECD (2013); it is considered in this chapter as a measure of well-being "later" because of its forward-looking characteristics.

From a human capital perspective, the *educational attainment* of the youngest generation is particularly important, as it reflects the stock of skills that will be carried forward in future years. Figure 3.7 shows the proportion of people aged 25-34 who have attained at least an upper secondary education in 2000, 2007 and 2013. Rates of attainment differ between countries: in Korea and Japan, upper secondary education rates among young adults are twice those in Turkey and Mexico. Portugal, Spain, Italy and Iceland also have low attainment rates among young adults, relative to the OECD average.

Most OECD countries recorded steady increases in the educational attainment of young adults (aged 24-34) since 2000, and this is particularly true for those countries starting from a lower base. The OECD average cumulative growth in upper secondary attainment from 2000 to 2007 was 5 percentage points, and growth then slowed to 3 percentage points between 2007 and 2013. The largest cumulative increases in attainment from 2000 to 2013 occurred in Portugal (29 percentage points), Turkey (20 points), the United Kingdom (19 points), Luxembourg (18 points), and Australia (17 points). Over the same time period, growth in young adult upper secondary educational attainment was much weaker (less than 2 percentage points) in the Slovak Republic, Switzerland, the United States, the Czech Republic and Germany – though these countries each started from a much stronger position in 2000. In sharp contrast to most countries, young adult attainment in 2013 was lower than in 2000 levels in Estonia (-3 percentage points) and Denmark (-5 points).

Figure 3.7. **Educational attainment among 25-34 year olds**
Percentage attaining at least an upper secondary education

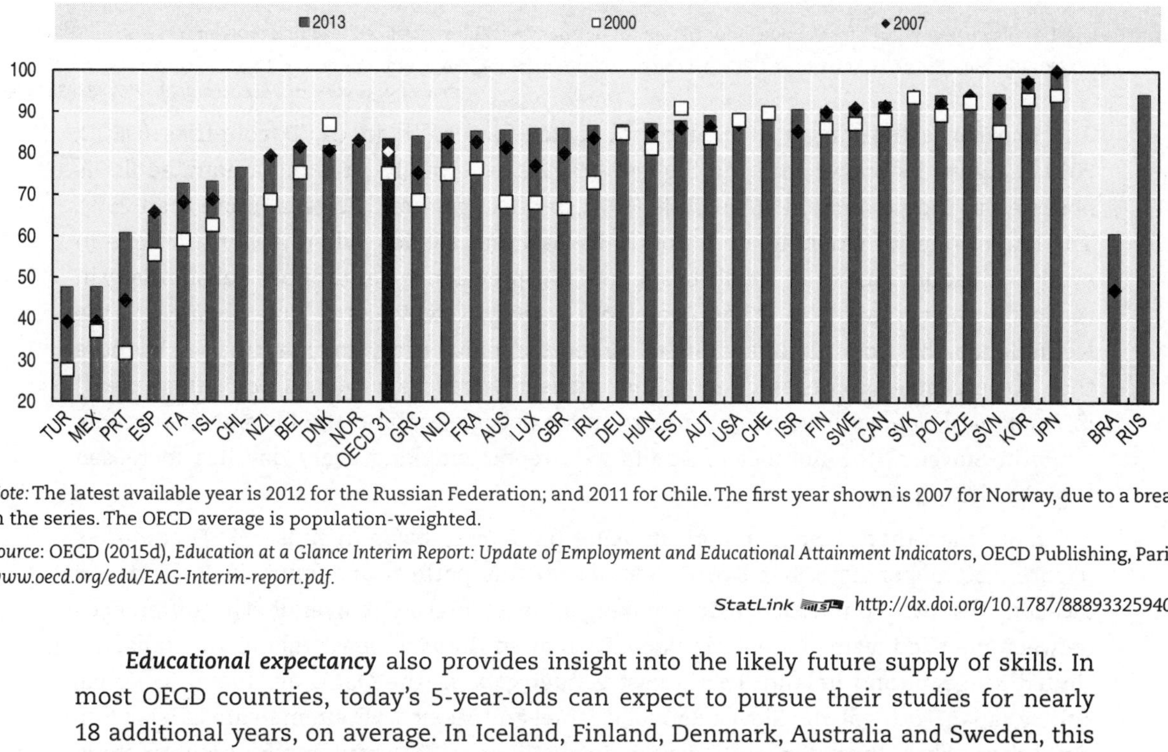

Note: The latest available year is 2012 for the Russian Federation; and 2011 for Chile. The first year shown is 2007 for Norway, due to a break in the series. The OECD average is population-weighted.

Source: OECD (2015d), *Education at a Glance Interim Report: Update of Employment and Educational Attainment Indicators*, OECD Publishing, Paris, *www.oecd.org/edu/EAG-Interim-report.pdf*.

StatLink ⬛⬛ *http://dx.doi.org/10.1787/888933259405*

Educational expectancy also provides insight into the likely future supply of skills. In most OECD countries, today's 5-year-olds can expect to pursue their studies for nearly 18 additional years, on average. In Iceland, Finland, Denmark, Australia and Sweden, this number rises to 19 additional years or more (Figure 3.8), while in Mexico, Luxembourg and Israel, it is limited to 16 years or fewer. When compared to measures of the average years of schooling of the current working-age population, this indicator suggests that the process of generational replacement may increase the average years of schooling in 2050 by close to 6 years for the OECD on average, ranging from less than 3 years in Japan and the United Kingdom, to 9 years or more in Portugal, Slovenia and Turkey.

As described in Chapter 2 of this edition, life expectancy at birth has been increasing in all OECD countries in recent years, even among those with the highest longevity (see also Oeppen and Vaupel, 2002; Wilmoth, 2011). At the same time, several risk factors (ranging from hypertension to excessive intake of sugar and salt) might potentially affect people's health status in the future, in particular smoking and obesity. While these factors may not necessarily affect a person's health "here and now", they can present a heightened risk to health status over the life-span.

Figure 3.8. **Educational expectancy**

Average number of years in education that a child aged 5 can expect to undertake (before age 39), 2012

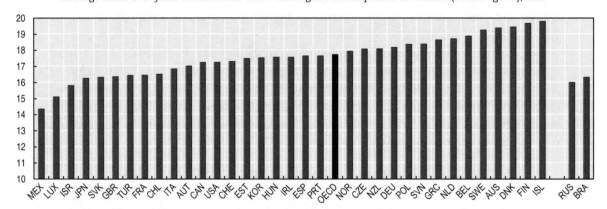

Note: The latest available year is 2011 for Canada. Information for Germany excludes advanced research programmes.

Source: OECD (2014b), *Education at a Glance 2014: OECD Indicators*, OECD Publishing, Paris, *http://dx.doi.org/10.1787/eag-2014-en.*

StatLink ᵐˢᵖ *http://dx.doi.org/10.1787/888933259414*

Smoking is the largest avoidable risk factor for health in OECD countries (OECD, 2013d). Figure 3.9 shows that the highest prevalence of daily smoking among adults is observed in Greece (around 40%), Chile (30%), and Hungary and Estonia (more than 25%). The lowest rates of smoking are found in Iceland and Mexico, where fewer than one in every eight adults smoke on a daily basis. Smoking prevalence has dropped substantially in the last decade in many countries. In Iceland, Norway, New Zealand, Luxembourg and the Netherlands, the proportion of adults who report smoking every day has dropped by more than 10 percentage points since 2000. The smallest decreases (around 1 percentage point) in smoking incidence have been recorded in Mexico, Greece and the Russian Federation, while in Slovenia, the number of adults who report smoking every day has increased slightly since 2000.

More men than women report smoking on a daily basis in most OECD countries (Figure 3.10, upper half), but two exceptions to this pattern are found in Iceland and Sweden, the two countries where smoking is least prevalent overall. The differences between men and women are also relatively small in Norway, New Zealand, Australia, the United Kingdom and Ireland. The largest gender gaps in the OECD are found in Korea, Turkey, Japan, Portugal, the Slovak Republic, Israel and Mexico, where men are at least two times more likely than women to smoke. In the Russian Federation, men are over three times more likely than women to smoke on a daily basis.

Between 2000 and 2013, smoking rates generally declined for both men and women (Figure 3.10, lower half), with the exceptions of Korea and the Russian Federation – where smoking among women increased even as it declined among men – and Slovenia. In around half of OECD countries, there has been a much sharper decline (in absolute terms) in smoking among men than among women. However, in the large majority of countries, a larger proportion of men were smokers to begin with. There are also socio-economic differences in smoking behaviour: lower incomes tend to be associated with a higher prevalence and intensity of smoking (OECD, 2013d).

Figure 3.9. **Smoking prevalence**

Percentage of people aged 15 and over who report smoking every day

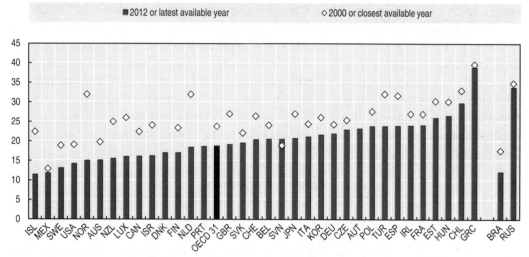

Note: The latest available year is 2013 for Denmark, Iceland, Israel, Italy, Luxembourg, New Zealand and Norway; 2011 for Spain and the United Kingdom; 2010 for Australia, and Greece; 2009 for Chile, Germany, Hungary, Poland, the Slovak Republic, and the Russian Federation; 2008 for Belgium; 2007 for Ireland; and 2006 for Austria and Portugal. The first year shown is 2001 for Australia, Belgium, Canada, Korea, Luxembourg, Poland, and Spain; 2002 for Ireland and Switzerland; 2003 for Chile, Germany, the Slovak Republic, Turkey, and Brazil; 2004 for the Czech Republic; 2007 for Slovenia; and 2008 for Greece. The OECD average is population-weighted.

Source: "Non-medical determinants of health", *OECD Health Statistics* (database), *http://dx.doi.org/10.1787/data-00546-en.*

StatLink ᵐˢ🔗 *http://dx.doi.org/10.1787/888933259422*

Figure 3.10. **Smoking prevalence among men and women**

Percentage of people aged 15 and over who report smoking every day, in 2012, and the change since 2000

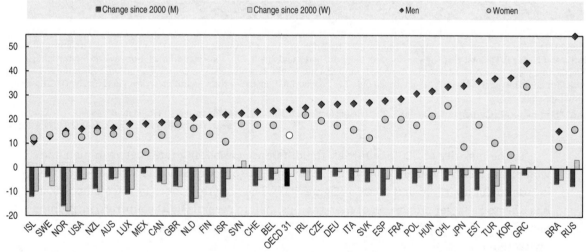

Note: The latest available year is 2013 for Denmark, Iceland, Israel, Italy, Luxembourg, New Zealand and Norway; 2011 for Spain and the United Kingdom; 2010 for Australia and Greece; 2009 for Chile, Germany, Hungary, Poland, the Slovak Republic, and the Russian Federation; 2008 for Belgium; 2007 for Ireland; and 2006 for Austria and Portugal. The year shown is 2001 for Australia, Belgium, Canada, Korea, Luxembourg, Poland, and Spain; 2002 for Ireland, and Switzerland; 2003 for Chile, Germany, the Slovak Republic, Turkey, and Brazil; 2004 for the Czech Republic; 2007 for Slovenia; and 2008 for Greece. The OECD average is population-weighted.

Source: "Non-medical determinants of health", *OECD Health Statistics* (database), *http://dx.doi.org/10.1787/data-00546-en.*

StatLink ᵐˢ🔗 *http://dx.doi.org/10.1787/888933259434*

In contrast to falling rates of smoking, the proportion of adults classified as *obese* has increased across the OECD since 2000 (Figure 3.11). The prevalence of obesity in 2012 ranged from 4% or 5% in Japan and Korea to more than 30% in Mexico and the United States – although comparability is limited by different data collection methodologies (see Box 3.3 for details). Obesity has increased since 2000 in most OECD countries, with especially large increases recorded in countries where obesity rates were already high (e.g. more than 8 percentage points in Mexico and 4 points in the United States). Sizeable increases in obesity prevalence were also recorded in Iceland (9 points), the Czech Republic and Luxembourg (7 points), as well as in France and Estonia (5 points). The smallest increases in obesity rates were recorded in the Slovak Republic, Chile and Japan (less than 1 percentage point).

Figure 3.11. **Obesity**

Percentage of the population aged 15 and older, as reported or measured

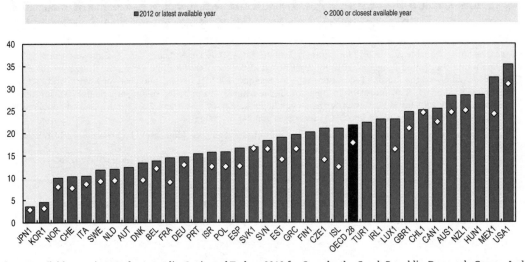

Note: The latest available year is 2011 for Australia, Spain and Turkey; 2010 for Canada, the Czech Republic, Denmark, Greece, Iceland and Israel; 2009 for Chile, Germany, Hungary and Poland; 2008 for Belgium and the Slovak Republic; 2007 for Finland and Ireland; and 2006 for Austria and Portugal. The first year shown is 2001 for Belgium, Korea and Spain; 2002 for Iceland, Israel, Norway and Switzerland; 2003 for Chile, Germany and New Zealand; 2004 for Canada, Poland and the Slovak Republic; 2006 for Greece; and 2007 for Australia and Slovenia. Results for countries marked with a "1" are based on a health examination rather than health interview surveys. The OECD average is population-weighted.

Source: "Non-medical determinants of health", *OECD Health Statistics* (database), *http://dx.doi.org/10.1787/data-00546-en.*

StatLink ᴍꜱᴸ *http://dx.doi.org/10.1787/888933259449*

In the majority of OECD countries, the differences in obesity rates between men and women are relatively small. More men than women are obese in Slovenia, while the reverse is true in Turkey, Chile and Mexico (Figure 3.12). The growth in obesity rates since 2000 has affected a larger proportion of men than women in several OECD countries, including Slovenia, Iceland, Luxembourg, the United States, Estonia, Greece, Spain, Norway and Switzerland.

Figure 3.12. **Obesity among men and women**
Percentage of the population aged 15 and older, in 2012, and the change since 2000

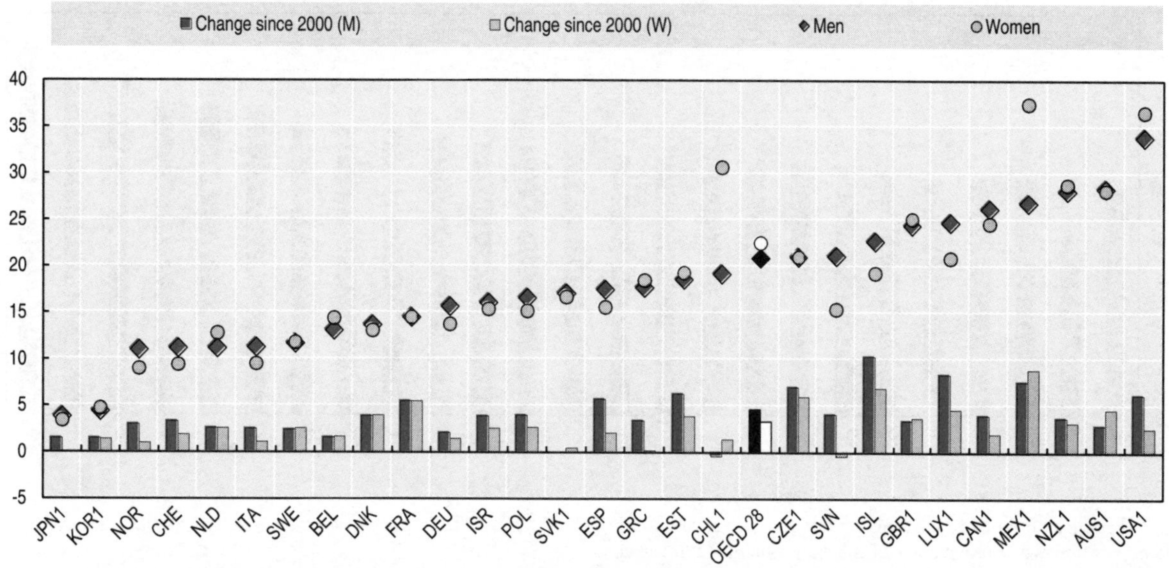

Notes: The latest available year is 2011 for Australia, Spain and Turkey; 2010 for Canada, the Czech Republic, Denmark, Greece, Iceland and Israel; 2009 for Chile, Germany, Hungary and Poland; 2008 for Belgium and the Slovak Republic; 2007 for Finland and Ireland; and 2006 for Austria and Portugal. The first year shown is 2001 for Belgium, Korea and Spain; 2002 for Iceland, Israel, Norway and Switzerland; 2003 for Chile, Germany and New Zealand; 2004 for Canada, Poland and the Slovak Republic; 2006 for Greece; and 2007 for Australia and Slovenia. Results for countries marked with a "1" are based on a health examination rather than health interview surveys. The OECD average is population-weighted.

Source: "Non-medical determinants of health", *OECD Health Statistics* (database), *http://dx.doi.org/10.1787/data-00546-en.*

StatLink ⟨⟨⟨⟨⟩ *http://dx.doi.org/10.1787/888933259453*

Social capital

The term "social capital" is used differently in different contexts. Scrivens and Smith (2013) distinguish among four aspects, or interpretations, of social capital: personal relationships; civic engagement; social network support; and trust and cooperative norms. They emphasise trust and cooperative norms as the components of social capital that are most pertinent to assessing well-being over time. This perspective, reflected in the illustrative indicators shown below (see Box 3.4), is also consistent with the recommendations by the Conference of European Statisticians (UNECE, 2014) on measuring sustainable development, which – in addition to trust – also highlight the role of institutions in social capital.

Social capital can contribute to sustaining well-being outcomes over time by enabling collective action to promote the efficient allocation of resources, the production of public goods (such as security or financial stability) and the preservation of shared assets (such as ecosystems). Through these roles, social capital contributes to the formation and maintenance of human, natural and economic capital (OECD, 2013a; Scrivens and Smith, 2013; UNECE, 2014).

The notion of **trust** captures some of the persistent features that regulate how a community functions (i.e. its capacity to achieve common goals and to overcome coordination failures) and, more generally, how people live together. Survey questions on "generalised trust" aim to capture people's perceptions of the trustworthiness of others. In 2013, the data collection for the European Union Statistics on Income and Living Conditions (EU SILC) included a general question about trust in others (Figure 3.13, see Box 3.4 for the definition). Across Europe, feelings of trust in others were highest in the Nordic countries (Denmark, Finland, Norway, Iceland and Sweden) and lowest in France, the Czech Republic, Greece, Hungary and Portugal.

Figure 3.13. **Trust in others, European countries**

Mean average response, 0-10 scale, 2013

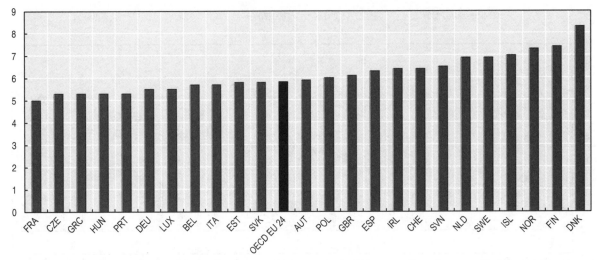

Note: Response options ranged from 0 ("You do not trust any other person") to 10 ("Most people can be trusted"). The OECD EU average is the population-weighted average of the values included in the chart.

Source: Eurostat (2015), European Union Statistics on Income and Living Conditions (EU-SILC), *http://appsso.eurostat.ec.europa.eu/nui/show. do?dataset=ilc_pw03&lang=en.*

StatLink ⬛⬛⬛ *http://dx.doi.org/10.1787/888933259460*

Box 3.4. **Illustrative indicators for measuring social capital**

The following measures are used to illustrate the concept of social capital:

● **Trust in others** is based on the survey question: "Would you say that most people can be trusted?" Respondents answer using an 11-point scale, ranging from 0 ("You do not trust any other person") to 10 ("Most people can be trusted"). These data were collected as part of the EU SILC 2013 ad hoc module on well-being (Eurostat, 2015), and are nationally representative of the population aged 16 years and above. However, coverage is limited to European countries only.

● **Trust in public institutions** is based on three different survey questions about trust in the political system, the legal system, and the police. The lead-in question is phrased: "How much do you personally trust each of the following national institutions…" Respondents answer using an 11-point scale, ranging from 0 ("No trust at all") to 10 ("Complete trust"). These data were also collected as part of the EU SILC 2013 ad hoc module on well-being (Eurostat, 2015).

● **Trust in the national government** is based on the question: "In this country, do you have confidence in each of the following, or not? … How about national government?". The data shown here reflect the percentage of the sample responding "yes" (the other response categories being "no", and "don't know"). The source for these data is the Gallup World Poll, which samples around 1 000 people per country, per year. The sample is *ex ante* designed to be nationally representative of the population aged 15 and over (including rural areas), and to correct for non-random response patterns, the sample data are weighted to the population using weights supplied by Gallup.˙

Trust in public institutions is particularly difficult to assess; ideally measures would capture the enduring aspects of trust that foster the capacity to act collectively, but there is a risk that questions may be interpreted by respondents in more narrow political terms. For example, in response to questions about confidence in national government, there is a risk that respondents refer to their confidence in the incumbent administration, rather than to their trust in government as a public institution more broadly.

Although national statistical offices are increasingly involved in capturing measures related to social capital (see Siegler, 2015, and Scrivens and Smith, 2013), with the exception of EU SILC the degree of

---

Box 3.4. Illustrative indicators for measuring social capital *(cont.)*

harmonisation across these datasets is low. As a result, several of the available indicators for social capital for non-European countries come from non-official sources and are best considered as placeholders.

The OECD is currently undertaking methodological work to develop better and more policy relevant measures of trust, with a focus on trust in institutions, and this includes the development of tools to observe how people behave in quasi-experimental settings, for large numbers of participants. This statistical work is part of the OECD Trust Strategy, with the objective of promoting open, informed and fair policy-making. This stream of OECD work will be contributing to the activities of the recently established UN Praia Group on Governance Statistics.

Further reading:

● Eurostat (2015) "Quality of life in Europe – facts and views – governance", in *Quality of Life*, an online publication: *http://ec.europa.eu/eurostat/statistics-explained/index.php/Quality_of_life_indicators*.

● The OECD Trust Strategy: *www.oecd.org/gov/trust-in-government.htm*.

● Scrivens, K. and C. Smith (2013), "Four Interpretations of Social Capital: An Agenda for Measurement", *OECD Statistics Working Papers*, No. 2013/06, OECD Publishing, Paris, *http://dx.doi.org/10.1787/5jzbcx010wmt-en*.

● Siegler, V. (2015), "Measuring National Well-Being – An Analysis of Social Capital in the UK", Office for National Statistics, *www.ons.gov.uk/ons/rel/wellbeing/measuring-national-well-being*.

*The weighting procedure used for data in the Gallup World Poll has multiple stages: first, an adjustment is made for geographic disproportionalities (e.g. due to oversampling in major cities); second, an adjustment is applied for sample selection probabilities (number of adults in the household; landline and mobile dual users); and third, weights are adjusted to reflect the distribution of the population by age, gender and educational attainment.

Trust in others has also been assessed in a broader range of countries through the Gallup World Poll in 2009/10, which featured a single yes/no question about whether most people can be trusted. These data were shown in *How's Life?* 2011 (OECD, 2011) and suggested across the OECD area as a whole, around 1 in 3 people feel that most other people can be trusted. In common with several Northern European countries, people in Canada, the United States and Japan reported above-average levels of trust in others, while people in Mexico, Korea and Chile reported levels of trust below the OECD average.

European data on trust in public institutions suggest that, in comparative terms, trust in the police tends to be highest, followed by trust in the legal system, and finally trust in the political system (Figure 3.14). Country differences mirror those for trust in others to some extent, with people in the Nordic countries, Northern Europe and Switzerland generally reporting higher levels of trust in public institutions, and people in Southern and Eastern Europe and France generally reporting lower levels. Countries' relative positions do change, however, depending on whether trust in the police, legal system or political system is considered.

The European data also provide some insights into feelings of trust among different groups within the population. Across EU countries in 2013, feelings of trust were very similar for men and women, and there were relatively few differences in trust among different age groups. However, larger differences in trust were visible in relation to income, education, employment status and household type (Eurostat, 2015). More specifically, both trust in others and trust in institutions were higher among higher income groups (compared to lower income groups); and among people with higher levels of educational attainment (compared to those with lower educational attainment). Unemployed people reported markedly lower levels of trust than employed people, people in education or training, and those in retirement. Single person households with at least one dependent child reported the lowest level of trust in others of all household types (Eurostat, 2015).

Figure 3.14. **Trust in public institutions, European countries**
Mean average response, 0-10 scale, 2013

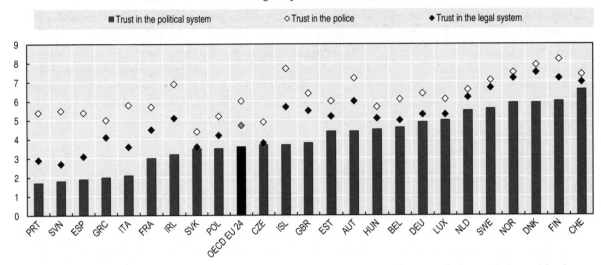

Note: Response options range from 0 ("No trust at all") to 10 ("Complete trust").The OECD EU average is the population-weighted average of the values included in the chart.

Source: Eurostat (2015), European Union Statistics on Income and Living Conditions (EU-SILC), *http://appsso.eurostat.ec.europa.eu/nui/show.do?dataset=ilc_pw03&lang=en.*

StatLink 🔗 *http://dx.doi.org/10.1787/888933259477*

Across the OECD area as a whole, data from the Gallup World Poll suggest that 2006-2014 has been a volatile period for people's trust in national governments (Figure 3.15). In 2014, around 38% of respondents in the OECD reported having trust in their national government, down from around 44% in 2009. People in countries that are characterised by higher trust in the national government also tend to report higher trust in the judicial system.

Figure 3.15. **OECD average trust in governments over time**
Percentage of the population reporting confidence in the national government, 2006-2014

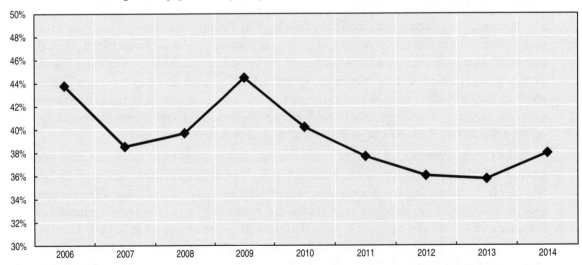

Note: The OECD average is based on 28 countries, as it excludes countries with more than two consecutive time-points missing in the series (i.e. Iceland, Luxembourg, Norway, the Slovak Republic, Slovenia and Switzerland). Among countries where a single time point is missing in the time series, the average of the two adjacent years is taken.The OECD 28 average is population-weighted.

Source: Gallup World Poll, *www.gallup.com/services/170945/world-poll.aspx.*

StatLink 🔗 *http://dx.doi.org/10.1787/888933259482*

While the notion of trust corresponds to a stock, measuring the investments in and depletion of this aspect of social capital is far from straightforward. At the individual level, investments in social capital might include pro-social activities such as volunteering (see Chapter 5), time spent on activities that strengthen social networks and community cohesion, and forms of civic engagement such as voting (see Chapter 2). Conversely, conflict between groups and opportunistic behaviours (such as cheating and corruption) can damage social capital. While information about these activities and their changes over time can be a source of more policy-relevant data, internationally comparable measures of this type are rarely available.

Economic capital

Economic capital plays a direct role in supporting people's material living conditions (e.g. housing, jobs and earnings) and a much wider role in determining the goods and services that people can afford to consume in pursuit of their well-being today and in the future. Crucially, economic capital also provides a store of value, providing a buffer against income shocks and enabling people, firms and governments to plan for the future.

Economic capital refers to both *produced capital* (tangible assets, such as buildings, machinery, transport infrastructure, inventories; knowledge assets, such as computer software, capitalised research and development (R&D) outputs, and entertainment, literary and artistic originals); and *financial capital* (which can include various financial assets such as currency and deposits, and liabilities in the form of loans and debt securities, and which may represent claims on produced capital). This section draws extensively on measures of economic capital from the System of National Accounts (see Box 3.5), using the OECD *National Accounts Database* and selected indicators featured in the *National Accounts at a Glance* publication (OECD, 2014c).

From an individual well-being perspective, the economic capital of households is particularly relevant, both for well-being "here and now" and "later". Data on household net financial wealth per capita (from National Accounts sources) and total household wealth (as measured in micro data) are discussed in Chapter 2. These indicators suggest large differences across OECD countries in both the level and the distribution of household wealth. The present chapter additionally considers the indebtedness of households, as this was a critical factor in the sub-prime crisis, and is also relevant for assessing the maintenance of well-being over time.

Figure 3.16 shows household debt as a percentage of net disposable income (see Box 3.5 for a full definition), which in 2013 ranged from below 60% in Mexico, Hungary, the Slovak Republic, Chile and Slovenia, to around 200% or more in Switzerland, Australia, Ireland, the Netherlands and Denmark. In over half of OECD countries for which data are available, household debts in 2013 were higher than in either 2007 or 2000. Exceptions to this pattern include the United States, Spain and the United Kingdom, where household debts rose from 2000, peaked in 2007 and fell thereafter; Ireland, Estonia and Denmark, where the peak occurred in 2009 (not shown); and Portugal, where the peak occurred in 2012 (also not shown). In sharp contrast to other countries, household debts were highest in Germany and Japan in 2000 and 2001 respectively, and have fallen since then.

Turning to economy-wide measures of economic capital, the main type of *produced capital* in the majority of OECD countries is fixed assets such as dwellings, non-residential buildings and infrastructure, machinery and equipment (see Box 3.5 for the definition).

In 2012, the total value of fixed assets per capita varied widely among the 19 OECD countries for which comparable data are available (Figure 3.17). The value was highest in Austria, the United States, Denmark, Germany, Australia and Sweden (at around 140 000 USD or more) and lowest in Chile, Mexico, Israel, Estonia and Greece (below 90 000 USD per capita).

Figure 3.16. **Household debt**

Percentage of net disposable income

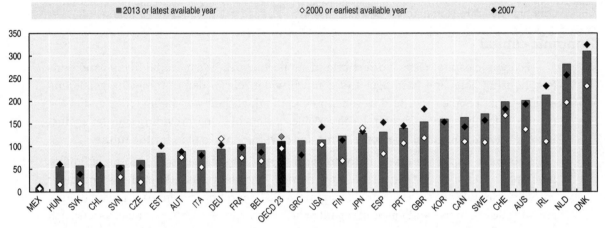

Note: The latest available year is 2014 for Portugal and Sweden; 2012 for Korea and Switzerland; and 2009 for Mexico. The first year shown is 2001 for Ireland and Slovenia; 2003 for Mexico; 2008 for Chile and Estonia, and 2010 for Korea. The OECD average is population-weighted.

Source: "National Accounts at a Glance", OECD National Accounts Statistics (database), http://dx.doi.org/10.1787/data-00369-en.

StatLink ᴬᴵˢᴸ http://dx.doi.org/10.1787/888933259495

Figure 3.17. **Net fixed assets per capita**

USD at current PPPs, 2012

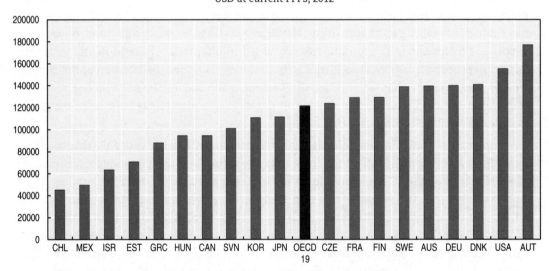

Note: The OECD average is the population-weighted average of the values in the chart.

Source: OECD calculations based on OECD National Accounts Statistics (database), http://dx.doi.org/10.1787/na-data-en.

StatLink ᴬᴵˢᴸ http://dx.doi.org/10.1787/888933259508

Box 3.5. **Illustrative indicators for measuring economic capital**

Data on household net financial wealth per capita (from National Accounts sources) and total household wealth (as measured in micro data) are discussed in Chapter 2 (under "income and wealth").The additional measures used to illustrate elements of economic capital here are all sourced from the OECD *National Accounts Database* and include:

- **Household debt**, which refers to the total outstanding debt of households as a percentage of their disposable income. Debt is calculated by summing liability categories such as loans, debt securities except financial derivatives, and other accounts payable. For most households, debt mainly consists of home mortgage loans and other liabilities such as credit lines, credit cards and other consumer credit (including automobile loans or student loans).

- **Net fixed assets** (such as dwellings, non-residential buildings, infrastructure, machinery and equipment) are shown here in US dollars per capita, at current prices for 2012, using PPPs for GDP. The data refer to net fixed assets for the total economy, as defined according to the System of National Accounts (SNA) 2008. Annual growth in **gross fixed capital formation** (i.e., investment in dwellings, buildings and other structures, transport equipment, other machinery and equipment, cultivated assets and intangible fixed assets) is also described.

- Knowledge capital is represented by the stock of **intellectual property assets**, shown here in US dollars per capita, at current prices for 2012, using PPPs for GDP. The data refer to intellectual property assets (e.g. research and development, software and databases, mineral exploration and evaluation, and entertainment, artistic and literary originals) for the total economy, as defined according to the System of National Accounts (SNA) 2008.

- **Investment in R&D** is expressed as a percentage of GDP. It consists of the value of expenditure of resident producers on creative work undertaken on a systematic basis in order to increase the stock of knowledge, including knowledge of man, culture and society, and the use of this stock of knowledge to devise new applications. Research is treated as capital formation except in cases where it is clear that the activity does not entail any economic benefit for its owner in which case it is treated as intermediate consumption.

- **Financial net worth of the total economy** refers to total financial assets minus total liabilities, expressed here in per capita terms. This includes monetary gold, currency and other forms of bank deposits, debt securities, loans, equity and investment fund shares/units, insurance pension and standardised guarantees, and other accounts receivable/payable. Tradable instruments are recorded at current market values, whereas other instruments are valued at nominal or book values. The original data (in national currencies) have been converted to US dollars using current PPPs for GDP.

- The **leverage of the banking sector** refers to the ratio between selected financial assets of the banking sector (i.e. currency and deposits, securities other than shares except financial derivatives and loans, as recorded on the asset side of the financial balance sheet) and their total equity (i.e. shares and other equity, except mutual fund shares, as reported on the liability side of the financial balance sheet). The banking sector is defined as the Central bank (S121) and other depository corporations (S122), as well as other financial intermediaries, with the exception of insurance corporations and pension funds (S123). However, there can be some country variations in this definition: in particular, "other financial intermediaries" can include financial auxiliaries (S124) in Australia, Canada, Iceland, Switzerland, the Slovak Republic and the United Kingdom. The data are non-consolidated for all OECD countries, except Australia and Israel.

- **Financial net worth of general government** is the total value of financial assets minus the total value of outstanding liabilities held by the general government sector, which consists of central, state and local governments, as well as social security funds. Consistent with standard practice, it is expressed here as a percentage of GDP. The SNA defines financial assets of the government sector as: currency

Box 3.5. **Illustrative indicators for measuring economic capital** (*cont.*)

and deposits; loans; shares and other equity; securities other than shares; insurance technical reserves; and other accounts receivable. Monetary gold and special drawing rights (SDRs) are part of government financial assets in a very few countries, such as the United Kingdom and the United States. Outstanding liabilities refer to the total liabilities as recorded in the financial balance sheet of the general government.

Despite the existence of well-established international standards on data collection, the availability of comparable data on economic capital across countries is still somewhat limited. For example, the cross-country comparability of produced capital data is not straightforward to assess, and may in some cases be affected by differences in the coverage of fixed assets, and for those countries that use the PIM model, by the length of time series available for gross fixed capital formation by asset category.

The international comparability of household debt is generally good, but debt ratios can be affected by different institutional arrangements, such as the tax deductibility of interest payments. When calculating the leverage of the banking sector, it would be preferable to use own funds (total net worth plus shares and other equity) as the denominator rather than equity alone, to avoid the undue influence of stock market fluctuations. Unfortunately, however, data on the non-financial assets of the banking sector are not available for many OECD countries, and thus the total net worth cannot be calculated.

The indicators shown here represent a first step in understanding the stock of economic capital – and do not provide a comprehensive basis for understanding financial or economic stability. There are important data gaps for measures of non-financial assets, in particular non-produced assets such as land and natural resources, both at the household and the government level; and assets such as cultural goods and historic monuments are also not well accounted for. Changes in financial net worth from one year to another can occur not only due to financial transactions over the period but also to price changes in financial assets and liabilities. Thus, growth in financial capital can give a misleading impression of future security if rapid gains over time are caused by unsustainable bubbles in asset prices. A fuller assessment of economic sustainability and stability therefore requires a much wider set of indicators – taking into account a variety of flow measures and risk factors.

Further reading:

● OECD (2014c), *National Accounts at a Glance 2014*, OECD Publishing, Paris, *http://dx.doi.org/10.1787/na_glance-2014-en*.

● OECD (2009), *Measuring Capital – OECD Manual: Second Edition*, OECD Publishing, Paris, *http://dx.doi.org/10.1787/9789264068476-en*.

● French Conseil d'Analyse Économique and German Council of Economic Experts (2010), *Monitoring Economic Performance, Quality of Life and Sustainability: Joint Report as requested by the Franco-German Ministerial Council, the German Council of Economic Experts Occasional Reports series, www.sachverstaendigenrat-wirtschaft. de/expertisen.html*.

OECD (2014c) details changes in the net stock of fixed assets between 2000 and 2010 for 15 OECD countries with comparable data. Expressed in volume terms, growth since 2005 has been strongest in Estonia (40%), Australia (22%), Korea (21%) and Norway (16%) and weakest in Germany (5%), Denmark (6%), Italy (6%), Hungary and the Netherlands (both 7%).

Gross fixed capital formation (see Box 3.5) in the OECD area as a whole has been volatile over the years since 2000 (Figure 3.18). A slump in the early 2000s was followed by strong annual growth from 2003 to 2004. Annual growth then slowed from 2005 to 2007, before turning negative in 2008 (-2.5%) and 2009 (-11.8%) in the midst of the economic and financial crisis. In 2010 annual growth was positive again, but remained weak in the years that followed, contributing to the slowness of the ongoing recovery.[4]

Figure 3.18. **Gross fixed capital formation, OECD average volume**
Annual growth rates in percentage, 2000-2013

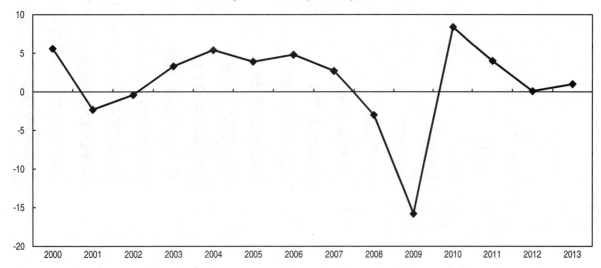

Note: OECD average values for 2000 - 2002 and 2013 are estimated. The OECD average is population-weighted.

Source: OECD National Accounts Statistics (database), *http://dx.doi.org/10.1787/na-data-en.*

StatLink ᴀᴤᴘ *http://dx.doi.org/10.1787/888933259517*

There is a case for highlighting "knowledge capital" in particular given its expected role in productivity growth and improvements in the quality of life in the future, including through a more efficient use of resources than at present (UNECE, 2014). Knowledge capital is nonetheless difficult to both define and to measure, thus, the average value of intellectual property products (IPPs, see Box 3.5 for the definition) is used here as a proxy. In 2012, the highest levels of IPPs were found in Denmark, the United States and Sweden, with an estimated value of over 10 000 USD per capita (Figure 3.19). By contrast, in Mexico, Estonia and Greece, the total value of IPPs was less than 2 000 USD per capita. In most OECD countries, knowledge capital represents a growing share of economic capital; it is also subject to faster depreciation than produced capital.

Investment in research and development (R&D) is key to building the overall stock of knowledge capital. For the 11 countries shown in Figure 3.20, R&D investment as a proportion of GDP in 2012 was highest in Finland (3.3%), and lowest in Greece (0.7%). Investment in R&D as a proportion of GDP was generally higher in 2012 than in 2000; though the level remained relatively stable in the Netherlands and Finland.

Financial capital can also act as a store of wealth to support well-being in the future. While, within a closed economy, financial capital is a zero-sum stock (i.e. for every asset there is a liability of equal value) – in open economies a country's financial assets can exceed its financial liabilities. As financial assets are claims on real assets in the end, the (net) external financial position of a country has consequences for the economic sustainability of well-being, providing a buffer in the event of shocks and a source of revenue in the future.

Figure 3.19. **Intellectual property products**
USD at current PPPs, per capita, 2012

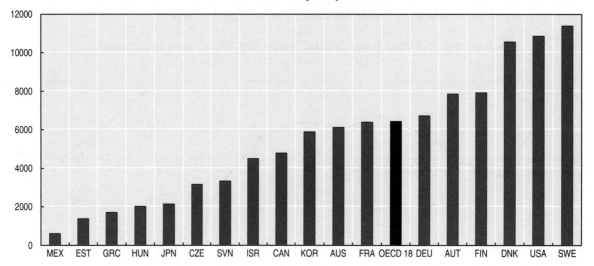

Note: The OECD average is the population-weighted average of the values included in the chart.

Source: OECD calculations based on *OECD National Accounts Statistics* (database), *http://dx.doi.org/10.1787/na-data-en.*

StatLink ⬛🖐 *http://dx.doi.org/10.1787/888933259521*

Figure 3.20. **Investment in R&D**
As a percentage of GDP

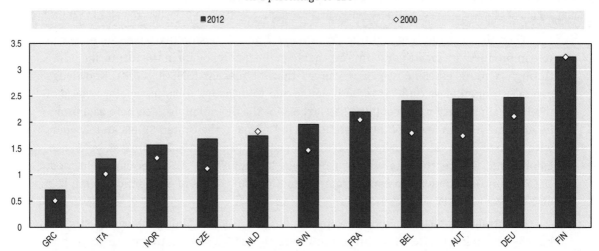

Source: OECD calculations based on *OECD National Accounts Statistics* (database), *http://dx.doi.org/10.1787/na-data-en.*

StatLink ⬛🖐 *http://dx.doi.org/10.1787/888933259538*

The economy-wide per capita financial positions of countries vary widely across the OECD (Figure 3.21). Among the 33 OECD countries for which comparable data are available, twelve had a positive net worth in 2013, meaning that the stock of their financial claims on the rest of the world exceeded their liabilities. Norway and Switzerland led the field with a financial net worth of over 80 000 USD per capita at current PPPs. Net worth was most negative in Iceland, Ireland, Luxembourg, Greece, Portugal and Spain, where liabilities exceeded assets by at least 30 000 USD per capita in 2013, and where net debts have increased at least fourfold since 2000. By contrast, Germany's financial position improved from around -250 USD per capita in 2000 to 14 885 USD in 2013. Norway's financial net worth increased thirteen-fold over the same time period.

Figure 3.21. **Financial net worth of the total economy**
USD per capita at current PPPs

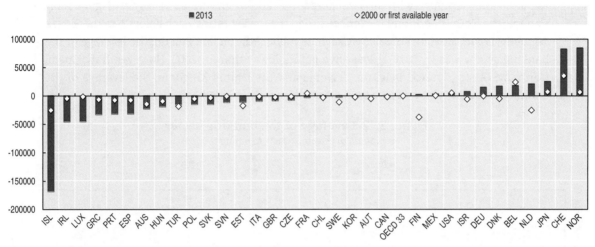

Note: The latest available year is 2012 for Korea; 2011 for Switzerland and 2009 for Mexico. The first year shown is 2001 for Ireland, Israel and Slovenia; 2002 for Korea; 2003 for Iceland; 2005 for Chile; 2008 for Estonia and Luxembourg; and 2010 for Turkey. The OECD average is the population-weighted average of the values included in the chart.

Source: OECD calculations based on *OECD National Accounts Statistics* (database), *http://dx.doi.org/10.1787/na-data-en.*

StatLink ⟨≡⟩ *http://dx.doi.org/10.1787/888933259546*

Beyond looking at the economic capital of a country as a whole, it is also important to examine the balance sheet positions of different sectors within the economy. Unfortunately, fully-fledged sectoral balance sheets, including non-financial assets, are only available in a few OECD countries, implying that most assessments are limited to their financial position (i.e. information on non-financial assets are generally not available). While this is an important omission from the perspective of applying the "capital approach" to measuring sustainability (one that has real implications for the way policies are assessed), some important insights can still be derived from the information that is currently available.

The stability of the banking and financial sector is, for example, particularly important for the economic stability of a country as a whole. In order to assess the strengths and vulnerabilities of financial systems in different countries, the International Monetary Fund (IMF) has developed a set of *Financial Soundness Indicators*, or FSIs (IMF, 2015), covering a wide dashboard of measures. The G20 "Data Gaps Initiative" is also following up a set of recommendations to improve the availability of relevant statistics in the wake of the financial crisis (IMF-FSB 2009; 2010; 2012), so that economic and financial developments can be better monitored by policy-makers. An Inter-Agency Group on Economic and Financial Statistics, established in 2008 and including the Bank of International Settlements, the European Central Bank, Eurostat, the IMF, OECD, United Nations and the World Bank, is playing a central role in the data gaps initiative.

The leverage of the banking sector refers to the ratio between the sector's financial assets (e.g. currency and deposits, recorded on the asset side of the financial balance sheet) and its equity (e.g. shares and other equity, as reported on the liability side of the financial balance sheet). Although this measure is somewhat crude – and only one indicator of many that would be needed to fully assess the sustainability of the financial sector – a high ratio (or leverage) represents a risk factor as it can increase exposure to risk and cyclical downturns.

In 2012, the leverage of the banking sector was highest in Chile, Italy, the Slovak Republic and Germany, with an asset-to-equity ratio of around 25 or higher (Figure 3.22). Canada, the Netherlands and Luxembourg had the lowest ratios, each below 3. In the Slovak Republic, Japan, Mexico, Korea, the Czech Republic, Austria and Poland, the leverage of the banking sector was in 2012 at least five points lower than in 2000. However, Italy, Spain, Germany, Greece, France, Belgium, Slovenia and the United Kingdom, the leverage of the banking sector in 2012 was at least 5 points higher than in 2000.

Figure 3.22. **Leverage of the banking sector**
Ratio of selected assets to equity

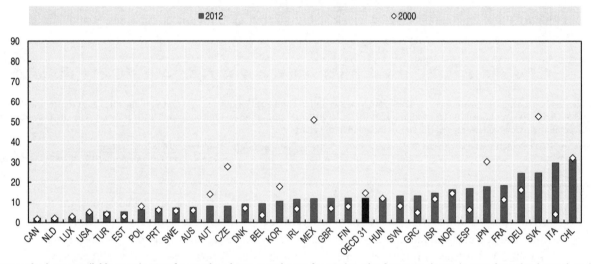

Note: The latest available year is 2011 for Israel and Japan; and 2009 for Mexico. The first year shown is 2001 for Ireland, Israel, and Slovenia; 2002 for Korea; 2003 for Denmark; 2005 for Chile; 2006 for Luxembourg; and 2010 for Turkey. The OECD average is the population-weighted average of the values included in the chart.

Source: "National Accounts at a Glance", *OECD National Accounts Statistics* (database), *http://dx.doi.org/10.1787/data-00369-en*

StatLink 📊 *http://dx.doi.org/10.1787/888933259554*

The financial position of general government is another important consideration for maintaining well-being over time, and because of implicit government guarantees, private debt can quickly become public debt. Governments may run deficits in order to support economic activity and the build-up of economic, human and social capital (e.g. through financing investment in fixed assets such as public infrastructure, or through investment in education and skills) or to prevent a deterioration of natural capital. On the other hand, a high government debt can also represent a risk factor for future well-being if, for example, sudden pressure to reduce that debt were to lead to large, rapid cuts in public expenditure.

The financial position of government (Figure 3.23; see Box 3.5 for the definition) is assessed here through a measure of financial net worth (i.e. the difference between liabilities and financial assets), rather than through measures of gross debt that are typically considered in economic policy discussion, where the focus is on liquidity rather than on sustainability *per se*. In 2013 (or the latest available year), the financial net worth of general government ranged from a positive value of 242% of GDP in Norway, 54% in Finland, and

49% in Luxembourg, to a negative position of -118% of GDP in Italy, -122% in Greece, and -123% in Japan. However, financial balance sheet data for the government sector excludes non-financial assets (infrastructure, cultural heritage, preserved landscape and works of art), and thus government financial net worth does not capture the total stock of wealth held by governments.

Between 2000 and 2013, most OECD countries experienced a reduction in net financial worth of government as a percentage of GDP, by an average of 31.3 percentage points. Exceptions to this included Norway, Sweden, Finland, Denmark and Canada, where government financial net worth as a percentage of GDP increased by 10 percentage points or more since 2000. The largest deteriorations in government net financial position between 2000 and 2013 occurred in Portugal, Ireland, Japan and the United States, where the net position worsened by over 50 percentage points.

Figure 3.23. **Financial net worth of general government**
As a percentage of GDP

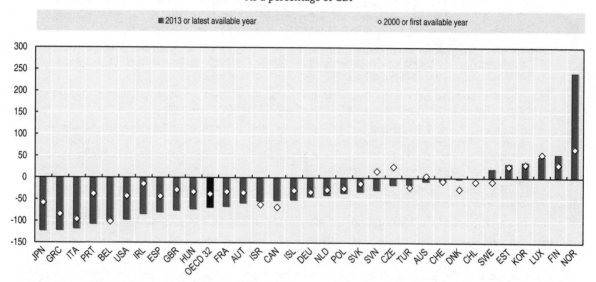

Note: The latest available year is 2014 for Australia, Austria, Belgium, Chile, Hungary, Norway, Portugal, Slovenia, Spain, Sweden, the United Kingdom and the United States; and 2012 for Korea and Switzerland. The first available year is 2001 for Israel and Slovenia; 2002 for Korea; 2003 for Iceland and Poland; 2005 for Chile; 2008 for Estonia and Luxembourg; and 2009 for Turkey. The OECD average is the population-weighted average of the values included in the chart.

Source: OECD National Accounts Statistics (database), *http://dx.doi.org/10.1787/na-data-en.*

StatLink ᴍ᠍ᔑᴘ *http://dx.doi.org/10.1787/888933259562*

Notes

1. While the focus of this chapter is the stocks of resources that can shape well-being outcomes over time, there are obvious synergies with the Sustainable Development Indicator sets (SDIs) used by many OECD governments and statistical offices. These indicator sets often feature additional measures that are not included in Table 3.1: for example, data on energy consumption from renewable sources; waste and recycling; international aid expenditure; early school leavers and young people not in employment, education or training (NEET); poverty; social cohesion; and measures of gender inequalities. Some of these topics are given more detailed treatment in other OECD work, such as the *Green Growth Indicators* initiative (e.g. OECD, 2014a); the *OECD Employment Outlook* (e.g. 2015e); work on income inequality and poverty (e.g. *In It Together*, OECD 2015f); the *OECD Gender Portal* (OECD, 2015g); and OECD work on Development Co-operation (e.g. OECD 2015h).

2. The six greenhouse gases included in the Kyoto Protocol are: carbon dioxide (CO_2), methane (CH_4), nitrous oxide (N_2O), hydrofluorocarbons (HFCs), perfluorocarbons (PFCs), and sulphur hexafluoride (SF_6).

3. In order to have a 50% probability of limiting the global mean temperature increase to 2 °C above pre-industrial levels, it is estimated that the atmospheric concentration of the six greenhouse gases included in the Kyoto Protocol would need to be stabilised below about 491 ppm CO_2 equivalent (European Environment Agency, European Environment Agency, 2015).

4. Following the Great Recession, all OECD countries have experienced sharp falls in the growth rate of "potential output", which was driven by lower stocks of capital per worker rather than by a slower pace of technological progress (OECD, 2015e). This decline in the stock of economic capital has re-opened discussion on the possibility that OECD countries may be confronting a period of "secular stagnation" in the future, where (with interest rates close to zero levels) investment is continually falling short of available savings. For further discussion, see the special chapter on investment in the *OECD Economic Outlook, Volume 2015* (OECD, 2015i), and also the analysis in OECD (2015j).

References

Boarini, R., M. Mira d'Ercole and G. Liu (2012), "Approaches to Measuring the Stock of Human Capital: A Review of Country Practices", *OECD Statistics Working Papers*, No. 2012/04, OECD Publishing, Paris, *http://dx.doi.org/10.1787/5k8zlm5bc3ns-en*.

European Environment Agency (2015), "Atmospheric greenhouse gas concentrations" (CSI 013/CLIM 052) – Assessment published Feb. 2015. *www.eea.europa.eu/data-and-maps/indicators/atmospheric-greenhouse-gas-concentrations-4/assessment* (accessed on 26 May, 2015).

Eurostat (2015), "Quality of life in Europe – facts and views – governance", in *Quality of Life*, an online publication, *http://ec.europa.eu/eurostat/statistics-explained/index.php?title=Quality_of_life_in_Europe_-_facts_and_views_-_governance&oldid=237687* (accessed on 4 July 2015).

FAO (The UN Food and Agriculture Organisation) (2010), *Global Forest Resources Assessment 2010 Main Report*, FAO Forestry Paper 163, *www.fao.org/docrep/013/i1757e/i1757e.pdf*.

French Conseil d'Analyse Économique and the German Council of Economic Experts (2010), *Monitoring Economic Performance, Quality of Life and Sustainability: Joint Report as requested by the Franco-German Ministerial Council*, the German Council of Economic Experts Occasional Reports series, *www.sachverstaendigenrat-wirtschaft.de/expertisen.html*.

IEA (2014), *Energy, Climate Change and Environment: 2014 Insights*, IEA, Paris, *http://dx.doi.org/10.1787/9789264220744-en*.

IMF (2015), "Financial Soundness Indicators", *http://fsi.imf.org/Default.aspx* (accessed on 8 July 2015).

IMF-FSB (Financial Stability Board)(2009), *The Financial Crisis and Information Gaps: Report to the G-20 Finance Ministers and Central Bank Governors*, *www.imf.org/external/np/g20/pdf/102909.pdf*.

IMF-FSB (2010), *The Financial Crisis and Information Gaps – Action Plans and Timetables*, *www.financialstabilityboard.org/2010/05/r_100510/?page_moved=1*.

IMF-FSB (2012), The Financial Crisis and Information Gaps – Progress Report on the G-20 Data Gaps Initiative: Status, Action Plans, Timetables, *www.imf.org/external/np/G20/pdf/093012.pdf*.

IUCN (2013), The IUCN Red List of Threatened Species, *www.iucnredlist.org/about* (accessed on 12 April 2015).

Liu, G. (2011), "Measuring the Stock of Human Capital for Comparative Analysis: An Application of the Lifetime Income Approach to Selected Countries", *OECD Statistics Working Paper* No. 41, 2011/06, OECD Publishing, Paris, *http://dx.doi.org/10.1787/5kg3h0jnn9r5-en*.

OECD (2015a), *Aligning Policies for a Low-carbon Economy*, OECD Publishing, Paris, *http://dx.doi.org/10.1787/9789264233294-en*.

OECD (2015b), "Carbon dioxide emissions embodied in international trade", *www.oecd.org/sti/inputoutput/co2*, (accessed on 15 July 2015).

OECD (2015c), *Water Resources Allocation: Sharing Risks and Opportunities*, OECD Studies on Water, OECD Publishing, Paris, *http://dx.doi.org/10.1787/9789264229631-en*.

OECD (2015d), *Education at a Glance Interim Report: Update of Employment and Educational Attainment Indicators*, OECD Publishing, Paris, *www.oecd.org/edu/EAG-Interim-report.pdf*.

OECD (2015e), *OECD Employment Outlook 2015*, OECD Publishing, Paris, *http://dx.doi.org/10.1787/empl_outlook-2015-en*.

OECD (2015f), *In It Together: Why Less Inequality Benefits All*, OECD Publishing, Paris, *http://dx.doi. org/10.1787/9789264235120-en*.

OECD (2015g), *OECD Gender Portal*, *www.oecd.org/gender/data/* (accessed on 12 May 2015).

OECD (2015h), *OECD International Development Statistics (database)*, *http://dx.doi.org/10.1787/dev-data-en* (accessed on 10 July 2015).

OECD (2015i), "Lifting Investment for Higher Sustainable Growth", in OECD, *OECD Economic Outlook*, Volume 2015 Issue 1, OECD Publishing, Paris, *http://dx.doi.org/10.1787/eco_outlook-v2015-1-46-en*.

OECD (2015j), *OECD Business and Finance Outlook 2015*, OECD Publishing, Paris, *http://dx.doi. org/10.1787/9789264234291-en*.

OECD (2014a), *Green Growth Indicators 2014*, OECD Green Growth Studies, OECD Publishing, Paris, *http:// dx.doi.org/10.1787/9789264202030-en*.

OECD (2014b), *Education at a Glance 2014: OECD Indicators*, OECD Publishing, Paris, *http://dx.doi. org/10.1787/eag-2014-en*.

OECD (2014c), *National Accounts at a Glance 2014*, OECD Publishing, Paris, *http://dx.doi.org/10.1787/na_glance-2014-en*.

OECD (2013a), *How's Life? 2013: Measuring Well-being*, OECD Publishing, Paris, *http://dx.doi.org/10.1787/9789264201392-en*.

OECD (2013b), *Environment at a Glance 2013: OECD Indicators*, OECD Publishing, Paris, *http://dx.doi. org/10.1787/9789264185715-en*.

OECD (2013c), *Water Security for Better Lives*, OECD Studies on Water, OECD Publishing, Paris, *http:// dx.doi.org/10.1787/9789264202405-en*.

OECD (2013d), *Health at a Glance 2013: OECD Indicators*, OECD Publishing, Paris, *http://dx.doi.org/10.1787/ health_glance-2013-en*.

OECD (2012), *OECD Environmental Outlook to 2050: The Consequences of Inaction*, OECD Publishing, Paris, *http://dx.doi.org/10.1787/9789264122246-en*.

OECD (2011), *How's Life? Measuring Well-Being*, OECD Publishing, Paris, *http://dx.doi. org/10.1787/9789264121164-en*.

OECD (2009), *Measuring Capital – OECD Manual: Second Edition*, OECD Publishing, Paris, *http://dx.doi. org/10.1787/9789264068476-en*.

Oeppen, J. and J.W. Vaupel (2002), "Broken Limits of Life Expectancy", *Science*, Vol. 296, No. 5570.

Scrivens, K. and C. Smith (2013), "Four Interpretations of Social Capital: An Agenda for Measurement", *OECD Statistics Working Papers*, No. 2013/06, OECD Publishing, Paris, *http://dx.doi. org/10.1787/5jzbcx010wmt-en*.

Siegler, V. (2015), "Measuring National Well-Being – An Analysis of Social Capital in the UK", Office for National Statistics, *www.ons.gov.uk/ons/rel/wellbeing/measuring-national-well-being*.

Statistics New Zealand (2011). Key findings on New Zealand's progress using a sustainable development approach: 2010, Statistics New Zealand, Wellington, *www.stats.govt.nz/browse_for_ stats/snapshots-of-nz/Measuring-NZ-progress-sustainable-dev-%20approach/key-findings-2010.aspx* (accessed on 29 May 2015).

Swiss Federal Statistical Office (2013): *Sustainable Development – A Brief Guide 2013: 17 key indicators to measure progress*, *www.bfs.admin.ch/bfs/portal/en/index/themen/21/01/new.html?gnpID =2013-267* (accessed on 10 July 2015).

United Nations (2009a) *Measuring Sustainable Development*, United Nations Economic Commission for Europe, prepared in cooperation with the OECD and the Statistical Office for European Communities (Eurostat), New York and Geneva, *https://sustainabledevelopment.un.org/index. php?page=view&type=400&nr=801&menu=35*.

United Nations Economic Commission for Europe (UNECE) (2014), *Conference of European Statisticians Recommendations on Measuring Sustainable Development*, United Nations, New York and Geneva, *www.unece.org/fileadmin/DAM/stats/publications/2013/CES_SD_web.pdf*.

UNU-IHDP and UNEP (2014) *Inclusive Wealth Report 2014. Measuring progress towards sustainability.* Cambridge: Cambridge University Press, *http://inclusivewealthindex.org*.

UNU-IHDP and UNEP (2012) *Inclusive Wealth Report 2012. Measuring progress towards sustainability.* Cambridge: Cambridge University Press, *http://inclusivewealthindex.org.*

Wilmoth, J.R. (2011), "Increase in Human Longevity: Past, Present and Future", *The Japanese Journal of Population,* Vol. 9, No. 1.

World Meteorological Organisation (WMO) (2014), *World Meteorological Organisation Greenhouse Gas Bulletin,* No. 10, 6 November 2014, *www.wmo.int/pages/prog/arep/gaw/ghg/GHGbulletin.html* (accessed on 10 July 2015).

Database references:

Eurostat (2015), *European Union Statistics on Income and Living Conditions (EU-SILC), http://appsso.eurostat.ec.europa.eu/nui/show.do?dataset=ilc_pw03&lang=en* (accessed on 03 July 2015).

Gallup World Poll, *www.gallup.com/services/170945/world-poll.aspx* (accessed on 03 July, 2015).

OECD Environment Statistics (database), *http://dx.doi.org/10.1787/env-data-en* (accessed on 4 July 2015).

OECD Health Statistics (database), *http://dx.doi.org/10.1787/data-00546-en* (accessed on 10 July 2015).

OECD National Accounts Statistics (database), *http://dx.doi.org/10.1787/data-00652-en* (accessed on 10 July 2015).

Chapter 4

How's life for children?

Childhood is a unique period of human development, and a critical phase for preparing future societies to be prosperous and sustainable. This chapter discusses the main measurement issues in child well-being, and then presents evidence of how children fare in 10 aspects of their lives. The analysis shows that a significant number of children live in poverty and in workless households in many OECD countries, and that risk of poverty has increased amid the Great Recession. While risks to health in early infancy are low in most OECD countries, they are substantially higher among adolescents. Most children grow up in a friendly social environment and many of them are socially engaged. However, a non-negligible share of children are at risk of being victimised. Children's experiences are also extremely diverse across ages, between genders, and according to the socio-economic background of their families. As children grow older, their relationships with schoolmates and parents become more difficult, and their life satisfaction and self-reported health fall. Children from poorer families experience lower well-being than children from richer families in almost all dimensions considered in this chapter.

The statistical data for Israel are supplied by and under the responsibility of the relevant Israeli authorities. The use of such data by the OECD is without prejudice to the status of the Golan Heights, East Jerusalem and Israeli settlements in the West Bank under the terms of international law.

Introduction: Why child well-being matters

Children and young people make up a large part of the population in all OECD countries: more than 1 in 4 people in the OECD are under the age of 20, with around 6% under the age of 5, 12% under the age of 10, and 13% between the age of 11 and 19 (OECD, 2015a). While inequalities in well-being outcomes across age groups have been extensively discussed in previous editions of *How's Life?*, the report has, so far, not included any child-specific well-being measures, or any comparison between households with and without children, or between children with different characteristics.

A rich literature has highlighted the link between well-being in childhood and in adulthood, especially as far as educational outcomes are concerned.[1] Understanding childhood conditions can, therefore, inform about well-being in later life and help in identifying opportunities or needs for early-stage policy intervention. Furthermore, the well-being of children, as *dependent members* of society, will in part depend on the well-being of their families and of society as whole. This link has been evident during the Great Recession, as highlighted by higher rates of child poverty (UNICEF, 2014), youth inactivity (Scarpetta, Sonnet and Manfredi, 2010; Carcillo et al., 2015) and homelessness (OECD, 2015c).

Child outcomes, as measured by traditional indicators of income poverty, infant health, education and youth activity have evolved in different directions over recent years (OECD, 2009, 2011 and 2015d). This has led to questions on how policy makers can do better to improve life outcomes for all children, and thereby contribute to improving general well-being in the future. The lack of consistent progress across key areas such as child poverty and youth activity has led many OECD countries and international agencies to launch initiatives in recent years to better measure child well-being (Box 4.1).

The OECD started working on child well-being in 2009 and developed a measurement framework that was used to provide an extensive analysis of child well-being in the report *Doing Better for Children* (OECD, 2009). Some of the indicators included in that report have been used since then in the *OECD Family Database,* which is routinely updated to monitor progress in selected outcomes of families with children. More recently, an OECD in-depth review of available survey data on children highlighted the main measurement gaps in this field (Richardson and Ali, 2014). This chapter builds on these various efforts to assess child well-being in a way that is consistent with the *How's Life?* approach.

The chapter is organised as follows. First, measurement issues in child well-being are discussed, including how the measurement of child well-being fits into the *How's Life?* framework. Then, the indicators used in this chapter are presented, along with the criteria that have guided their selection. The following section reviews the evidence on child well-being across OECD countries, looking at both cross-country differences in average child well-being, and at inequalities across children with different characteristics. The final section then concludes by discussing the statistical agenda ahead.

Box 4.1. **International and national initiatives on measuring child well-being**

The past decade has witnessed a growing number of initiatives on measuring child well-being. These have been undertaken by international agencies – e.g. UNICEF (2007, 2009 and 2013), the OECD (2009 and 2011), the European Commission (2008) – academics, NGOs and research institutions (Bradshaw, Hoelscher and Richardson, 2007; Richardson, Hoelscher and Bradshaw, 2008; Save the Children, 2008 and 2011; and TARKI, 2010). Measuring child well-being has also been a topical subject in many OECD countries. For instance:

● In Australia, the *Child Health, Development and Well-being* studies undertaken by the Australian Institute of Health and Welfare (*www.aihw.gov.au/child-health-development-and-wellbeing/*) measure key well-being outcomes for children below the age of 14 (through 56 indicators) and below the age of 12 (through 19 indicators). These outcomes are clustered into 7 dimensions: health, healthy development, learning and development, risk factors, families and communities, safety and security, and systems performance.

● In the United Kingdom, the Office for National Statistics has been focusing on children under age 15 as part of the UK's Measuring National Well-being Programme (ONS 2012, 2014). Building on the well-being framework designed for the general population, the ONS developed a provisional set of 31 headline measures of children's well-being (covering both objective and subjective aspects) across 7 domains (personal well-being, relationships, health, what we do, where we live, personal finance, education and skills). A baseline measurement of 22 of these 31 indicators was undertaken in 2014, with a view to updating the set in 2015 following a public consultation (ONS, 2014).

Many other countries have undertaken official studies in the past to assess or monitor the state of children's well-being nationally. The review by Ben-Arieh et al. (2001) highlighted regularly produced child well-being reports dating back to the mid-1990s in Belgium (Flemish and Walloon communities), Canada, Finland, Germany, Italy and Japan (on maternal and child health statistics), with a frequentcy ranging from yearly to every 5 years. The authors also highlighted a number of one-off national reports on child well-being conducted in Denmark and Portugal (on child labour, children in institutions and child abuse). In some cases, initiatives monitoring child well-being are undertaken by non-government agencies but with government financial support (e.g. Child Trends in the United States, undertaken with the support of the Department of Health and Human Services) or have been regularly reported to government upon completion (e.g. The State of the Child in Israel).

Measuring child well-being

How to define child well-being?

Child well-being can be defined and operationalised in multiple ways. The approach used in this chapter, and in previous OECD analysis on this issue (OECD, 2009), defines child well-being in terms of a number of life dimensions that matter to children, now and in the future. This approach emphasises the importance of looking at children's lives in a multidimensional way, in the same spirit *How's Life?* adopts for the overall population.

Looking at child well-being as a multidimensional construct is common to most recent research on the issue (see e.g. Bradshaw et al., 2007 and 2009). Pollard and Lee (2003), for instance, define child well-being as "a multidimensional construct incorporating mental/psychological, physical and social dimensions", while Ben-Arieh and Frones (2007) refer to the "economic conditions, peer relations, political rights and opportunities for development" available to children. The emphasis on multidimensionality was partly a response to the more limited approach to monitoring child life outcomes that prevailed until around the mid-2000s, where international indicator sets focussed mostly on income poverty measures for households with children. Growing dissatisfaction with this approach, the increased availability of child-related data from surveys covering many aspects of their lives, and the increased demand for evidence-based policies for children all contributed to the development of a multidimensional approach. In practice, all multidimensional approaches start from choosing the range of relevant domains that are important to children's lives and then selecting indicators that best measure these domains.[2]

As with the broader *How's Life?* methodology, this chapter also adopts a multidimensional approach. More specifically, it assumes that the relevant dimensions of child well-being should relate to aspects of children's lives that are *intrinsically valuable to children today* and that *might impact on their future*. This distinction builds on the two main perspectives on child development (i.e. the "developmental" and the "child rights" perspective) that are discussed in the relevant literature (Box 4.2).

Box 4.2. **Defining child well-being: insights from the academic literature**

The literature on child well-being has emphasised two major perspectives:

● The *developmental perspective* stresses that good child well-being today implies good adult well-being tomorrow. This approach therefore underscores the importance of building human capital and social skills for the future (Brofenbrenner, 1979).

● The *child-rights perspective* focuses on children as human beings who experience well-being in the "here-and-now". One important feature of this perspective is that it relies on the direct input of children in the process of deciding what aspects are important to them and how they might be measured (Casas, 1997; Ben-Arieh et al., 2001).

These two perspectives can sometimes be complementary: for instance, good educational outcomes for children today are typically an important precondition to good labour market outcomes tomorrow. However, good educational outcomes today may also imply stress and school pressure on children that might be detrimental to their well-being "here-and-now". Whenever there are trade-offs between current and future well-being, the child-rights perspective will provide a different picture of child well-being than the developmental perspective.

From a conceptual viewpoint, however, both these perspectives are well in line with the conceptual framework used in the *How's Life?* report. This framework makes two important distinctions: first, between what matters intrinsically (as the child-rights perspective assumes) and what matters instrumentally (as the developmental perspective posits); and second, between well-being outcomes "here and now" and well-being outcomes "later". In practice, this chapter discusses evidence of child well-being outcomes that are both important today *and* that will affect their future tomorrow.

An additional distinction in the child well-being literature is made between approaches that focus on poor child well-being outcomes ("deficit" approaches) and approaches that think of child well-being as a positive concept ("strengths-based" approaches). The analysis of child well-being made in this chapter reconciles these two perspectives because it looks at both average living conditions and at inequalities in child well-being and the well-being of the most deprived children.

Dimensions of child well-being and selection of indicators

In practice, most of the international and national initiatives in this field define child well-being in terms of a similar set of dimensions (Annex 4.A1, Table 4.A.1) covering items that children own or have access to, their experiences and conditions of daily life, as well as their subjective feelings about life as a whole.

The measurement framework used in this chapter builds on the methodology outlined in the first OECD report on child well-being, *Doing Better for Children* (OECD, 2009). This report operationalised the concept of child well-being in terms of six main dimensions covering both material conditions and quality of life (i.e. material well-being, housing and environment, health and safety, risk behaviours, quality of school life, and educational well-being). These dimensions were identified through a review of the cross-country research on child well-being, which has roots in the international standards agreed in the United Nations Convention on the Rights of the Child (UNCRC, United Nations, 1990).[3] These six dimensions which apply to the specificities of children align quite closely to those used in *How's Life?* for the population as a whole.

With this in mind, the chapter considers 10 of the 11 dimensions in *How's Life?* (see Chapter 1 and Table 4.1, left-hand column) to measure child well-being. The dimension "work-life balance" is excluded as it is an issue that concerns adults only. In addition, the scope of the "social connections" dimension is extended to include both relationships with the family (which are central to child development) as well as interactions within schools (which is where children spend a significant part of the day, and which shapes much of their identity as well as their future well-being outcomes in a range of fields). This dimension is henceforth labelled "social and family environment". Finally, it also worth noting that, as in *Doing Better for Children*, some of the dimensions do not refer to child outcomes directly, but rather to the outcomes of the families in which children live. This is the case, for instance, for all aspects of material conditions (e.g. household income) as well as for environmental quality, where the focus is the household in which children are dependent members.

The 10 dimensions of child well-being are thus organised into two groups: on the one hand, the well-being conditions of families where children live, which mainly capture material aspects as well as the conditions of the home environment in which children grow up; on the other, the well-being conditions specific to children that focus on the individual level, mostly child-centred well-being factors (i.e. health, education, civic engagement, social and family environment, personal security and subjective well-being).

The criteria used to select the indicators of child well-being listed in Table 4.1 are the same as those that have been used to select indicators for *How's Life?* (i.e. indicators should have face validity; focus on summary outcomes; be amenable to change and sensitive to policy interventions; be commonly used and accepted in the relevant literature; ensure comparability across countries and maximum country coverage; and be collected through a recurrent instrument). Two additional criteria, based on the *Doing Better for Children* methodology (OECD, 2009),[4] have guided the selection of the indicators used in this chapter, namely:

● The indicators should ideally cover *all children* from birth to age 17 inclusive at a minimum.[5]

● For the well-being conditions specific to children, whenever possible, the *child*, rather than the family, should be the unit of analysis: this child-centred approach is common to all recent studies of child well-being.

Table 4.1. **Dimensions and indicators of child well-being**

Well-being conditions of families where children live	
Income and Wealth	Disposable income of households with children*
	Child income poverty*
Jobs and earnings	Children in workless households
	Children with a long-term unemployed parent
Housing conditions	Average rooms per child
	Children in homes that lack basic facilities
Environmental quality	Children in homes with poor environmental conditions
Well-being conditions specific to children	
Health status	Infant mortality*
	Low birth weight*
	Self-reported health status
	Overweight and obesity*
	Adolescent suicide rates
	Teenage birth rates
Education and skills	PISA mean reading score**
	PISA creative problem solving score**
	Youth neither in employment nor in education or training*
	Educational deprivation*
Civic engagement	Intention to vote
	Civic participation
Social and family environment	Teenagers who find it easy to talk to their parents
	Students reporting having kind and helpful classmates
	Students feeling a lot of pressure from schoolwork
	Students liking school*
	PISA sense of belonging index
	Time children spend with their parents
Personal security	Child homicide rates*
	Bullying*
Subjective well-being	Life satisfaction

Notes: Indicators marked with a * were also included in *Doing Better for Children*. Indicators marked with a ** were included in *Doing Better for Children* with a slightly different definition.

These various selection criteria define the minimum standards for inclusion and justify the selection of one indicator over another where multiple choices are possible. These considerations have led to the selection of 28 indicators, which in most cases are aligned with those used in *Doing Better for Children*. These indicators are drawn from a variety of sources. In some cases, they come from administrative records (e.g. death certificates or data from hospital records), labour force statistics and household surveys covering the population as a whole, which allow identifying respondents based on their age or their household characteristics (e.g. presence of children). In other cases they come from specialised surveys that assess specific aspects of children's quality of life, such as the OECD *Programme for International Student Assessment* (PISA), the *Health Behaviour in School-aged Children* (HBSC) and the *International Civic and Citizenship Education Study* (ICCS) (see Box 4.3).

While each of these sources focuses on a different aspect of children's experiences, taken together they provide a comprehensive overview of child well-being in OECD countries. However, these surveys have an uneven country and time coverage; therefore the analysis of child well-being presented in this chapter is somewhat limited. Similarly, the available evidence is often insufficient to assess how well-being has evolved over time; for this reason, trends in child well-being described in this chapter are limited to a subset of dimensions and indicators. Where household data are used, survey weights were adjusted to compute measures for children experiencing each well-being outcome. The child survey data were also checked for possible biases due to differential non-response to different questions (Box 4.4).

Box 4.3. **International surveys on children's quality of life**

The indicators on children's quality of life presented in this chapter come from three main surveys:

- The OECD *Programme for International Student Assessment* (PISA) covers all OECD countries and 23 non-OECD countries. It is a triennial survey, first launched in 2000 and comprising 4 additional waves (2003, 2006, 2009 and 2012). PISA measures cognitive skills in the domains of reading and mathematical and scientific literacy. It also assesses students' performance on cross-curricular competencies like ICT skills, communications and problem-solving. The data are obtained through the administration of background and assessment questionnaires that include pencil-and-paper tests. Assessments last a total of two hours. The unit of analysis is students aged from 15 years and 3 months to 16 years and 2 months at the beginning of the assessment period. PISA relies on a two-stage stratified sample: the first stage samples individual schools with 15-year-old students, and the second stage samples students within schools. Tests are administered to between 5 000 and 10 000 students from at least 150 schools in each country.

- The *Health Behaviour in School-aged Children* (HBSC) study, conducted by the HBSC network in collaboration with WHO Europe, covers countries in the WHO European region, the United States and Canada. It has been carried out in 1983/84, 1985/86, 1989/90, 1993/94, 1997/98, 2001/02, 2005/06 and 2009/10. The HBSC measures health behaviours, health outcomes, individual and social resources as well as background factors of students aged 11, 13 and 15. The data are collected through the administration of a standard student questionnaire. The school-based survey collects data through a self-completion questionnaire administered in classrooms. The sample consists of approximately 1 500 pupils from each age group (i.e. a total of 4 500 from each country). Various sampling methods have been used across different waves.

- The *International Civic and Citizenship Education Study* (ICCS), conducted by the International Association for Evaluation Achievement, covers Austria, Belgium (Flemish region), Chile, the Czech Republic, Denmark, England, Estonia, Finland, Greece, Ireland, Italy, Korea, Luxembourg, Mexico, the Netherlands, New Zealand, Norway, Poland, the Slovak Republic, Slovenia, Spain, Sweden, Switzerland and 15 non-OECD countries. It was carried out once in 2008/2009. The ICCS focuses on four themes: civic society and systems, civic principles, civic participation and civic identities. The data are collected through the administration of tests and questionnaires to students, and of questionnaires to their teachers and school principals. In addition, an on-line questionnaire for national research centres collects data on the national context for civic and citizenship education. The target populations are children in their 8th year of schooling, provided that their average age is above 13.5 years. The typical sample size for each country is around 150 schools and between 3 500 and 5 000 students. Probability Proportionate by Size sampling is used to select the schools; within schools, one classroom is randomly selected to take the tests.

Source: Richardson, D. and N. Ali (2014), "An Evaluation of International Surveys of Children", *OECD Social, Employment and Migration Working Papers*, No. 146, OECD Publishing, Paris. *http://dx.doi.org/10.1787/5jxzmjrqvntf-en.*

Box 4.4. **Correcting for non-response biases in survey data**

Non-response bias in surveys, e.g. when particular children are missing from the sampling frame or when participants refuse to answer certain questions, can lead to flawed estimates of how child well-being outcomes in a country evolve over time or compare with other countries (Richardson and Ali, 2014).

For example, many overweight teenagers do not answer survey questions on bodyweight, resulting in underestimates of obesity. Logistic regression analysis on body weight questions in the 2010 wave of the HBSC shows that the probability of non-response is significantly affected by students' characteristics; in particular, in most countries, students who are younger, come from poorer households, and do not live with both parents are less likely to respond to bodyweight questions (Richardson and Ali, 2014). As these groups tend to have higher bodyweights, this differential non-response may lead to biased estimates of the prevalence of overweight as measured in this survey.

To overcome this problem, all survey-based indicators presented in this chapter have been checked for non-response biases based on socio-economic background characteristics, following the same procedure as the one proposed by Richardson and Ali, 2014 to adjust overweight and obesity indicators using gender, family composition and family affluence as grouping variables.

An alternative approach to assess the validity of estimates is to use variables that might represent "co-variates" (e.g. in the case of obesity, asking a question about how children feel about their body size).

The results show that, with both approaches, the adjusted estimates were not statistically different from the unadjusted ones in most countries, pointing to the absence of non-response biases or indicating that such biases are small (see Figure 4.1 for the results of the second approach applied to obesity data). All survey indicators shown in this chapter are therefore unadjusted.

Figure 4.1. **Overweight children**
Percentage of 11,13 and 15-years-old, 2010

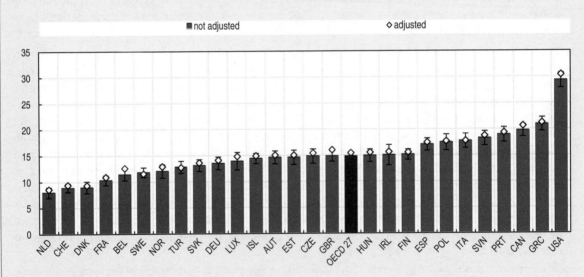

Note: The error bar indicates the 95% confidence interval of the unadjusted estimates. Adjusted indicators are estimated using the co-variate approach described above.

Source: OECD calculations on the Health and Behaviour in School-aged Children Study (HBSC): www.hbsc.org/.

StatLink 🔗 http://dx.doi.org/10.1787/888933259570

Measurement challenges

Despite the growing efforts and interest in measuring child well-being, significant challenges remain. One critical issue is the limited involvement of children in the development of child well-being measures (OECD, 2009). While theory and measurement work on child indicators has moved towards recognising children as participants with their own perspectives, it can be difficult to involve young children in designing survey instruments, and even sometimes to elicit responses from them.[6] It is also impossible to ignore the parental perspective, as parents have the primary responsibility for their children's well-being. This is why, for instance, the measurement unit underlying most indicators of child *material* well-being is the family (or the household), based on the implicit (and strong) assumption that household resources are distributed equally among adults and children, and irrespective of children's age.

Other important challenges in measuring child well-being include limited data availability and, for those data that are available, sometimes low data quality. While these issues can be more or less severe – depending on the data source used (survey and administrative data) and the country considered – they imply that all reporting initiatives face challenges in producing a *comprehensive* picture of children's lives and in covering *all children*. In particular, as stressed by Richardson and Ali (2014), research in this area has to contend with:

- A lack of purpose-built surveys focused on child well-being. This means that existing data cover only some child well-being outcomes. Existing surveys tend to focus on income and deprivation, with some also interested in health, risky behaviour and time use. Less is known, in general, about housing and children's relationships, which provide contextual information necessary for understanding the environment (emotional and physical) in which children grow up. More comparative information on key dimensions such as child protection, neglect, play, mental health, civic engagement, quality of the environment and access to safe spaces, among others, is also lacking.

- A largely adolescent-focus in most available data. Most indicators on school achievement, social connections, civic engagement and health behaviours refer to children over the age of 11, while none of the survey-based indicators shown in this chapter are available for children under age 9.

- A limited possibility to disaggregate indicators by the full range of relevant socio-economic/demographic characteristics. Further, the data cannot effectively distinguish disabled children, children not living at home, and in some cases, migrant children.

- An absence of information about the duration and persistence (or development) of experiences in each of the well-being dimensions. Indeed, most children surveys are cross-sectional, not longitudinal.

- The exclusion from all surveys of children in special-needs schools or otherwise "hard-to-reach" children (e.g. children not in school, in institutions, or in transitionally or chronically homeless families).

- Changes to the surveys over time – see Richardson and Ali (2014) for more details and examples of reliability tests on key indicators.

● Bias due to non-responses to specific items or modules in the child and household surveys due to the complexity of questions, stigma or cultural bias.

● Insufficient involvement of disadvantaged children in the measures produced. Achieving representative participation by children with different socio-economic and demographic characteristics represents a challenge that all surveys of children have yet to overcome.

The evidence presented in this chapter is based on existing data that suffer from some of the shortcomings discussed above, both in terms of the conceptual underpinnings and the coverage of the child population. These limitations have to be kept in mind when interpreting the analysis on child well-being presented here. The efforts currently underway to address some of these problems should help to improve the situation in the future (Box 4.5).

Box 4.5. **New international surveys on child well-being**

New international surveys are planned that will improve data availability and coverage in the future:

● The *Measuring Youth Well-Being* (MYWEB) project is presently scoping the feasibility of a longitudinal survey of well-being among children and young people in Europe. Implemented by a consortium of 13 research institutions across Europe, and funded by the European Commission's Seventh Framework Programme for Research, this project is designed to assess the most effective way to develop longitudinal data across a range of child well-being measures and dimensions. The output from the feasibility study includes a study of the needs and uses of longitudinal child well-being data, a discussion of how policies may be informed by such data, and a pilot survey of a preferred longitudinal design (i.e. an accelerated birth cohort design, with participants ageing out in their mid-to-late 20s). For further information see *http://fp7-myweb.eu/about*.

● *Children's World*, an International Survey of Children's Well-Being (ISCWeB) carried out by the International Society for Child Indicators (ISCI), is a subjective well-being survey covering children aged 8, 10 and 12. It reported its second round of findings in mid-2015. *Children's World* is the first international survey that collects information on children's own evaluations of their well-being in a comprehensive way. This cross-sectional survey also collects information on children's daily activities and time use. At present, *Children's World* is being undertaken in 15 countries (Algeria, Colombia, England, Estonia, Ethiopia, Germany, Israel, Nepal, Norway, Poland, Romania, South Africa, Korea, Spain and Turkey), with samples of at least 1 000 school children per age group. For further information see *www.isciweb.org/*.

● The *OECD PISA* survey included in its 2015 wave a life evaluation question that is in line with the one recommended by the *OECD Guidelines on Measuring Subjective Well-being* (OECD, 2013), which is also used by many OECD National Statistical Offices. Further, an optional module for measuring the subjective well-being of students on a more extended basis is being considered for inclusion in PISA 2018.

● Finally, as part of the OECD's ongoing work to develop data in the area of children's education and well-being, two new data collections are being planned. The first is *the International Longitudinal Study of Skills Development in Cities*, a city-level longitudinal survey of children's non-cognitive skills and life outcomes from Grade 1 (i.e. around age 6) into early adulthood (OECD, 2015b). This survey will extend knowledge on what drives educational achievement in childhood, with a focus on the role of social and emotional skills in the development of various well-being outcomes (e.g. life satisfaction, health and educational outcomes, and civic engagement). The second proposed OECD data collection is a survey to measure the quality of the learning and well-being environment for early childhood education and care and child development.

Evidence on child well-being

This section presents evidence on child well-being based on the existing information to date. First, it presents a comparative analysis of the indicators of child well-being outlined in Table 4.1 above, starting with evidence on the well-being of families where children live and then on well-being conditions specific to children. For each dimension included in these two groups, the section describes the indicators used and how they are linked to child well-being. Where data are available, outcomes based on each indicator are compared to those observed before the Great Recession, and with those referring to the population as a whole. All the evidence discussed in the first sub-section considers children aged 0-17 as a "homogeneous" group within a country, without considering characteristics such as gender, ethnic and socio-economic background. Because children are however a very heterogeneous group, the second sub-section analyses how their well-being and experience of life depends on a number of individual and family factors. In particular, the sub-section discusses differences in terms of age, gender, family socio-economic background and composition and migrant origin, but it does not look at ethnic differences. While the latter are very important in some OECD countries (e.g. Canada, New Zealand), they cannot be easily captured with the statistics used in this chapter as these are not available at a very disaggregated level.

Comparative analysis of various aspects of child well-being

Well-being of families where children live

Income and poverty

In line with *Doing Better for Children*, the income of families where children live is measured by the average disposable income of households with children under 18; in addition, the relative income poverty rate for children under 18 is also shown in order to capture the number of children living in deprived households.

A higher income enables families to better provide for their children's material needs, from items necessary for school, to suitable housing and more nutritious diets. Poverty during childhood has been linked to worse health conditions and school performance, and to lower earnings when an adult (e.g. Case, Fertig and Paxson, 2005; and Currie et al., 2012). The UNCRC commits governments to ensure that children have an adequate standard of living and defines the right of all children to access educational items that are important for their development, such as children's books. For the purpose of comparing disposable income per child and calculating relative income poverty, the same (equivalised) household income is attributed to each individual member of the household, including children.

The average disposable income per child varies greatly across OECD countries. Children in Luxembourg, Norway and Switzerland have the highest average disposable income, which is more than six times higher than the average disposable income of Mexican children (Figure 4.2). The average disposable income for the total population, including children, is higher than the average disposable income of 0-17 year-olds in almost all countries, with the exceptions of Denmark and Estonia. The largest gaps between overall income and children's income are observed in Luxembourg, the United States and Switzerland.

Figure 4.2. **Disposable income per child**

Average equivalised disposable income, per child aged 0-17, thousands of USD in PPPs

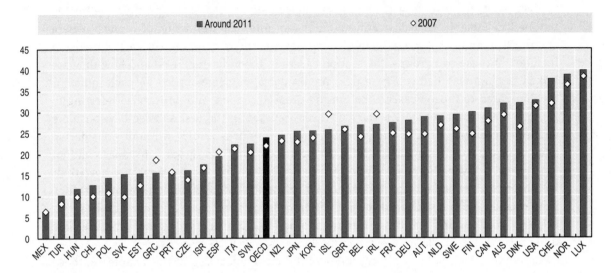

■ Around 2011   ◇ 2007

Note: The latest available year is 2012 for Australia, Hungary, Mexico and the Netherlands, 2010 for Belgium; and 2009 for Japan. PPPs are those for private consumption.

Source: OECD Income Distribution Database, http://dx.doi.org/10.1787/459aa7f1-en.

StatLink ⬛⬛ *http://dx.doi.org/10.1787/888933259586*

Comparing the average disposable income of children with its pre-crisis levels highlights both a widening of the gap between countries with the highest and the lowest income and a slight increase in the OECD average. The countries most affected by the financial crisis, i.e. Iceland, Greece, Ireland, Spain and Portugal, experienced declines in children's mean disposable income compared to 2007, while Switzerland and the Slovak Republic experienced the largest increase.

Mean income does not provide a relevant picture of the material well-being of all groups in the population if income is distributed unequally. Child poverty, measured as the proportion of children living in households with an equivalised disposable income of less than half of the median income of the total population, depicts the situation of children living in the worst-off families. While most Nordic countries have very low child poverty rates, more than a quarter of children in Mexico, Turkey and Israel live in poor households (Figure 4.3). Child income poverty is more than seven times higher in Turkey and Israel than in Denmark, the country where it is the lowest. Child poverty rates are higher than overall poverty rates in most OECD countries. In Korea, Finland, Norway and Denmark, however, children face a lower risk of poverty compared to the overall population. Although this is not an exclusive group (other countries have been increasing childcare investment) all of the Nordic countries, and more recently Korea, have invested relatively more of their family spending on childcare services compared to other OECD countries. This means that in the balance of family policies, parental support services for care, which are a form of employment support and promote dual earner families, have been prioritized against cash income subsidies. Helping families into good quality employment is commonly understood to be the most sustainable way to address long term child poverty risks, and this approach may be behind the relative success of Korea and the Nordic countries.

Relative to 2007, child poverty rates have increased in more than two-thirds of OECD countries. The increase in child poverty was largest in Hungary (where child poverty has more than doubled), followed by Turkey and Spain (about 5 percentage points higher in both countries). Child poverty also increased quite significantly in Greece (3.2 percentage points), Belgium (2.7) and Sweden (2.5). Conversely, the largest drop in child poverty was recorded in the United Kingdom (-3.6 percentage points), followed by Portugal (-1.9), Finland (-1.3) and Korea (-1.2).

Figure 4.3. **Child poverty rate**

Percentage of children aged 0-17 living in households whose disposable income is below 50% of the median

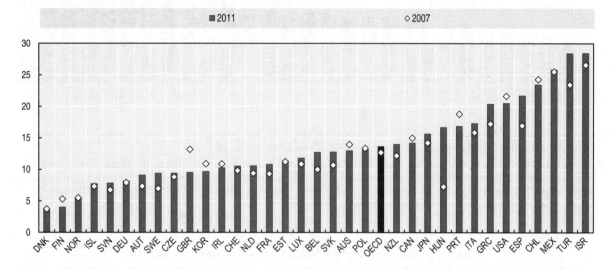

Note: The latest available year is 2012 for Australia, Hungary, Mexico and the Netherlands, 2010 for Belgium; and 2009 for Japan.

Source: OECD Income Distribution Database, http://dx.doi.org/10.1787/459aa7f1-en.

StatLink ᴍᴵˢ￫ *http://dx.doi.org/10.1787/888933259595*

Jobs and earnings

Adult employment outcomes may affect children not only through the financial situation of the family, but also through the effect that employed parents can have as role models for their children. In addition, stigmatisation due to unemployment may affect children in and outside the family. Two employment-related indicators are presented below. These are the share of children (up to age 17) living in households with no employed adult, and the share of children with at least one parent who is long-term unemployed.

Many children in OECD countries see their parents experience spells of unemployment. In 2012, almost one in five Irish children were living in a household with no employed adult household member. In Hungary, the United Kingdom and Spain, over 15% of children did not have an employed adult in the household. Luxembourg, Slovenia, Switzerland and Norway are the countries with the lowest share of children living in households where there is no employed adult, with rates of around 5% (Figure 4.4).

The percentage of children who live in a household where at least one parent has been unemployed for 12 months or more is negligible in the Netherlands, Switzerland and Australia and small in most other OECD countries. However, around 15% of children in Ireland and Portugal have at least one long-term unemployed parent (Figure 4.5).

Figure 4.4. **Children living in workless households**

Percentage of children living in households where there is no employed adult, 2012

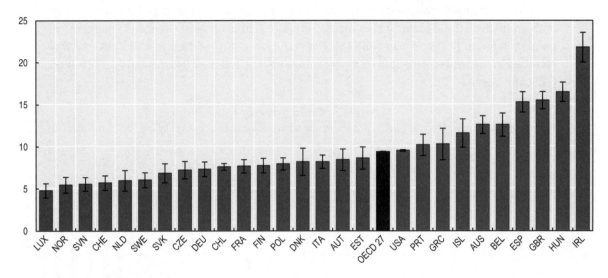

Note: Calculated as the percentage of all children 0-17 for which data on the employment status of at least one adult (18-65) in the household is available. Error bars represent the 95% confidence interval of the national estimate.

Source: EU-SILC 2012, HILDA 2012 (Australia), CASEN 2011 (Chile), ACS 2012 (United States). EU-SILC is the EU Statistics on Income and Living Conditions. HILDA is the Household, Income and Labour Dynamics in Australia longitudinal survey carried out by the University of Melbourne. CASEN is the Encuesta de Caracterización Socioeconómica Nacional, carried out by the Ministry of Social Development. ACS is the American Community Survey carried out by the US Census Bureau.

StatLink 🔗 *http://dx.doi.org/10.1787/888933259601*

Figure 4.5. **Children with a long-term unemployed parent**

Percentage of children living in a household with at least one long-term (12 months or more) unemployed parent, 2012

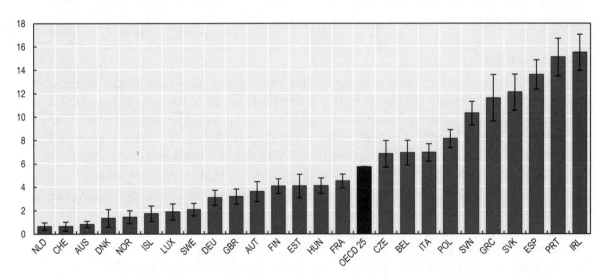

Note: Calculated as the percentage of all children 0-17 for which information on the employment status of at least one parent living in the same household is available. Error bars represent the 95% confidence interval of the national estimate.

Source: For European countries, EU-SILC 2012; for Australia, Household, Income and Labour Dynamics (HILDA) survey, 2012.

StatLink 🔗 *http://dx.doi.org/10.1787/888933259611*

Housing conditions

All children need adequate housing conditions for their physical and mental health and for their social development. This is specifically acknowledged by Article 27.3 of the UNCRC. The housing dimension of child well-being is described below through two indicators of the quality of children's housing, i.e. the average rooms per children and the share of children living in homes that lack basic facilities.

The number of rooms in a dwelling is computed as the number of rooms (or bedrooms) divided by household size of families with children.[7] This measure indicates whether families live in overcrowded conditions. On average, children in OECD countries live in households with one bedroom per person (Figure 4.6). Ireland and Belgium have the largest number of rooms per child across the OECD, while children in Mexico live on average in the most crowded conditions. In all countries except Ireland, the average number of rooms increases with the age of the youngest child. These findings should however be interpreted with caution, as the indicator is based on slightly different definitions across countries.[8]

Figure 4.6. **Average rooms per person in households with children**
Rooms per child, around 2012

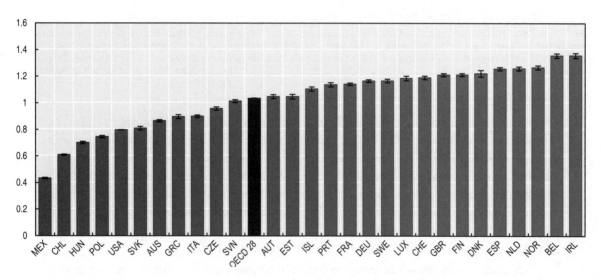

Note: The number of rooms is assessed through the question on "number of rooms available to the household" in EU-SILC, and the number of bedrooms in the other surveys. Error bars represent the 95% confidence interval of the national estimate.

Source: EU-SILC 2012, HILDA 2012 (Australia), ENIGH 2012 (Mexico), CASEN 2011 (Chile), ACS 2012 (United States). HILDA is the Household, Income and Labour Dynamics (HILDA) survey carried out by the University of Melbourne. ENIGH is the Encuesta Nacional de Ingresos y Gastos de los Hogares carried out by the Mexican National Statistical Office. CASEN is the Encuesta de Caracterización Socioeconómica Nacional, carried out by the Ministry of Social Development. ACS is the American Community Survey carried out by the US Census Bureau.

StatLink ᴍᴤᴘ *http://dx.doi.org/10.1787/888933259627*

A dwelling is considered as lacking basic facilities when it has no indoor flushing toilet for the sole use of the household, which is detrimental to families' hygiene. In most OECD countries, very few households with children live in dwellings lacking these basic facilities (Figure 4.7). In Hungary and Ireland, around 1 in 10 children live in households lacking a private flushing toilet in their dwelling.[9] A more detailed analysis would be necessary to explain these patterns, which could also reflect the specific building styles prevailing in various countries.

Figure 4.7. **Children living in households without basic facilities**
Number of children per 1 000 living in dwellings that lack a private flushing toilet, 2012

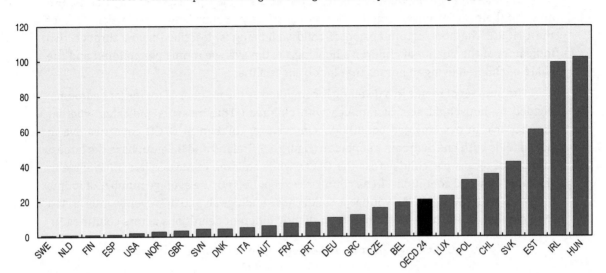

Note: Households are classified as having basic facilities if they have an indoor flushing toilet for the sole use of the household.

Source: EU-SILC 2012. HILDA 2012 (Australia), CASEN 2011 (Chile), ACS 2012 (United States). HILDA is the Household, Income and Labour Dynamics (HILDA) carried out by the University of Melbourne. CASEN is the Encuesta de Caracterización Socioeconómica Nacional, carried out by the Ministry of Social Development. ACS is the American Community Survey carried out by the US Census Bureau.

StatLink ⏵ http://dx.doi.org/10.1787/888933259637

Environmental quality

Children are particularly vulnerable to air pollution and other environmental hazards. Respiratory infections are estimated to account for 20% of mortality among children under the age of five. There is also evidence that the increasing prevalence of asthma among children has been aggravated by air pollution (WHO, 2005). However, comparative data on children's exposure to air pollution and other environmental threats is limited. For this reason, environmental quality is described by an indicator on the share of households with children who report being exposed to pollution and noise in the neighbourhood where they live, which is available only for European countries and Australia.

This indicator is defined as the percentage of 0-17 year-old children living in homes with poor environmental conditions. The environmental conditions are assessed using questions on whether the household has experienced noise, pollution and other environmental problems (see note to Figure 4.8 for the exact definition in the various surveys).

Australia had the lowest share of children living in poor environmental conditions, followed by Ireland and the Nordic countries, Poland and Hungary (Figure 4.8). At the other end of the spectrum, Greece, Germany, the Netherlands and Belgium recorded the largest share of households with children living in poor environmental conditions.

Well-being conditions specific to children

Health status

Children's health data have long been collected by health professionals and in health systems. Thanks to studies such as Health Behaviour in School-aged Children (see Box 4.3), both administrative and survey data are available for a broad range of health aspects. Two indicators – infant mortality and low birth weight – are used here to measure the health status of infants. Two other indicators – self-reported health status and prevalence of overweight and obesity – are reported for children aged 11, 13 and 15. These are complemented by two additional indicators – suicide rates among children aged 10 to 19 and teenage birth rates – that capture development in later childhood.

Figure 4.8. **Children living in poor environmental conditions**
Percentage of 0-17 year-old children living in homes with self-reported poor environmental conditions, around 2012

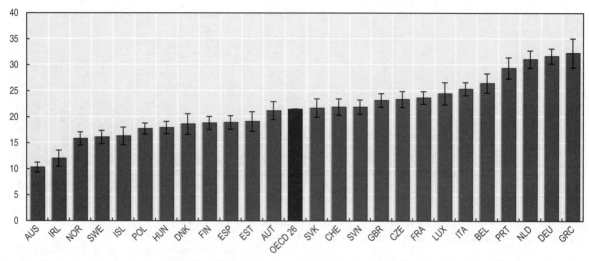

Note: For European countries, environmental conditions are assessed using the question whether the household has experienced any of the following problems: i) too much noise in your dwelling from neighbours or from outside (traffic, business, factory, etc.); or ii), pollution, grime or other environmental problems in the local area such as: smoke, dust, unpleasant smells or polluted water. In Australia, households were asked whether they experienced i) traffic noise, ii) rubbish and litter lying around, or iii) vandalism and deliberate damage to property in their neighbourhood. Error bars represent the 95% confidence interval of the national estimate.

Source: EU-SILC 2012, HILDA 2012 (Australia). HILDA is the Household, Income and Labour Dynamics (HILDA) carried out by the University of Melbourne.

StatLink ᴴᵗᵗᵖ http://dx.doi.org/10.1787/888933259646

Infant mortality, defined as the death rate of children under the age of one, captures a number of observed and unobserved factors in maternal and infant health. It also reflects the characteristics and effectiveness of different health systems (OECD, 2009). Most OECD countries have low or very low infant mortality rates, with the lowest rates observed in Iceland, Slovenia and Japan (Figure 4.9). Mexico has an infant mortality rate above 1%, much higher than in other OECD countries. Overall infant mortality fell slightly in the OECD since 2007. Over this period, Turkey's infant mortality rate decreased more than in any other country, followed by Mexico. These results should be taken with some caution, however, in particular when low levels are attained, due to different national practices in registering premature infants.[10]

Low birth weight, defined by the WHO as a weight of less than 2 500 grams at an infant's birth, is an important indicator of infant health because of its association with infant morbidity and mortality and later child outcomes (Hack, Klein and Taylor, 1995). Several Nordic countries have the lowest rates of low birth weight in the OECD (Figure 4.10). Children born in Greece and Japan are most likely to be underweight, an outcome which, in the case of Japan, contrasts with the very low level of infant mortality achieved in the country (OECD, 2011). Over the period from 2007 to 2012, the largest improvements in reducing the prevalence of low birth weight were recorded in Mexico and Turkey, while the rates in Luxembourg and Greece deteriorated. The overall OECD average remained unchanged (Figure 4.10).

Figure 4.9. **Infant mortality**

Number of deaths of children under age one per 1 000 live births

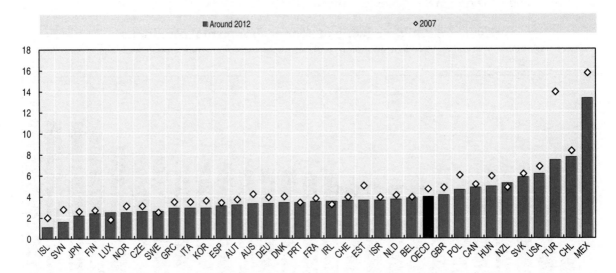

Note: For the United States, New Zealand, Canada and Chile the latest available year refers to 2011.

Source: OECD Health Statistics Database, http://dx.doi.org/10.1787/health-data-en.

StatLink 🔢📊 *http://dx.doi.org/10.1787/888933259655*

Figure 4.10. **Children born underweight**

Number of live births weighing less than 2 500 grams as a percentage of total number of live births

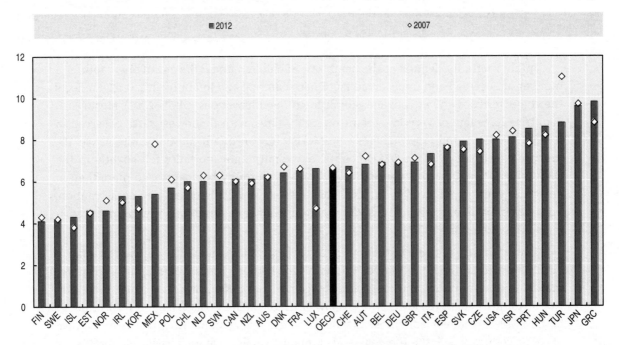

Note: The latest available year refers to 2010 for Belgium, and to 2011 for Australia, Canada, Chile and France.

Source: OECD Health Statistics Database, http://dx.doi.org/10.1787/health-data-en.

StatLink 🔢📊 *http://dx.doi.org/10.1787/888933259667*

Self-reported health is a summary measure that represents how respondents feel about their overall health status. Figure 4.11 shows the percentage of 11, 13 and 15 year-old school children who report their health as fair or poor. The countries with the highest share of adolescents who report their health as fair or poor are the United States, the United Kingdom, Hungary and Belgium (Figure 4.11). Greece and Spain are the top performers in terms of self-reported health.

Overweight and obesity among children are associated with several health-related problems and can have health consequences that last into adulthood. Therefore overweight and obesity among young people are not only a public health issue but also an indicator of both child well-being and future life chances. Indeed, obesity has serious psychological and social impacts through harmed self-esteem as well as increased depression and stigmatisation (Griffiths, Parsons and Hill, 2010). The consequences of being overweight or obese at an early age can be tracked into adulthood (Singh et al., 2008) and may include an increased risk of cardiovascular diseases and diabetes. Children in the United States are most likely to report being overweight or obese (Figure 4.12), both overall and when looking at 11, 13 and 15 year-olds separately. The Netherlands, Switzerland and Denmark are among the countries with the lowest share of overweight children.

Mental health is an important aspect of well-being. However, objectively-measured data on children's mental health are not available. Suicide rates provide an indication of the prevalence of severe mental health problems. Child suicide rates, measured as the annual number of deaths caused by intentional self-harm (i.e. deaths classified as ICD10 by WHO) per 100 000 children aged 10 to 19 are very low across the OECD. The lowest rates are observed in Greece and Spain. New Zealand has the highest incidence of child suicides, followed by Finland, Chile and Ireland (Figure 4.13).

Figure 4.11. **Teenagers reporting poor health**
Percentage of 11, 13 and 15 year-old children with self-perceived fair or poor health, 2010

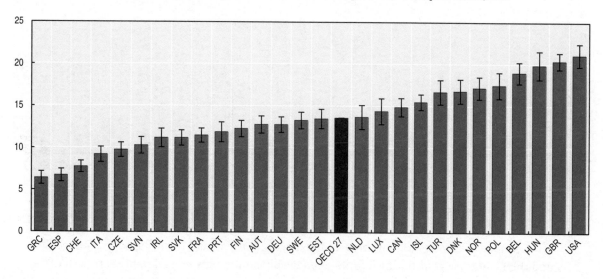

Note: Error bars represent the 95% confidence interval of the national estimate.

Source: Health and Behaviour in School-aged Children Study (HBSC) 2010, *www.hbsc.org/.*

StatLink ⟶ *http://dx.doi.org/10.1787/888933259675*

Figure 4.12. **Children who are either overweight or obese**

Percentage, 2010

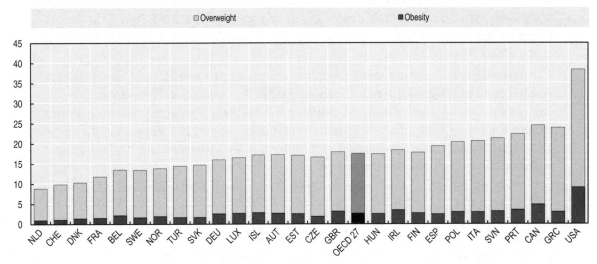

Note: Percentage of overweight and obese girls and boys aged 11, 13 or 15. Bars are ordered by obesity rates.

Source: Health and Behaviour in School-aged Children Study (HBSC) 2010, *www.hbsc.org/.*

StatLink ᴍ⁵ᴸ *http://dx.doi.org/10.1787/888933259687*

Figure 4.13. **Child suicide rates**

Death rates by intentional self-harm per 100 000 children, 3-year average around 2011

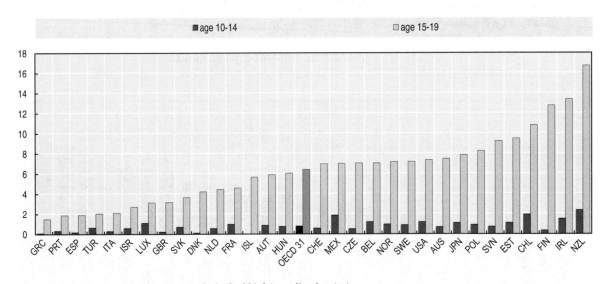

Source: WHO Mortality Database, *http://www.who.int/healthinfo/mortality_data/en/.*

StatLink ᴍ⁵ᴸ *http://dx.doi.org/10.1787/888933259691*

Teenage birth rates are an important aspect of both sexual health among teenagers and the health risk confronting infants. Teenage birth rates vary considerably across OECD countries, ranging between almost no cases in Slovenia, Switzerland and Korea to over 55 births per 1 000 teenage girls in Chile and Mexico (Figure 4.14). The United States, the United Kingdom and New Zealand also record some of the highest rates of teenage fertility. Compared to 2007, most OECD countries experienced declines in teenage birth rates, with the largest improvements recorded in Ireland and Israel. Other types of risky behaviours among children are described in Box 4.6.

Figure 4.14. **Teenage birth rates**

Teenage births per 1 000 women aged 15-19

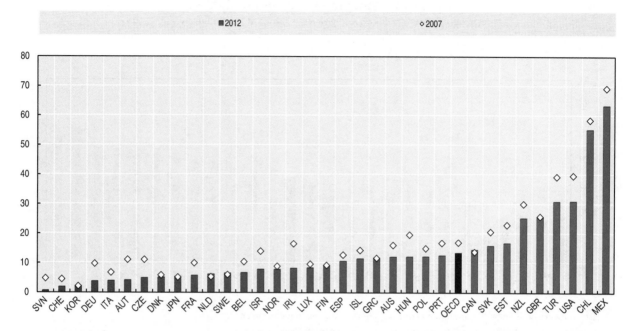

Source: World Development Indicators, World Bank, *http://data.worldbank.org/data-catalog/world-development-indicators*.

StatLink ⬛ ⬚ *http://dx.doi.org/10.1787/888933259705*

Box 4.6. **Risky behaviour among children**

Unlike other health outcome indicators, smoking, drinking and physical activity are not well-being outcomes *per se* but rather indicators of health behaviours and future health risks. Adolescent smoking and drinking and a lack of physical activity are risk factors because they often have adverse consequences for physical and mental health. Tobacco is the leading cause of preventable death, and tobacco consumption creates large social and health costs for all countries in the OECD (Currie et al., 2012). Adolescents establish addictions more quickly than adults, and most adult smokers had their first cigarette or were already addicted to nicotine by age 18 (ibid.). Alcohol use is another major factor in determining ill-health and preventable death worldwide (WHO, 2002). Regular drinking and drunkenness are associated with poorer psychological, social and physical health outcomes, as well as poorer educational outcomes, violence, injuries, smoking, drug use and risky sexual behaviour (Currie et al., 2012; OECD, 2015e). Finally, physical activity promotes physical and mental health (musculoskeletal and cardiovascular health and reduced anxiety and depression) in the short and long term and may improve cognition and academic performance among young people (Currie et al., 2012). At the same time, it should be acknowledged that taking some risks may not necessarily be bad, and in some respects is a normal part of growing up (OECD, 2009).

Indicators of risky behaviour include 15-year-olds who smoke regularly, 13- and 15-year-olds who report having been drunk on more than two occasions, and the percentage of 11, 13 and 15 year-olds who do moderate to vigorous physical activity daily in the past week.

Smoking and drinking. Overall smoking rates (for boys and girls) range from 7.8% in Iceland to over 27.3% in Austria (Figure 4.15). While, on average, smoking rates are higher for girls than for boys, the opposite pattern prevails in Ireland, the United Kingdom, Sweden, Germany, the Netherlands, Belgium, Spain, Italy, the Czech Republic and Austria. Lower family affluence is generally associated with a higher prevalence of child smoking in all countries, with the exceptions of Portugal, Poland, Estonia and the Slovak Republic.

Box 4.6. **Risky behaviour among children** (cont.)

Figure 4.15. **Smoking rates among children**

Percentage of 15 year-old boys and girls who smoke at least once a week, 2010

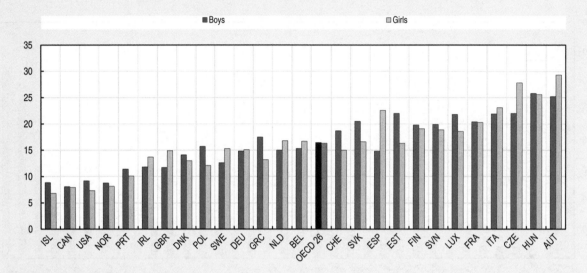

■ Boys   ▫ Girls

Note: Data are ordered by the combined percentage (boys and girls) in increasing order.

Source: Health and Behaviour in School-aged Children Study (HBSC) 2010, www.hbsc.org/.

StatLink ᵐˢᵖ http://dx.doi.org/10.1787/888933259710

The incidence of drunkenness rises strongly between ages 13 and 15 in all countries (Figure 4.16). While drinking rates are higher on average for 15-year-old girls than for 15-year-old boys, in the United Kingdom, Sweden, Norway, Denmark, Spain, Finland and Canada the opposite pattern occurs (Currie et al., 2012). The measures are limited in terms of child coverage because surveys of smoking and drinking are undertaken in schools. It is likely that those at extreme risk do not attend school regularly and are hence not surveyed.

Figure 4.16. **Children drinking alcohol to excess**

Percentage of 13 and 15 year-olds who have been drunk at least twice in their life, 2010

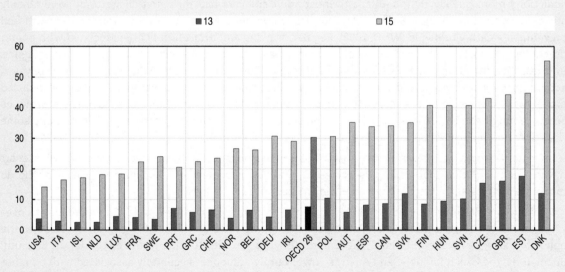

■ 13   ▫ 15

Note: Data are ordered by the combined percentage (13 and 15-year-olds) in increasing order.

Source: Health and Behaviour in School-aged Children Study (HBSC) 2010, www.hbsc.org/.

StatLink ᵐˢᵖ http://dx.doi.org/10.1787/888933259726

Box 4.6. **Risky behaviour among children** (*cont.*)

Physical activity. Based on their extensive review of the literature, Strong et al. (2005) recommended that children participate in at least 60 minutes of moderate-to-vigorous physical activity (MVPA) daily; this minimum standard is now included in the guidelines issued by some government and professional organisations. Evidence shows that most young people do not meet it (Figure 4.17). The share of children participating in at least 60 minutes of MVPA daily ranges from 7.5% in Sweden to 30.8% in Ireland. Daily physical activity is much more common for boys than for girls, and among children aged 11 than those aged 15.

Figure 4.17. **Children engaging in daily physical activity**

Percentage of 11, 13 and 15 year-olds doing moderate to vigorous physical activity daily in the past week, 2010

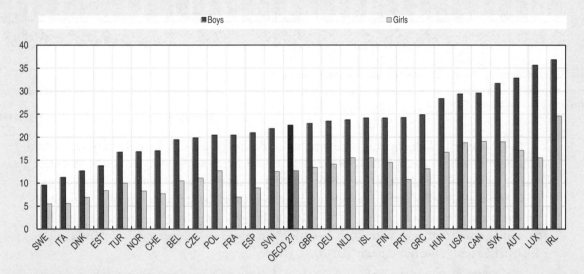

Note: Moderate-to-vigorous physical activity as defined by the Health Behaviour in School-aged Children (HBSC) report refers to exercise undertaken for at least an hour that increases both heart rate and respiration (and sometimes leaves the child out of breath). Each country estimate uses reported physical activity rates and sample numbers for 11, 13 and 15-year-old boys and girls to calculate country percentages. The data are drawn from school-based samples.

Source: Health and Behaviour in School-aged children Study (HBSC) 2010, *www.hbsc.org/*.

StatLink ⟨⟨⟨ *http://dx.doi.org/10.1787/888933259735*

Education and skills

The first indicator of education and skills for children used here is the average reading literacy score of 15 year-old students, taken from PISA 2012. To capture a broader set of cognitive and non-cognitive skills that are relevant for success in school and life, the PISA creative problem-solving score is also described below. This section also provides evidence on the percentage of 15 to 19 year-olds who are not in education, employment or training (NEET) as well as on educational deprivation, which is measured by asking 15-year-olds about their access to certain items that are important for school performance.

Japan and Korea perform best in terms of the PISA average reading scores among all OECD countries (Figure 4.18), while Chile and Mexico have the lowest average scores.[11] Chile, Estonia, Germany, Hungary, Israel, Japan, Korea, Luxembourg, Mexico, Poland, Portugal, Switzerland and Turkey all improved their reading performance across successive PISA waves (OECD, 2014a). Mexico and Chile combine the lowest average reading scores and the highest shares of students who do not meet the baseline level of proficiency in reading. Between 2000 and 2012, Israel and Poland increased the share of top-performing students in reading while simultaneously reducing the share of low performers (OECD, 2014a).

Figure 4.18. **PISA reading scores among children**
Average reading literacy scores of 15 year-olds, 2012

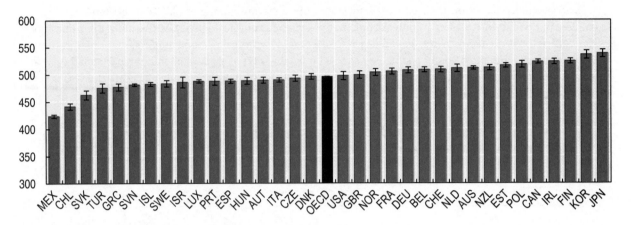

Note: Error bars represent the 95% confidence interval of the national estimate.

Source: PISA 2012, OECD (2014a), *PISA 2012 Results: What Students Know and Can Do (Volume I)*, Revised edition, February, OECD Publishing, Paris, *http://dx.doi.org/10.1787/19963785*.

StatLink ⟨≣⟩ *http://dx.doi.org/10.1787/888933259747*

Cognitive skills like reading, mathematics and science are not the only determinants of success in school and in life, which depends on a much wider range of competencies (Rychen and Salganik, 2003).[12] Problem-solving competence is defined by PISA as: "... an individual's capacity to engage in cognitive processing to understand and resolve problem situations where a method of solution is not immediately obvious. It includes the willingness to engage with such situations in order to achieve one's potential as a constructive and reflective citizen" (OECD, 2014b).[13]

The PISA 2012 problem-solving assessment focuses on general cognitive processes, rather than on the ability to solve problems in particular school subjects. Computer-based simulated scenarios are used as part of the assessment to generate so-called "interactive problems". Problem-solving performance is positively related to performance in reading, mathematics and science; however, the relationship is weaker than that observed between these subjects (OECD, 2014b).

As in the case of reading, students in Korea and Japan perform best in the complex problem-solving assessment among all the participating countries (Figure 4.19).[14] On average, 20% of students in the OECD do not achieve the minimum level of problem-solving proficiency deemed to be required to participate effectively and productively in 21st century societies.

The indicator shown in Figure 4.20 measures the share of 15 to 19 year-olds who are not in employment, education or training (NEET). This indicator captures the incidence of school dropouts, the length of school-to-work transitions and the importance of youth unemployment, all of which have severe impacts on both individual well-being and economic performance. Turkey, Mexico, Italy, Spain and Ireland have a NEET rate of more than 10% (Figure 4.20). In Turkey, the share of young people who are not in education, employment or training is almost 8 times higher than in Germany, where the share is only 2.8% among 15-19 year-olds. The Czech Republic, Poland, Luxembourg, Slovenia and Norway also have very low NEET rates.

Figure 4.19. **Students' performance in PISA computer problem-solving**

Average computer problem-solving scores of 15 year-olds, 2012

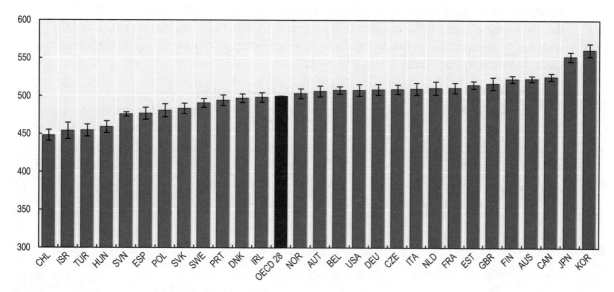

Note: Error bars represent the 95% confidence interval of the national estimate.

Source: PISA 2012, OECD (2014b), *PISA 2012 Results: Creative Problem Solving (Volume V), Students' Skills in Tackling Real-Life Problems*, OECD Publishing, Paris, *http://dx.doi.org/10.1787/19963785.*

StatLink ᴍᴸᴾ *http://dx.doi.org/10.1787/888933259759*

Between 2007 and 2013, the numbers of NEET youth have increased significantly in Ireland (by more than 5 percentage points), while they have fallen substantially in Israel (minus 19 percentage points) and Turkey (-12 points).

Figure 4.20. **Young people who are neither in employment nor in education or training**

Percentage of 15-19 year-olds

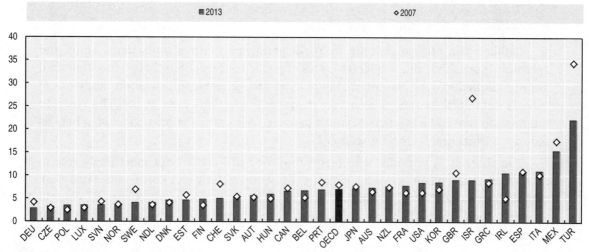

Note: The latest available data for Chile refer to 2011.

Source: *OECD Education at a Glance Database, http://dx.doi.org/10.1787/19991487.*

StatLink ᴍᴸᴾ *http://dx.doi.org/10.1787/888933259768*

Educational deprivation is defined as the share of 15-year-old students who report possessing less than four educational items, based on the 2012 wave of PISA. On this measure, most OECD countries have very low rates of 15-year-olds who are educationally deprived (below 5 per 1 000). However, in Mexico almost 30 in 1 000 children are educationally deprived according to this definition. Other low-performing countries include Turkey and Chile, followed by the United States (Figure 4.21).

Figure 4.21. **Educational deprivation**
Number of 15-year olds reporting having less than the four educational items, per 1 000 15-year-olds
in the school population, 2012

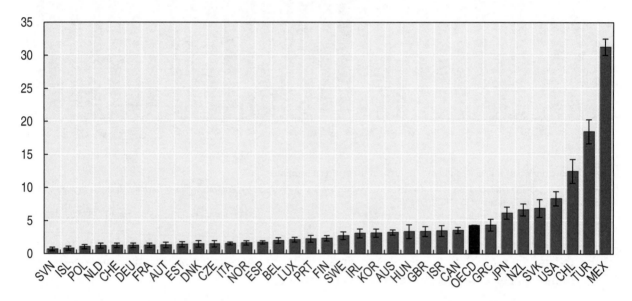

Note: The educational items include a desk to study, a quiet place to study, a computer for school work, educational software, internet, books for school and a dictionary.

Source: OECD calculations on PISA 2012, OECD, *http://dx.doi.org/10.1787/19963785.*

StatLink ᴍᴌ🔊 *http://dx.doi.org/10.1787/888933259778*

Civic engagement and participation

Children can engage civically by participating in youth organisations, clubs and voluntary groups that aim to address issues of public concern. Even though most children are not allowed to vote, the International Civic and Citizenship Education Study (ICCS) collects data on their intention to vote in national elections later in life. The reported intention to vote and a measure of young peoples' civic participation are included here as indicators of children's civic engagement.

The share of 14 year-olds who report that they will probably or most likely vote in national elections when grown up is highest in Denmark, Italy and Korea, with rates close to 90% (Figure 4.22). Conversely, in the Czech Republic, less than half of 14 year-olds intend to vote in adulthood. These results have to be interpreted while bearing in mind that current intentions to vote are not necessarily predictive of future voting.

In Chile and Mexico, more than half of the 14 year-olds participating in the ICCS survey reported having participated in organisations, groups or clubs in the last 12 months (Figure 4.23). In Finland, Denmark and Korea, less than 1 in 4 respondents indicated having participated in one of the different types of organisations covered by the ICCS survey.

Figure 4.22. **Children's intentions to vote**
Percentage of 14-year-old students who intend to vote in national elections when they are adults, 2009

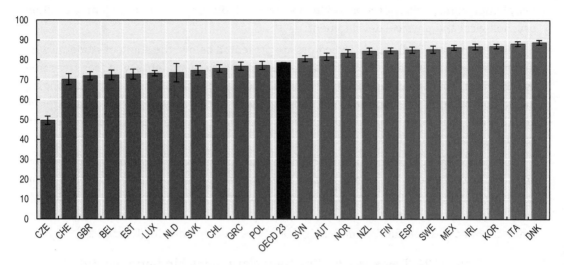

Note: BEL = Belgium (Flemish teenagers only). Error bars represent the 95% confidence interval of the national estimate.

Source: The International Civic and Citizenship Education Study (ICCS) 2009, *http://iccs.acer.edu.au.*

StatLink ᴍᴙᴨ *http://dx.doi.org/10.1787/888933259781*

Figure 4.23. **Teenagers socially engaged**
Percentage of 14 year-old students who participated in organisations, groups or clubs in the last 12 months, 2009

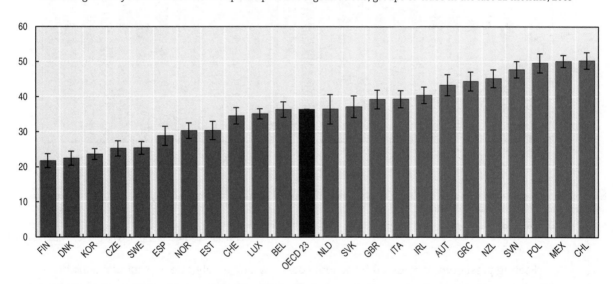

Note: Participation in a youth organisation affiliated with a political party or union, an environmental organisation, a human rights organisation, a voluntary group doing something to help the community, an organisation collecting money for a social cause, a cultural organisation based on ethnicity, a religious group or organisation, a group of young people campaigning for an issue to help the community, or an organisation collecting money for a social cause. Error bars represent the 95% confidence interval of the national estimate.

Source: The International Civic and Citizenship Education Study (ICCS) 2009, *http://iccs.acer.edu.au.*

StatLink ᴍᴙᴨ *http://dx.doi.org/10.1787/888933259793*

Social and family environment

Peers and the family are crucial determinants of children's well-being. Currie et al. (2012), based on HBSC data, have shown that positive peer relationships serve as a protective factor, with positive effects in terms of improving adolescent health and reducing psychological complaints. Adolescents who are part of dense social networks have higher self-perceived health and a better sense of well-being, and are less likely to engage in risky behaviours. Similarly, there is extensive research on the impact of the family on child psychological and physical development.

Based on these findings, six indicators are presented below: the share of students who report having kind and helpful classmates; the percentage of students who feel pressured by schoolwork; the percentage of students who report liking school; the "sense of belonging index" computed in PISA; the share of teenagers who find it easy to talk to their parents; and the time that parents spend with children doing basic childcare activities as well as in educational and recreational activities.

School experiences can be crucial to children's development of self-esteem, self-perception and healthy behaviours. Classmate support increases feelings of belonging to a social group or setting (Currie et al., 2012). Peer groups at school are therefore very important for children's well-being. Swedish children are most likely to report having kind and helpful classmates, while only 44% of Greek children find their classmates kind and helpful (Figure 4.24).

Figure 4.24. **Teenagers finding their classmates kind and helpful**

Percentage of students who agree that most of their classmates are kind and helpful, 2010

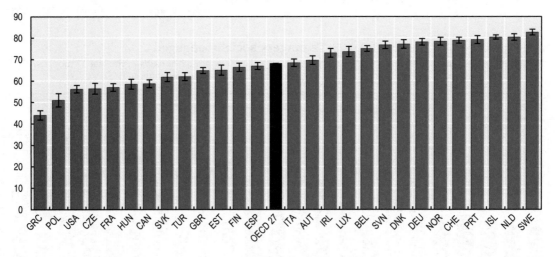

Note: Percentage of girls and boys aged 11, 13 and 15 who report that their classmates are kind and helpful. Error bars represent the 95% confidence interval of the national estimate.

Source: Health and Behaviour in School-aged Children Study (HBSC) 2010, www.hbsc.org/.

StatLink ᕯᗄ⅀ http://dx.doi.org/10.1787/888933259807

Feeling pressured or stressed by schoolwork may negatively affect students' learning as well as non-academic outcomes such as health, risky behaviour and general well-being (Currie et al., 2012). While some pressure may have a positive effect on students' educational outcomes, too much pressure is not desirable. In the HBSC survey, students aged 11, 13 and 15 are asked how pressured they feel by the schoolwork they have to do, with response options ranging from "a lot" to "not at all". The indicator presented here is the share of students who reported feeling a lot of pressure from schoolwork. On average, one in ten children in the OECD reports feeling a lot of pressure (Figure 4.25). The variation across OECD countries is high, with almost 30% in Turkey feeling pressured as compared to only 4% in Germany and Austria. It is however important to note this indicator is not available for Japan and Korea, two countries where school pressure is known to be high.[15]

Figure 4.25. **Children feeling pressured by schoolwork**

Percentage of girls and boys aged 11, 13 and 15 who report that they feel a lot of pressure from schoolwork, 2010

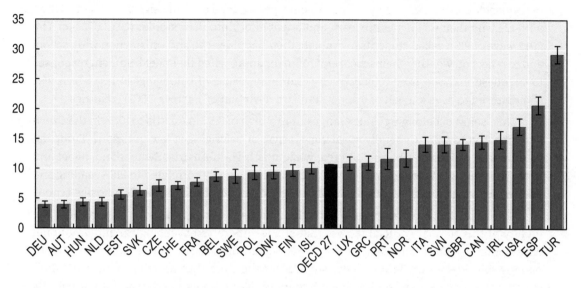

Note: Error bars represent the 95% confidence interval of the national estimate.

Source: Health and Behaviour in School-aged Children Study (HBSC) 2010, *www.hbsc.org/.*

StatLink ᨀᨆᨊ *http://dx.doi.org/10.1787/888933259816*

Young people's experiences in school can either support the development of their self-esteem, self-perceptions and health behaviours, or conversely represent a risk factor, adversely affecting students' mental and physical health. Students who dislike school or do not feel connected to it are more likely to fail academically, drop out and develop mental health problems (Currie et al., 2012). Overall, 3 out of 4 students aged 11, 13 and 15 in OECD countries reported liking school in the 2010 wave of the HBSC (Figure 4.26). Students in Iceland like school the most, while those in Estonia are least likely to report liking it.

Figure 4.26. **Children liking school**

Percentage of 11, 13 and 15 year-old children who report liking school, 2010

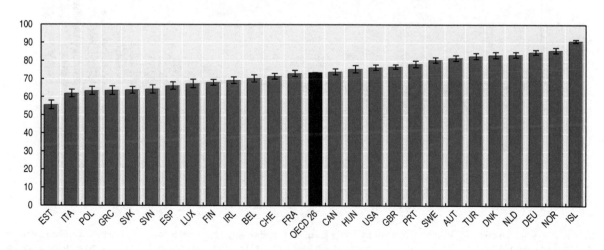

Note: Error bars represent the 95% confidence interval of the national estimate.

Source: Health and Behaviour School-aged children Study (HBSC) 2010, *www.hbsc.org/.*

StatLink ᨀᨆᨊ *http://dx.doi.org/10.1787/888933259827*

Another indicator of students' well-being in school is the PISA "sense of school belonging" index, which reflects how connected students feel with their school and their peers. A lack of connectedness can adversely affect students' perceptions of themselves, their satisfaction with life, and their willingness to learn and to put effort into their studies (OECD, 2014c). The 2012 wave of PISA asked students to evaluate their happiness at, and satisfaction with, school and to reflect on whether their school environment approached their ideal. Student responses to six questions were used to construct a summary "sense of belonging" index, which was standardised to have a mean of 0 and a standard deviation of 1 across OECD countries.

This "sense of belonging" index ranges from a high of 0.55 in Austria to -0.36 in the Czech Republic (Figure 4.27). Generally speaking, a sense of belonging is low in Eastern European countries as well as in Japan and Korea, while it is high in Austria, Switzerland, Israel and Spain. The sense of belonging to school index is also inversely correlated to PISA reading and problem-solving scores and positively correlated to the number of students who like school.

The time that children spend with their parents and, even more importantly, the quality of this time are crucial factors that shape children's psychological and emotional development (Monna and Gauthier, 2009). Research also shows the importance of both parents' involvement. There is wide variation in the time that parents spend with their children, with Australian children spending more than 4 hours per day with their parents and Korean children spending less than one hour (Figure 4.28). In the OECD area, the time mothers spend with their children is more than the double that of fathers. Mothers cover a significant share of physical care and supervision while fathers spend most of their time with children in teaching and recreational activities. The share of parental time spent in basic childcare and in teaching and recreational activities is much more similar for mothers and fathers in the Nordic countries, in Canada and in the United States.

Figure 4.27. **Children who feel they belong in their school**

The PISA Sense of Belonging Index is based on a Rasch scaling of six items, 2012

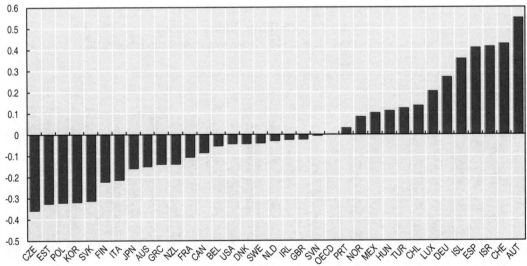

Note: Based on a Rasch scaling of six items (I feel like an outsider, I make friends easily, I feel like I belong, I feel awkward and out of place, Other students seem to like me, I feel lonely), and standardised to have a mean of 0 and a standard deviation of 1 across all participating OECD countries.

Source: PISA 2012, OECD (2014c), *PISA 2012 Results: Ready to Learn (Volume III) Students' Engagement, Drive and Self-Beliefs*, *http://dx.doi. org/10.1787/19963785*.

StatLink 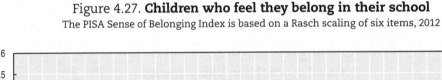 *http://dx.doi.org/10.1787/888933259831*

Figure 4.28. **Parental time with children**

Daily minutes, 2013 or latest available year

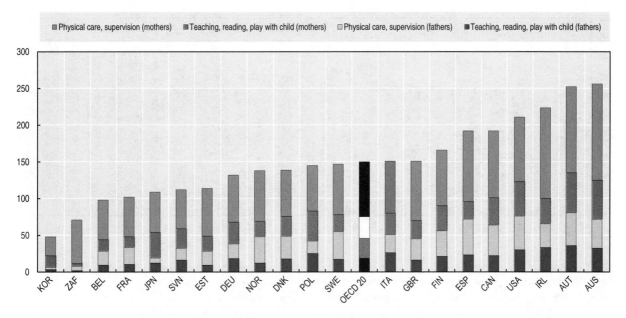

Note: Data refer to the amount of time spent on childcare that respondents report themselves in their time-use diaries as a primary activity (i.e. without doing other activities at the same time). Basic childcare includes childcare and child supervision, as well as time spent in transporting children, with the exception of Ireland and Korea where time spent transporting children is not included. Data refer to care for children under the age of 18, except for Australia and Canada (less than 15 years).Data for Ireland and Korea do not include time spent transporting children. Data refer to 1999-2000 for Estonia; 2000 for South Africa; 2000-01 for Norway, Slovenia, Sweden, the United Kingdom; 2001 for Denmark; 2001-02 for Germany; 2003-4 for Poland; 2005 for Belgium and Ireland; 2006 for Japan; 2008-09 for Australia, Italy; 2009 for Korea; 2009-10 for Finland, France and Spain; 2010 for Canada; and 2013 for the United States.

Source: OECD calculations based on the Harmonised European Time Use Survey web application for European countries (*https://www.h2.scb.se/ tus/tus/*), public-use time use survey micro-data and tabulations from national statistical offices for non-European countries,

StatLink ⟲ *http://dx.doi.org/10.1787/888933259841*

Children's communication with their parents is important in establishing the family as a protective factor. Family support helps children to deal with stressful situations and buffers them against several negative influences (Currie et al., 2012). Children's relationships with their parents can be measured by the percentage of students who report that they can easily talk with their mother or father. Hungary and the Netherlands have the highest percentages of teenagers who report finding it easy to talk to at least one of their parents (Figure 4.29). However, there is little variation across the OECD countries, and most countries have values above 80%. An exception is France, where more than 1 in 4 teenagers report that it is difficult for them to talk to at least one of their parents.

Personal security

Two indicators are used to describe children's personal security. These relate to child deaths by intentional injury (homicides) among 0-19 year-old children, and children's exposure to bullying in school. Bullying is defined as hostile physical or verbal actions that cause distress to victims. Victims of bullying are likely to experience several problems, such as depression, anxiety and loneliness, which can persist into adulthood (Currie et al., 2012). While these two indicators capture relevant elements of personal security, research has also consistently shown that other forms of childhood victimisation, as well as neglect, can affect child well-being, both in the sense of developmental and child-rights perspectives. There are not considered here because of the lack of comparative data.

Figure 4.29. **Teenagers finding it easy to talk to their parents**
Percentage of students who can easily talk to at least one of their parents, 2010

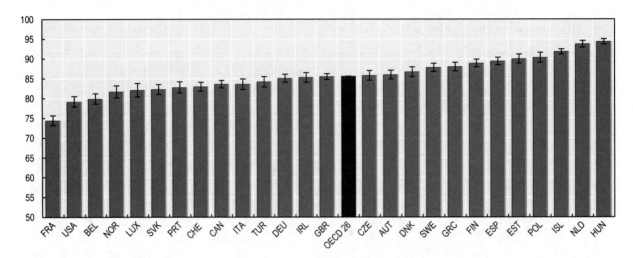

Note: Percentage of girls and boys aged 11, 13 and 15 who report they find it easy to talk to their mother (or stepmother) or father (or stepfather). Error bars represent the 95% confidence interval of the national estimate.

Source: Health and Behaviour in School-aged Children Study (HBSC) 2010, *www.hbsc.org/*.

StatLink ᘡᛯᓴ *http://dx.doi.org/10.1787/888933259857*

On average in the OECD, the child homicide rate is 1 in 100 000. However, there is a large variation across countries, with more than twice as many child homicides in Mexico and the United States as in any other OECD country (Figure 4.30). Homicides rates also show large variations among children of different ages, as well as by types of perpetrator (i.e. whether the perpetrator is a family member or not); these variations are not documented here.

Figure 4.30. **Child homicide rates**
Death rates by intentional injury per 100 000 children, 3-year average around 2011

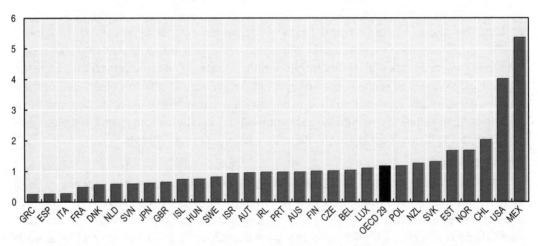

Note: Data for Canada are not available on a comparable definition. National figures of child homicides rates are available here *http://www.statcan.gc.ca/pub/85-002-x/2014001/article/14114/tbl/tbl31-eng.htm#tbl31n_1).*

Source: WHO Mortality Database, *www.whi.int/healthinfo/statistics/mortality/en/index/html.*

StatLink ᘡᛯᓴ *http://dx.doi.org/10.1787/888933259861*

For the indicator shown in Figure 4.31, a student is considered to be "bullied" if other students say or do nasty or unpleasant things to him or her, or if the student is deliberately excluded from activities repeatedly. However, when two students of about the same strength or power argue or fight, or when a student is teased in a friendly and playful way, this is not considered to be bullying by this definition. The indicator also refers to bullying occurred at school and therefore excludes new types of bullying through social media that are becoming increasingly common. Based on the aforementioned definition, the incidence of bullying among school children is high in some OECD countries, such as Estonia, Austria and Belgium, where more than 15% of teenagers report having experienced bullying twice or more over the past 2 months (Figure 4.31). Italy and Sweden have the lowest rates of bullying across the OECD countries based on the available data.

Being bullied is just one side of the phenomenon, as bullying others is also known to have a negative impact on the health of perpetrators themselves, through higher health risk behaviours and other disruptive behaviours some of which may persist through life. Children who bully others also report more disconnectedness with families and with their peers, and are more likely to commit more crimes when they become adults (Currie et al., 2012).

Figure 4.31. **Children who report having been bullied**
Percentage of children who have been bullied at least twice in the last two months, 2010

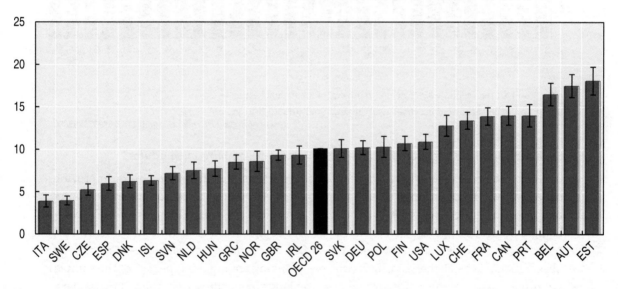

Note: Percentage of girls and boys aged 11, 13 and 15 who report that they have been bullied at school at least twice over the last two months. Error bars represent the 95% confidence interval of the national estimate.

Source: Health and Behaviour School-aged children Study (HBSC) 2010, *www.hbsc.org/*.

StatLink 🔍 *http://dx.doi.org/10.1787/888933259876*

Subjective well-being

Life satisfaction in childhood and youth is an important aspect of well-being that is associated with social competence and coping skills that lead to more positive outcomes in adulthood (Currie et al., 2012). Subjective well-being is measured in the HBSC as the mean life satisfaction score of 11, 13 and 15 year-olds; the measure reported below is based on the Cantril Ladder, which asks students to rate their current life relative to the best possible life (10) for them and the worst possible life (0). Data on life satisfaction are based on individual assessments and can therefore be affected by cultural norms, which can limit comparability across countries.

Based on this measure, children in Spain, the Netherlands and Iceland are most satisfied with their lives (Figure 4.32), while those in Turkey and Poland are the least satisfied. Interestingly, the outcomes for adults on life satisfaction measured through the same question in the Gallup World Poll (see Chapter 2) are quite different from those reported by young people, with large differences in Spain and Denmark.[16] Overall, the OECD average score is lower for adults than for children.

Figure 4.32. **Children's life satisfaction**

Average life satisfaction score of girls and boys aged 11, 13 and 15 on a scale from 0 to 10 (highest), 2010

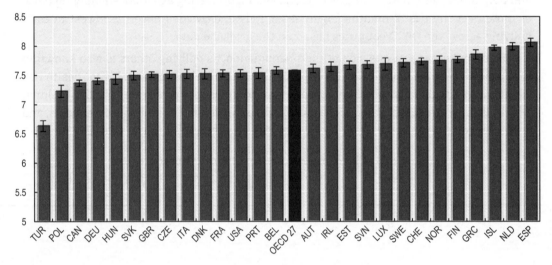

Note: Error bars represent the 95% confidence interval of the national estimate.

Source: Health and Behaviour in School-aged Children Study (HBSC) 2010, *www.hbsc.org/.*

StatLink ⟨⟨⟩⟩ *http://dx.doi.org/10.1787/888933259880*

Summing up: how's life for children and how does it compare with adults?

Taken together the evidence presented above shows that there is room for improving children's well-being in almost every OECD country. For all the dimensions and indicators discussed, countries' outcomes vary widely across the different domains of child well-being. Some country patterns in overall child well-being outcomes are shown in Figure 4.33, based on an analysis that covers only indicators and countries with a sufficient number of observations.[17] The Netherlands performs best, ranking among the top third of the sample performers in 80% of the indicators and never ranking among the bottom third of performers. Child well-being is also very high in Germany, Switzerland and Denmak ranking among the top third performers with around half of the indicators and among the bottom third performers in 20% or less of the indicators. Conversely, the United States, Poland and Turkey rank among the bottom third performers in a majority of indicators, while positioning themselves among the top third performers only in a handful of indicators.

A country's performance on child well-being tends to be correlated with its performance on general well-being, as measured by the *How's Life?* headline indicators shown in Chapter 2, though the correlation is far from perfect (Figure 4.33, Panel B). For instance, Switzerland records excellent results in child well-being as well as in general well-being, but Canada, the United States and Luxembourg do much better on the general *How's Life?* indicators than on the child-specific ones. By contrast, child well-being is comparatively high in Slovenia and the Czech Republic, while the performance of these two countries is less favourable when looking at the *How's Life?* indicators in Chapter 2.

Figure 4.33. **A bird's eye view of child well-being outcomes across OECD countries**

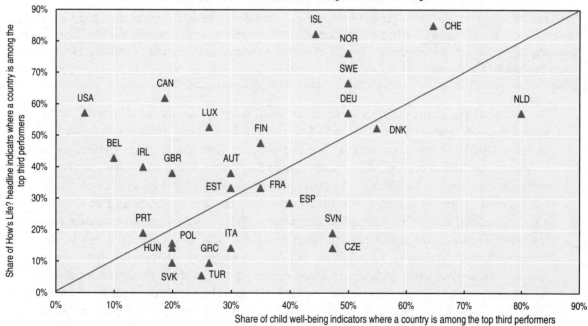

Notes: Panel A shows, on the y-axis, the share of child well-being indicators where a country performs in the top third and, on the x-axis, the share of child well-being indicators which rank a country in the bottom third of performers. Only 20 indicators out of the 28 analysed in this chapter have been retained for this analysis to ensure an even country coverage throughout. Countries with low indicator coverage (i.e. less than 15 indicators) are not shown here.

Panel B shows, on the y-axis, the share of 21 headline indicators of *How's Life?* which ranks a country in the top third and, on the x-axis, the share of the child well-being indicators which ranks a country in the top third, as shown in the y-axis of Panel A. Only 21 headline indicators out of the 23 included in Chapter 1 were retained in this analysis to ensure an even country coverage throughout. The diagonal denotes that countries record an equally good performance when assessed with either *How's Life?* headline indicators or child well-being ones.

StatLink ᵐˢᵖ http://dx.doi.org/10.1787/888933259896

These results should be interpreted with caution, as they are partly dependent on the threshold used to assess countries' performance as well as on the countries included in the sample. In addition, this analysis cannot be used to inform a discussion of how child well-being affects adult well-being, or to infer trade-offs between adult and child well-being.

Inequalities in child well-being by age, gender and socio-economic status

All the indicators described above are characterised by substantial differences in outcomes across different groups of children within the same country, whether disaggregating by age, gender or socio-economic status. Unfortunately, not all the indicators can be broken down by all of these characteristics. In general, most indicators drawn from OECD databases cannot be disaggregated, while those based on surveys can. However, surveys like PISA, the HBSC and the ICCS limit their collection to children of certain ages, implying that the age breakdown is limited to the age of the survey respondents. Family-based indicators such as household disposable income, relative income poverty, parental employment, housing and environmental conditions can be disaggregated by the age of the youngest child and by the socio-economic status of the household head. Some of the most significant differences between groups are summarised below, with more detailed information available online (see Box 4.7).

Box 4.7. Inequalities in child well-being: where to find the data

All the data supporting the analysis of inequalities in child well-being of this section can be found in the corresponding statlinks shown at the bottom of the charts shown in the chapter. For instance, detailed information on life satisfaction by age, gender and socio-economic background of children can be found in the statlink of Chart 4.32.

Some of the main differences in child well-being by the *age* of the child (or by age of the youngest child in the case of household-level data) include the following. In some OECD countries, parents with small children face the greatest challenges in accessing the labour market, with children aged 5 or below being more likely to live in workless households. Families with small children generally have less space at home: the number of rooms per household increases with the age of the youngest child in almost all OECD countries, with a few exceptions. There is no clear association across countries between the age of the youngest child and a lack of basic facilities in the houses where children live, although children aged 5 or below are more likely to live in households lacking basic facilities in some countries. The share of children reporting poor health increases with age, while the rate of overweight children falls as children grow older. The life satisfaction of students decreases as they get older in all OECD countries, while pressure from schoolwork increases as children get older; similarly, the share of students who like school decreases with the cohort's age from 11 to 15 years in almost all OECD countries. Communicating with one's parents also becomes more challenging with age in all the countries participating in the HBSC, and the share of students who agree that most of their classmates are kind and helpful also declines with age in most countries. However, the percentage of 11, 13 and 15 year-old children who report that they have been bullied at school at least twice in the last two months declines with age in almost all countries.

Many of the selected indicators also vary substantially when disaggregated by *gender*. Girls are more likely to report poor health than boys in almost all countries. Conversely, boys in all OECD countries are more likely to be overweight and more likely to commit suicide than girls. In all OECD countries, 15 year-old girls perform better in reading than boys, while boys of the same age have a small advantage in mathematics and science scores, as well as in creative problem-solving in most countries. In countries where the share of youth not in education, employment or training is high overall, girls are much more likely than boys to be in this situation. Overall, girls are slightly less likely to be educationally deprived. In most countries, boys are more likely than girls to find it easy to talk to their mother or father. Boys are, however, more likely to be bullied than girls in almost all countries. Life satisfaction is higher for boys than for girls in all OECD countries participating in the HBSC. More girls than boys report liking school in all OECD countries covered by this same study. More boys than girls die by intentional injury in almost all countries.

Finally, when disaggregating child well-being data by *socio-economic status, family composition and migrant background*, the main stylised facts are the following. In all OECD countries, children living in jobless families are more common among households in which only one parent is present. In most OECD countries, children from migrant backgrounds[18] are more likely to live in jobless households, to have long-term unemployed parents, and to live in more over-crowded conditions. In most OECD countries, children in households with lower income and living with only one parent are more likely to report poor environmental conditions.

Greater family affluence (measured using the number of cars, holidays, PCs in the family home and whether the child has their own bedroom) is associated with higher self-perceived health by children in all countries. Family affluence is also associated with lower rates of child overweight and obesity in most OECD countries. Students whose parents have a higher economic, social and cultural status have higher scores in reading and problem-solving in all countries. Low socio-economic status is associated with higher rates of educational deprivation in all OECD countries. The gap in educational deprivation between students with high and low socio-economic status is largest in countries with a high overall rate of educationally deprived children. Not living with both parents is associated with higher deprivation rates in most countries, while the association with migration background varies across OECD countries. The share of teenagers who intend to vote increases with socio-economic background in all the participating countries and, in most countries, non-native children are less likely to intend to vote. Civic participation rates increase with the family's socio-economic status in most OECD countries, but is less frequent among non-native teenagers in many countries. However, non-native children are more likely to participate in youth clubs or organisations in several OECD countries.

In most OECD countries, children in less wealthy families are more likely to feel pressured by schoolwork and less likely to report liking school. The likelihood of both liking school, and feeling a sense of belonging in school, declines with socio-economic status in all OECD countries. The higher a family's socio-economic background, the more likely are children to talk easily with their parents. Furthermore, students with more affluent families are more likely to report having kind and helpful classmates in most OECD countries. The share of 11, 13 and 15 year-old children who have been bullied at school at least twice in the last two months decreases with family affluence in almost all OECD countries. Average life-satisfaction is lower for 11, 13 and 15 year-olds in the bottom third of the family affluence scale than for those in the top third.

The statistical agenda ahead for child well-being

As in previous OECD efforts to measure child well-being, the analysis presented in this chapter has limitations. One fundamental issue is that the framework (and the indicators used) are very much data-driven rather than based on an *ex ante* conceptualisation of the most relevant aspects of child well-being, with data specifically collected for that purpose. As no existing survey captures the key factors for children's well-being across all age groups and OECD countries, this chapter has relied on the available data. This inevitably leads to gaps in how the concepts selected are operationalised as well as in the age range of the children who are covered.[19]

Moreover, as highlighted in Section 4.2.3, all surveys of children or households – though particularly school-based surveys – can miss the children most at risk of social exclusion, due to homelessness, institutionalisation, poor health or special educational needs. These surveys are therefore not fully representative of all children, and may exhibit this form of bias to varying degrees across countries and years (Richardson and Ali, 2014). Finally, all of the data are derived from cross-sectional collections. This means that it is impossible to determine how various outcomes are causally linked at the individual level, how well-being in one dimension affects well-being in another, or how policy interventions may shape the evolution of the well-being of a given cohort. Until longitudinal and purpose-built surveys of child well-being become more widely available, it might be challenging to untangle policy influences for different children at different times, possibly leading to misinterpretation of how these outcomes relate to one another.

While this chapter has relied on the best available data, it has also highlighted areas where further statistical work is needed. The main priorities for advancing the statistical agenda for monitoring well-being, as outlined by Richardson and Ali (2014), include:

- Efforts should be made to fill gaps in the measurement of child well-being in terms of age-related indicators (children under nine are missing from comparative child survey data), children with special needs, and dimensions of child well-being not covered by existing studies. Some survey data for European countries are already available for this purpose (e.g. data on mental health from the European School Survey Project on Alcohol and Other Drugs – ESPAD – survey[20]), but for non-European countries new data collection efforts are needed (possibly via adjustments or additions to existing surveys, or through supplemental out-of school surveys). More indicators related to inequalities in child well-being are also needed to identify priority intervention groups.

- Efforts should be made to harmonise data collections among the major international surveys. This will facilitate the analysis of interactions between well-being indicators and provide new evidence for policy. Funding bodies or governmental bodies that work with more than one survey should encourage these efforts.

- Where the harmonisation of available data is not possible, or does not produce adequate information for informing policies for *all* children (which is likely to be the case in most countries, given the restrictions on age coverage and at-risk groups of children), the development of longitudinal datasets of child well-being should be pursued. Longitudinal datasets, with multiple cohorts, have the potential to provide data for both monitoring and policy evaluation. At present, the lack of data needed to identify spill-overs across well-being dimensions restricts the development of an optimal child policy portfolio (OECD, 2009).

Notes

1. Family conditions and children's early experiences have a strong influence on educational outcomes in later life. For instance, evidence shows that parental employment and earnings (Machin, 1998), poverty in childhood (Bladnen and Gregg, 2004), parental economic status (after controlling for cognitive ability, Bukodi et al., 2014), leisure and physical activity (Dregan and Gulliford, 2013) and bullying (Brown and Taylor, 2008) are all linked to educational outcomes in later life. Other studies show that parental resources (Faas et al., 2012), parent incarceration (Miller et al., 2105) and alcohol consumption (Balsa et al., 2011) are linked to children's educational attainment (and, in some cases, to the likelihood of experiencing mental health and welfare dependency). Further studies show how mother's educational attainment mediates the link between health behaviours during pregnancy and the health of infants (Conti et al., 2012), as does family instability and child behaviour (Fomby, 2012). The effects in adulthood of educational outcomes in childhood are also well established. Birth cohort studies show that in the United Kingdom educational outcomes (e.g. childhood cognitive ability and educational attainment) are linked to occupational outcomes (Cheng and Furnham, 2012) and mental well-being upon reaching adult age (Cheng and Schoon, 2013). Research has also found links between educational factors (attainment, attendance, aspiration) and health behaviours such as smoking (Maralani, 2014) and alcohol use (Crosnoe, 2006).

2. Conceptually, these studies treat child well-being as a latent variable made up of aspects or dimensions that are not necessarily correlated. They sometimes combine all indicators pertaining to the same dimension and then combine these dimensional indicators into a single child well-being score using averages of standardised scales (e.g. z-scores). Most studies that rely on composite indicators apply equal weights (both within and across dimensions).

3. The UNCRC commits governments to ensuring that children have a standard of living adequate to ensure their physical, mental, spiritual, moral and social development, and in particular to provide material assistance to children "in need" (UNCRC, Art. 27), to access education (Art. 28) and through it to develop their fullest potential (Art. 29a), to secure adequate housing conditions (Art. 27.3), to ensure children's survival and physical development (Art. 6); to provide for their health and safety, and to develop institutions, services and facilities that provide for the care and protection of children (Art. 3.3).

4. Some additional criteria for the selection of indicators discussed in *Doing Better for Children* were not retained here. For instance, this chapter does not include indicators aimed at balancing efficiency and equity considerations. Another criterion that guided the selection of indicators in *Doing Better for Children* was to limit the selection to "policy amenable" indicators, namely indicators suitable for policy evaluations and considered to fall primarily within the responsibility of public bodies (rather than of parents or children themselves). The choice in this chapter to look at a broader range of well-being outcomes (rather than being limited to those that are within the remit of public policies) is in line with most recent studies based on a multi-dimensional approach to the well-being in adulthood and childhood, e.g. UNICEF (2013).

5. This implies that the United Nations definition of a child as a person under age 18 is used in this chapter.

6. For instance, Richardson and Ali (2014) show that non-response rates decrease with age for some survey items such as life satisfaction.

7. The figures based on EU-SILC may be slightly different from the corresponding Eurostat figures (http://ec.europa.eu/eurostat/statistics-explained/index.php/Housing_statistics) as, in contrast with the Eurostat methodology, this report does not make use of children weights. This choice has been made to build comparable indicators in non-EU countries whose corresponding surveys do not include children weights. In addition, the use of children weights builds on the assumption that children are excluded from the relevant statistical population when they are heads of households. This chapter does not make this assumption and considers children all individuals under 18-years-old, in line with UNECE definitions, and irrespective of their role in the household.

8. For European countries, the indicator is based on the number of rooms available to the household, including living rooms, and comes from the EU Statistics on Income and Living Conditions (EU-SILC); for Australia, Chile, Mexico and the United States, the indicator is based on the number of bedrooms only and the sources are HILDA, ENIGH, CASEN and ACS (see note to Figure 4.6).

9. The indicator of children living in dwellings without indoor flushing toilets does not include shared sanitation facilities across multigenerational households (i.e. parents and grandparents living together). When considering shared toilets across multigenerational households, the share of children living in dwellings without toilets is lower in both Hungary (i.e. 7.4% as opposed to 10.2%) and Ireland (i.e. 1.9% versus 9.9%).

10. In Canada and the United States, premature births are registered as live births; this implies higher measures of infant mortality and low birth weight compared to European countries, where live births require a minimum gestational age (OECD, 2009).

11. The PISA reading proficiency scale was constructed to have a mean score of 500 among OECD countries, with a standard deviation of 100 in the first PISA reading assessment, which was administered in 2000. In 2012, the mean score among OECD countries was 496 with a standard deviation of 94.

12. The OECD Survey of Adult Skills (PIAAC) finds that complex problem solving skills are of growing importance in the labour market (OECD, 2014b).

13. Like the reading score, the problem-solving scale was constructed to have a mean score among OECD countries of 500, with about two-thirds of students across OECD countries scoring between 400 and 600.

14. Problem-solving tests are optional for countries participating in PISA.

15. See for instance OECD 2014c and *www.oecd.org/pisa/keyfindings/PISA-2012-results-japan.pdf*.

16. Spanish children are much more satisfied with their lives than Spanish adults, while adults in Denmark report a slightly higher average life satisfaction score than children in Denmark.

17. The analysis looks at countries' overall performance in child well-being by considering the proportion of indicators used in this chapter where a country records a good performance (i.e. ranks in the top third of the countries) and the proportion of indicators where a country records a bad performance (i.e. ranks in the bottom third).

18. Results on child well-being outcomes by migrant status should be taken with caution as the household surveys used in this chapter cover migrants to a limited extent.

19. For instance, in the case of data from administrative sources, it is often impossible to disaggregate the indicators as would be desirable: this is the case, for example, of the indicators on birth weight and child homicides, where no breakdown by age or socio-economic characteristics is available. Where the data come from surveys, the information is typically limited to children of a specific age (e.g. those aged 15 in the case of PISA; those aged 11, 13 and 15 in the case of the HBSC) and to specific aspects (competences in PISA, health and behaviours in the HBSC), thus omitting other important aspects, such as child protection or neglect, children's access to green spaces, or time use. Together, these limitations lead to a lack of information on, say, the educational outcomes of children in primary school or the health outcomes of pre-schoolers.

20. The European School Survey Project on Alcohol and Other Drugs (ESPAD) covers Austria, Belgium, the Czech Republic, Denmark, Estonia, Finland, France, Germany, Greece, Hungary, Iceland, Ireland, Italy, the Netherlands, Norway, Poland, Portugal, the Slovak Republic, Slovenia, Sweden, Switzerland, Turkey, the United Kingdom and another 14 non-OECD countries. ESPAD covers issues of integration, psychological problems, cannabis use as well as the use of alcohol, tobacco and drugs. Data are collected through a standardised school questionnaire administered to students turning 16 in the calendar year of the survey.

References

Ben-Arieh, A., N.H. Kaufman, A.B. Andrews, R.M. George, B.J. Lee and J.L. Aber (2001), *Measuring and Monitoring Children's Well-being*, Springer Publishing, The Netherlands.

Ben-Arieh, A. and I. Frønes (2007), "Indicators of Children's Well being: What should be Measured and Why?", *Social Indicators Research*, Vol. 84, pp. 249-250.

Blanden, J. and P. Gregg (2004), *Family Income and Educational Attainment: A Review of Approaches and Evidence for Britain*, Discussion Paper No.41, London: Centre for the Economics of Education.

Bradshaw, J., P. Hoelscher and D. Richardson (2007), "An Index of Child Well-being in the European Union", *Social Indicators Research*, 80 (1), pp. 133-77.

Bradshaw, J. and D. Richardson (2009), "An Index of Child Well-being in Europe", *Child Indicators Research*, Vol. 2, No. 3, pp. 319-351.

Bronfenbrenner, U. (1979), *The Ecology of Human Development. Experiments by Nature and Design.* Cambridge, MA, Harvard University Press.

Brown, S. and K. Taylor (2008), Bullying, education and earnings: Evidence from the National Child Development Survey. *Economics of Education Review*, 27 (4), pp. 387-401.

Bukodi, E., R. Erikson and J.H. Goldthorpe (2014), The effects of social origins and cognitive ability on educational attainment: Evidence from Britain and Sweden. *Acta Sociologica*, 57(4), pp. 293-310.

Carcillo, S., R. Fernández, S. Königs and A. Minea (2015), "NEET Youth in the aftermath of the crisis" OECD Social, *Employment and Migration Working Papers*, No. 164.

Casas, F. (1997), "Children's Rights and Children's Quality of Life: Conceptual and Practical Issues", *Social Indicators Research*, Vol. 42, pp. 283-298.

Case A., A. Fertig and C. Paxson (2005), "The lasting impact of Childhood Health and Circumstance", *Journal of Health Economics*, Vol. 24, No. 2, pp. 365-89.

Cheng, H. and A. Furnham (2012), Childhood cognitive ability, education, and personality traits predict attainment in adult occupational prestige over 17 years. *Journal of Vocational Behaviour*, 81(2), pp. 218-226.

Cheng, H. and I. Schoon (2013), The Role Of School Engagement in Young People's Career Development and Mental Well-Being: Findings from Two British Cohorts. In H. Helve and K. Evans (ed.), *Youth, and Work Transitions in Changing Social Landscapes*. London: Tufnell Press.

Conti, G., J. Heckman, P. Pinger and A. Zanolini (2012), *Transmission of Inequality: Maternal skills, Behavior and Birth Outcomes*. EEA/ESEM Conference, Malaga, 27-31 August 2012.

Crosnoe, R. (2006), The Connection Between Academic Failure and Adolescent Drinking in Secondary School. *Sociology of Education*, 79(1), pp. 44-60.

Currie, C., C. Zanotti, A. Morgan, D. Currie, M. de Looze, C. Roberts, O. Samdal, O.R.F. Smith and V. Barnekow (2012), Social determinants of health and well-being among young people. Health Behaviour in School-aged Children (HBSC) study: international report from the 2009/2010 survey. Copenhagen, WHO Regional Office for Europe (Health Policy for Children and Adolescents, No. 6).

Dregan, A and M.C. Gulliford (2013), "Leisure-Time Physical Activity over the Life Course and Cognitive Functioning in Late Mid-Adult Years: A Cohort-Based Investigation", *Psychological Medicine*, 43(11), pp. 2447-2458.

European Commission (2008), *Child poverty and well-being in the EU: Current status and way forward*, Social Protection Committee, Office for Official Publications of the European Communities, Luxembourg. *http://www.libertysecurity.org/IMG/pdf_ke3008251_en.pdf*.

Griffiths, L.J., T.J. Parsons and A.J. Hill (2010), "Self-esteem and quality of life in obese children and adolescent: a systematic review", *International Journal of Pediatric Obesity*, 2010, Vol. 11, No. 12, pp. 835-846

Hack, M., N.K. Klein and H.G. Taylor (1995), "Long-term developmental outcomes of low birth weight infants" *Future Child* 1995 Spring; Vol. 5, No. 1, pp. 176-96.

Faas, C., M.J. Benson and C.E. Kaestle (2012), "Parent Resources during Adolescence: Effects on Education and Careers in Young Adulthood", *Journal of Youth Studies*, 16(2), pp. 151-171.

Fomby, P. (2012), "Family Instability and School Readiness in the United Kingdom", *Family Science*, 2(3), pp. 171-185.

Machin, S. (1998), Childhood Disadvantage and Intergenerational Transmissions of Economic Status, in *'Exclusion, Employment and Opportunity'* Atkinson, A.B., J. Hills (eds), LSE Centre for Analysis of Social Exclusion.

Maralani, V. (2014), "Understanding the Links between Education and Smoking", *Social Science Research*, 48, pp. 20-34.

Miller, H.V. and J.C. Barnes (2015), "The Association Between Parental Incarceration and Health, Education, and Economic Outcomes in Young Adulthood", *American Journal of Criminal Justice*, pp. 1-20.

OECD (2009), *Doing Better for Children*, OECD Publishing, Paris, *http://dx.doi.org/10.1787/9789264059344-en*

OECD (2011), *Doing Better for Families*, OECD Publishing, Paris, *http://dx.doi.org/10.1787/9789264098732-en*

OECD (2013), *OECD Guidelines on Measuring Subjective Well-Being*, OECD Publishing, Paris, *http://dx.doi.org/10.1787/9789264191655-en*.

OECD (2014a), *PISA 2012 Results: What Students Know and Can Do (Volume I)*, Revised edition, February, OECD Publishing, Paris, *http://dx.doi.org/ 10.1787/9789264208780-en*.

OECD (2014b), *PISA 2012 Results: Creative Problem Solving (Volume V), Students' Skills in Tackling Real-Life Problems*, OECD Publishing, Paris, *http://dx.doi.org/10.1787/9789264208070-en*.

OECD (2014c), *PISA 2012 Results: Ready to Learn (Volume III) Students' Engagement, Drive and Self-Beliefs*, OECD Publishing, Paris, *http://dx.doi.org/ 10.1787/9789264201170-en*.

OECD (2015a), *OECD Population Database*. Retrieved from *http://stats.oecd.org/Index.aspx?DatasetCode=POP_FIVE_HIST#*.

OECD (2015b), *International Longitudinal Study of Skills Development in Cities*, *www.oecd.org/edu/ceri/internationallongitudinalstudyofskillsdevelopmentincities.htm*.

OECD (2015c), *Integrating the Delivery of Social Service for Vulnerable Groups*, forthcoming, OECD Publishing, Paris.

OECD (2015d), *OECD Family Database*, OECD Publishing, Paris.

OECD (2015e), *Tackling Harmful Alcohol Use: Economics and Public Health Policy*, OECD Publishing, *http//dx.doi.org/10.1787/9789264181069-en*.

ONS (2012), *Measuring National Well-being – Children's Well-being 2012*, *www.ons.gov.uk/ons/dcp171766_283988.pdf*.

ONS (2014), *Measuring National Well-being – Exploring the Well-being of Children in the UK, 2014*, *www.ons.gov.uk/ons/dcp171776_379712.pdf*.

Pollard, E. and P. Lee (2003), "Child Well-Being: A Systematic Review of the Literature", *Social Indicators Research*, Vol. 61, pp. 59-78.

Richardson, D., P. Hoelscher and J. Bradshaw (2008), "Child Well-being in Central and Eastern European Countries (CEE) and the Commonwealth of Independent States (CIS)", *Child Indicators Research*. Vol. 1, pp. 211-250.

Richardson, D. and N. Ali (2014), "An Evaluation of International Surveys of Children", *OECD Social, Employment and Migration Working Papers*, No. 146, OECD Publishing, Paris, *http://dx.doi.org/10.1787/5jxzmjrqvntf-en*.

Rychen, D.S. and L.H. Salganik (2003), *Key competencies for a successful life and a well-functioning society*, Hogrefe & Huber Publishers.

Save The Children (2012), The Child Development Index 2012, Progress, Challenges and Inequality, Save The Children, London, *www.savethechildren.org.uk/sites/default/files/docs/Child_Development_Index_2012_UK_low_res.pdf*. Accessed October 2012.

Save the Children (2008), The Child Development Index: Holding Governments to account for children's wellbeing, Save The Children, London, *www.savethechildren.org.uk/sites/default/files/docs/Child_Development_Index%281%29_1.pdf*. Accessed October 2012.

Scarpetta, S., A. Sonnet and T. Manfredi (2010), "Rising Youth Unemployment During The Crisis: How to Prevent Negative Long-term Consequences on a Generation?", *OECD Social, Employment and Migration Working Papers*, No. 106, OECD Publishing, Paris.

Singh, A.S., C. Mulder, J.W. Twisk, W. van Mechelen and M.J. Chinapaw, "Tracking of childhood overweight into adulthood: a systematic review of the literature", *Obesity Review*, Vol. 9, No. 5, pp. 474-488.

Tarki (2010), *Child Poverty and Child Well-being in the European Union: Report for the European Commission*. Tarki Social Research Institute, Budapest.

UNCRC (1990), *United Nations Convention on the Rights of the Child*, United Nations, New York, *www.unhchr.ch/html/menu3/b/k2crc.htm*.

UNICEF (2014), *Children of the Recession: The impact of the Economic Crisis on Child Well-being in Rich Countries*, Innocenti report card 11, UNICEF, Florence.

WHO (2005), Air Quality Guidelines, Global Update 2005. World Health Organisation Regional Office for Europe, Copenhagen, Denmark.

WHO (2002), The World Health Report 2002 – Reducing risks, promoting healthy life. Geneva, World Health Organization.

Databases referred to in this chapter

EU Statistics on Income and Living Conditions, *http://ec.europa.eu/eurostat/help/new-eurostat-website* (accessed on 17 July 2015).

Health Behaviour in School-aged Children Study, *www.hbsc.org/* (accessed on 17 July 2015).

International Civic and Citizenship Study, *http://iccs.acer.edu.au* (accessed on 17 July 2015).

OECD Population database, *http//dx.doi.org/10.1787/lfs-lfs-data-en* (accessed on 17 July 2015).

OECD Family database, *www.oecd.org/els/family/database.htm* (accessed on 17 July 2015).

OECD Income distribution database, *http//dx.doi.org/10.1787/socwel-data-en* (accessed on 17 July 2015).

WHO Mortality Database, *www.whi.int/healthinfo/statistics/mortality/en/index/html* (accessed on 17 July 2015).

World Development Indicators, World Bank, *http://data.worldbank.org/data-catalog/world-development-indicators* (accessed on 17 July 2015).

ANNEX 4.A

An overview of dimensions and indicators used in comparative child well-being analysis

Table 4.A.1. An overview of dimensions and indicators used in comparative child well-being analysis

	European multidimensional indices (Bradshaw et al. 2007 and 2009)[1]	Unicef Report Cards 7 (2007) and 9 (2010)[1]	CEE CIS index (Richardson et al., 2008)	Doing Better for Children (OECD, 2009)[2]	Save the children (2008 and 2012)[1]	European Commission Child poverty and Well-being (2008)[2]	European Commission TARKI (2010)	US Dept. of Commerce (Hobbs and Lippman, 1990)[3]	OECD Family Database (since 2007)
Health and safety	Child health from birth (infant mortality; low birth weight). Health behaviour (dental; nutrition x 2; physical activity; BMI). Mortality rates (all, 0-19, suicide). Vaccinations (measles; DPT3; Pol3)	Child health from birth (infant mortality; low birth weight). Health @ behaviour (nutrition x 2 and [dist., 2010]; physical activity [dist., 2010]; BMI); Health Problems (morbidity [dist., 2010]); Mortality rates (all, 0-19). Vaccinations (measles; DPT3; Pol3)	Child health from birth (infant mortality; low birth weight; breastfeeding x 2). Mortality rates (under 5; accidental). Vaccinations (DPT3; Pol3; measles). Health Problems (morbidity, respiratory; morbidity, diarrhoea; dental; stunting; underweight; wasting). Health behaviour (nutrition; physical activity)	Child health from birth (low birth weight; infant mortality; breastfeeding). Health behaviour (physical activity). Mortality rates (all, 0-19; suicide). Vaccinations (pertussis; measles)	Health Problems (BMI); Mortality rates (under 5)	Child health from birth (breastfeeding[c]; life expectancy[a]; infant mortality[b]; low birth weight[b]). Health behaviour (nutrition[b] - breakfast; nutrition[c] - 5 a day; dental[c] x 2; physical activity x 2[b,c]). Health Problems (BMI[b] and [c]; mental health[c]; morbidity – chronic[c]; morbidity – infectious[c]). Mortality rates (suicide[b]; suicide and self-harm 10-24[c]). Vaccinations[c]	Child health from birth (breastfeeding; low birth weight; infant mortality). Health behaviour (dental; nutrition x 2). Vaccinations	Child health from birth (AIDS transmission; infant mortality x 2 [inc. first day rate]; low birth weight). Health Problems (morbidity); Mortality rates (suicide; male youth motor accidents)	Child health from birth (breastfeeding; infant mortality; life expectancy; low birth weight). Health Problems (morbidity diabetes and asthma; BMI). Mortality rates (suicide). Vaccinations
Subjective well-being	Subjective well-being (life; peers x 3 [2007]; health).	Subjective well-being (health; life; peers x 3)				Subjective well-being (home[c]; school safety[c] x 2)	Subjective well-being (life)		
Personal family and peer relationships	Family relations (mother, 2009; father, 2009). Peer relations (classmates)	Family relations (meals; talking). Peer relations	Family relations (x 2). Peer relations (x 2).			Peer relations x 2[b,c]			
Material well-being and economic security	Income poverty (relative; gap). Deprivation (household x 2 [one in 2009]; educational items). Economic strain (2009). Jobless households	Average disposable income [dist., 2010]. Income poverty (relative; household x 2; educational items and [dist., 2010]). Jobless households	Income poverty (absolute). Deprivation (educational items x 2; household)	Average disposable income. Income poverty (relative). Deprivation (educational items)		Income poverty (relative[a]; relative gap[a]; persistent[a]; in-work[a]; anchored[c]; minimum income threshold[c]; absolute[c]). Economic strain[b]. Deprivation (educational items[b]; environment[b]; household[b]; ICT outside school[c]; services[c] x 2; services[b]; care services[b])	Income poverty (relative x 2). Deprivation (educational items; household x 2 [inc. severe forms])	Average disposable income; Income poverty (absolute x 2; poor earnings; poor transfers)	Average disposable income. Income poverty (relative)

Table 4.A.1. An overview of dimensions and indicators used in comparative child well-being analysis (cont.)

	European multidimensional indices (Bradshaw et al. 2007 and 2009)[1]	Unicef Report Cards 7 (2007) and 9 (2010)[1]	CEE CIS index (Richardson et al., 2008)	Doing Better for Children (OECD, 2009)	Save the children (2008 and 2012)[1]	European Commission Child poverty and Well-being (2008)[2]	European Commission TARKI (2010)	US Dept. of Commerce (Hobbs and Lippman, 1990)[3]	OECD Family Database (since 2007)
Educational Well-being	Educational achievement (reading; mathematics; science). Educational participation (youth; pre-primary). Aspirations (2007)	Aspirations. Educational achievement (reading; mathematics; science and [dist., 2010]). Educational participation (youth)	Educational achievement (reading; mathematics; science). Educational participation (pre-primary; primary; secondary).	Educational achievement (mean literacy; distribution)	Educational participation (primary)	Educational achievement (dist. in reading skills[c]; literacy[a]). Educational attainment (early leavers[a]; failure rate in lower secondary[c]; pass rates secondary[c]; failure rate in secondary[a]). Educational participation (truancy[a])	Educational achievement (literacy at 10; literacy at 15)	Educational participation. Educational attainment (x 2)	Educational attainment (years in; graduation rates). Educational achievement (literacy at 10; literacy at age 15)
Behaviour and risks	Risk behaviour (smoking; alcohol; drugs, cannabis; drugs, inhalants, [2007]). Sexual health (Fertility 15-19; active <15; safe sex). Violence and violent behaviour (fights; bullying)	Risk behaviour (smoking; alcohol; drugs). Sexual health (pregnancy 15-19; active <15; safe sex). Violence and violent behaviour (fights; bullied)	Crime (juvenile rate; petty). Risk behaviour (smoking; alcohol; drugs x 2). Sexual health (Fertility 15-19; safe sex x3; active <15). Violence and violent behaviour (bullied x 2).	Risk behaviour (smoking; alcohol). Sexual health (Fertility 15-19). Violence and violent behaviour (bullied)		Crime (offered drugs[c]; offending[c]; victimisation[c]). Risk behaviour (accidents x 2[b,c]; alcohol[c]; smoking x 3[c]; drugs[c]). Sexual health (pregnancy 15-19[b]; fertility 15-19[c]). Violence and violent behaviour (bullied[c]; experiences of[c])	Risk behaviour (smoking; alcohol x 2; drugs - illicit; drugs - medicinal)	Sexual health (abortions 15-24; pregnancy 15-19; fertility 15-19); Violence and violent behaviour (mortality)	Risk behaviour (smoking; drugs)
Housing and the local environment	Environment (crime; dirt, etc., 2009). Housing problems. Overcrowding	Overcrowding [dist., 2010].	Overcrowding. Housing problems (sanitation; water)	Overcrowding. Environment (dirt, etc.)		Environment (climate[c]; dirt, etc.[c]; play space < 5[b]; space for activities[c]). Housing problems[b] (comfort[b]; basic standards[b]). Overcrowding (space[b]; % of children[c]; own room[c] x 2)			

Table 4.A.1. An overview of dimensions and indicators used in comparative child well-being analysis (cont.)

	European multidimensional indices (Bradshaw et al. 2007 and 2009)[1]	Unicef Report Cards 7 (2007) and 9 (2010)[1]	CEE CIS index (Richardson et al., 2008)	Doing Better for Children (OECD, 2009)	Save the children (2008 and 2012)[1]	European Commission Child poverty and Well-being (2008)[2]	European Commission TARKI (2010)	US Dept. of Commerce (Hobbs and Lippman, 1990)[3]	OECD Family Database (since 2007)
Quality of school life	Well-being at school (pressure; enjoyment)	Well-being at school		Well-being at school (enjoyment)		Well-being at school[c]. Deprivation (education services[b] x 2; ICT at school[b]; school health services[c]; school food services[c])			
Family forms and care		Family form (single families; step families)	Family form (divorce). Child discipline (x 2). Children in care (foster; residential; infant homes).			Family form (break-ups[c])		Family form (early marriage; single youth; median age – marriage; median age – first birth)	
Social, economic and civic participation	Civic participation (x 2 in 2007). Youth employment (NEET)	Youth employment	Child labour	Youth employment (NEET)		Civic participation (social[b]). Youth employment (NEET[c])		Youth activity (employment x 2 [inc. by sector]; unemployment x 3)	Civic participation (voluntary work; voting). Youth employment (NEET)

Notes: 1) Indicators included in both studies have not been dated. "dist" refers to indicators presented as distributional measures; "x 2" means that multiple indicators of that type are included in the framework. 2) Indicators from the European Commission report are labelled with postfix "a" (commonly agreed EU indicators), "b" (not common EU indicators, but available across EU sources, and used by some EU countries), and "c" (alternatives to EU indicators used in some countries for which EU sources are not suited, EC, 2008). 3) Indicators for children above the age of 17 have been excluded.

Chapter 5

The value of giving: Volunteering and well-being

This chapter analyses the importance and features of volunteer work – i.e. the time devoted to unpaid non-compulsory activities whose concern is the common good – across OECD countries. The evidence shown in this chapter suggests that one in three adults volunteers through an organisation at least once a year. This proportion is potentially higher when informal help to friends, neighbours and strangers is considered. Volunteering produces benefits not only for the beneficiaries but also for the volunteers themselves: volunteering helps people to acquire skills and knowledge that may enhance career development or employment prospects, and is also associated with higher levels of life satisfaction and positive moods. Moreover, volunteering is beneficial to society at large and plays an important economic role. The lack of a standard definition and of comparable data makes it difficult to paint a definitive picture of the level and extent of volunteer work in the OECD area; the main steps to be implemented in order to improve the measurement of volunteering are discussed.

Introduction: Why volunteering matters for well-being

Volunteering matters a great deal for people's well-being, and it impacts on many of the dimensions used in the *How's Life?* framework. First, the goods and services produced by volunteers contribute to households' material conditions and well-being. Second, most volunteering is typically undertaken in the sectors of social provision, health care, education, environmental preservation or development cooperation, which often target the homeless, migrants, and others who are very poor and disadvantaged. This means that volunteering can be expected to affect many of the quality-of-life dimensions included in *How's Life?* – such as health status, skills and competencies, and environmental quality – by both increasing the levels of these outcomes overall, and by narrowing inequalities in their distribution. Third, volunteering is both an important type of "work" (based on the third-party criterion, i.e. an activity undertaken by others) and an activity that is personally rewarding, undertaken as a form of leisure or civic participation.

Who benefits from volunteering? The most obvious beneficiaries are those receiving the goods and services produced by volunteering. These are often people who are hard to reach through conventional social programmes, and who lack the resources to purchase basic goods and services on the market. But volunteering also benefits the volunteers themselves. Volunteering is a tool for the integration of youth facing difficult situations or of seniors after retirement. For those who suffer social isolation and exclusion, volunteering allows them to participate in the life of the community as valued and valuable citizens. For older people, it can ensure a successful transition from paid employment to retirement.

Volunteering has been found to have a positive impact on the physical and mental health of the people engaged in it, helping working-age people to acquire the hard and soft skills that enhance their career development or employment prospects. Time spent volunteering is also more associated than other unpaid work activities with higher life satisfaction and more positive moods. Once these advantages – in terms of health, skills, subjective well-being – are factored in, the benefits of volunteering for the volunteers might be as large, if not larger, than those for the recipients.

Volunteering also benefits society at large. As an expression of a vibrant civil society, volunteering helps create social capital, building and consolidating bonds of trust and cooperation, while cultivating norms of altruism, solidarity, civic mindfulness and respect for diversity (Putnam, 1995, 2000). In other terms, volunteering is an essential component of the fabric of a "good society".

The subject of volunteering has gained widespread public and political interest in recent years. Policy debates have taken place in many countries on how to preserve and encourage volunteering, or whether to establish quasi-mandatory civic service programmes for young people. Various government commissions have studied ways to stimulate volunteering among diverse groups such as the young and adults aged 50 and over, working parents and immigrants (Box 5.1). However, despite the political momentum and a number of international initiatives, little sustained effort has gone into measuring the scope, scale and impacts of volunteering.

This chapter attempts to partly address this gap, drawing on existing comparative information. The chapter is organised as follows. First, the main challenges in defining and measuring volunteering are outlined, before introducing the indicators that are used for the empirical analysis. The prevalence, frequency and distribution of volunteering in OECD countries are then described, while the section that follows investigates some of the linkages between volunteering and various well-being outcomes, and presents a rough estimate of the economic value of volunteering activities. Some of the statistical gaps that should be filled to provide a better understanding of volunteering are then identified.

Box 5.1. **Volunteering in policy debates**

In its 2001 recommendations on support for volunteering, the United Nations General Assembly identified volunteering as "an important component of any strategy aimed at ... poverty reduction, sustainable development, health, disaster prevention and management and ... overcoming social exclusion and discrimination" (United Nations, 2001). In 2008, the European Parliament spoke of volunteering as "[the] most sustainable form of renewable energy" and encouraged Member States and regional and local authorities to "recognise [its] value ... in promoting social and economic cohesion" (European Parliament, 2008). The year 2011 was declared the European Year of Volunteering by the European Commission, in an effort to "raise awareness of the value and importance of volunteering" (Council of the European Union, 2009).

National governments have also been progressively encouraging volunteering as a means to improve well-being, engage citizens in society and meet the demand for new services and needs. In many countries, governments have increasingly focused on providing opportunities for voluntary engagement by citizens (e.g. the British government's "Big Society" initiative, the French "Service Civique", and the Danish "Social Service Act") and they have launched widespread educational campaigns on the benefits of voluntary work.

Defining and measuring volunteering

Defining volunteering

A teacher volunteering for an extra-curricular after-school activity, a factory worker giving some of her time to restore a social housing building, a teenager shovelling an elderly neighbour's walkway, a professional lawyer providing legal assistance to people who cannot afford it: all of these are examples of volunteering. The very diversity of these activities, ranging from the distribution of flyers once a year to being a full-time volunteer worker all year-round, makes defining what specifically constitutes volunteering a very challenging task.

Being a relatively "new" subject of inquiry, volunteering has been conceptualised in many different ways. Definitions differ in terms of both scope and exhaustiveness: some combine voluntary work and charitable activities, blurring the distinction between donations of time and donations of money. Some include informal activities, while others are restricted to volunteering in organisations or, in some cases, in non-profit organisations or in organisations in which the volunteer is a member.

A broad perspective on volunteering has been provided by the Conference of European Statisticians, which proposed a framework for measuring volunteering in 2013 based on the distinction between *volunteer work* (i.e. an activity that could have been performed by others) and *participatory actions*. The latter include activities beyond "work" that do not produce services for which demand exists or that cannot be performed on one's behalf by another person. These "participatory actions" may involve the provision of either time or money. In the approach proposed by the Conference of European Statisticians, the common feature of the activities that fall under the umbrella term of "volunteering" is that they all aim to increase the common good and that they are neither mandatory nor paid. All of the empirical evidence in this chapter refers to "volunteer work", i.e. it excludes various forms of "participatory actions".

One critical element of volunteering is the provision of work. The International Labour Organization's *Manual on the Measurement of Volunteer Work* defines volunteer work as "[un]paid non-compulsory work; that is, time individuals give without pay to activities performed either *through an organisation* or *directly* for others outside their own household" (ILO, 2011).[1] This definition – which provides the conceptual framework for measuring volunteering in various cultural and legal settings – differentiates volunteer work from leisure activities by the criterion that volunteer work must generate goods or services that have value to people other than the volunteers themselves. It also differentiates volunteering from paid work by emphasising that this work is unpaid and performed without any legally sanctioned compulsion.

One way to further categorise all types of volunteering activities is by their degree of formality (Wilson and Musick, 1997). *Formal volunteering* (referred to as "indirect volunteer work" by the ILO) consists in activities undertaken *through organisations* (e.g. non-profit institutions or private companies). Examples include collecting money for an NGO, or working for associations, schools, nurseries, neighbourhood groups or committees, etc. *Informal volunteering* (referred to as "direct volunteer work" by the ILO) relates instead to informal help *for other households*.[2] This includes looking after children, cleaning and tidying up, helping in legal matters, counselling and advising about problems, caring for the elderly/ill, looking after pets, preparing meals, etc. (Lee and Brudney, 2012). Helping those who are in need is an important aspect of both formal and informal volunteering, and activities carried out toward this end can be very similar in the two settings.

Measuring volunteering

Volunteering and the System of National Accounts

The challenges to measurement are not only conceptual. Data on volunteering are scarce and fragmented, and cross-country comparability is limited. Within the System of National Accounts (SNA) – the set of international guidelines used by countries when compiling national economic statistics – non-profit institutions (NPIs) are classified as either "market producers" (included in the corporate sector), when the income they gain from fees and charges covers most of their costs, or as "non-market producers", and included in either the government sector (when they are financed and controlled by government) or else separately identified as Non-Profit Institutions Serving Households (NPISH). In each of these cases, national account measures of the value added by non-profit institutions are limited to the monetary costs of running these institutions. Since 1968, the SNA distinguishes NPISH from households in the narrower sense, although not all countries separately report measures referring to NPISH in all their economic accounts. As a significant part of the economic activity of NPIs is included in the accounts for the corporate sector and general government, leaving only a fraction visible in the NPISH sector, it is difficult to get a clear appreciation of the economic scale and composition of the non-profit sector. In addition, the SNA only measures the value of *paid* work in the NPISH sector, hence missing much of the economic contribution of these institutions.

To uncover the economic activities of these "hidden" NPIs, in 2003 the United Nations Statistical Commission approved the *Handbook on Non-profit Institutions in the System of National Accounts (UN NPI Handbook)*, developed by the Johns Hopkins Center for Civil Society Studies in cooperation with the UN Statistics Division and an international team of experts (United Nations, 2003). The Handbook offered a set of guidelines for identifying the NPIs "hidden" in the economic accounts of each institutional sector. It also called upon countries to take these NPIs "out" of the sectors to which they had been allocated, and to include data on them into an NPI *satellite account*, which would also record the value of *unpaid* volunteer work that these NPIs use (Table 5.1).[3] NPI satellite accounts offer a comprehensive way to generate reliable and comparable data on the economic importance of NPIs. Close to 40 countries have now committed to implementing the UN NPI Handbook, and 16 of them have completed at least an initial NPI satellite account.

Table 5.1. **Treatment of non-profit institutions in the NPI satellite account of the System of National Accounts**

ACCOUNT	SECTORS OF THE SNA									NON-PROFIT SECTOR
	Non-financial corporations sector		Financial corporations sector		General government sector		Household sector		NPISH sector	
	(S.11)		(S.12)		(S.13)		(S.14)		(S.15)	
	Total	NPIs	Total	NPIs	Total	NPIs	Total	NPIs	NPIs	
Production										ΣN_i
Generation of income										
Assets										ΣNi

Source: United Nations (2003), *Handbook on Non-profit Institutions in the System of National Accounts*, United Nations Publication, Sales No. E.03.XVII.9 ST/ESA/STAT/SER.F/91, New York, *http://unstats.un.org/unsd/publication/seriesf/seriesf_91e.pdf*.

On average, the size of the NPI sector described through the NPI satellite account is twice as large as that of the non-profit institutions serving households which is visible through standard 1993 SNA methods. In Canada, the NPI sector is nearly five times larger than what was formerly visible through standard SNA methods. Changes introduced in the 2008 revision of the System of National Accounts (2008 SNA) – which require national statistical agencies to distinguish between NPI and non-NPI components in the core accounts, and to report the NPI sub-totals separately – should make the production of NPI satellite accounts easier in the future.

Volunteering in Labour Force Surveys

In 2009, the 18th International Conference of Labour Statisticians (ICLS) stressed "the importance of measuring volunteer work" not only "to acknowledge [its] significant contribution in disaster assistance, rural education and other programmes" but also because of the importance of such measurement "for labour statistics, as one of the objectives of these statistics is to measure all aspects of labour" (ILO, 2009). As a follow-up, in 2013 the

19th International Conference of Labour Statisticians adopted a resolution that expanded the concept of work to distinguish between its different forms, with the goal *inter alia* to highlight the "contribution of all forms of work to economic development, to households' livelihoods and to the well-being of individuals and society". Volunteer work is one of the five forms of work that statistical offices are invited to identify and measure (Box 5.2).

Box 5.2. **Volunteer work in the 19th International Conference of Labour Statisticians resolution**

In 2013, the ICLS proposed new standards for measuring "work", asking National Statistical Offices to report on five mutually exclusive forms of work (Table 5.2): a) *own-use production work*, comprising production of goods and services for own final use; b) *employment work*, comprising work performed for pay or profit; c) *unpaid trainee work*, comprising work performed without pay to acquire workplace experience or skills; d) *volunteer work*, comprising non-compulsory work performed for others without pay; and e) *other work activities* (not defined in the resolution).

Table 5.2. **Forms of work and the System of National Accounts 2008**

Intended destination of production	For own final use		For use by others					
Forms of work	Own-use production work		Employment (work for pay or profit)	Unpaid trainee work	Other work activities	Volunteer work		
	of services	of goods				in market and non-market units	in households producing	
							goods	services
Relation to 2008 SNA		Activities within the SNA production boundary						
	Activities inside the SNA General production boundary							

Source: International Labour Organization (ILO) (2013), *Report of the Conference. 19th International Conference of Labour Statisticians*, Geneva, 2-11 October 2013, *www.ilo.org/wcmsp5/groups/public/---dgreports/---stat/documents/normativeinstrument/wcms_230304.pdf*.

The resolution defines **persons in volunteer work** as all people of working age who, during a short reference period, performed any unpaid, non-compulsory activity to produce goods or provide services for others, where: i) "any activity" refers to work for at least one hour; ii) "unpaid" is interpreted as the absence of remuneration in cash or in kind for work done, with the exception of some small form of support or stipend in cash or in kind; iii) "non-compulsory" is interpreted as work carried out without civil, legal or administrative requirements that are different from the fulfilment of social responsibilities of a communal, cultural or religious nature; and iv) production "for others" refers to work performed either through organisations comprising market and non-market units or for households other than the household of the volunteer worker or of related family members (i.e. direct volunteering).

It should be noted that this definition of volunteer work differs from that provided in the *ILO Manual on the Measurement of Volunteer Work*, as it excludes unpaid work done for "family members living in other households"; this narrower definition reflects the view that informal caring is often considered obligatory, rather than voluntary, when the recipient is a family member, even when they belong to a separate household (e.g. older parents living alone).

By recognising volunteering as a form of "work", the 2013 ICLS resolution opened the door to making the gathering and reporting of basic data on volunteering standard, and strengthened the case for developing and adopting "supplements" to national labour force surveys (LFS) or other household surveys on a periodic basis, as recommended by the *ILO Manual on the Measurement of Volunteer Work*. Because of the characteristics of national

LFS (frequent and regular collection; large sample size; compulsory participation in many countries; highly professional administration), data collected through special modules of these can be used to determine the amount of various kinds of volunteer work (e.g. by institutional and economic sector, by form of activity, by region or level of urbanisation of the area where it is delivered, etc.) and to identify the demographic profile of volunteers (e.g. age, gender, income level, education, urban or rural residence, paid occupation if any).[4]

Unfortunately, as of today, only a few countries (e.g. Poland, Hungary, Switzerland and Italy) have fielded the LFS ad hoc module,[5] while others are working towards its implementation (e.g. Belgium, Ireland) or are exploring ways to make their existing data-gathering on volunteering comparable with the ILO methodology (e.g. the United Kingdom and Germany).

Volunteering in social and time use surveys

No international survey exists that is specifically designed to measure volunteering. Most evidence on volunteering is national-based, relying on surveys that have different definitions, sampling frames and reference periods. This makes it difficult to compare the numbers and profile of volunteers across countries based on these surveys.[6] At the international level, questions about participation in volunteer activities are typically included in surveys addressing a wide range of other topics. Also, these surveys rely on small samples and on diverse and often not comparable methodologies, and are exposed to the risk of being cancelled or delayed in times of tight budget constraints (Rochester, Paine and Howlett, 2009). Research has shown that volunteers are more likely than the general population to respond to small-scale surveys and opinion polls; as a result, small-scale surveys or opinion polls may lead to an over-estimation of the scale of volunteering relative to larger-scale official surveys (Pew Research Center, 2015).[7]

Moreover, international surveys most often rely on catch-all questions that could be interpreted differently by different respondents, rather than building on the ICLS definition of volunteer work.[8] An example of the type of question often used in general social surveys is: "In the past 12 months did you do unpaid voluntary work for an organisation?" Stand-alone questions such as this one place only a minimum burden on the respondent. However, data quality problems arise when using a direct question on volunteering that is not introduced by a short lead-in text helping to fix the concept of unpaid volunteer work in the mind of the respondent (Toppe and Groves, 2007).[9] Another important limitation is that survey questions treat volunteering as a uniform category, whereas in reality the phenomenon to be captured is a complex one.[10] As a consequence, even simple statistics on the share of the population engaged in volunteering have significant margins of uncertainty.

While questions on engagement in formal volunteering generally follow a quite standard phrasing, questions on informal help are more likely to vary across surveys. Some include help to family members living outside the household (e.g. older parents) in the list of activities; others refer only to help provided to friends, acquaintances and strangers.

Some surveys go beyond general questions about volunteering, defined in one way or another, to include a list of prompts about the types of organisations or activities to which people devote their time, as well as questions about the motivations for volunteering. However, only a few of these surveys ask questions about the amount of time spent on volunteer work.[11]

An additional source for analysing volunteer work is Time Use Surveys (TUS). These surveys collect information on the amount of time people allocate to their everyday activities. In these surveys, participants describe their daily activities in their own words in a diary over a reference period (usually a day or a week); activities are then grouped by the organisation undertaking the survey, and volunteer work, both direct and organisation-based, is typically included as one of the main categories (Miranda, 2011). The diary method reduces the risk that respondents are influenced by social desirability, thus offering a credible way to collect accurate information on individuals' behaviour, but it may impose a large burden on respondents.[12]

In terms of the measurement of volunteer activities, TUS typically generate three types of data: i) population-wide estimates of the average time spent on a standard list of activities, including both organisation-based and direct volunteering; ii) estimates of the average time spent by participants in those activities; and iii) participation rates, i.e. the share of the population reporting these activities. Although the definition and classification of activities used in national surveys are usually similar to those in the International Classification of Activities for Time Use (ICATUS) – which has 15 major groups, each with 2 to 5 subgroups – there are persistent differences in terms of survey features, the number of diary days sampled, and the categorisation of activities. The recent release of the UNECE *Guidelines for Harmonising Time Use Surveys* should help to improve cross-country comparability in this field (UNECE, 2013).

The general presumption is that TUS are more reliable than general surveys in recording information on the amount of time that individuals spend volunteering.[13] However, volunteering may be heavily concentrated in specific periods of time; it follows that people may happen not to volunteer on the day they are sampled, so the TUS is thus likely to underestimate participation in volunteering. Moreover, as TUS are conducted with low frequency, they tend to produce information that often becomes outdated over time.

In summary, data on volunteering are either in their infancy (i.e. satellite accounts and ad hoc modules of LFS) or unable to elicit accurate information on the various facets of volunteer work (i.e. social surveys and TUS). The lack of systematic comparative data on volunteering makes it difficult to generate support for and design policies that bolster volunteering efforts.

Choice of indicators and data sources to measure volunteering

Despite data constraints and methodological issues, this section uses existing information to provide some estimates of the scale and features of volunteering. The focus of the empirical analysis presented in this section is on volunteer work (rather than on other types of participatory actions, such as donations), based on the definition adopted in the ICLS. In some cases, however, this definition is adjusted to fit the available data. Both formal and informal aspects of volunteering are investigated, although most of the available information relates to activities undertaken through an organisation. As the nature of involvement may change as people move through their lives, the analysis also assesses attitudes towards volunteering for different population groups: students as well as working-age and older people.

In the absence of international surveys that focus specifically on volunteering, and reflecting the limited country-coverage of satellite accounts and ad hoc LFS modules on volunteering, the evidence presented below is mainly drawn from "secondary" sources, such as social surveys and time use surveys. To shed light on various aspects of volunteering, this chapter makes use of a wide range of sources. The possible discrepancies between different surveys and studies imply that the statistical analysis of volunteering is open to interpretation and should be seen as indicative only. For instance, it will not be possible to state conclusively that volunteering rates are lower among older people than among the working-age population, as the evidence for these two groups draws on different surveys.

Evidence on the prevalence and frequency of formal volunteering is drawn from the OECD Survey of Adult Skills (PIAAC). The PIAAC survey covers 20 OECD countries (Australia, Austria, Canada, the Czech Republic, Denmark, Estonia, Finland, France, Germany, Ireland, Italy, Japan, Korea, the Netherlands, Norway, Poland, the Slovak Republic, Spain, Sweden and the United States), three OECD sub-national entities (Flanders in Belgium; England and Northern Ireland in the United Kingdom), as well as the Russian Federation (OECD, 2013). Although the main focus of this survey is on the skills and competencies of the working-age population, it also includes a question on volunteering, asking respondents whether they did volunteer work in the preceding 12 months, including unpaid work for a charity, a political party, a trade union or other non-profit organisation. The possible answers are: i) never; ii) less than once a month; iii) less than once a week but at least once a month; iv) at least once a week but nor every day; and v) every day.[14]

Participation rates for informal help are computed for European countries alone using the well-being module of the 3rd wave of the European Social Survey (ESS), which contains a question on informal help: "Not counting anything you do for your family, in your work, or within voluntary organisations, how often, in the past 12 months, did you actively provide help for other people?" The possible answers are: i) at least once a week; ii) at least once a month; iii) at least once every three months; iv) at least once every six months; v) less often; and vi) never.[15] Information on the amount of time devoted to both formal volunteering and informal help is gathered through the OECD Time Use Database.[16]

The PIAAC survey focuses on the working-age population, leaving aside other population groups that make important contributions to the volunteer sector: students and older people. To take into account the contribution of these two groups, additional data sources are considered below:

● The International Civic and Citizenship Study (ICCS), a comparative research programme of the International Association for the Evaluation of Educational Achievement (IEA) covering 23 OECD countries (Austria, Belgium, Chile, the Czech Republic, Denmark, Estonia, Finland, Greece, Ireland, Italy, Korea, Luxembourg, Mexico, the Netherlands, New Zealand, Norway, Poland, the Slovak Republic, Slovenia, Spain, Sweden, Switzerland and the United Kingdom), as well as 15 non-OECD countries. The ICSS is used to assess the participation in volunteer activities of students aged around 14 (i.e. in Grade 8 or equivalent). Students are asked whether they have ever volunteered in an organisation (i.e. youth organisation, environmental organisation, human rights organisation, fund-raising organisation, cultural organisation, or youth campaigning). To improve the comparison of volunteering rates among students with the rates among adults and the older population, the analysis is restricted to students who declare that they have volunteered at least once in the 12 months preceding the interview.

● The Survey of Health, Ageing and Retirement in Europe (SHARE)[17] provides evidence on different aspects of the life of people aged 50 years or more in 18 European OECD countries (Austria, Belgium, the Czech Republic, Denmark, Estonia, France, Germany,

Hungary, Israel, Italy, Luxembourg, the Netherlands, Poland, Portugal, Slovenia, Spain, Sweden and Switzerland).[18] The question on formal volunteering is: "Have you done any of these activities in the last 12 months: voluntary or charity work"; while information on informal help is based on the question: "In the last 12 months, have you personally given personal care or practical household help to a family member living outside your household, a friend or neighbour?"

Complementary information on volunteering (e.g. field of activity) as well as on the relationships between volunteering and various well-being outcomes for the volunteers is drawn from the European/World Value Survey (EVS/WVS) and the Gallup World Poll. These surveys allow for full country-coverage, but suffer from small sample sizes and other methodological issues. Table 5.3 provides an overview of the statistical quality of the different sources used in the next section to assess volunteering in OECD countries.

Table 5.3. **The quality of various data sources on volunteering**

Indicator	Source	Statistical quality			
		Well-established instrument collected	Comparable definition (ILO)	Country coverage	Latest available year
Formal volunteering (prevalence rates)	PIAAC	~	√	~	2012
	ESS	~	√	~	2006
	EQLS	~	√	~	2012
	Eurobarometer	~	√	~	2012
	Gallup World Poll	X	√	√	2014
	EVS/WVS	X	√	√	2008
	OECD Time Use Database	√	~	√	1 data point from 1999 to 2013
Informal volunteering (prevalence rates)	PIAAC	~	~	~	2012
	ESS	~	√	~	2006
	EQLS	~	X	~	2012
	Eurobarometer	~	~	~	2012
	Gallup World Poll	X	~	√	2014
	EVS/WVS	X	X	√	2008
	OECD Time Use Database	√	~	√	1 data point from 1999 to 2013
Frequency of volunteering	PIAAC	~	~	~	2012
	ESS	~	~	~	2006
	EQLS	~	~	~	2012
	Eurobarometer	~	~	~	2012
	Gallup World Poll	X	X	√	2014
	EVS/WVS	X	X	√	2008
	OECD Time Use Database	√	~	√	1 data point from 1999 to 2013

Note: The symbol √ shows that the indicator selected meets the criterion shown in the table; the symbol ~ that the indicator meets the criterion to a large extent; the symbol X that the indicator does not meet the criterion or it meets it only to a limited extent.

StatLink ᠍ᡕ᠍ http://dx.doi.org/10.1787/888933260112

Evidence on volunteering

Prevalence and frequency of volunteering

Figure 5.1 below shows that, on average, across OECD countries, about one in three adults reports having volunteered through an organisation in the past 12 months, with the share ranging from 18% in Spain and the Czech Republic to more than 55% in the

United States and Norway. These results are in line with previous research (e.g. Plagnol and Huppert, 2010), which has reported higher volunteering rates in the Nordic and English-speaking countries, and lower ones in Southern and Eastern Europe. The general finding that formal volunteering rates are higher in English-speaking countries seems to hold also at the regional level. In particular, for Canada, when English- and French-speaking respondents of the PIAAC survey are considered separately, volunteering rates stand at 52% and 36% respectively.[19]

Figure 5.1. **Participation rates in formal volunteering**

Percentage of the working-age population who declared having volunteered through an organisation in the preceding 12 months, by frequency, 2012

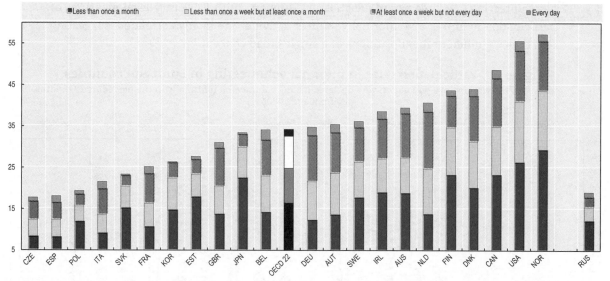

Note: Data for Belgium refer to Flanders; data for England and Northern Ireland are presented combined (GBR). Data for the Russian Federation exclude the Moscow municipal area.

Source: OECD calculations based on data from OECD (2012), OECD Survey of Adult Skills (PIAAC database), *www.oecd.org/site/piaac/*.

StatLink ⟨⟩ http://dx.doi.org/10.1787/888933259909

Countries also differ in the frequency with which formal volunteer work takes place (Figure 5.1). In Norway, where the prevalence of volunteering is highest, only 3.2% of volunteers declare having spent time in volunteer activities on a daily basis over the preceding 12 months. The largest share of those who volunteer every day is recorded in Spain (9.5%), where the overall prevalence of volunteering is low (less than one in five people does any voluntary activity). Many volunteers report doing voluntary work only sporadically (less than once a month), with the rate ranging from 34% in the Netherlands to 67% in Japan. The share of those who volunteer at least once a week is lowest in Japan (9%) and highest in the Netherlands (34%).

Volunteering for organisations is not the only way in which people provide time and energy for unpaid non-compulsory activities whose concern is the common good. Evidence from the European Social Survey shows that informal volunteering is widespread in OECD European countries where, on average, seven in ten individuals of working-age report having provided some form of informal help to people other than family members, such as friends, neighbours and strangers (Figure 5.2). The rates are below the OECD average in most Southern and Eastern European countries, while in the Nordic countries around 90% of respondents declare having spent time in informal volunteer activities over the preceding

12 months. In terms of frequency, on average, half of those who volunteer informally do so on a regular basis (once a month or once a week), with this percentage being highest in Germany (70%) and lowest in Portugal (26%).

The low rates of informal volunteering observed in Southern and Eastern European countries may be partly due to the fact that in these countries, which are characterised by tight family bonds and low welfare services, care for older parents and pre-school children is provided mostly by other family members (e.g. daughters and grandparents) and is not reported by respondents as a form of informal volunteering (Dykstra and Fokkema, 2011; Hank, 2007). Moreover, besides social, psychological and cultural aspects, it is also likely that contextual factors such as a country's historical background determine levels of volunteering to a large extent (Plagnol and Huppert, 2010).[20] Country-level measures of participation in formal and informal volunteer activities are highly correlated, suggesting that they are different manifestations of a single broad concept.[21]

Figure 5.2. **Participation rates in informal volunteering in European countries**

Percentage of the working-age population who declared having volunteered informally in the preceding 12 months, by frequency, 2006

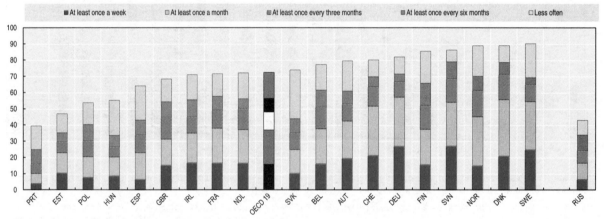

Source: OECD calculations based on data from the European Social Survey (2006), European Social Survey Round 3 Data, Data file edition 3.5. (database), Norwegian Social Science Data Services, Norway – Data Archive and distributor of ESS data, *www.europeansocialsurvey.org/*.

StatLink ⚊ *http://dx.doi.org/10.1787/888933259919*

The use of different sources seriously hampers data comparability and does not enable a direct comparison of the participation rates in formal volunteer activities shown in Figure 5.1 with the participation rates in informal help shown in Figure 5.2. However, it is possible to compute participation rates in formal volunteering based on data from the European Social Survey. Although those rates do not match exactly those from the PIAAC survey, the country ranking is broadly similar, with Nordic and English-speaking countries showing higher participation rates in formal volunteer activities than their Southern and Eastern European peers. Moreover, when participation rates in informal help and formal volunteer activities are both computed on data drawn from the European Social Survey, the former are consistently higher than the latter ones, suggesting that in the OECD area informal helpers are potentially more numerous than formal volunteers.

Data on the frequency of volunteering gathered through the type of international surveys used above give only a rough idea of the *amount of time* dedicated to volunteer work. Additional information on this aspect can be obtained from Time Use Surveys, which are available for a number of OECD countries. As not everybody volunteers, it is interesting to look at the time spent on formal and informal volunteer activities by the *entire population* (within the 15-64 age category; Figure 5.3, left vertical axis) alongside the time spent on those activities by those who report volunteer work in their time use diaries, which is used here as a proxy for *those who actually perform the activity* in a given day (Figure 5.3, right vertical axis). With respect to the first aspect, little time is spent on average on formal volunteering by the population as a whole, ranging from less than 5 minutes per day in most OECD countries to 13 minutes in New Zealand. The picture is different when considering the average amount of time spent by those who actually volunteer time in a given day. Indeed, in this case, the time spent per day on formal volunteer work ranges from less than one hour per day in Mexico to nearly three hours per day in Belgium, Japan and Italy. Across the OECD countries considered, on days that people volunteer, they devote on average more than two hours per day to formal voluntary work (Figure 5.3, Panel A).

Figure 5.3. **Time spent in formal and informal volunteering**
Average minutes of volunteering per day, by all respondents and by volunteers only, among people aged 15-64

Panel A: Formal volunteering, 2013 or latest available year

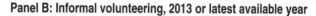

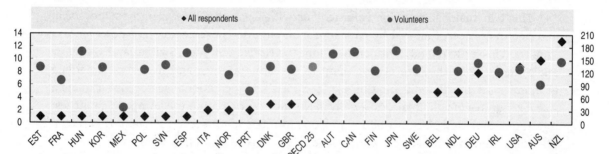

Panel B: Informal volunteering, 2013 or latest available year

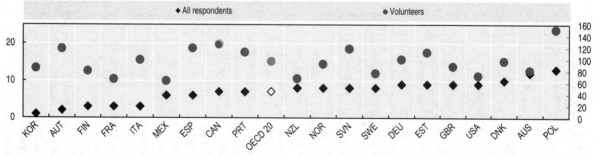

Note: Countries are ranked in ascending order of time allocated to formal volunteering (Panel A) and informal volunteering (Panel B) by all respondents. Data refer to 2013 for the United States; 2011 for Japan; 2010 for Canada; 2009-10 for Estonia, Finland, New Zealand and Spain; 2009 for Korea and Mexico; 2008-08 for Austria, France and Italy; 2006 for Australia; 2005-06 for the Netherlands; 2005 for Belgium, Ireland, and the United Kingdom; 2003-04 for Poland; 2001-02 for Germany; 2001 for Denmark; 2000-01 for Norway, Slovenia and Sweden; 1999-2000 for Hungary and 1999 for Portugal. Data refer to respondents aged 20 to 74 for Belgium, Germany, Norway, Poland, Slovenia and Sweden; to respondents aged 15 and over for Australia; and to respondents aged 10 and over for Korea.

Source: OECD calculations based on the Harmonised European Time Use Survey web application, *https://www.h2.scb.se/tus/tus/;* Eurostat *Time Use Database, http://appsso.eurostat.ec.europa.eu/nui/show.do?dataset=tus_00selfstat&lang=en;* public-use time use survey micro-data; and tabulations from national statistical offices.

StatLink ᴍ⬚⬚ᴨ *http://dx.doi.org/10.1787/888933259929*

In terms of informal volunteering, the population at large across the OECD countries considered spends on average 7 minutes per day helping other households' members informally. Little time is spent in Korea (1 minute per day), while in Poland people devote 13 minutes per day to informal help (Figure 5.3, Panel B). The length of time spent in informal volunteering by those who perform this activity also varies greatly across countries. In France and Mexico, the time spent by volunteers in informal voluntary work (67 and 64 minutes, respectively) is well below the OECD average of more than one hour and a half; at the other end of the spectrum, in Spain and Canada, volunteers devote more than two hours per day to informal activities (Figure 5.3, Panel B). These findings suggest that a small group of people is responsible for the vast majority of both formal and informal volunteering. While this emphasises the generosity of the so-called "civic core", it also highlights the vulnerability of the volunteer sector, in that it heavily relies on a small group of individuals.

Information on the sectors where volunteers are most active can be obtained through the 2008 European/World Values Survey (EVS/WVS). Based on this source, volunteers are mainly active in the social and health services; education and culture; social movements (i.e. environment, human rights, peace, women's rights); and sports and recreation (Figure 5.4).

The two main sectors for volunteer activities across OECD countries are social and health services, followed by education and culture. Those sectors are however less important in Northern and Continental Europe (i.e. Norway, Sweden, Switzerland, Germany and France), while they are predominant in the United States and in several emerging economies (i.e. Brazil, India and China). The sports and recreational sector also attracts a sizeable number of volunteers, especially in Northern and Continental European countries: in Iceland, Germany, Norway and Ireland, one in three volunteers is active in this sector. The social movements sector is widespread in South Africa and in a number of Southern European countries (e.g. Greece and Spain).

Figure 5.4. **Distribution of volunteers by field of activity**
Percentage of volunteers, 2008 or latest available year

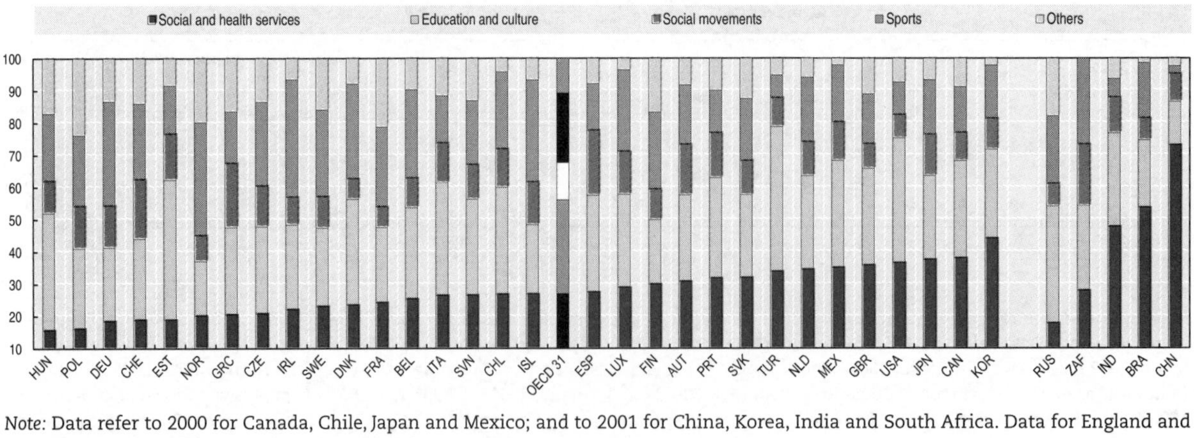

Note: Data refer to 2000 for Canada, Chile, Japan and Mexico; and to 2001 for China, Korea, India and South Africa. Data for England and Northern Ireland are presented combined (GBR).

Source: OECD calculations based on data from the European Values Survey (2011), European Values Study 2008, Integrated Dataset (EVS 2008), Data file version 3.0.0, GESIS Data Archive, http://dx.doi.org/10.4232/1.11004, for European countries; and the World Values Survey Association (2009), World Values Survey, Wave 5 2005-2008, Official Aggregate v.20140429, World Values Survey Association (database), www.worldvaluessurvey.org, for non-European countries.

StatLink ⏹⏺🔗 http://dx.doi.org/10.1787/888933259931

The socio-demographic profile of the volunteers

Many factors underpin people's decisions to volunteer. These include traditional socio-demographic characteristics such as income, education and health (Schlozman, Burns and Verba, 1994; Day and Devlin, 1998) but also subjective dispositions, attitudes and social roles (Curtis, Baer and Grabb, 2001). The propensity to volunteer also varies over different stages of the life cycle (Erlinghagen, 2010; Oesterle, Johnson and Mortimer, 2004; Tang, 2006). Tables 5.A.1 and 5.A.2 in the Annex provide an overview of the socio-demographic characteristics of volunteers for the OECD area in the formal and informal sectors, respectively.[22] Figures 5.5 and 5.6 show the participation rates and prevalence of regular (i.e. more often than once a month) volunteering for various population groups.[23]

With respect to formal volunteering (Figure 5.5 and Table 5.A.1 in the Annex), men and women tend to volunteer at fairly similar rates, even though they engage in different types of activities (men are much more likely than women to volunteer in sports associations, while women volunteer predominantly in the social and health sectors).[24] Age has an effect on both the decision to volunteer and the time commitment. Those aged 25 to 34 volunteer the least, followed by adults aged 55 to 65 (34%). This suggests an inverted U-shape for the relationship between age and volunteering up to age 65: from young adulthood (25-34) the incidence of volunteer work increases, reaching a peak between the ages of about 35 to 55, and then declines again among pre-retirees (Wilson, 2000).[25]

Volunteering increases strongly with people's education (Erlinghagen, 2010; Hank and Erlinghagen, 2010; Hank and Stuck, 2008). Several factors contribute to this pattern. First, education provides the cognitive skills that are necessary for many volunteering tasks but also fosters civic values.[26] Second, the highly educated have larger social networks and are therefore more likely to know members of associations (Bekkers et al., 2007; McPherson, Popielarz and Drobnic, 1992). Since "being asked" is an important incentive to join an organisation (Oesterle, Johnson and Mortimer, 2004; Prouteau and Wolff, 2008), this tends to boost participation within circles of highly educated people.[27] Figure 5.5 (and Table 5.A.1 in the Annex) confirms that people with a university degree are twice as likely to volunteer (48%) as those with primary education (24%).

Education and income are strongly related; it hence follows that participation in formal volunteering increases with household income. For instance, while one individual in four among those with low household income reports having volunteered in the previous 12 months, this proportion almost doubles among higher-income people (Table 5.A.1 in the Annex). In addition, people working part-time, or even full-time, volunteer in larger proportions than inactive individuals.[28] Country-based research shows, however, that part-time or full-time employees tend to volunteer less hours on average than the unemployed or those not in the labour force (Vézina and Crompton, 2012).

Married or common-law couples are more likely than singles to volunteer in formal settings. Another factor increasing participation in formal volunteering is having school-aged children (i.e. aged 4 to 17) in the household. Many parents of school-aged children participate in school and after-school activities (Gee, 2011)[29] as a way of investing in the human capital of their offspring (Albertini and Radl, 2012). Figure 5.5 confirms that parents of school-aged children have higher rates of volunteering (39%) than both people without children (35%) and parents with younger children in the household (32%).

In an increasingly multicultural society, volunteering may represent a vehicle for integrating immigrants and promoting the values of inclusive citizenship. Immigrant volunteers are also of significant benefit to the volunteer sector, as they can broaden the organisational and linguistic capacity and add new outlooks and perspectives to an organisation. Figure 5.5 shows that immigrants are less likely than their native-born counterparts to volunteer within an organisation.

Figure 5.5. **Participation and frequency of formal volunteering for selected population groups on average in the OECD area**

Percentage, working-age population, 2012

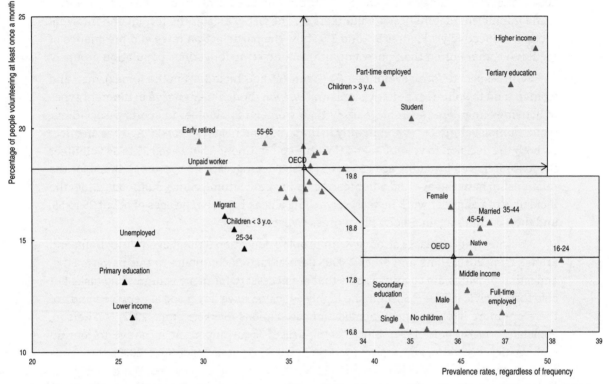

Note: Locating the different socio-demographic groups on a coordinate plane makes it possible to identify those who have both higher participation and frequency than the OECD average (these groups are shown in blue, in the upper right quadrant), those with participation and frequency below the OECD average (in black, in the lower left quadrant) and those who are close to the OECD average (in grey, near the origin of the coordinate plane).

Source: OECD calculations based on data from OECD (2012), OECD Survey of Adult Skills (PIAAC database), *www.oecd.org/site/piaac/*.

StatLink ⬛️⬛️ http://dx.doi.org/10.1787/888933259941

Turning to informal volunteering (Figure 5.6 and Table 5.A.2. in the Annex), volunteers are again more likely: i) to be better-educated than people who do not volunteer (80% of university graduates compared with 56% of people without a high school diploma); ii) to be employed (73% of those with jobs versus 65% of the unemployed); and iii) to have higher household income (77% of those with higher income compared with 61% of those with fewer economic resources). Participation in informal volunteer activities is quite stable across age groups, ranging from 68% to 73% until age 64. The frequency of informal volunteering is also similar across most age groups: about 20% to 26% of people in all age groups who report having volunteered informally in the previous 12 months do so at least once a week, while almost one in three informal volunteers contributes at least once a month.

Overall, these findings suggest that people from higher socio-economic backgrounds are more likely to volunteer, possibly because they have larger networks and more opportunities to volunteer, as well as higher social and cognitive skills that prove to be valuable in performing volunteer activities. In contrast, disadvantaged people face significant barriers to volunteering (Bekkers, 2005; Schlozman, Verba and Brady, 1999). Some of these barriers are financial; some stem from a lack of awareness about volunteering and how to access it; some arise from the false perception of having little to offer. This in turn raises the question of the existence and perpetuation of an opportunity gap in volunteering. Given that volunteer work is done by those who have ample resources, members of lower socio-economic groups are further marginalised and deprived of opportunities for enhancing their human and social capital.

Figure 5.6. Participation and frequency of informal volunteering for selected population groups on average in European countries

Percentage, working-age population, 2006

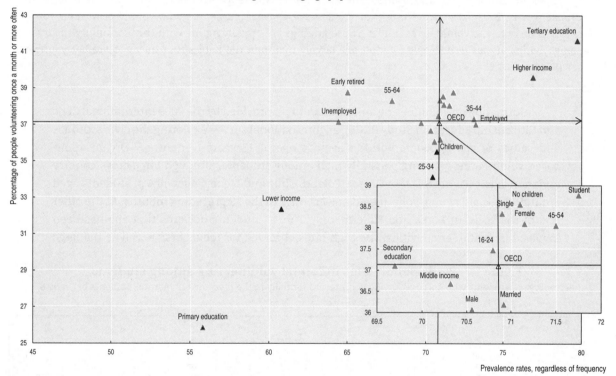

Note: Locating the different socio-demographic groups on a coordinate plane makes it possible to identify those who have both higher participation and frequency than the OECD average (these groups are shown in blue, in the upper right quadrant), those with participation and frequency below the OECD average (in black, in the lower left quadrant) and those who are close to the OECD average (in grey, near the origin of the coordinate plane).

Source: OECD calculations based on data from the European Social Survey (2006), European Social Survey Round 3 Data, Data file edition 3.5. (database), Norwegian Social Science Data Services, Norway – Data Archive and distributor of ESS data, *www.europeansocialsurvey.org/*.

StatLink ᴀᴍᴅ *http://dx.doi.org/10.1787/888933259955*

Special focus on two population groups: students and older people

The PIAAC survey covers people of working age, and hence largely misses two groups who have long been identified as recipients of services, rather than givers: students and older people. This omission is important, as volunteering can be performed over a wide span of the life course, starting from early age. Shannon (2009) studied volunteerism among children aged 8 to 12, showing that even the youngest participate in a large range of volunteer activities, and that performing volunteer work provides lasting tangible and intangible benefits (Box 5.3).

Box 5.3. **Life-time effects of volunteering at a young age**

Research has shown that volunteering at a young age promotes healthy lifestyles, discourages risky behaviour and is an important resource for addressing some of the pressing issues that young people face, such as teenage pregnancy, dropping out of school, substance abuse, and violence (Hart et al., 2007; Wilson and Musick, 2000). Volunteering can also nurture important life skills and values in children, which can be particularly important for children with fewer opportunities to develop such skills and interests, such as those in low-income urban areas. Moreover, volunteering enhances the psychological development of children by increasing self-esteem, positive self-confidence, responsibility, and an interest in learning (Lewis, 2002; Phalen, 2003).

Early volunteering also has an influence that lasts well into adulthood. Developmental theorists suggest that experiences during childhood and early adolescence shape lifelong values and provide a sense of purpose (Lewis, 2002). Moreover, Hart et al. (2007) have shown that people who volunteer in their youth are also more likely to volunteer as adults. These findings are broadly in line with the "continuity theory of ageing", which argues that people in adult age largely maintain the habits that they acquired at younger ages (Wilson, 2012).

Information on volunteering among students is provided by the 2009 International Civic and Citizenship Education Study (ICCS), an international survey exploring the civic attitudes and values of young people with an average age of 13 years 6 months.[30] Organisation-based volunteering rates are generally high among students, although large cross-country variation exists (Figure 5.7).[31] In Greece, Poland, Chile and Mexico over 40% of students aged around 14 declare having volunteered at least once in the 12 preceding months. At the other end of the scale, in Korea and Finland, only 1 in 10 students declares that she has been involved in volunteer activities. The high rates observed for teenagers as well as the large

Figure 5.7. **Participation rates in formal volunteering among students**

Percentage of students who declared having volunteered formally in the preceding12 months, students in Grade 8, aged around 14, 2009

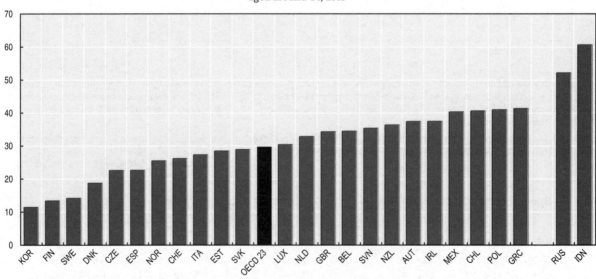

Note: The chart shows the percentage of students who declared that they volunteered at least once in the preceding 12 months in *at least one* of the following sectors: youth organisations; environmental organisations; human rights organisations; fund-raising organisations; cultural organisations; and youth campaigning. Data for Belgium refer to Flanders; data for the United Kingdom refer to England only.

Source: OECD calculations based on data from the International Association for the Evaluation of Educational Achievement (IEA) (2009), International Civic and Citizenship Education Study (ICCS) (database), *www.iea.nl/iccs_2009.html.*

StatLink ⚇ *http://dx.doi.org/10.1787/888933259961*

cross-country variations should be interpreted with caution, as they may be influenced by the requirement in some national school systems to perform community service in order to graduate from high school. Across OECD countries, most students are active in fund-raising and youth campaigning. In Greece, Poland and the Russian Federation, it is also quite common for young people to volunteer in environmental associations. Conversely, the humanitarian and cultural sectors attract only a small share of young volunteers.

As people get older, they often find volunteering a good substitute for the social roles that they have lost, such as work and active parenthood. Volunteering in old age can have a positive social impact on both society and the volunteers: it can reduce isolation, strengthen community ties, enhance volunteers' self-esteem, change stereotypes, and promote social and political consciousness (Haski-Leventhal, 2009). Van Willigen (2000) found that the positive psychological effect of volunteering increases in older age, as older volunteers experience greater psychological benefits for each hour that they contribute.

According to the Survey of Health, Ageing and Retirement in Europe (SHARE), overall 16% of the population aged 50 and over in the OECD European countries covered by the survey volunteered in an organisation at least once over the 12 months preceding the interview. The Netherlands (38%) and Denmark (29%) are characterised by the highest shares of adults above the age of 50 volunteering, followed by France and Switzerland (at 27-28%) and by Luxembourg, Belgium and Germany (at 21-22%). The shares of older people who volunteered in Italy (12%) and in Portugal and Spain (5-6%) are significantly below the average for Continental Europe. Low rates of volunteering among adults above 50 are also reported in Eastern Europe (Figure 5.8). Volunteering rates in old age remain roughly stable until the age of 64 (21% on average in the OECD area) and drop (to the level of 12%) among those aged 65 and more, probably due to functional limitations.

Figure 5.8. Participation rates in formal volunteering among people aged 50 and over in European countries

Percentage of people aged 50 and over who declared having volunteered formally in the preceding 12 months, 2015 or latest available year

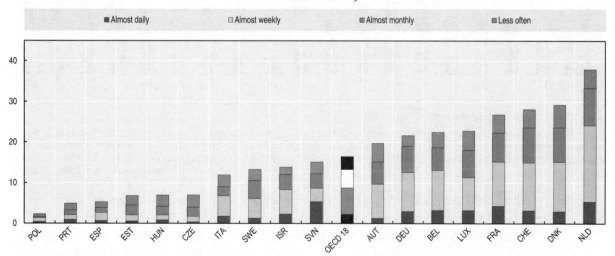

Note: Data for Hungary, Poland and Portugal refer to 2011.

Source: OECD calculations based on data from the Survey of Health, Ageing and Retirement in Europe (SHARE) (2015), Survey of Health, Ageing and Retirement in Europe, Wave 5, Release 1.0.0 (database), *http://dx.doi.org/10.6103/SHARE.w5.100*; and SHARE (2013), Survey of Health, Ageing and Retirement in Europe, Wave 4, Release 1.1.1 (database), *http://dx.doi.org/10.6103/SHARE.w4.111*.

StatLink ᐧᐧᐧ *http://dx.doi.org/10.1787/888933259970*

Among the people aged 50 and more who reported having volunteered in a formal setting in the previous year, almost one-sixth (15%) did so almost daily, two in five were active almost every week (40%), and slightly more than one-fourth volunteered almost monthly (Figure 5.8). Cross-country variations are notable, but rather unsystematic and unrelated to the overall level of engagement.

As for informal volunteering, one-fourth of respondents provided informal help to family, friends or neighbours (Figure 5.9). Cross-country differences follow a pattern similar to that observed for formal volunteering, with high levels of participation in Denmark (48%), followed by Sweden, Belgium, the Netherlands and the Czech Republic (34-40%) and, further down the league, France, Switzerland and Austria (26-29%). Participation in informal volunteering is much lower in Spain, Hungary and Poland (15-18%) as well as in Israel and Portugal (10-11%). On average, in the OECD countries covered by the survey, informal volunteering is highest among those younger than 65 (37%), reaches the level of 28% among the 65-74 years old and drops to 13.5% among the elderly.

Figure 5.9. **Participation in informal volunteering among people aged 50 and over in European countries**

Percentage of people aged 50 and over who declared having volunteered informally in the preceding 12 months, 2015 or latest available year

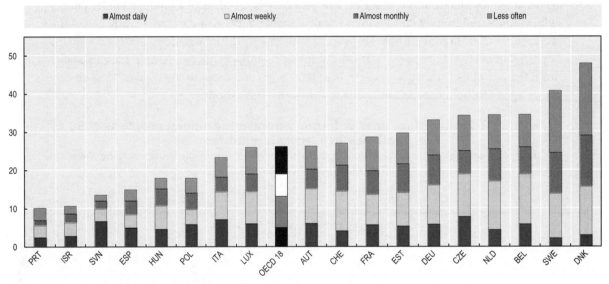

Note: Data for Hungary, Poland and Portugal refer to 2011.

Source: OECD calculations based on data from the Survey of Health, Ageing and Retirement in Europe (SHARE) (2015), Survey of Health, Ageing and Retirement in Europe, Wave 5, Release 1.0.0 (database), http://dx.doi.org/10.6103/SHARE.w5.100; and SHARE (2013), Survey of Health, Ageing and Retirement in Europe, Wave 4, Release 1.1.1 (database), http://dx.doi.org/10.6103/SHARE.w4.111.

StatLink ⫘⫘⫘ http://dx.doi.org/10.1787/888933259983

Half of those providing informal help do so weekly or even more often. However, there is an inverse relationship between the overall prevalence and the frequency of helping. In Slovenia, while the proportion of older helpers is low, about half of those who help are active almost daily (plus another 25% of "weekly" helpers). In Denmark and Sweden, on the other hand, while the prevalence of informal helping is much higher than in Southern Europe, more than two-thirds of the helpers do not engage on a regular basis.

Volunteerism varies across the life course not only in terms of participation, frequency of engagement, activity and organisation type, but also with respect to the motivation to volunteer. While little comparative evidence is available on the motivation to do volunteer work among the young and adult population, information from the 2nd wave of SHARE – which covers a somewhat different and smaller set of European countries – suggests that an important driver for the decision by older people to volunteer is the willingness to meet new people and to contribute something useful (Figure 5.10). In Israel and Southern Europe the major motivation to volunteer in older age seems to be related to the feeling of doing something useful; while in Continental and Northern Europe people aged 50 and over engage in voluntary activities mainly to develop new social relationships.

Figure 5.10. **Motivations to volunteer among people aged 50 and over in European countries**
Percentage of volunteers, 2008

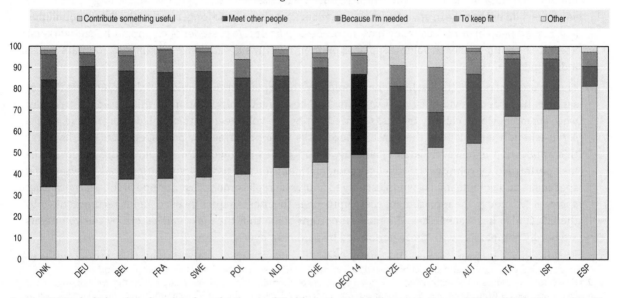

Source: OECD calculations based on data from the Survey of Health, Ageing and Retirement in Europe (SHARE) (2013), Survey of Health, Ageing and Retirement in Europe, Wave 2, Release 2.6.0 (database), *http://dx.doi.org/2010.6103/SHARE.w2.260*.

StatLink ᴍᴸᴸᴸ *http://dx.doi.org/10.1787/888933259992*

Measuring the well-being benefits of volunteering

The economic value of volunteering

When volunteers give their time to paint a building, take an elderly neighbour to hospital or feed the homeless, what is the value of the output that they are producing? Two methods for calculating the economic value of non-market production have been proposed (Box 5.4): the *output method* and the *input method* (O'Neill, 2001; Prouteau, 2006; Prouteau and Wolff, 2004; Sajardo and Serra, 2011). As the output method is closer to the approach used in national accounts, it allows direct comparison with market production (Abraham and Mackie, 2005). However, this requires identifying similar goods and services produced in a market setting; hence, due to data constraints, the input method is used in most practical applications (e.g. Ahmad and Koh, 2011; Salamon, Sokolowski and Haddock, 2011) and is also used here.

Box 5.4. **Valuing the economic value of volunteer work**

The economic value of volunteer work can be estimated in two different ways. The *output method* values the goods or services generated by volunteer work. While being conceptually closer to the conventions used for compiling economic accounts, there are major obstacles to putting this approach into practice (Prouteau, 2002). First, it requires clear and full identification of the outputs generated by volunteer work, which is not always possible. Second, there is often no close substitute on the market for the output produced by volunteers.[1]

The *input method* attributes a monetary value to the inputs entering the production of the goods and services produced by volunteering. In most practical applications, the inputs considered are limited to the work provided by volunteers. This input approach is usually implemented in two ways:

● The *opportunity cost* method quantifies the wage income that the volunteers forego to carry out their unpaid voluntary work. This approach has some weaknesses. First, it ignores that a large part of the volunteers do not engage in any paid work, either because they are no longer part of the active population (e.g. retired people) or because they have never been part of it (e.g. students or unpaid house-workers). Second, the value that each volunteer places on their free time is subjective and hard to compare across individuals.

● The *replacement cost* method values what would have been paid for the services of the volunteers if these services had been provided by paid workers. The best-practice application of this approach (*specialist wage approach*) would classify the tasks carried out by the volunteers into detailed categories (e.g. legal services) and then calculate their cost if these tasks were performed by paid specialists (e.g. lawyers); this application is however data demanding, as it requires detailed information on the nature of the task performed by volunteers, as well as an adjustment for any productivity differential between paid specialists and volunteers. The simplest way to apply the replacement cost method is the *generalist wage approach*.[2] Although the replacement cost approach is the most frequently used and is recommended by the ILO, it also has weaknesses, the most important being that the tasks carried out by the volunteers are hardly comparable with those performed by paid employees.

1. This is the case in the great majority of the outputs produced by the voluntary sector, particularly in contexts of little or no financial solvency on the demand side, or where outputs of a public nature are affected by "free-rider" problems.
2. The few international studies on this topic have used a number of alternatives as the benchmark salary: the average wage in the social services sector (United Nations, 2003); the mean non-agricultural wage (Anheier and Salamon, 2001); and the wages paid by non-profit organisations in their respective spheres of action (Mertens and Lefevre, 2004).

Source: Abraham, K.G. and C. Mackie (eds.) (2005), *Beyond the Market: Designing Nonmarket Accounts for the United States*, Washington, DC: National Academies Press.

To evaluate the economic value of volunteer work across OECD countries, Table 5.4 combines information on the number of hours volunteered (formally and informally) from TUS with information on the average hourly wage in each country from the *OECD Employment and Labour Market Statistics Database* and data on GDP from the *OECD National Accounts Statistics Database*. A replacement cost approach is used to assign a monetary value to the hours devoted to volunteering. As no information is available on the price of specialised labour in specific volunteer activities, Table 5.4 relies on the average hourly labour cost of each country. Hourly wages are converted to an annual full-time equivalent, assuming a 40-hour work-week and 52 weeks in a year (including paid vacations). For the purpose of cross-country comparison, nominal values are converted into 2013 US dollars using purchasing power parities for private consumption.[32]

Table 5.4. **Estimates of the economic value of volunteering in the OECD area**

2013 or latest available year

	Estimates of the economic value of volunteering	
	Amount (2013 value, US$ billion, PPPs)	% of national GDP (2013 value, US$, PPPs)
Australia	49.4	4.7
Austria	4.5	1.2
Belgium	5.1	1.1
Canada	36.3	2.4
Denmark	6.7	2.7
Estonia	0.5	1.4
Finland	2.9	1.3
France	19.2	0.8
Germany	117.6	3.3
Hungary	0.5	0.2
Ireland	3.5	1.7
Italy	19.6	0.9
Japan	33.2	0.7
Korea	7.8	0.5
Mexico	19.7	1.0
Netherlands	7.7	1.0
New Zealand	6.4	4.1
Norway	5.9	1.8
Poland	25.3	2.8
Portugal	4.3	1.5
Slovenia	1.2	2.0
Spain	22.1	1.4
Sweden	11.3	2.6
United Kingdom	60.2	2.5
United States	621.7	3.7
OECD25	**1 093**	**1.9**

Note: Data on time use refer to: 2013 for the United States; 2011 for Japan; 2010 for Canada; 2009-10 for Estonia, Finland, New Zealand and Spain; 2009 for Korea and Mexico; 2008-08 for Austria, France and Italy; 2006 for Australia; 2005-06 for the Netherlands; 2005 for Belgium, Ireland, and the United Kingdom; 2003-04 for Poland; 2001-02 for Germany; 2001 for Denmark; 2000-01 for Norway, Slovenia and Sweden; 1999-2000 for Hungary and 1999 for Portugal. Information on the number of hours volunteered informally is not available for Belgium, Hungary, Ireland, Japan and the Netherlands.

Source: OECD calculations based on the Harmonised European Time Use Survey web application, *https://www.h2.scb.se/tus/tus/*; *Eurostat Time Use Database*, *http://appsso.eurostat.ec.europa.eu/nui/show.do?dataset=tus_00selfstat&lang=en*; public-use time use survey micro-data; tabulations from national statistical offices; OECD (2015a), "Aggregate National Accounts, SNA 2008: Gross domestic product", *OECD National Accounts Statistics* (database), *http://dx.doi.org/10.1787/data-00001-en*; and OECD (2015b), "Annual full time earnings and annual labour costs in equivalent USD, 25-64 year-old population", *OECD Employment and Labour Market Statistics* (database), *http://dx.doi.org/10.1787/eag-2010-table88-en*.

StatLink ⟶ http://dx.doi.org/10.1787/888933260129

Table 5.4 shows rough estimates of the economic value of volunteer work in real US dollars (2nd column) and as a share of countries' GDP (3rd column). While the range of uncertainty is large, due to data constraints and the methodological shortcuts used, these estimates suggest that the volunteer sector is a considerable economic force – accounting for 1 trillion US dollars in the OECD area and representing a substantial share of GDP (1.9%). The economic value of volunteering is particularly high in Australia, Germany, New Zealand and the United States (at 3% of GDP or above).

When we give, how much do we receive?

The benefits from volunteering flow not only to others but also to the volunteers themselves: they include meeting people, making new friends, broadening life experience, boosting confidence, experiencing positive moods, and acquiring new skills. Following the OECD well-being framework, these benefits are classified here under three main headings: i) health status; ii) skills and earnings; and iii) subjective well-being.

Health status

Previous research has shown a positive link between volunteering and health status: volunteers are more likely to enjoy good physical and mental health and to exhibit lower rates of mortality than people who do not volunteer (Box 5.5).

Box 5.5. **The relationship between volunteering and health status**

By helping others, people develop stronger networks that buffer stress and reduce the risk of illness. The benefits of volunteering for health are especially evident at later stages of life, when physical health problems are more likely to occur and when other forms of social integration, such as work and marriage, are no longer available.

A number of studies (see Wilson and Musick (2000) for a review) suggest that there are physical health benefits to volunteering, in terms of both lower morbidity and higher life expectancy. Several epidemiological studies have relied on longitudinal data to investigate the causal relationship between volunteer engagement and health status: most have concluded that volunteering causes good health, rather than healthy people being more likely to volunteer. More research is however needed to understand the importance of mediating variables or mechanisms through which volunteering improves health status.

Most of the health benefits of volunteering are concentrated in old age.[33] The SHARE survey provides a wealth of information on the life status and well-being of people in later life, and it is well-suited to assess the relationship between volunteering and health. Table 5.5 shows significant differences in several health indicators between old-age volunteers and non-volunteers across the surveyed countries.

The table highlights a significant correlation between health and volunteering, although nothing can be inferred on the causal pathway. In general, older people who volunteer formally are more likely than non-volunteers to report a better health status. The relationship between informal help and health is somewhat milder, especially in the case of depression. However, large variations exist across countries. In countries where participation rates in informal volunteering are high (e.g. Denmark and Sweden) informal help is generally associated with lower levels of depression, while the reverse holds in countries showing low levels of participation in informal volunteer activities (e.g. Portugal). In countries where volunteering rates are low, informal helping roles usually occur within close social networks and are associated with stronger social responsibilities and low social recognition. Informal help providers are thus more likely to experience volunteering fatigue and burnout that may offset the salubrious effect of volunteering on depression (Li and Ferraro, 2005).

Table 5.5. **Health outcomes of people aged 50 and over in European countries,
by participation in volunteer work**

Percentage, 2015 or latest available year

	Self-reported health			Depression (Euro-D scale)			Chances to live up to an older age[1]		
	Good/very good			Low/no depression			Expected chances higher than 50%		
	Do not volunteer	Volunteer formally	Volunteer informally	Do not volunteer	Volunteer formally	Volunteer informally	Do not volunteer	Volunteer formally	Volunteer informally
Austria	64.5	79.7	75.0	79.1	83.5	80.6	62.1	78.6	71.4
Belgium	68.7	80.6	78.4	71.3	76.1	69.5	51.3	66.2	62.7
Check Republic	54.1	72.4	58.9	70.1	75.3	71.3	34.6	46.2	44.0
Denmark	70.5	84.6	79.8	79.1	86.6	83.1	65.4	79.7	73.7
Estonia	26.1	52.6	37.4	59.4	78.9	65.3	46.6	64.5	57.8
France	57.1	78.5	73.0	63.1	70.2	61.6	48.1	62.3	59.8
Germany	51.4	72.1	66.4	73.6	81.5	74.5	51.8	63.6	62.7
Hungary	33.6	47.3	37.8	56.6	71.5	57.7	27.5	49.1	34.2
Israel	64.1	77.5	69.2	79.7	83.1	77.2	51.0	78.6	66.2
Italy	54.9	72.0	64.9	63.6	68.5	60.0	58.0	73.5	72.1
Luxembourg	61.2	82.3	71.5	71.0	77.7	71.3	58.8	71.5	67.5
Netherlands	61.4	81.0	71.5	78.5	85.7	78.7	59.9	72.4	72.3
Poland	38.9	36.3	58.4	58.1	33.3	55.5	54.4	35.2	42.7
Portugal	36.9	48.6	44.3	61.3	68.9	41.6	53.8	56.9	56.3
Slovenia	57.7	77.3	71.6	73.2	81.4	77.0	54.9	67.2	63.3
Spain	54.0	70.9	62.5	66.4	73.5	66.6	57.4	75.1	63.8
Sweden	72.6	79.9	80.5	79.0	85.5	80.5	53.5	66.6	70.4
Switzerland	79.6	90.5	86.1	81.4	84.7	84.2	63.9	69.9	69.9
OECD 18	**55.9**	**71.3**	**65.9**	**70.3**	**75.9**	**69.8**	**53.0**	**65.4**	**61.7**

Note: Data for Hungary, Poland and Portugal refer to 2011.

1. Respondents were asked to grade on a scale from 0 to 100 the likelihood that they will live to be of a certain age or older age (such as 75 among the 50-65 age group).

Source: OECD calculations based on data from the Survey of Health, Ageing and Retirement in Europe (SHARE) (2015), Survey of Health, Ageing and Retirement in Europe, Wave 5, Release 1.0.0 (database), http://dx.doi.org/10.6103/SHARE.w5.100; and SHARE (2013), Survey of Health, Ageing and Retirement in Europe, Wave 4, Release 1.1.1 (database), http://dx.doi.org/10.6103/SHARE.w4.111.

StatLink ᵃᵍᵖ http://dx.doi.org/10.1787/888933260138

Skills and earnings

Volunteering also delivers labour-market benefits (Box 5.6), during early- and mid-life (Strauß, 2008) and the later career (Lancee and Radl, 2012). Some authors have suggested that the impact of volunteering may be limited because it does not provide volunteers with skills that they can easily transfer to paid work (Vegeris et al., 2010). However, volunteers generally report that volunteering enhances both their "hard skills", such as skills in information technology, language, business management and customer relations, and their "soft skills", such as in communications, teamwork, time keeping and discipline (Hirst, 2001; Corden and Sainsbury, 2005; Newton, Oakley and Pollard, 2011; Nichols and Ralston, 2011).[34] Likewise, managers believe that workplace skills can be gained from volunteering (Volunteering England, 2010).[35]

The PIAAC results show that in the large majority of OECD countries people who engage in volunteering have higher literacy, numeracy and problem-solving skills and receive higher wages than non-volunteers (Table 5.6). These findings should however be taken with caution. First, the correlation between volunteering and workplace skills/ earnings may be spurious and driven by omitted variables (e.g. age). Second, the positive relation highlighted in Table 5.6 is not informative about causality (if any) between the

Table 5.6. **Adult proficiency levels and hourly wages, by volunteer engagement and country**

Average values, working-age population, 2012

	Proficiency in literacy		Proficiency in numeracy		Proficiency in problem solving		Hourly wages[1]	
	Do not volunteer	Do volunteer	Do not volunteer	Do volunteer	Do not volunteer	Do volunteer	Do not volunteer	Do volunteer
Australia	272	293	259	281	284	295	18.3	19.8
Austria	266	276	270	285	282	287	18.6	20.0
Belgium	269	288	273	295	277	288	21.6	23.5
Canada	262	285	254	277	273	291	18.9	21.1
Czech Republic	272	283	273	287	280	294	8.8	9.9
Denmark	264	279	271	287	280	287	23.3	24.4
Estonia	272	287	269	284	274	286	14.5	17.1
Finland	282	295	276	291	288	291	9.4	10.2
France	257	277	247	275			18.6	20.2
Germany	263	283	263	288	278	290	18.1	20.1
Ireland	261	275	249	266	274	280	20.4	23.4
Italy	248	260	244	260			15.8	17.4
Japan	295	298	285	294	295	293	15.6	17.1
Korea	270	280	260	272	282	284	17.1	20.4
Netherlands	279	291	275	289	284	290	20.8	22.7
Norway	269	286	267	287	281	290	23.0	25.3
Poland	264	280	257	273	272	284	8.8	11.1
Slovak Republic	272	281	273	285	280	285	8.6	9.9
Spain	248	267	243	261		.	16.3	19.3
Sweden	273	291	271	293	284	295	18.4	19.3
United Kingdom	265	288	254	280	275	291	15.1	16.8
United States	256	281	236	266	267	284	19.5	23.1
OECD 22[2]	**267**	**283**	**262**	**281**	**279**	**289**	**16.8**	**18.7**
Russian Federation	273	285	268	277	275	282	5.0	5.3

Note: Data for Belgium refer to Flanders; data for the United Kingdom refer to England and Northern Ireland only. Data for the Russian Federation exclude the Moscow municipal area.

1. Hourly wages include bonuses and are expressed in PPP-adjusted US dollars. The sample includes only working-age employees. The wage distribution was trimmed to eliminate the 1st and 99th percentiles.
2. Except for proficiency in problem solving, for which it is OECD 19.

Source: OECD calculations based on data from OECD (2012), OECD Survey of Adult Skills (PIAAC database), *www.oecd.org/site/piaac/*.

StatLink ⬛⬛⬛ *http://dx.doi.org/10.1787/888933260140*

variables at hand. However, econometric analysis controlling for a number of individual characteristics, sample selection bias and causality issues suggests that volunteering fosters the acquisition of skills used in the workplace and yields a wage premium (see Box 5.6 and Annex 5.B).

Subjective well-being

Most of the research on the effects of volunteering on subjective well-being finds that people who engage in unpaid work to help others benefit in some way (Becchetti, Pelloni and Rossetti, 2008; Dolan, Peasgood and White, 2008; Helliwell, 2003; OECD, 2011; Post, 2005), although a few studies conclude that, after controlling for a number of individual characteristics (e.g. age, gender, personal traits, employment status, income), the impact of volunteering is considerably reduced or may even be negative (Bjørnskov, 2006; Meier and Stutzer, 2008; Li, Pickles and Savage, 2005). Most of this research on volunteering and subjective well-being, however, is based on cross-sectional data, which makes it difficult to systematically assess causal effects. Moreover, the channels through which volunteer engagement might benefit subjective well-being are diverse (Box 5.7).

Box 5.6. **The relationship between volunteering, earnings and skills**

Several studies conclude that volunteering contributes to "individual employability" by enhancing knowledge, skills, work attitudes, confidence, self-esteem, mental and physical health and well-being (Corden and Sainsbury, 2005; Hirst, 2001; Newton et al., 2011; Nichols and Ralston, 2011). However, evidence on the extent to which these "employability" gains translate into higher paid employment is mixed (Kamerāde and Ellis Paine, 2014; Ellis Paine, McKay and Moro, 2013). Moreover, the detailed channels through which volunteer engagement might benefit workers still remain unclear, and may differ across countries and workers' characteristics.

While the relevance of education as a determinant of volunteer engagement is well-established, less is known about the effects of volunteering on the level of skills acquired by the adult population, mostly due to data constraints. In this respect, the analysis shown in Table 5.B.1 in the Annex represents a first attempt to investigate the link between volunteer involvement and workplace skills. A number of variables have been included to control for spurious relations, while the issue of causality has been addressed in a two-stage least squares regression framework using the level of trust in others as an instrumental variable. After controlling for reverse causality and selection biases, PIAAC-based estimates suggest that volunteering increases workplace skills.

Concerning the impact of voluntary work on earnings, the existing evidence is limited – mostly due to the absence of data sets suitable for testing this relationship properly. Most of these studies, however, find a wage premium for volunteering that ranges between 7% and 19%. The last column of Table 5.B.1 in the Annex shows the results of an analysis carried out to assess the "true" earnings return to volunteering. Two methodological approaches have been considered to estimate the effect of voluntary work on earnings. First, an instrumental variable technique has been used to address the endogeneity bias when estimating the effect of volunteering – similar to that employed in the case of a skills premium. Second, a self-selection framework of labour market participation has been used to correct for potential sample selection bias (Heckman technique). After controlling for reverse causality and selection biases, PIAAC-based estimates suggest that volunteering increases the average hourly earnings by 14%, which is in line with estimates reported in previous studies (Day and Devlin, 1998; Hackl, Halla and Pruckner, 2007; Prouteau and Wolff, 2006).

Table 5.7 summarises the main findings of the empirical analysis carried out on the PIAAC data to investigate the effects of volunteering on proficiency and earnings (the full set of results is provided in Annex 5.B). The analysis of the effect of formal volunteering on skills proficiency and earnings deserves further research and will benefit from the release of the second wave of the PIAAC survey.

Table 5.7. **Coefficients of formal volunteering on skills proficiency and earnings**

	Literacy skills	Numeracy skills	Problem-solving skills	Hourly earnings[1]
Formal volunteering	11.0**	10.8**	8.0**	0.14***
Socio-economic controls	YES[2]	YES[2]	YES[2]	YES[3]
Reverse causality	YES	YES	YES	YES
Self-selection bias				YES[4]
Country fixed-effects	YES	YES	YES	YES

Note: ** Significant at 5%, *** significant at 1%.

1. The dependent variable "hourly earnings" refers to the natural logarithm of hourly earnings. Hourly earnings include bonuses and are expressed in PPP-adjusted US dollars. The wage distribution was trimmed to eliminate the 1st and 99th percentiles. The sample includes only working-age employees.

2. Coefficients adjusted for age, gender, foreign-born status, job tenure and type of occupation.

3. Coefficients adjusted for age, gender, foreign-born status and job tenure.

4. The labour force participation equation controls for age, gender, presence of children, marital status and partner's employment.

Source: OECD calculations based on data from OECD (2012), OECD Survey of Adult Skills (PIAAC database), *www.oecd.org/site/piaac/*.

StatLink ⏩ *http://dx.doi.org/10.1787/888933260158*

> ## Box 5.7. **The relationship between volunteering and subjective well-being**
>
> A growing number of studies have investigated the association between volunteering and psychological characteristics such as life satisfaction and self-esteem. The bulk of this research points to volunteer participation enhancing subjective well-being.
>
> Different channels through which volunteering may exert a positive effect on subjective well-being have been identified. First, volunteering benefits subjective well-being by providing a sense of meaning and purpose in life, by helping to offset role losses such as those associated to retirement and widowhood, and can even relieve stress in times of personal crisis (Van Willigen, 2000). Second, volunteering may lead to better subjective well-being because it facilitates social support and social interactions (Wilson and Musick, 2003). Finally, volunteering can bolster the self-esteem of support providers (Krause and Shaw, 2000).
>
> Each of these is a reasonable pathway in the relationship between volunteering and subjective well-being, but the outcome may not always be beneficial. Some studies show a non-linear effect of hours of formal volunteering on subjective well-being (Van Willigen, 2000), suggesting that a moderate amount of volunteering is optimal. In addition, engagement in different volunteer activities such as formal volunteering and informal helping may lead to different outcomes.

Table 5.8 shows the relation between engagement in formal volunteering and two different indicators of subjective well-being – life satisfaction and affect balance – based on data from the Gallup World Poll.[36] The question on formal volunteering from the Gallup World Poll reads: "In the past month, have you volunteered your time to an organisation?" Data show that, on average, volunteers tend to report higher satisfaction with life and experience positive feelings more frequently than non-volunteers.[37] Table 5.C.1 in the Annex presents the distribution of feelings included in the affect balance metric, by volunteer engagement and country; this evidence shows that volunteers tend to report more positive feelings than non-volunteers, while no clear pattern emerges when it comes to negative emotions. Studies found, for instance, that helping people whose conditions may not be improved (e.g. people living in hospice or runaway youth) can generate sadness and burnout among the helpers (Gabard, 1997; Haski-Leventhal and Bargal, 2008).

Even after controlling for a number of individual characteristics (i.e. gender, age, income and education levels, marital and parental status, and area of residence), the relationship between volunteering and life satisfaction remains large and significant (Figure 5.11, black horizontal line). However, focusing on the average effect of volunteering might hide a non-linear relationship (Binder, 2015; Binder and Freytag, 2013). Figure 5.11 shows that volunteering is positively related to life satisfaction over all quintiles, although the relation weakens at higher levels of life satisfaction (see Table 5.C.2 in Annex for more details). The strong link between volunteering and life satisfaction in the lowest quintile seems to support the view that volunteering provides a protective role as it allows the volunteers to mitigate their own unhappiness (Binder and Freytag, 2013).

Table 5.8. **Subjective well-being indicators, by volunteer engagement and country**

Average values, 2014 or latest available year

Country	Life satisfaction 0-10 Cantril Ladder		Affect balance % of respondents reporting a positive affect balance	
	Do not volunteer	Volunteer formally	Do not volunteer	Volunteer formally
Australia	7.2	7.5	75.9	76.2
Austria	7.0	7.5	79.5	83.5
Belgium	6.8	7.1	75.9	77.9
Canada	7.2	7.4	76.9	77.7
Chile	6.8	6.9	77.2	79.4
Czech Republic	6.5	6.6	70.4	78.2
Denmark	7.5	7.7	80.0	85.8
Estonia	5.4	6.2	72.1	81.2
Finland	7.4	7.6	81.7	84.7
France	6.4	6.8	77.4	81.3
Germany	7.0	7.3	77.0	85.3
Greece	4.7	5.9	59.2	72.7
Hungary	5.1	5.3	67.3	85.9
Iceland	7.5	7.7	84.5	86.5
Ireland	6.7	7.1	76.9	80.8
Israel	7.3	7.7	66.6	70.7
Italy	6.0	6.1	63.5	64.6
Japan	5.7	6.1	77.0	86.9
Korea	5.7	6.3	66.5	71.2
Luxembourg	6.8	6.9	81.3	83.9
Mexico	6.4	6.9	81.5	84.4
Netherlands	7.2	7.4	85.5	84.5
New Zealand	7.3	7.7	78.4	84.0
Norway	7.4	7.7	79.2	84.4
Poland	5.1	5.6	74.3	75.6
Portugal	5.1	5.7	61.5	67.3
Slovak Republic	5.8	6.0	71.9	78.8
Slovenia	5.4	6.4	64.5	78.5
Spain	6.4	6.4	70.3	69.2
Sweden	7.2	7.6	80.7	79.0
Switzerland	7.4	7.7	83.4	86.2
Turkey	5.4	5.7	61.0	70.8
United Kingdom	6.5	6.8	78.9	79.6
United States	6.9	7.3	75.5	76.7
OECD	6.5	6.8	74.5	79.2

Note: Data refer to 2013 for Iceland and Turkey.

Source: OECD calculations based on data from the Gallup World Poll, *www.gallup.com/strategicconsulting/en-us/worldpoll.aspx*.

StatLink ᔕᐱᓚ *http://dx.doi.org/10.1787/888933260165*

An alternative approach to assess the relationship between volunteering and subjective well-being is to rely on the affect module of time use surveys collected in a number of OECD countries (e.g. France, the United States). These modules allow exploring the effects of specific activities on experienced well-being assessed at a particular point in time. An analysis of these data suggests that volunteering is among the most pleasant activities and that, on the days when they volunteer, people spend less time in unpleasant states than non-volunteers do (Box 5.8).

Figure 5.11. **The effect of formal volunteering on life satisfaction**

Coefficients of volunteering on life satisfaction, by quintile of life satisfaction

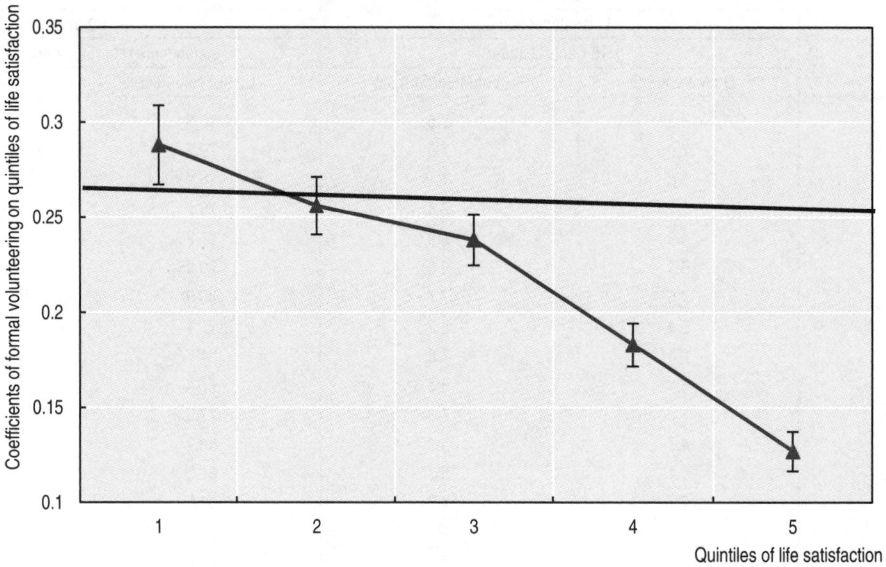

Note: The analysis includes all OECD countries. Data are pooled across all available years from 2006-2014. The horizontal line gives the coefficient of volunteering on the whole sample (0.264***). Error bars for coefficients over life satisfaction quintiles correspond to the 95% confidence intervals. Coefficients of volunteering over life satisfaction quintiles vary from 0.288*** at the lowest to 0.127*** at the highest quintiles.

Source: OECD calculations based on data from the Gallup World Poll, www.gallup.com/strategicconsulting/en-us/worldpoll.aspx.

StatLink ⊟ http://dx.doi.org/10.1787/888933260006

Box 5.8. **Volunteering and subjective well-being in the American Time Use Survey**

The well-being module from the 2013 American Time Use Survey is used here to investigate the link between daily "happiness" and volunteer activities. The analysis considers two measures of the feelings experienced during the day: the affect balance and the proportion of time spent in an unpleasant state (U-index). Table 5.9 shows a list of the 15 most enjoyable activities (out of 90) ranked by the average value of affect balance. Together with non-basic childcare, entertainment, religious practices and out-of-home leisure, voluntary activities are in the group of activities most likely to lead to positive feelings; this result is consistent with prior research (Kahneman et al., 2004; Krueger et al., 2009; White and Dolan, 2009).

Figure 5.12 confirms that volunteering has a significant impact on people's experienced well-being. For instance, people who did not volunteer on the day they were sampled spent almost one-fourth of their daily time in an unpleasant state, while this proportion is less than one-fifth for those who performed volunteer activities on the day (24% and 19%, respectively, Panel A). In terms of hours, this implies that, in the days when they volunteered, volunteers spent one hour more than their counterparts in a pleasant state. Similarly, on those same days, the proportion of respondents reporting more pleasant than unpleasant feelings was higher for volunteers (95%) than for non-volunteers (87%, Panel B).

Box 5.8. **Volunteering and subjective well-being
in the American Time Use Survey** (cont.)

Table 5.9. **Affect balance and U-index in the American Time Use Survey,
by activity**

Average values, working-age population, 2013

Activities	Affect balance	U-index
Volunteer activities: not elsewhere classified	4.25	0.0278
Arts and entertainment (other than sports)	3.90	0.0548
Volunteer activities: social service and care activities (except medical)	3.75	0.0682
Attending or hosting social events	3.74	0.0702
Religious or spiritual practices	3.59	0.0962
Informal help: caring and helping for non-household children	3.45	0.0991
Volunteer activities: participating in cultural activities	3.42	0.0625
Volunteer activities: attending meetings and training	3.40	0.2105
Participating in sports, exercise, or recreation	3.40	0.1290
Socialising and communicating	3.33	0.1481
Caring for and helping household children	3.29	0.1706
Shopping	3.22	0.1206
Attending sporting or recreational events	3.09	0.0435
Gardening and houseplant care	2.93	0.1534
Helping non-household adults	2.85	0.1890

Note: Affect balance is defined as the difference between the average score the respondent gives to all positive feelings, and the average score of all negative feelings. It can take any value between –6 and 6. The "U-index" measures the proportion of time that is spent in an unpleasant state; for a given episode, this is defined as equal to 1 if the maximum rating of any of the negative emotions (stress, tiredness, sadness, pain) exceeds the rating of happiness, and 0 if not. Activities with less than 15 observations are not shown in the table.

Source: OECD calculations based on data from the United States Department of Labor (2015), American Time Use Survey (ATUS) 2013 (database), Bureau of Labor Statistics, *www.bls.gov/tus/#database.*

StatLink ᵐˢᵖ *http://dx.doi.org/10.1787/888933260176*

Figure 5.12. **Time spent in an unpleasant state and positive affect balance in the American Time Use Survey, by presence of volunteering**

Working-age population, 2013

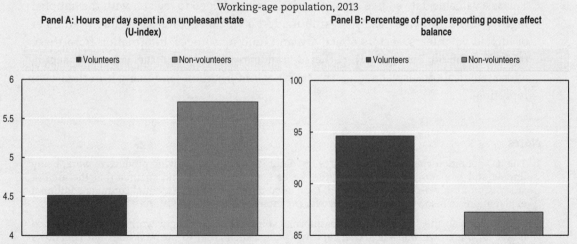

Panel A: Hours per day spent in an unpleasant state (U-index)

Panel B: Percentage of people reporting positive affect balance

Note: The term "volunteers" refers to people who volunteered on the day; the term "non-volunteers" refers to the people who did not volunteer on the day. Affect balance is defined as the difference between the average score the respondent gives to all positive feelings, and the average score of all negative feelings. The "U-index" measures the proportion of time that is spent in an unpleasant state; for a given episode, this is defined as equal to 1 if the maximum rating of any of the negative emotions (stress, tiredness, sadness, pain) exceeds the rating of happiness, and 0 if not.

Source: OECD calculations based on data from the United States Department of Labor (2015), American Time Use Survey (ATUS) 2013 (database), Bureau of Labor Statistics, *www.bls.gov/tus/#database.*

StatLink ᵐˢᵖ *http://dx.doi.org/10.1787/888933260011*

The statistical agenda ahead for volunteering

While some comparative statistical information on volunteering is available, and has provided the basis for the analysis presented in this chapter, it remains limited in many important respects. To respond to the demand for better information on the size, structure and effects of volunteering, steps should be taken in the following areas:

● *Consistently applying a common definition of volunteer work across different surveys along the lines recommended by the 2013 ICLS resolution* (by both official and non-official data producers). This would avoid the current situation where surveys (e.g. labour force surveys, time use surveys, general household surveys) differ in terms of the activities included (in particular with respect to caring for family members living alone or in separate households), the time period used for assessing whether respondents have performed volunteer work (e.g. the previous four weeks or the previous 12 months), the frequency and duration of the work done, and the type of service produced.

● *Developing experimental measures of the economic value of volunteering*, through the periodic compilation of *satellite accounts* covering the full range of non-profit institutions and including the economic value of volunteer work, along the lines pursued by the ongoing UNECE Task Force on Valuing Unpaid Household Service Work.

● *Developing metrics for other aspects of volunteering beyond "work".* These include donations (cash and in-kind) and non-work activities such as being a member of a volunteering organisation or participating in a campaign launched by such organisations. While these types of non-work activities are better understood as a form of "political and civic participation" (Boarini and Diaz, 2015), they are important to gauge how volunteering contributes to social capital and to maintaining a vibrant civil society.

● *Using additional sources.* Most OECD countries have a national registry of non-profit associations or organisations, normally managed by a public body and updated regularly. This is a valuable data source when associations are obliged to register with the national registry and to provide consistent information about their professional staff, number of unpaid volunteers, sectors of activity, and funding sources. Information from these registries should be regularly gathered and disseminated by the voluntary sector, with statistical offices validating this statistical information (and using it in their own reporting).

Notes

1. The ILO definition spells out the features of volunteer work (i.e. involving productive work; being unpaid and non-compulsory; and not for use by own household), and ensures that the area of study is uniformly defined, regardless of local circumstances. The ILO Manual contains additional explanations to resolve possible doubts over the interpretation of the criteria.

2. In this approach, the defining feature for informal volunteering is that any work or service provided is not for one's own household: hence, driving one's own child to hospital does not constitute volunteering, while driving a neighbour does.

3. "Satellite accounts" pull together data on particular types of institutions that are scattered among a variety of institutional sectors or economic activities in the SNA classification systems. In the case of NPIs, the satellite account is designed to pull together data on NPIs that have been allocated to the financial corporations, nonfinancial corporations, government, NPISH, and household sectors in order to provide a complete picture of the NPI "sector".

4. However, reliance on LFS as the platform for measuring volunteer work also limits the range of issues that can be explored. The volunteering module proposed by the ILO Manual consists of 1.5 pages of questions focusing on five issues: i) who are the volunteers?; ii) what activity do they perform?; iii) what is the amount of time they spend on each activity during a specific reference period?; iv) whether the activity is performed directly for a person or through an organisation and, if the latter, what type of organisation it is (e.g. non-profit, for-profit, public, co-operative); and v) what field or sector does this volunteering contribute to (e.g. health, education, social services, environment, culture, sport, etc.)? The Manual adopts a four-week reference period for questions on volunteer work, which is significantly shorter than the 12-month time frame used in most social surveys, and translates into lower estimates of the magnitude of volunteer work (number of volunteers).

5. Evidence from the LFS ad hoc module for Poland shows that formal and informal volunteering represented around 10% of all those working, and close to 3% of (broadly defined) GDP. Although referring to the ILO Manual, the ad hoc LFS module on volunteer work in Hungary uses a longer reference period (the 12 months preceding the interview, rather than the previous 4 weeks).

6. One of the few surveys that gathered comparative data on volunteer work in a sizeable cross-section of countries was carried out as part of the Johns Hopkins Comparative Nonprofit Sector Project (Salamon et al., 1999). This exercise collected information about the number of volunteers, the hours volunteered, and the field of activity. Most of these data were collected through specially commissioned inserts to omnibus population surveys; in some countries, special organisational surveys were used instead.

7. Recent analysis by the Pew Research Center highlights a large decline in response rates to opinion polls in the United States (from around 36% in 1997 to 9% today), and a tendency for volunteers to be over-represented in these surveys relative to the population at large (Pew Research Center, 2015). While the study concludes that, for most variables, small-sample polls provide unbiased estimates of most household characteristics, the share of people who reported having volunteered over the past year is much higher in these small-scale polls than in larger-scale official surveys (at 55% and 27% respectively).

8. For example, the question asking whether respondents helped a stranger or someone they did not know could be interpreted by respondents as meaning anything from providing hours of assistance to incidental acts, such as giving someone directions on the street. Likewise, answers to questions about whether respondents volunteered time to an organisation may include compulsory community service required as a condition of graduation or mere attendance at events (e.g. religious services).

9. Toppe and Groves (2007) found that "a non-trivial percentage of people did things they did not consider volunteering, but which should be considered volunteering".

10. In other terms, the complex reality of volunteering is reduced to a unidimensional measure: one predicts volunteer participation in general (yes or no), as if it were a uniform and robust entity (Cnaan and Amrofell, 1994; Cnaan, Handy and Wadsworth, 1996).

11. Organisational surveys could in principle be used to record the time spent in volunteer activities by organisations that maintain written records of volunteer inputs. However, these surveys capture only organisation-based volunteering. Also, a key obstacle to their use is that the voluntary sector is characterised by high turnover, a relatively informal approach and poor recording of information, implying that data are often not reliable.

12. While the use of a self-administered diary is widespread in the Europe and North America, the majority of countries in Latin America use a list of activities for measuring time use.

13. However, TUS do not provide much information about the institutional settings in which activities of interest take place, such as the types of organisations for which respondents volunteer or the types of jobs they perform.

14. The Gallup World Poll (GWP) includes a question on formal volunteering: "In the past month, have you volunteered your time to an organisation?" Despite being more recent and covering all OECD countries, those data are not used in this section as the survey question is not informative about the frequency of volunteering involvement.

15. The Gallup World Poll (GWP) also includes a question on informal volunteering. Despite being more recent and covering all OECD countries, these data are not used in this section as the survey question is very different from the ICSL definition of informal volunteering. The GWP question is: "In the past month, have you helped a stranger?"; this question could be interpreted by respondents

as a proxy for being a "good citizen" rather than as a measure of informal help, which is usually provided to persons who are close to the helper.

16. In the OECD Time Use Database, informal volunteering is defined as the time devoted to help non-household members (hence it may include help to family members living in a different household).

17. This chapter uses data from SHARE Wave 5 release 1.0.0, as of 31 March 2015 (DOI: 10.6103/SHARE. w5.100), from SHARE Wave 4 release 1.1.1, as of 28 March 2013 (DOI: 10.6103/SHARE.w4.111), and from SHARE Wave 2 release 2.6.0, as of 29 November 2013 (DOI: 10.6103/SHARE.w1.260 and 10.6103/ SHARE.w2.260). See *www.share-project.org* for a full list of funding institutions.

18. For further information see: *www.share-project.org* and Malter and Börsch-Supan (2015).

19. This finding is in line with the evidence shown in Vézina and Crompton (2012), according to which volunteering rates are lowest in Québec (37%) and highest in the English-speaking provinces of Canada (ranging from 41% to 58%).

20. For instance, the lower rates of volunteering in some Eastern European countries have been explained by the fact that citizens in those countries now feel free *not* to volunteer, while under communism they were required to provide unpaid work for the common good (Hodgkinson, 2012).

21. The Pearson's correlation between the two forms of volunteering (formal and informal) is 0.73, and is significant at the 1% confidence level.

22. Besides analysing socio-economic determinants, social psychologists have also assessed the psychological traits of volunteers. However, the importance of personality as a driver of volunteering seems to be weak relative to social conditions and norms (Bekkers, 2005; Musick and Wilson, 2008).

23. For the purpose of the analyses shown in Figures 5.5 and 5.6, the OECD average values are population-weighted. Hence, they are slightly different from the OECD average values shown in Figures 5.1 and 5.2, which are simple averages.

24. In Mexico, for instance, the percentage of men volunteering in the sports and recreational sector is three times higher than that of women, while in Chile almost 70% of volunteers in the social and health sector are women. These patterns of gender differences closely mirror those found in the paid labour market.

25. Figure 5.5 covers only the working-age population. Volunteering rates are likely to increase in retirement.

26. According to Wilson (2000), "education boosts volunteering because it heightens awareness of problems, increases empathy, and builds self-confidence".

27. Oesterle, Johnson and Mortimer (2004) claim that people with higher levels of education have a greater interest in volunteering because they have a greater stake in the community. This perspective would imply that volunteering is, ultimately, self-interested.

28. This tends to corroborate the view that participation in the labour market fosters volunteering (Wilson, 2000), possibly because work experience yields skills, which makes people more able to volunteer. This relationship is further discussed and analysed later in the chapter.

29. Research has shown that when volunteering in parent-pupil associations is excluded, parents volunteer less than individuals without children (Prouteau and Wolff, 2008).

30. The 2009 International Civic and Citizenship Education Study gathered data from more than 140 000 students studying in Grade 8 (or equivalent) at more than 5 300 schools from 38 countries. The questionnaire covers four different content domains (Civic society and systems, Civic principles, Civic participation, and Civic identities), which include a variety of topics.

31. Percentage values shown in Figure 5.7 are slightly different from those reported in Figure 4.23, as here participation in religious and political organisation is not considered.

32. The calculations are made as follows: *Value of labour used in volunteer activities in nominal currency = Average hourly post-tax labour cost * Average hours worked per day * Days in a year * Population (16 years and above)*. This method is broadly consistent with the one used by Ahmad and Koh (2011) to value home production, i.e. the services produced by households for their own use.

33. The health benefits of volunteering are not limited to older adults (Omoto and Snyder, 1995). However, the differences in health outcomes between helpers and non-helpers are more difficult to detect in younger people, where health is not affected by susceptibilities associated with aging.

34. Volunteers are often interested in acquiring skills through volunteering activities that are formally recognised by certificates. Passeport Bénévole (*www.passeport-benevole.org*), issued by France Bénévolat, documents the skills and qualifications acquired and the experiences gained through voluntary work. Since its introduction in 2007, 100 000 such passes have been distributed. These passes improve the description of volunteers' skills and formalise the volunteering, thus making it more verifiable. The point is also to make the skills and qualifications usable for the respective volunteer's career. Similarly, in the Czech Republic, a personal skills and qualifications portfolio has been developed that certifies the competences and qualifications acquired during volunteering.

35. See: *www.volunteering.org.uk/who-we-can-help/employers/the-business-case-for-esv* (accessed 29 May 2015).

36 The indicator on life satisfaction used in the Gallup World Poll is based on the Cantril Ladder, which asks people to rate their current life relative to the best and worst possible lives for them on a scale from 0 to 10. Conversely, the measure of affect balance captures experienced well-being rather than evaluative well-being, and is based on three positive emotions (enjoyment, feeling well-rested, and smiling or laughing a lot) and three negative emotions (worry, anger and sadness) experienced yesterday; this indicator takes a value of 1 if the positive emotions experienced by each respondent outnumber the negative ones, and of 0 otherwise.

37. These results should be interpreted with caution. Due to data constraints it is not possible to take into account reverse causality (do people volunteer more when they are happy?) and simultaneity biases (some third factor, such as religion, leading to higher volunteering and more happiness).

References

Abraham, K.G. and C. Mackie (eds.) (2005), "Beyond the Market: Designing Nonmarket Accounts for the United States", Washington, DC, National Academies Press.

Ahmad, N. and S. Koh (2011), "Incorporating Estimates of Household Production of Non-Market Services into International Comparisons of Material Well-Being", *OECD Statistics Working Papers*, 2011/07, OECD Publishing, Paris, *http://dx.doi.org/10.1787/5kg3h0jgk87g-en*.

Albertini, M. and J. Radl (2012), "Intergenerational Transfers and Social Class: Inter-Vivos Transfers as Means of Status Reproduction?", *Acta Sociologica*, Vol. 55, No. 2, pp. 107-123.

Anheier, H.K. and L.M. Salamon (2001), "Volunteering in cross-national perspective: Initial comparisons", *Civil Society Working Paper series*, No. 10, Centre for Civil Society, London School of Economics and Political Science, London, *http://eprints.lse.ac.uk/29049/1/CSWP_10_web.pdf*.

Becchetti, L., A. Pelloni and F. Rossetti (2008), "Relational goods, sociability, and happiness", *Kyklos*, Vol. 61, pp. 343-363.

Bekkers, R. (2005), "Participation in Voluntary Associations: Relations with Resources, Personality, and Political Values", *Political Psychology*, Vol. 26, No. 3, pp. 439-454.

Bekkers, R., B. Völker, M. van der Gaag and H. Flap (2007), "Social Networks of Participants in Voluntary Associations", in *Social Capital: Advances in Research*, N. Lin and B.H. Erickson (eds.), Oxford University Press, Oxford.

Binder, M. (2015), "Volunteering and life satisfaction: A closer look at the hypothesis that volunteering more strongly benefits the unhappy", *Applied Economics Letters*, Vol. 22, No. 11, pp. 874-885.

Binder, M. and A. Freytag (2013), "Volunteering, subjective well-being and public policy", *Journal of Economic Psychology*, Vol. 34, pp. 97-119.

Bjørnskov, C. (2006), "The multiple facets of social capital", *European Journal of Political Economy*, Vol. 22, No. 1, pp. 22-40.

Boarini, R. and M. Díaz (2015), "Cast a Ballot or Protest in the Street – Did our Grandparents Do More of Both?: An Age Period-Cohort Analysis in Political Participation", *OECD Statistics Working Papers*, 2015/02, OECD Publishing, Paris, *http://dx.doi.org/10.1787/5js636gn50jb-en*.

Cnaan, R.A. and L.M. Amrofell (1994), "Mapping volunteer activity", *Nonprofit and Voluntary Sector Quarterly*, Vol. 23, No. 4, pp. 335-51.

Cnaan, R.A., F. Handy and M. Wadsworth (1996), "Defining who is a volunteer: Conceptual and empirical considerations", *Nonprofit and Voluntary Sector Quarterly*, Vol. 25, No. 3, 364-83.

Corden, A. and R. Sainsbury (2005), *Volunteering for employment skills: A qualitative research study*, University of York: Social Policy Research Unit, York.

Council of the European Union (2009), "Council decision of 27 November 2009 on the European Year of Voluntary Activities Promoting Active Citizenship (2011)", *Official Journal of the European Union*, (2010/37/EC), *http://ec.europa.eu/citizenship/pdf/20091127_council_decision_en.pdf*.

Curtis, J.E., D.E. Baer and E.G. Grabb (2001), "Nations of Joiners: Explaining Voluntary Association Membership in Democratic Societies", *American Sociological Review*, Vol. 66, No. 6, pp. 783-805.

Day, K.M. and R.A. Devlin (1998), "The Payoff to Work without Pay: Volunteer Work as an Investment in Human Capital", *Canadian Journal of Economics*, Vol. 31, No. 5, pp. 1179-1191.

Dolan, P., T. Peasgood and M. White (2008), "Do we really know what makes us happy? A review of the economic literature on the factors associated with subjective well-being", *Journal of Economic Psychology*, Vol. 29, pp. 94-122.

Dykstra, P.A. and T. Fokkema (2011), "Relationships between parents and their adult children: a West European typology of late-life families", *Ageing and Society*, Vol. 31, No. 04, pp. 545-569.

Ellis Paine, A., S. McKay and D. Moro (2013), "Does volunteering improve employability? Insights from the British Household Panel Survey and beyond", *Voluntary Sector Review*, Vol. 4, No. 3, pp. 333-353.

Erlinghagen, M. (2010), "Volunteering after Retirement. Evidence from German Panel Data", *European Societies*, Vol. 12, No. 5, pp. 603-625.

European Parliament (2008), *Report on the role of volunteering in contributing to economic and social cohesion*, Committee on Regional Development, *www.europarl.europa.eu/sides/getDoc.do?type=REPORT&reference=A6-2008-0070&language=EN*.

Gabard, D.L. (1997), "Volunteer burnout and dropout: issues in AIDS service organizations", *Journal of Health and Human Service Administration*, Vol. 19, No. 3, pp. 283-303.

Gee, L.K. (2011), "The Nature of Giving Time to Your Child's School", *Nonprofit and Voluntary Sector Quarterly*, Vol. 40, No. 3, pp. 552-565.

Hackl, F., M. Halla and G.J. Pruckner (2007), "Volunteering and income – The fallacy of the good Samaritan?", *Kyklos*, Vol. 60, pp. 77-104.

Hank, K. (2007), "Proximity and contacts between older parents and their children: a European comparison", *Journal of Marriage and Family*, Vol. 69, No. 1, pp. 157-173.

Hank, K. and M. Erlinghagen (2010), "Dynamics of Volunteering in Older Europeans", *Gerontologist*, Vol. 50, No. 2, pp. 170-178.

Hank, K., and S. Stuck (2008), "Volunteer Work, Informal Help, and Care among the 50+ in Europe: Further Evidence for 'Linked' Productive Activities at Older Ages", *Social Science Research*, Vol. 37, No. 4, pp. 1280-1291.

Hart, D., T.M. Donnelly, J. Youniss and R. Atkins (2007), "High School Community Service as a Predictor of Adult Voting and Volunteering", *American Educational Research Journal*, Vol. 44, No. 1, pp. 197-219.

Haski-Leventhal, D. and D. Bargal (2008), "The volunteer stages and transitions model: Organizational socialization of volunteers", *Human Relations*, Vol. 61, No. 1, pp. 67-102.

Haski-Leventhal, D. (2009), "Elderly Volunteering and Well-Being: A Cross-European Comparison Based on SHARE Data", *Voluntas*, Vol. 20, No. 4, pp. 388-404.

Helliwell, J.F. (2003), "How's life? Combining individual and national variables to explain subjective well-being", *Economic Modelling*, Vol. 20, pp. 331-360.

Hirst, A. (2001), *Links between volunteering and employability: Research report*, Department of Education and Skills, London.

Hodgkinson, V. (2012), "Volunteering in Global Perspective", *The Values of Volunteering: Nonprofit and Civil Society Studies*, Dekker, P. et al. (eds.), Kluwer Academic/Plenum Publishers, New York.

ILO (2013), 19th International Conference of Labour Statisticians, Report of the Conference, Geneva, 2-11 October, *www.ilo.org/wcmsp5/groups/public/---dgreports/---stat/documents/normativeinstrument/wcms_230304.pdf*.

ILO (2011), *Manual on the Measurement of Volunteer Work*, International Labour Office, Geneva, *www.ilo.org/wcmsp5/groups/public/---dgreports/---dcomm/---publ/documents/publication/wcms_167639.pdf*.

ILO (2009), "Report of the Conference – 18th International Conference of Labour Statisticians, Geneva", 24 November-5 December 2008, *www.ilo.org/wcmsp5/groups/public/---dgreports/---stat/documents/meetingdocument/wcms_101467.pdf*.

Kahneman, D., A.B. Krueger, D.A. Schkade, N. Schwarz and A.A. Stone (2004), "A Survey Method for Characterizing Daily Life Experience: The Day Reconstruction Method", *Science*, Vol. 3, pp. 1776-1780.

Kamerade, D. and A. Ellis Paine (2014), "Volunteering and employability: implications for policy and practice", *Voluntary Sector Review*, Vol. 5, No. 2, pp. 259-273.

Krause, N. and B.A. Shaw (2000). "Giving Social Support to Others, Socioeconomic Status, and Changes in Self-Esteem in Late Life", *Journal of Gerontology: Social Sciences*, Vol. 55B, No. 6, pp. 323-333.

Krueger, A.B., D. Kahneman, C. Fischler, D. Schkade, N. Schwarz and A.A. Stone (2009), "Time Use and Subjective Well-Being in France and the U.S.", *Social Indicators Research*, Vol. 93, pp. 7-18.

Lancee, B. and J. Radl (2012), "Social Connectedness and the Transition from Work to Retirement", *Journals of Gerontology Series B: Psychological Sciences and Social Sciences*, Vol. 67, No. 4, pp. 481-490.

Lee, Y. and J.L. Brudney (2012), "Participation in formal and informal volunteering: Implications for volunteer recruitment", *Nonprofit Management and Leadership*, Vol. 23, No. 2, pp. 159-180.

Lewis, M. (2002), "Service Learning and Older Adults", *Educational Gerontology*, Vol. 28, pp. 655-667.

Li, Y. and K.F. Ferraro (2005), "Volunteering and Depression in Later Life: Social Benefit or Selection Processes?", *Journal of Health and Social Behavior*, Vol. 46 (March), pp. 68-84.

Li, Y., A. Pickles and M. Savage (2005), "Social capital and social trust in Britain", *European Sociological Review*, Vol. 21, pp. 109-123.

Malter, F. and A. Börsch-Supan (eds.) (2015), *SHARE Wave 5: Innovations & Methodology*, MEA, Max Planck Institute for Social Law and Social Policy, Munich.

McPherson, J.M., P.A. Popielarz and S. Drobnic (1992), "Social Networks and Organizational Dynamics", *American Sociological Review*, Vol. 57, pp. 153-170.

Meier, S. and A. Stutzer (2008), "Is Volunteering Rewarding in Itself?", *Economica*, Vol. 75, pp. 39-59.

Mertens, S. and M. Lefebvre S. (2004), "La difficile mesure du travail bénévole dans les institutions sans but lucratif", in *Institut des Comptes Nationaux, Le compte satellite des institutions sans but lucratif 2000 et 2001*, Banque Nationale de Belgique and Centre d'Economie Sociale d'HEC-Ecole de Gestion de l'Université de Liège, Brussels.

Miranda, V. (2011), "Cooking, Caring and Volunteering: Unpaid Work around the World", *OECD Social, Employment and Migration Working Papers*, No. 116, OECD Publishing, Paris, *http://dx.doi.org/10.1787/5kghrjm8s142-en*.

Musick, M.A. and J. Wilson (2008), *Volunteers: A social profile*, Bloomington, IN: Indiana University Press.

Newton, B., J. Oakley and E. Pollard (2011), *Volunteering: Supporting transitions*, Institute for Employment Studies, *https://vinspired.com/content_packages/636*.

Nichols, G and R. Ralston (2011), "Social inclusion through volunteering: the legacy potential of the 2012 Olympic Games", *Sociology: The Journal of the British Sociological Association*, Vol. 45, No. 5, pp. 900-914.

O'Neill, M. (2001), "Research on living and volunteering: Methodological considerations", *Nonprofit and Voluntary Sector Quarterly*, Vol. 30, pp. 505-514.

OECD (2013), *OECD Skills Outlook 2013: First Results from the Survey of Adult Skills*, OECD Publishing, Paris, *http://dx.doi.org/10.1787/9789264204256-en*.

OECD (2011), *How's Life? Measuring Well-Being*, OECD Publishing, Paris, *http://dx.doi.org/10.1787/9789264121164-en*.

Oesterle, S., M.K. Johnson and J.T. Mortimer (2004), "Volunteerism during the Transition to Adulthood: A Life Course Perspective", *Social Forces*, Vol. 82, No. 3, pp. 1123-1149.

Omoto, A.M. and M. Snyder (2002), "Considerations of community: The context and process of volunteerism", *American Behavioral Scientist*, Vol. 45, No. 5, pp. 846-67.

Pew Reaserch Centre (2015), "Assessing the Representativeness of Public Opinion Surveys", March, Washington, DC, *http://www.people-press.org/files/legacy-pdf/Assessing%20the%20 Representativeness%20of%20Public%20Opinion%20Surveys.pdf*.

Phalen, K.F. (2003), "Kids of Character", *Volunteer Leadership Journal*, Summer, pp. 4-9.

Plagnol, A.C. and F.A. Huppert (2010), "Happy to help? Exploring the factors associated with variations in rates of volunteering across Europe", *Social Indicators Research*, Vol. 97, pp. 157-176.

Post, S.G. (2005), "Altruism, happiness, and health: It's good to be good", *International Journal of Behavioral Medicine*, Vol. 12, pp. 66-77.

Prouteau, L. (2006), "La mesure et la valorisation du bénévolat", Colloque ADDES (7 Mars), Université de Nantes, Nantes Atlantique Universités, *http://addes.asso.fr/wp-content/uploads/2015/03/2006-Prouteau-definitif.pdf*.

Prouteau, L. (2002), "Le bénévolat sous le regard des économistes", *Revue française des affaires sociales*, Vol. 4, No. 4, pp. 117-134.

Prouteau, L. and F.C. Wolff (2008), "On the relational motive for volunteer work", *Journal of Economic Psychology*, Vol. 29, No. 3, pp. 314-335.

Prouteau, L. and F.C. Wolff (2006), "Does volunteer work pay off in the labor market?", *Journal of Socio-Economics*, Vol. 35, pp. 992-1013.

Prouteau, L. and F.C. Wolff (2004), "Le travail bénévole : un essai de quantification et de valorisation", *Economie et statistique*, Vol. 373, pp. 33-56.

Putnam, R.D. (2000), *Bowling Alone: The Collapse and Revival of American Community*, Simon and Schuster, New York.

Putnam, R.D. (1995), "Bowling alone: America's declining social capital", *Journal of Democracy*, Vol. 6, No. 1, pp. 65-78.

Rochester, C., E. Paine, A. and S. Howlett (2009), *Volunteering and Society in the 21st Century*, Palgrave Macmillan, Hampshire, England.

Sajardo, A. and I. Serra (2011), "The Economic Value of Volunteer Work. Methodological Analysis and Application to Spain", *Nonprofit and Voluntary Sector Quarterly*, Vol. 40, No. 5, pp. 873-895.

Salamon, L.M., S. Sokolowski and M. Haddock (2011), "Measuring the economic value of volunteer work globally – concepts, estimates and a roadmap to the future", *Annals of Public and Cooperative Economics*, Vol. 82, No. 3, pp. 217-252.

Salamon, L.M., H.K. Anheier, R. List, S. Toepler, S.W. Sokolowski and Associates (1999), *Global Civil Society: Dimensions of the Nonprofit Sector*, Johns Hopkins Comparative Nonprofit Sector Project, Baltimore.

Schlozman, K.L., N. Burns and S. Verba (1994), "Gender and the Pathways to Participation: The Role of Resources", *Journal of Politics*, Vol. 56, No. 4, pp. 963-990.

Schlozman, K.L., S. Verba and H.E. Brady (1999) "Civic Participation and the Equality Problem", in T. Skocpol and M.P. Fiorina (eds.), *Civic Engagement in American Democracy*, Russell Sage Foundation, New York.

Shannon, C.S. (2009), "An untapped resource: Volunteers aged 8 to 12", *Nonprofit and Voluntary Sector Quarterly*, Vol. 38, No. 5, pp. 828-845.

Strauß, S. (2008), *Volunteering and Social Inclusion: The Interrelation between Unemployment and Civic Engagement in Germany and Great Britain*, VS-Verlag, Wiesbaden.

Tang, F. (2006), "What Resources are needed Volunteerism? A Life Course Perspective", *Journal of Applied Gerontology*, Vol. 25, No. 5, pp. 375-390.

Toppe, C. and R. Groves (2007), "What is Volunteering and How Can It Be Measured", Paper prepared and presented at the JHU/UNECE Workshop on Volunteer Measurement, Geneva.

United Nations (2003), *Handbook on Nonprofit Institutions in the System of National Accounts*, United Nations Publication, Sales No. E.03.XVII.9 ST/ESA/STAT/SER.F/91, New York, *http://unstats.un.org/ unsd/publication/seriesf/seriesf_91e.pdf*.

United Nations (2001), *Role of Volunteerism in the Promotion of Social Development*, Resolution Adopted by the General Assembly fifty-sixth session (A/RES/56/38), *www.unv.org/en/news-resources/resources/un-resolutions/doc/role-of-volunteerism-in.html* (accessed on 29 May 2015).

UNECE (2013), *Guidelines for Harmonising Time Use Surveys*, United Nations, Geneva, *www.unece.org/fileadmin/DAM/stats/publications/2013/TimeUseSurvey_Guidelines.pdf*.

Van Willigen, M. (2000), "Differential benefits of volunteering across the life course", *Journal of Gerontology: Social Sciences*, Vol. 55B, pp. 308-318.

Vegeris, S., K. Vowden, C. Bertram, R. Davidson, F. Husain, K. Mackinnon and D. Smeaton (2010), "Support for newly unemployed and Six Month Offer evaluations: A report on qualitative research findings", DWP Research Report No. 691, Department for Work and Pensions, London, *https://www.gov.uk/government/uploads/system/uploads/attachment_data/file/214463/rrep691.pdf*.

Vézina, M. and S. Crompton (2012), "Volunteering in Canada", *Canadian Social Trends*, Statistics Canada Catalogue No. 11-008-X, Statistics Canada, *www.statcan.gc.ca/pub/11-008-x/2012001/article/11638-eng.pdf*.

Volunteering England (2010), *Policy briefing: Get Britain working*, November, London.

White, M.P. and P. Dolan (2009), "Accounting for the richness of daily activities", *Psychological Science*, Vol. 20, pp. 1000-1008.

Wilson, J. (2012), "Volunteerism research: A review essay", *Nonprofit and Voluntary Sector Quarterly*, Vol. 41, pp. 176-212.

Wilson, J. (2000), "Volunteering", *Annual Review of Sociology*, Vol. 26, pp. 215-240.

Wilson, J. and M.A. Musick. (2000), "The effects of volunteering on the volunteer", *Law and Contemporary Problems*, Vol. 62, No. 4, pp. 141-168.

Wilson, J. and M.A. Musick (1997), "Who Cares? Toward an Integrated Theory of Volunteer Work", *American Sociological Review*, Vol. 62, pp. 694-713.

Database references

European Social Survey (2006), *European Social Survey*, Round 3 Data, Data file edition 3.5. (database), Norwegian Social Science Data Services, Norway – Data Archive and distributor of ESS data, *www.europeansocialsurvey.org/* (accessed on 29 May 2015).

European Values Survey (2011), *European Values Study 2008*, Integrated Dataset (EVS 2008), Data file version 3.0.0 (database), GESIS Data Archive, *http://dx.doi.org/10.4232/1.11004* (accessed on 29 May 2015).

Eurostat (2015), *Time Use Database*, *http://appsso.eurostat.ec.europa.eu/nui/show.do?dataset=tus_00selfstat&lang=en* (accessed on 5 July 2015).

Gallup World Poll, *www.gallup.com/strategicconsulting/en-us/worldpoll.aspx* (accessed 10 June 2015).

Harmonised European Time Use Survey web application, *https://www.h2.scb.se/tus/tus/* (accessed on 1 July 2015).

International Association for the Evaluation of Educational Achievement (IEA) (2009), *International Civic and Citizenship Education Study (ICCS)* (database), *http://www.iea.nl/iccs_2009.html* (accessed on 29 May 2015).

OECD (2015a), "Aggregate National Accounts, SNA 2008: Gross domestic product", *OECD National Accounts Statistics* (database), *http://dx.doi.org/10.1787/data-00001-en* (accessed on 24 May 2015).

OECD (2015b), "Annual full time earnings and annual labour costs in equivalent USD, 25-64 year-old population", *OECD Employment and Labour Market Statistics* (database), *http://dx.doi.org/10.1787/eag-2010-table88-en* (accessed on 24 May 2015).

OECD (2012), *OECD Survey of Adult Skills* (PIAAC database), *www.oecd.org/site/piaac/* (accessed on 1 July 2015).

SHARE (2013), *Survey of Health, Ageing and Retirement in Europe*, Wave 4, Release 1.1.1 (database), *http://dx.doi.org/10.6103/SHARE.w4.111* (accessed on 29 May 2015).

SHARE (2013), *Survey of Health, Ageing and Retirement in Europe*, Wave 2, Release 2.6.0 (database), *http://dx.doi.org/2010.6103/SHARE.w2.260* (accessed on 29 May 2015).

Survey of Health, Ageing and Retirement in Europe (SHARE) (2015), Survey of Health, Ageing and Retirement in Europe, Wave 5, Release 1.0.0 (database), *http://dx.doi.org/10.6103/SHARE.w5.100* (accessed on 29 May 2015).

United States Department of Labor (2015), American Time Use Survey (ATUS) 2013 (database), Bureau of Labor Statistics, *www.bls.gov/tus/#database* (accessed on 24 April 2015).

World Values Survey Association (2009), *World Values Survey*, Wave 5 2005-2008, Official Aggregate v.20140429, World Values Survey Association (database), *www.worldvaluessurvey.org* (accessed on 15 May 2015).

ANNEX 5.A

Characteristics of the volunteers

Table 5.A.1. **Prevalence and frequency of formal volunteering, by individual and household characteristics**

Percentage, working-age population, 2012

Individual and household characteristics	Prevalence rates, regardless of frequency	Prevalence rates by frequency of engagement			
		Every day	At least once a week	Less than once a week	Less than once a month
GENDER					
Male	36.0	1.6	7.2	8.4	18.7
Female	35.9	1.8	8.1	9.3	16.6
AGE					
16-24	38.2	1.32	7.56	9.31	20.0
25-34	32.4	1.26	5.43	7.93	17.8
35-44	37.1	1.95	7.97	9.02	18.2
45-54	36.5	1.81	8.16	8.83	17.7
55-65	33.6	1.71	8.25	9.38	14.4
EDUCATION					
Primary education	24.4	1.5	5.2	5.7	12.0
Secondary education	34.5	1.6	7.4	8.3	17.2
Tertiary education	47.9	1.9	9.2	10.9	25.9
EMPLOYMENT STATUS					
Full-time employed	36.9	1.4	7.0	8.8	19.8
Part-time employed	40.5	2.1	9.2	10.8	18.5
Unemployed	26.1	2.4	6.1	6.3	11.3
Student	42.2	1.3	8.4	10.8	21.7
Unpaid worker	30.3	2.1	8.4	7.6	12.2
Early retired	29.7	2.3	9.1	8.1	10.3
MARITAL STATUS					
Married	36.7	1.8	8.0	9.1	17.8
Single	34.8	1.5	7.1	8.4	17.9
HOUSEHOLD STRUCTURE					
No children	35.4	1.5	6.8	8.6	18.5
Children younger than 3 years	31.8	1.4	5.4	8.7	16.3
Children older than 3 years	38.6	1.9	8.5	11.0	17.3
HOUSEHOLD ECONOMIC STATUS					
Lower income	25.8	1.9	3.1	6.5	14.3
Middle income	36.2	1.5	7.7	8.5	18.6
Higher income	49.3	1.8	9.0	12.8	25.7
FAMILY BACKGROUND					
Migrant	31.3	1.76	7.4	7.0	15.2
Native	36.3	1.66	7.6	9.1	17.9

Source: OECD calculations based on data from OECD (2012), OECD Survey of Adult Skills (PIAAC database), *www.oecd.org/site/piaac/*.

StatLink ᴍᴸᴾ http://dx.doi.org/10.1787/888933260185

Table 5.A.2. **Prevalence and frequency of informal volunteering,
by individual and household characteristics**

Percentage, working-age population, 2006

Individual and household characteristics	Prevalence rates, regardless of frequency	Prevalence rates by frequency of engagement				
		At least once a week	At least once a month	At least once every three months	At least once every six months	Less often
GENDER						
Male	70.6	14.5	21.6	11.9	7.6	15.0
Female	71.2	17.8	20.3	10.0	8.3	14.7
AGE						
16-24	70.8	16.1	21.4	9.4	6.9	17.0
25-34	70.5	13.9	20.2	10.9	9.1	16.3
35-44	73.1	16.3	21.1	12.5	9.0	14.4
45-54	71.5	16.9	21.2	11.2	8.4	13.8
55-64	67.8	17.7	20.6	10.4	6.1	13.1
EDUCATION						
Primary education	55.8	12.3	13.6	8.0	6.8	15.2
Secondary education	69.7	16.3	20.8	10.3	7.3	15.0
Tertiary education	79.7	17.6	24.0	13.8	10.1	14.2
EMPLOYMENT STATUS						
Employed	73.2	15.7	21.3	12.2	8.8	15.2
Unemployed	64.5	17.6	19.5	9.3	7.2	10.8
Student	71.8	16.0	22.7	9.1	6.9	16.9
Early retired	65.0	18.0	20.8	7.5	5.3	13.5
MARITAL STATUS						
Married	70.9	15.7	20.5	11.8	8.6	14.4
Single	70.9	16.9	21.5	10.0	7.2	15.4
HOUSEHOLD STRUCTURE						
No children	71.1	17.1	21.5	10.1	7.1	15.3
Children	70.7	15.3	20.3	11.9	9.0	14.3
HOUSEHOLD ECONOMIC STATUS						
Lower income	60.8	14.9	17.5	8.9	6.5	13.1
Middle income	70.3	15.9	20.8	10.5	8.1	15.1
Higher income	76.9	17.0	22.6	13.0	8.5	15.8

Source: OECD calculations based on data from the European Social Survey (2006), European Social Survey Round 3 Data, Data file edition 3.5. (database), Norwegian Social Science Data Services, Norway – Data Archive and distributor of ESS data, *www.europeansocialsurvey.org/*.

StatLink ᐅᓬᖮ *http://dx.doi.org/10.1787/888933260194*

ANNEX 5.B

Volunteering and human capital

Table 5.B.1. **The effect of formal volunteering on skills proficiency and earnings**

Explanatory variables	Skills proficiency			Hourly earnings[3]
	Literacy[1]	Numeracy[1]	Problem-solving[2]	
Formal volunteering	10.998	10.791	7.993	0.14
	(12.05)**	(9.75)**	(7.30)**	(8.40)***
Female	-4.194	-14.186	-8.952	-0.232
	(6.01)**	(17.27)**	(11.90)**	(-14.1)**
Age	-0.456	-0.335	-0.837	0.016
	(11.66)**	(8.45)**	(20.75)**	(21.09)***
Permanent contract	10.976	17.218	13.222	0.09
	(8.65)**	(11.13)**	(9.47)**	(2.85)**
Temporary contract	8.538	13.39	11.625	-0.27
	(4.72)**	(6.06)**	(5.77)**	(-4.85)**
Born abroad	-28.861	-29.089	-20.635	-0.196
	(19.05)**	(17.78)**	(12.01)**	(-6.34)**
Skilled occupation	40.746	46.591	32.649	
	(26.10)**	(29.02)**	(14.98)**	
Semi-skilled white-collar occupation	21.798	23.789	15.812	
	(14.38)**	(14.75)**	(7.87)**	
Semi-skilled blue-collar occupation	8.444	11.258	1.332	
	(5.31)**	(6.83)**	(-0.55)	
Literacy skills				0.002
				(3.35)**
Numeracy skills				0.001
				(-0.66)
Problem-solving skills				0.002
				(3.62)**
Constant	264.116	248.799	289.218	1.574
	(109.03)**	(102.93)**	(99.40)**	(13.09)***
λ				-0.346
				(-22.26)***

1. The analysis includes 20 OECD countries (Australia, Austria, Canada, the Czech Republic, Denmark, Estonia, Finland, France, Germany, Ireland, Italy, Japan, Korea, the Netherlands, Norway, Poland, the Slovak Republic, Spain, Sweden and the United States) and three OECD sub-national entities (Flanders in Belgium; England and Northern Ireland in the United Kingdom).

2. The analysis includes 17 OECD countries (Australia, Austria, Canada, the Czech Republic, Denmark, Estonia, Finland, Germany, Ireland, Japan, Korea, the Netherlands, Norway, Poland, the Slovak Republic, Sweden and the United States) and three OECD sub-national entities (Flanders in Belgium; England and Northern Ireland in the United Kingdom).

Table 5.B.1. **The effect of formal volunteering on skills proficiency and earnings** (*cont.*)

3. The dependent variable "hourly earnings" refers to the natural logarithm of hourly earnings. Hourly earnings include bonuses and are expressed in PPP-adjusted US dollars. The wage distribution was trimmed to eliminate the 1st and 99th percentile. The sample includes only working-age employees. The analysis includes 20 OECD countries (Australia, Austria, Canada, the Czech Republic, Denmark, Estonia, Finland, France, Germany, Ireland, Italy, Japan, Korea, the Netherlands, Norway, Poland, the Slovak Republic, Spain, Sweden and the United States) and three OECD sub-national entities (Flanders in Belgium; England and Northern Ireland in the United Kingdom). A negative and statistically significant coefficient of λ means that there exists a self-selection bias.

Note: The coefficients in the table represent the impact of the explanatory variables on skills proficiency and hourly earnings. Country fixed-effects are not shown in the table. Z-values in parentheses: *** significant at the 1% level, ** significant at the 5% level, * significant at the 10% level.

Source: OECD calculations based on data from OECD (2012), OECD Survey of Adult Skills (PIAAC database), *www.oecd.org/site/piaac/*.

StatLink ⬛ᴵᴸˢ▸ *http://dx.doi.org/10.1787/888933260205*

ANNEX 5.C

Volunteering and subjective well-being

Table 5.C.1. **Positive and negative feelings, by volunteer engagement and country**

Percentage of people who declared having experienced positive emotions (enjoyment, feeling well-rested, and smiling or laughing a lot) and negative emotions (worry, anger and sadness) the previous day, 2014 or latest available year

Country	Positive feelings						Negative feelings					
	Well-rested		Experienced enjoyment		Smiled		Sadness		Anger		Worry	
	Do not volunteer	Volunteer formally	Do not volunteer	Volunteer formally	Do not volunteer	Volunteer formally	Do not volunteer	Volunteer formally	Do not volunteer	Volunteer formally	Do not volunteer	Volunteer formally
Australia	69.0	62.7	79.0	81.0	75.3	74.7	22.6	19.9	16.4	15.0	37.7	35.8
Austria	70.3	70.5	74.6	81.6	76.1	84.0	13.3	10.6	11.3	12.3	27.9	24.6
Belgium	63.9	66.4	76.1	80.8	81.9	82.2	21.5	22.1	12.5	15.6	40.1	41.7
Canada	66.8	68.1	83.9	83.6	82.6	84.1	22.5	25.0	13.0	17.3	40.6	36.6
Chile	58.6	65.1	86.8	93.4	85.8	86.7	21.9	23.0	17.7	15.0	43.4	45.0
Czech Republic	59.3	57.2	70.1	79.9	63.1	72.7	14.5	19.1	22.6	13.5	34.3	35.2
Denmark	66.7	69.1	88.4	90.6	76.4	81.9	18.5	17.5	15.9	13.3	37.7	30.6
Estonia	61.8	65.2	72.7	84.9	57.7	73.2	21.2	15.7	9.9	11.0	31.3	32.0
Finland	69.6	67.3	75.4	80.7	78.3	83.1	14.6	15.3	8.9	5.7	33.2	45.8
France	63.4	67.8	76.8	86.4	80.7	90.5	15.6	20.4	13.8	23.3	31.3	30.4
Germany	69.1	71.2	77.4	83.4	72.7	80.1	18.6	15.0	14.0	11.3	27.5	22.1
Greece	64.9	55.9	66.1	84.3	70.6	84.8	29.9	11.0	29.9	22.8	58.7	47.5
Hungary	56.8	49.8	68.5	88.0	56.8	72.9	21.4	16.8	14.5	9.3	37.8	28.5
Iceland	54.4	61.3	86.5	91.5	84.7	89.9	10.6	14.8	8.1	9.3	24.8	30.4
Ireland	69.9	72.1	78.7	86.8	72.8	78.1	20.9	18.8	13.3	14.5	35.1	34.5
Israel	60.0	66.2	60.6	70.6	57.7	58.9	23.2	19.5	25.3	19.5	35.8	33.2
Italy	63.1	59.2	70.0	65.9	74.0	71.7	35.1	42.0	15.2	20.5	53.4	60.1
Japan	68.9	79.9	63.6	80.7	76.6	86.7	10.5	10.5	15.4	15.0	32.7	27.3
Korea	64.8	74.5	58.0	77.7	64.5	79.4	21.8	17.4	20.0	13.2	47.7	37.1
Luxembourg	69.1	73.3	80.0	85.8	77.0	81.4	13.9	18.7	11.6	14.7	24.7	21.6
Mexico	70.0	69.9	72.6	80.2	77.2	78.6	16.7	22.8	8.6	8.0	44.5	33.3
Netherlands	68.2	70.1	87.6	90.7	83.3	87.4	18.0	19.7	10.6	7.9	36.8	40.2
New Zealand	64.9	60.9	85.2	85.3	84.6	83.2	15.7	18.4	12.3	14.6	28.0	31.4
Norway	61.6	70.7	85.9	90.3	76.8	85.5	17.4	16.4	13.2	10.0	30.2	26.6
Poland	56.5	60.0	76.2	81.7	76.8	85.0	17.9	18.2	21.8	18.2	27.7	28.5
Portugal	55.5	60.8	55.0	64.0	69.9	73.6	34.1	28.9	10.0	13.7	62.7	67.0
Slovak Republic	68.9	73.3	72.1	86.5	68.6	73.8	18.6	18.3	27.1	23.0	35.3	35.2
Slovenia	69.0	76.7	54.6	61.6	64.0	72.0	16.6	19.2	18.9	16.1	52.5	50.5
Spain	71.1	72.3	66.0	68.2	76.8	74.4	22.8	26.9	25.8	22.6	53.1	47.7
Sweden	64.7	62.3	86.6	90.6	79.1	82.1	19.7	19.9	14.0	17.0	28.7	28.8
Switzerland	72.7	71.2	82.2	84.0	82.3	80.6	17.6	14.3	14.4	13.2	25.0	28.2
Turkey	72.1	77.7	59.3	81.2	64.2	90.1	36.7	35.8	39.7	38.1	41.4	58.4
United Kingdom	64.3	64.6	78.0	81.8	76.5	85.4	18.6	24.4	15.1	18.5	39.2	36.7
United States	68.2	69.3	80.4	90.4	81.2	83.3	23.4	23.9	18.4	18.0	40.2	45.4
OECD	**65.2**	**67.1**	**74.5**	**82.2**	**74.3**	**80.3**	**20.2**	**20.0**	**16.4**	**15.6**	**37.7**	**37.0**

Note: Data for Iceland and Turkey refer to 2013.

Source: OECD calculations based on data from the Gallup World Poll, www.gallup.com/strategicconsulting/en-us/worldpoll.aspx.

StatLink http://dx.doi.org/10.1787/888933260211

Table 5.C.2. **Quantile regression analysis of the effects of formal volunteering on life satisfaction**

Explanatory variables	Life satisfaction				
	1st quintile	2nd quintile	3rd quintile	4th quintile	5th quintile
Formal volunteering	0.288	0.256	0.238	0.183	0.127
	(11.20)**	(16.79)**	(15.63)**	(16.12)**	(9.55)**
Male	-0.11	-0.003	-0.027	-0.067	-0.046
	(5.28)**	(-0.23)	(2.07)*	(6.51)**	(3.68)**
Married	-0.163	-0.236	-0.159	-0.08	-0.073
	(7.48)**	(17.45)**	(11.15)**	(6.84)**	(5.19)**
Age: 25-34 y.o.	-0.218	-0.074	-0.084	-0.049	0.019
	(4.44)**	(2.60)**	(3.08)**	(2.34)*	(-0.79)
Age: 35-54 y.o.	-0.261	-0.061	-0.077	-0.031	0.082
	(5.92)**	(2.33)*	(3.10)**	(-1.61)	(3.70)**
Age: 55-64 y.o.	-0.212	-0.049	-0.022	0.056	0.179
	(4.38)**	(-1.7)	(-0.77)	(2.62)**	(7.32)**
Age: 65+	-0.009	0.005	0.069	0.134	0.282
	(-0.2)	(-0.16)	(2.45)*	(6.31)**	(12.14)**
Secondary education	0.407	0.217	0.213	0.118	-0.027
	(14.69)**	(11.31)**	(9.66)**	(6.24)**	(-1.31)
Tertiary education	0.366	0.231	0.152	0.028	-0.205
	(9.93)**	(9.50)**	(5.92)**	(-1.33)	(8.77)**
Someone to count on	0.560	0.254	0.232	0.113	-0.047
	(19.29)**	(11.60)**	(8.63)**	(4.61)**	(-1.67)
Health problems	-0.229	-0.022	-0.067	-0.034	0.009
	(10.01)**	(-1.43)	(3.90)**	(2.34)*	(-0.52)
Household income	0.597	0.523	0.477	0.283	0.101
	(35.49)**	(49.51)**	(44.54)**	(31.69)**	(12.63)**
Small town or village	-0.104	-0.183	-0.182	-0.17	-0.167
	(3.24)**	(9.36)**	(8.79)**	(10.71)**	(9.06)**
Big city	-0.136	-0.227	-0.241	-0.144	-0.133
	(4.01)**	(11.11)**	(11.20)**	(8.77)**	(6.94)**
Suburb of a big city	0.081	0.07	0.031	0.054	0.046
	(2.13)*	(3.06)**	(-1.3)	(3.08)**	(2.22)*
Constant	-2.313	0.43	1.78	4.635	8.01
	(13.81)**	(4.03)**	(16.48)**	(49.97)**	(93.83)**
R^2	0.2	0.26	0.22	0.23	0.22
N	31,924	32,253	32,241	31,839	30,034

Note: The analysis includes all OECD countries. Data are pooled across countries and all available years from 2006-2014. The variable "household income" refers to the natural logarithm of the household disposable income. Z-values in parentheses: * indicates that values are significant at 10% confidence level; ** indicates that they are significant at 5% confidence level; and *** that they are significant at 1% confidence level.

Source: OECD calculations based on data from the Gallup World Poll, *www.gallup.com/services/170945/world-poll.aspx*.

StatLink ᓫᕽᓴᕽ *http://dx.doi.org/10.1787/888933260227*

Chapter 6

Going local: Measuring well-being in regions

This chapter provides a framework and a set of indicators to assess well-being in OECD sub-national regions. Circumstances in the place where people live are important elements to consider in order to obtain a thorough picture of their well-being, which is shaped by a combination of individual attributes and place characteristics. The indicators presented in this chapter cover nine dimensions of well-being and include aspects of both material conditions and quality of life. The chapter provides evidence on the regional disparities in the different well-being dimensions and includes an assessment of income inequality and poverty within regions. Finally, the main steps to be implemented in order to improve the measurement of well-being at sub-national level in the future are discussed.

The statistical data for Israel are supplied by and under the responsibility of the relevant Israeli authorities. The use of such data by the OECD is without prejudice to the status of the Golan Heights, East Jerusalem and Israeli settlements in the West Bank under the terms of international law.

Introduction: Why a regional perspective matters for measuring well-being

To get a complete picture of people's living conditions, it is important to consider the regional and local circumstances that affect their well-being. This can include, for example, how people's access to local public services shapes their choices, or how well-functioning infrastructures and services contribute to healthier lives, better job opportunities and more cohesive communities.

Sub-national data and indicators add information on the distribution of well-being across territories and can highlight how advantages or disadvantages in well-being dimensions are distributed not only among groups of people with different characteristics but also across locations. National averages for well-being indicators typically mask stark variations across regions within a country. For example, in 2013 the employment rate between Italy's regions varied by 33 percentage points, from 40% (in Campania) to 73% (in the region of Bolzano), a difference similar to that observed across OECD countries. Similarly, the number of years a person can expect to live in the United States varies across states by six years, only three years less than the variation between OECD countries.

Regional and local governments hold important responsibilities for many of the policies that bear most directly on people's lives. Around 40% of public spending in the OECD area is by sub-national governments, and 70% of sub-national public expenditure in the OECD area goes to education, health, social protection and general public services (OECD, 2013). In addition, many of the interactions among policies are location-specific: policies on land-use, transport and housing, for example, differ between locations and the interactions among these different strands of policy are more readily manageable where they occur, in specific places. Measuring well-being at the local level can help policy makers to prioritise public intervention where improvements are most needed, to better assess and monitor the spatial concentration of advantages or disadvantages, and to improve policy coherence by identifying synergies that policies can leverage. Finally, as measures of local well-being refer to conditions of everyday life, they can also help to empower citizens to demand action that responds to their expectations and needs and, thereby, to restore people's trust in the capacity of public institutions to address pressing challenges. Many initiatives to develop well-being metrics at the local level have been launched in recent years with the objectives of broadening the information available, helping the design and evaluation of local development policies, raising awareness on specific issues and increasing government accountability (Box 6.1).

The OECD report *How's Life in Your Region?* (OECD, 2014a), released in October 2014, builds on both the conceptual framework of the OECD *Better Life Initiative* and on the *Regions at a Glance* series to expand the measurement of people's well-being to the sub-national level. A set of comparable indicators for 362 regions in 34 OECD countries was developed in the context of this project, covering nine well-being dimensions.

Box 6.1. **Selected initiatives to measure well-being at sub-national level**

Regional well-being indicators can serve various purposes and be used by different stakeholders. Previous experience with these indicators suggest that they have been used by both national and regional authorities – often in partnership with independent institutions and universities – as well as by non-governmental organisations.

Recent national initiatives have aimed to broaden the information on well-being available at the sub-national level to cover the entire country. Since 2013, the Australian Bureau of Statistics (ABS) – recognising the important differences between its measures of well-being and progress across the nation – has included in its Measures of Australia's Progress (MAP) report a chapter that discusses indicators at the regional level for each well-being dimension of MAP. In Italy, in 2013 the National Statistical Office (ISTAT) and the National Council on the Economy and Labour (CNEL) published a report on Equitable and Sustainable Well-being (BES): most of the indicators (on 12 dimensions of well-being) are available at the regional level and, in the future, the BES framework will be adapted and applied to large cities and provinces. In 2013 the Turkish Statistical Institute expanded its annual Life Satisfaction Survey at the provincial level (Tl3 regions); the Survey gathers information on happiness, personal development and satisfaction with various public services. Turkey's Ministry of Development also published the Socio-Economic Development Study (SEDI) in 2013 that ranks provinces and regions according to 61 indicators grouped in 8 dimensions (demography, education, health, employment, competitiveness and innovation, financial capacity, accessibility, and quality of life).

In 2012, the Polish Ministry of Regional Development and the United Nations Development Program (UNDP) have developed a UNDP – Human Development Index (HDI) applied at the sub-national level ("powiat", corresponding to the local administration units (LAU1) in the Eurostat classification). The Index (referred to as the Local Human Development Index, LHDI) consists of three components: health (measured by life expectancy and infant mortality, deaths due to cancer and heart disease), education (percentage of children in pre-school and average results of secondary school final examinations) and welfare (average income level per capita). The survey, carried out by the UNDP, the Warsaw School of Economics and the Central Statistical Office (CSO), uses data from the CSO and administrative records for the years 2007-2010. The results show high disparities in social development, with cities, large towns and the areas around them generally displaying better performance than rural areas (*http://issuu.com/undp_poland/docs/lhdi_report_poland_2012_eng*). In its *Long-term National Development Strategy: Poland 2030*, the government declared that it would use HDI, alongside GDP, as the main indicator to measure the country's development. The LHDI index has led to better links between regional/local strategy goals and national strategy goals. The LHDI is an effective tool for planning, monitoring and evaluating the activities of local government, and the study is being used to improve public policies and monitor the implementation of strategic objectives at the regional and local level.

Local authorities can also use well-being indicators to monitor regional challenges or performance in specific dimensions of well-being, and to prioritise the allocation of public funding among territories. In the Netherlands, for example, increasing concern about personal safety brought the Dutch Central Bureau of Statistics to introduce the *Crime Survey* in the late 1990s and the *Safety Monitoring Survey* later on. The surveys collect information on physical, social and safety conditions as well as on fear of crime, victimisation, neighbourhood problems and the functioning of the police at the national, regional and local levels. In the United Kingdom, the *Well-being for Life Strategy* in Newcastle provides a plan for actions to undertake in the period 2013-2016 that focus on three specific domains of well-being: education, employment and health. To raise awareness about regional attractiveness and economic growth, the region of Southern Denmark launched the *Good Life* initiative in 2012. A broad set of well-being indicators is collected for each of the region's municipalities, with the goal of monitoring demographic and social phenomena and developing better-informed policy. The Australian Bureau of Statistics (2011) computes Socio-Economic Indexes for

Box 6.1. **Selected initiatives to measure well-being at sub-national level** *(cont.)*

Areas (SEIFA), which are then ranked according to their socio-economic situation: these indexes are used for different purposes, including targeting areas that require funding and services. In the United States, the *Partnership for Sustainable Communities* (PSC), a Federal initiative aimed at integrating housing, transport and environmental policies to build more economically and environmental sustainable communities, provides a set of comparable indicators for different territorial scales which are linked to five well-being dimensions. Communities applying for federal funding can use the well-being measures to inform different stages of the project cycle (design, implementation and evaluation).

Various regions and countries use well-being measures to identify priority areas for policy intervention. In Hungary, regions receiving EU Cohesion Policy funding are classified according to 24 indicators in four dimensions: society and demography; housing and living conditions; local economy and labour market; and infrastructure and environment. This kind of classification was used to define programmes that focused on economic development, employment, education and Roma integration in the 33 most disadvantaged micro-regions in the period 2007-2013. In the Netherlands, the Telos research centre measures economic, socio-cultural and ecological capital in order to alert citizens and policy makers about what needs policy attention and what is working well. In the Italian region of Sardinia, the implementation of the 2007-2013 EU Cohesion Policy was supported by the introduction of a performance scheme (*Obiettivi di Servizio*), which defined minimum standards for four policy areas that had been characterised by poor results in terms of the level and quality of public services: building on this initiative, the regional government identified a comprehensive set of well-being measures for the regional development plan for the period 2014-2020. The Province of Rome introduced a well-being strategy that led to the introduction of well-being measures in 2012: citizens were involved through community surveys designed to understand how they value different dimensions of well-being, and the provincial government used the well-being measures to define its territorial development strategy. In Mexico, the State of Morelos identified a series of indicators to monitor a set of well-being dimensions and included them in the State Development Plan for 2013-2018.

In 2010, New Zealand's Ministry of Social Development published the *Social Report*, which provides a comprehensive assessment of people's well-being at both national and regional level. The report includes a set of well-being indicators for the 16 regional council areas in several domains, such as health, knowledge and skills, jobs, economic standards of living, civil and political rights, cultural identity, leisure, safety, and social connectedness. A new release of the Report will be available in late 2015. In addition, the second edition of the *Regional Economic Activity Report* published in 2014 provides a comparative assessment of regional economic performance in the country's 16 regional council areas, which allows a better understanding of the roles that different regions play in the economy. Indicators cover several domains, such as demographic information, living standards and jobs (including regional GDP), skills and jobs, national and international connections, and public sector expenditure.

Well-being indicators measured at local level have also been used by non-governmental organisations with the aim of promoting social awareness and advocating policy actions. Examples of this sort can be found in Colombia (Bogotá, *Cómo Vamos*) and Mexico (Ciudad de México, *Cómo vamos*). Bogotá *Cómo Vamos* provides a series of indicators related to five aspects of quality of life: every year the organisation running the initiative publishes a quality of life report, a citizen perception survey and a monitoring and evaluation report on the results achieved by the Bogotá City Council. Finally, the Young Foundation introduced a measurement tool, called WARM (Wellbeing and Resilience Measure) in the United Kingdom to support local agencies and communities in prioritising the use of resources.

Source: Australian Bureau of Statistics (2011), "Socio-Economic Indexes for Areas", ABS, Canberra, *www.abs.gov.au/websitedbs/ censushome.nsf/home/seifa* (accessed 29 May 2015); Australian Bureau of Statistics (2013), "Measures of Australia's Progress"; Bogotà Cómo Vamos, "Bogotà Cómo Vamos", Bogota, Colombia, available at: *www.bogotacomovamos.org/media/uploads/documento/new/ librillo1_v4.pdf* (accessed 10 July 2014); Bogotà Cómo Vamos, available at: *www.bogotacomovamos.org* and *www.bogotacomovamos.org/ concejo* (accessed 10 July 2014); Hák, Tomás, Moldan Bedrich and Lyon Dahl Arthur (eds.) (2007), *Sustainability Indicators: A Scientific Assessment*, Island Press, Young Foundation, *www.youngfoundation.org* (accessed 29 May 2015); Istat (2014), "Il benessere equo e sostenibile"; Koopman, M., H.-J. van Mossel and A. Straub (eds.) (2009), *Performance Measurement in the Dutch Social Rented Sector,*

Box 6.1. **Selected initiatives to measure well-being at sub-national level** (cont.)

IOS Press, Amsterdam; New Zealand Ministry of Social Development (2010), *The Social Report 2010*, Ministry of Social Development, Wellington, New Zealand; New Zealand Ministry of Business, Innovation & Employment (2014), *Regional Economic Activity Report 2014*, Ministry of Business, Innovation & Employment, Wellington, New Zealand; OECD (2014a), "City of Newcastle (United Kingdom)", OECD (2014a), "Province of Rome (Italy)", OECD (2014a), "Region of Sardinia (Italy)", OECD (2014a), "Region of Southern Denmark (Denmark)", OECD (2014a), "State of Morelos (Mexico)", OECD (2014a), "US Partnership for Sustainable Communities", all in OECD (2014a), *How's Life in Your Region?: Measuring Regional and Local Well-being for Policy Making*, OECD Publishing, Paris; Telos website, *www.telos.nl/default.aspx* (accessed 29 May 2015); Zauberman, R. (2010), *Victimisation and Insecurity in Europe: A Review of Surveys and Their Use*, VUB University Press; Turkish Statistical Institute (2013), "Life Satisfaction Survey"; Turkey Ministry of Development (2013), "Socio-Economic Development Study (SEDI)", *http://www3.kalkinma.gov.tr/bolgesel.portal* (accessed 29 May 2015); National Human Development Report: Poland 2012. Regional and Local Human Development *http://issuu.com/undp_poland/docs/lhdi_report_poland_2012_eng* (accessed 29 May 2015).

Measuring well-being at the sub-national level poses formidable challenges. First, the geographical scales of interest may differ from country to country as well as within countries, e.g. administrative regions, functional areas, metropolitan areas, cities, or school districts. To adequately inform policy makers and citizens, data need to pertain to the scale of people's everyday lives and the sphere of influence of public policy. Second, sub-national data are typically sparser than national data, and need to draw on a much wider range of sources. In particular, survey data on households and individuals are seldom designed to provide information at small geographies.

This chapter provides evidence on the distribution of well-being across localities, based on the evidence included in OECD (2014a), and identifies some of the main priorities for statistical work in the future. The chapter is organised as follows: section 2 provides an overview of the framework for measuring regional and local well-being that underpins the OECD report *How's Life in Your Region?*, and identifies the main challenges to the measurement of well-being at the sub-national scale, providing some examples of innovative practices to develop more comprehensive sets of well-being indicators at the sub-national level. Section 3 provides evidence on regional disparities in selected well-being dimensions of the OECD regional well-being framework; the chapter looks in particular at the measurement of "access to services", one key dimension to well-being in regions that is absent from the *How's Life?* framework. The last section identifies the main statistical gaps in this field, and outlines the type of statistical work that should be pursued in the future to provide a more robust statistical description of the well-being conditions in different local areas.

Measuring regional well-being

An OECD *framework for measuring well-being at the local level*

Building on the OECD *How's Life?* framework, the OECD sub-national framework understands current well-being as a multi-dimensional concept that puts the accent on what matters to people, focuses on outcomes (rather than inputs and drivers) and emphasises the need to go "beyond averages" by looking at the distribution of well-being among individuals, social groups (for example, recent migrants, elderly people, etc.) and territories (Figure 6.1). A critical element that *How's Life in Your Region?* adds to the framework used for *How's Life?* is the notion that people's well-being is shaped by a combination of individual traits and placed-based characteristics. Being employed, for example, is a crucial aspect of people's well-being, and it is determined by both individual characteristics, such as skills and education, and contextual factors such as access to training and transport and labour market conditions. Table 6.1 includes some further examples of how place-based factors interact with individual characteristics to produce well-being outcomes at the local level.

Table 6.1. **People in places: The multiple drivers of place-based well-being**

Place-based factors	⇔	Individual characteristics	=	People's well-being
– Dynamism of regional economic context		– Family		– Employment
– Regional labour pool		– Education		– Income
– Access to training		– Skills		– Earnings
– Transport		– Motivation		– Poverty rates
– Information networks		– Biological and genetic factors		– Life expectancy at birth
– Education opportunities		– Lifestyle		– Infant mortality
– Social conditions (housing, heating, relative and absolute inequality, etc.)		– Risky behaviour		
– Environmental conditions (pollution, amenities, etc.)		– Income		

Information on individuals and places can help to better understand the spatial concentration of advantages and disadvantages, and whether the different sources of inequality (individual and place-based) reinforce each other (Sampson, 2008; Wilson, 1987). A similar approach to measuring well-being that combines individual and place characteristics has been adopted recently by the "Good Life" initiative in the region of Southern Denmark (OECD, 2014c) and by the Socio-Economic Indexes for Areas (SEIFA) in Australia (Australian Bureau of Statistics, 2011, Box 6.1). Building on these experiences, a range of place-based factors is included in the OECD regional framework.

Figure 6.1. **The OECD framework for measuring well-being at regional and local levels**

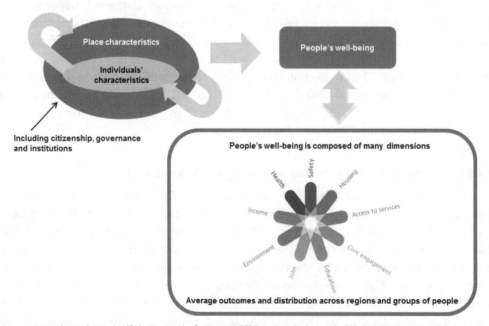

Source: OECD (2014a), How's Life in Your Region?, OECD Publishing, Paris, http://dx.doi.org/10.1787/9789264217416-en.

To make this regional framework operational, a set of comparable indicators has been developed to measure outcomes in nine well-being dimensions for the 362 OECD large regions. When available, the regional indicators used here are the same as those used in *How's Life?* at the national level. In addition, the well-being dimension of *access to services* is included in the regional framework, while the three dimensions "work-life balance", "social connections" and "subjective well-being" considered in *How's Life?* are not included in the regional framework due to lack of data. Subjective assessments of life circumstances can usefully complement objective measures and should be included to monitor people's well-being in greater depth. The OECD Better Life initiative at national level includes subjective well-being as an autonomous dimension, which is measured through life satisfaction. Other self-reported indicators are used to measure health and social connections. However, at this stage none of the indicators in the regional framework provide information about people's self-reported experiences of their own well-being (e.g. perceived social support, feelings about work-life balance, or life satisfaction measures, Table 6.2), mainly because of lack of information, since survey data are usually not representative at the regional and local level.

The regional well-being indicators are available in the OECD *Regional Well-Being Database* (*http://dx.doi.org/10.1787/region-data-en*); and the OECD *Regional Statistics Database* (*http://dx.doi.org/10.1787/region-data-en*). A limited set of headline indicators is also available through the OECD regional well-being web-tool (*www.oecdregionalwellbeing.org*); these indicators are shown in bold in Table 6.2.

Measurement challenges

The OECD regional well-being framework emphasises the dynamic relation between individual and place-based characteristics. The indicators selected refer to the individuals (e.g. life expectancy at birth) but also to the places where the individuals live (e.g. air quality in the region). The first measurement challenge relates to the geographical scale at which statistical analysis at the sub-national level should be carried out. To adequately inform policy, data need to capture the scale of people's everyday lives and the sphere of intervention of public policies. In practice, *regions* are defined in each country according to different notions (administrative, political, economic, geographical, etc.), and the availability of data on the different regions can vary widely. The OECD classification of regions distinguishes between administrative and functional borders when defining sub-national units. Administrative boundaries are used to define the OECD "large regions" (Box 6.2): these rely on national definitions and generally represent the first administrative tier of sub-national governments. Data on these large regions can be especially important to understand the role of sub-national governments in policy design and public service delivery – as more than 40% of public expenditure in OECD countries and two-thirds of public investments were made by sub-national governments in 2013.

At the same time, the places where individuals live, work and socialise may have little relation to the administrative boundaries around them. This implies that places interact with each other through a broad set of economic and social linkages, and that these linkages typically cross local and regional administrative boundaries. To capture these linkages, places are often grouped by National Statistical Offices into "functional regions". Data mapped to functional regions rather than to traditional administrative boundaries can improve the planning and implementation of policies for infrastructure, transport, housing, schools and spaces for culture and recreation, by better integrating these and adapting them to local needs. In 2012, the OECD/EU developed a harmonised definition of Functional Urban

Table 6.2. **Dimensions and indicators for measuring well-being at the regional and national levels**

Dimensions		Regional indicators included in *How's Life in Your Region?* or associated databases	National indicators included in *How's Life?* headline measures
Material conditions	Income (levels and distribution)	Level:	– Household adjusted disposable income
		– **Household adjusted disposable income** (mean and median)	– Household net financial wealth
		Distribution:	
		– Gini Index for household disposable and market income	
		– Quintile share ratio (S80/S20) for household disposable and market income	
		– Regional relative poverty (headcount ratios for disposable and market income, with poverty line set at 40%, 50% and 60% of the national median income)	
	Jobs	– **Employment rate**	– Employment rate
		– Long-term unemployment rate	– Long-term unemployment rate
		– **Unemployment rate**	– Average annual earnings per employee
			– Probability of becoming unemployed
	Housing	– **Number of rooms per person**	– Number of rooms per person
			– Housing expenditure
			– Dwellings without basic facilities
Quality of life	Health status	– **Life expectancy at birth**	– Life expectancy at birth
		– **Age adjusted mortality rate**	– Perceived health
	Education and skills	– **Educational attainment**	– Educational attainment
		– Students' cognitive skills (PISA)	– Students' cognitive skills (PISA)
			– Competencies in the adult population
	Environmental quality	– **Air quality (PM$_{2.5}$)**	– Air quality (PM$_{2.5}$)
		– Loss of forest and vegetation	– Satisfaction with water quality
		– Municipal waste recycled	
		– Access to green space	
	Personal security	– **Homicide rate**	– Homicide rate (deaths by assault)
		– Car theft rate	– Self-reported victimisation
		– Mortality due to transport accidents	
	Civic engagement and governance	– **Voter turnout**	– Voter turnout
			– Government stakeholder engagement
	Accessibility of services	– **Broadband connection**	
		– Average distance to the closest hospital	
		– Share of population with access to public transport (selected cities only)	
		– Unmet medical needs	
	Work-life balance	Not available	– Employees working very long hours
			– Time devoted to leisure and personal care
	Social connections	Not available	– Social network support
	Subjective well-being	Not available	– Life satisfaction

Note: For several indicators, data are available for only a limited number of countries, and coverage is particularly limited in the cases of Students' cognitive skills (PISA) measured at the regional level, municipal waste recycled, average distance to the closest hospital, share of population with access to public transport, and unmet medical needs. Indicators shown in bold are available through the OECD regional well-being web-tool (*www.oecdregionalwellbeing.org*).

Sources: OECD (2014a), *How's Life in Your Region?*, OECD Publishing, Paris, *http://dx.doi.org/10.1787/9789264217416-en;* "Regional well-being", OECD *Regional Statistics* (database), *http://dx.doi.org/10.1787/data-00707-en;* and OECD *Regional Statistics* (database), *http://dx.doi.org/10.1787/region-data-en.*

Box 6.2. **How are "regions" defined?**

To increase international comparability, regions are classified by the OECD on two territorial levels, reflecting the administrative organisation of countries. OECD large (TL2) regions represent the first administrative tier of sub-national government, e.g. Provinces in Canada, *Comunidades Autonomas* in Spain, *Régions* in France, or States in the United States. The well-being indicators presented in this chapter have been developed for the 362 OECD large regions. Data on these large regions also provide information on inter-regional disparities in the various well-being dimensions, showing that in some cases disparities within countries are larger than across countries. Because the large administrative regions include local governments and many areas with different economic functions (e.g. cities and rural areas), the OECD has also established a common classification of "smaller regions"; these are sub-divisions of the larger regions, and generally correspond to administrative units, with the exception of those in Australia, Canada, Germany and the United States. For these countries, the small regions refer to statistical or economic divisions established by countries and used for data collection. Relying on the criteria of population density, the share of people living in rural communities, the size of urban areas and the distance from urban centres, the OECD rural-urban typology classifies the small regions as "predominantly rural remote", "predominantly rural close to a city", "intermediate" and "predominantly urban" (Brezzi et al., 2011). Most OECD and non-OECD countries have a national definition of rural and urban regions whose criteria are the same as those used in the OECD rural-urban typology, although the thresholds chosen may differ.

Areas applied to 29 OECD countries, and started developing indicators for functional urban areas with a population larger than 500 000 people (OECD, 2012). Most of these indicators are estimates produced by the OECD by integrating different data sources to obtain values at the desired geographical level, and cover only a limited range of dimensions and countries.

The choice among different tiers of analysis implies different trade-offs in terms of measurement strategies. National Statistical Offices typically collect a large number of data for administrative regions, particularly for the larger ones, and much less for small regions and functional areas. Despite some national efforts to provide data for small units that could then be aggregated into different geographies, the availability of official statistics at very small geographical levels remains limited essentially to Census Population data. This represents a major constraint on comprehensive measures of well-being at local level.

Survey-based information for producing indicators of well-being is often not available at the regional or local scale, since surveys are usually designed to provide information that is statistically significant only at the national level (Wishlade and Yuill, 1997; OECD, 2013). Countries can, however, adopt various changes in survey practices to make more sub-national information available: these include changes in the sample structure, to attribute a larger weight to smaller regions; the use of multi-year averages; and the release of those survey details that are necessary to compute standard errors. Changes in the structure of the sample, however, may lead to additional costs to run the survey, or to trade-offs in terms of the analysis of the results (for example, regional samples may become available with a loss of information on other characteristics of the sampled population). To minimise these costs, National Statistical Offices and other data producers are developing alternative methods to compile well-being indicators at different territorial scales. For example, the Nordic countries typically rely extensively on register data and use personal identifiers to link administrative and survey data that refer to the same individual. Other options include using the respondent's localisation in on-line surveys or activities that can be monitored geographically, integrating registries of infrastructure or natural resources with other statistical data, and global (satellite-based) data to derive measures of environmental performance and land management. Some international and national examples of initiatives to develop sets of well-being indicators at sub-national level based on different sources are presented in Box 6.3.

Box 6.3. **New sources of data to measure well-being at different geographical scales**

Several initiatives have been undertaken in recent years to improve the measurement of well-being at different sub-national geographical levels by integrating different sources of data.

In 2011, the European Commission commissioned the World Bank to estimate "poverty maps" for small areas (i.e. cities and neighbourhoods). By combining national census data with data from the EU Statistics on Income and Living Conditions, this initiative generated estimates on income poverty and social exclusion in seven EU countries (Estonia, Hungary, Latvia, Poland, Romania, Slovakia and Slovenia) at municipal, district, sub-regional and regional level. These estimates highlighted large intra-regional income inequalities that were masked at a larger territorial scale and identified specific pockets of deprivation.

Danish national and regional health authorities have carried out the "*How are you?*" survey since 2010 to gather information on well-being, life-style, health and disease among adults. Most data are available at municipal level and are integrated with administrative data to plan and qualify activities within the health sector on a national, regional and municipal level. As part of the "*Good Life*" initiative, the region of Southern Denmark has collected yearly survey data since 2012 on personal safety, health, relationships, self-actualisation, and an assessment of local surroundings for the region's municipalities.

The French National Statistical Office (INSEE) published a report in 2015 on the quality of life at territorial level (*Une approche de la qualité de vie dans les territoires*). The report identifies 27 indicators related to 13 well-being dimensions that are potentially available at municipal level. The data sources range from administrative records to local and national surveys. A new map of the country has been produced using various characteristics of small areas (the final results refer to 2 677 areas defined as territories with less than 50 000 inhabitants differentiated by socio-economic characteristics).

In Hungary, the Regional Development and Spatial Planning Information System (TeIR) integrates statistical, geographical and policy data from different sources (Hungarian Central Statistics Office, government bodies, administrative registers, municipalities and satellite data) to provide evidence at different geographical scales. The TeIR is used to prepare territorial development programmes and to trace their impact in Hungary and in its regions. Additionally, it serves as a base for the Regional Development Monitoring and Assessment System (T-MER), which provides a unified framework for spatial monitoring and activity assessment, and includes indicators at different scales.

In 2014 and 2015, the Italian National Institute of Statistics (Istat) published a report on equitable and sustainable well-being in urban areas (Urbes) (*www.istat.it/it/archivio/153995*). The Urbes project uses data from administrative records, population census as well as national surveys. The project involves a network of 29 large Italian cities and aims to provide a data analysis and identify the best indicators of the state of well-being in Italy's urban areas. The report is based on 65 indicators that are broken down into 11 domains at municipality and provincial levels in order to give a fuller picture of well-being in urban areas. The report is disseminated by Istat and ANCI (the National Association of Italian Municipalities) at national level and presented to the citizens in the various municipalities.

The *Regiones Socioeconómicas de Mexico* is a product of the Mexican National Statistical Institute (INEGI) and has provided socio-economic data at Federal, Municipal and AGEB (*Áreas Geo-statisticas Básicas*) levels since 2004. This initiative followed the previous *Cuadernos de Información para la Planeación de los Estados*, which contained data at only the state and municipal levels. The aim of the *Regiones Socioeconómicas* is to better inform federal and local governments on outcomes in four dimensions (i.e. housing, health, education

Box 6.3. **New sources of data to measure well-being at different geographical scales** (*cont.*)

and employment) by computing a number of indicators from census data. The data are freely available on the INEGI web page, together with a web tool that allows mapping the different indicators across various territorial levels.

The Central Statistical Office of Poland provides well-being indicators at sub-national level. The *Social Cohesion Survey*, which was first conducted in 2011, was used to produce a set of indicators at different geographical levels, including the *voivodships* (TL2), on various domains such as the quality of life, poverty and social capital. The results of the survey analysis are included in the 2014 report *Quality of life, social capital, poverty and social exclusion in Poland* (*http://stat.gov.pl/en/topics/living-conditions/living-conditions/quality-of-life-social-capital-poverty-and-social-exclusion-in-poland,4,1.html*). The second edition of the Social Cohesion Survey is expected to be a source of even more extensive information on sub-national well-being in Poland.

Two initiatives by central administrations in Portugal provide web portals with open access to databases of central and local administrations, together with applications to use these data and access indicators. For example, on the Agency for Administrative Modernisation portal, open datasets have been classified according to different topics, and applications are provided to measure road accidents or citizens' use of local multipurpose administrative centres. The portal (igeo.pt) gathers geographical data from different national agencies on land management instruments, environmental performance, etc., that users can import to their Geographic Information System (GIS) for visualisation (Web Map Service – WMS) or querying (Web Feature Service - WFS). Statistics Portugal also intends to develop and implement an online platform (INE GeoPortal) consisting of an infrastructure to support spatial data management and visualisation, namely through a web service for geospatial information map viewing and downloading, and a service to explore an online metadata catalogue.

The Swiss Federal Statistical Office (FSO) published a report in 2014 on the quality of life at municipality level. Data are used by Urban Audit Switzerland, and show 24 indicators along 13 well-being dimensions in Switzerland's ten largest cities (above 50 000 inhabitants). The data sources range from administrative records to local and national surveys. The indicators presented may be complemented in the future so that a fuller picture of well-being in cities can be presented.

Indices of Multiple Deprivation (IMD) in the United Kingdom have been produced since 2000 by the Department for Communities and Local Governments to measure levels of deprivation in seven domains: employment; income; health; crime; education; living environment and barriers to services. The IMD use 40 indicators derived from administrative, survey and census data sources. Initially, the indices were built at district ward level (corresponding to the smallest geography for electoral districts) but, since 2004, they have been available for the smaller scale of "lower-layer super-output areas" (around 1 500 persons). The IMD have been used to guide the location of social services, like Sure Start Children's Centres, and to target regeneration programmes, like the Neighbourhood Renewal Fund and the Single Regeneration Budget.

In recent years, the OECD has used various types of satellite data developed by space agencies or academic consortia, e.g. exposure to particulate matter in the air ($PM_{2.5}$) for the entire world at different resolutions, combined with geographic information systems (GIS), to measure land cover and its changes, air quality and emissions and other environmental indicators. For example, the indicator of air pollution used in *How's Life in Your Region* (OECD, 2014; Table 6.2) is an estimate of the population's exposure to particulate matter ($PM_{2.5}$) derived from satellite observations. While satellite monitoring of air pollution is less precise than ground-based monitoring stations, it has the advantage of covering the entire globe (while many countries still lack enough ground monitoring stations) and to provide estimates that are consistent within and across countries.

Source: World Bank (2014), European Union Accession Countries – Poverty mapping of new members in EU: completion memo. Washington, DC, *http://documents.worldbank.org/curated/en/2014/06/19764353/european-union-eu-accession-countries-poverty-mapping-new-members-eu-completion-memo*; Danish Health and Medicines Authority (2014), "Danskernes Sundhed – Den Nationale Sundhedsprofil 2013"; Sundhedsstyrelsen, Copenhagen, *https://sundhedsstyrelsen.dk/~/media/1529A4BCF9C64905BAC650B6C45B72A5.ashx*;. Region of Southern Denmark (2015), "KONTUR Region Syddanmark 2014", pp. 42-51, *http://detgodeliv.regionsyddanmark*.

Alternative data derived from public and private sources also have great potential if their use for assessing well-being at sub-national level is harmonised across countries. The increased availability of data from new sources in the last few years – i.e. the explosion in the volume of data available and in the speed of data production – might be mobilised. Social network and crowd-sourced data are already being used to measure a wide range of issues at a detailed geographical scale. In Indonesia, for example, a joint project between the UN and the national government extracts daily food prices from public tweets, which helps to assess both access to food and local living costs (IEAG, 2014).

Significant methodological constraints limit the capacity to produce comparable well-being indicators at sub-national level based on individual responses to surveys, e.g. people's appraisal of the quality of public services, their life satisfaction, their self-reported experiences of victimisation or the social support available. Improvements in the availability of indicators for some well-being dimensions, such as access to services, housing, education and safety, will depend on the capacity to overcome these constraints. For the same reason, the well-being dimensions of "subjective well-being", "work-life balance" and "social connections" reported in *How's Life?* at national level are not currently included in the regional framework, as they are measured uniquely with survey data at the national level.

The geography of well-being

As in *How's Life?*, the well-being dimensions and indicators included in *How's Life in Your Region?* can be grouped into two broad domains: material conditions and quality of life. Jobs, income and housing are the three dimensions related to material conditions, while the six dimensions of quality of life are health, education, safety, civic engagement, environment and access to services. Regional differences within countries are large for most of the indicators considered, in some cases larger than the differences observed across countries. The evidence reviewed in *How's Life in Your Region?* also suggests that the economic crisis of 2008 has not only resulted in lower employment and income levels at the national level, but also in widened disparities between regions in around half of all OECD countries. This development has generally reflected a greater rise in unemployment in the most disadvantaged regions (OECD, 2014b). This section provides evidence on the size of regional disparities in selected well-being dimensions where such disparities were particularly large, such as income, jobs, education, environment and access to services. A description of the regional disparities in the remaining dimensions (housing, health, civic engagement and safety) can be found in OECD (2014b).

Lower regional disparities are associated with higher levels of national well-being

The focus on well-being at sub-national level makes it possible to highlight cases where nation-wide indicators provide only a partial picture of the living conditions that people experience. First, countries that have similar national average values in one dimension of well-being can experience very different regional disparities in the same dimension. This is the case of Turkey and the Czech Republic with respect to income per capita:[1] while in both countries, disposable income per capita averages around 11 500 dollars at the national level, regional values range between 6 000 and 15 500 dollars in Turkey, but only between 10 500 and 15 000 in the Czech Republic. Conversely, countries with similar inter-regional disparities may feature very different national average well-being scores. Australia and Italy, for example, have substantially different levels of disposable income per capita, but a similar magnitude of inter-regional disparities in the same indicator (Figure 6.2).

Figure 6.2. **National average levels plotted against regional disparities in four dimensions of well-being**

2013

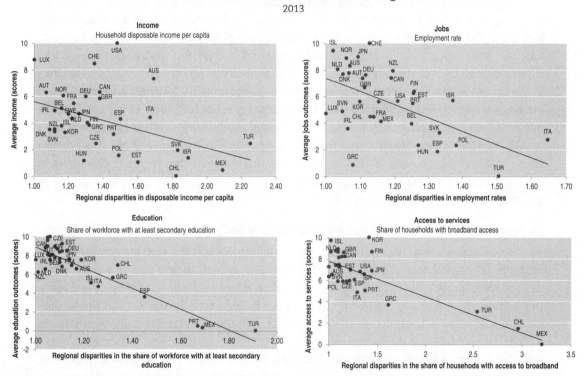

Note: The values of the indicators in the 362 OECD regions have been transformed into scores from 0 to 10, with higher values indicating higher well-being outcomes. The y-axis of each figure reports country average scores for each dimension. The regional disparities reported in the x-axes were computed as the ratio between the value of the top 20% (fifth quantile) and the bottom 20% (first quantile) of regions for the indicators considered for each dimension.

Source: OECD (2014a), *How's Life in Your Region?*, OECD Publishing, Paris, *http://dx.doi.org/10.1787/9789264217416-en.*

StatLink ᔎ *http://dx.doi.org/10.1787/888933260023*

Notwithstanding the significant heterogeneity in the association between regional disparities and overall levels of well-being, for some well-being dimensions (e.g. income, jobs, education and access to services), OECD countries with larger regional disparities often also experience lower national well-being scores. For each of these dimensions, Figure 6.2 plots the average well-being score at national level and the extent of regional disparities in the same dimension (measured as the ratio between the value of the indicator in the top 20% of regions and in the bottom 20%). The negative correlation observed for education and access to services seems to be driven by the three countries with the lowest scores, which might act as outliers; however, in both these cases the correlation remains robust when these countries are omitted from the analysis.[2] One possible explanation of the negative correlations plotted in Figure 6.2 is that cross-country differences in each well-being dimension are, on average, larger among the poorly-performing regions than among the best-performing ones.

Regarding the implications of spatial disparities in well-being outcomes, recent literature shows that the well-being outcomes experienced by individuals, especially the young, in the place where they live can affect their opportunities to achieve better outcomes later in life. In other words, individuals' choices are affected by the living conditions in the place where they are located, which in turn might affect their well-being achievements in the long run. This might be particularly relevant for the dimensions related to the provision of public services. In the case of education, for example, the availability of good schools for children can shape their future opportunities. Analyses for the United States show that average income in the neighbourhood has a large impact on individuals' future earnings capacity, an effect that is roughly half of that related to parental income (Rothwell and Massey, 2015). Other research finds that intergenerational social mobility differs substantially across cities in the United States. Cities characterised by higher social mobility feature, on average, lower income inequality, less segregation and better primary schools (Chetty et al., 2014). These patterns are partly explained by the "external effects" of education: individuals benefit from being surrounded by more educated people, i.e. education at local level generates positive social externalities (Moretti, 2004). On the whole, this suggests that regional disparities in well-being outcomes might have implications for people's overall well-being that should be investigated further.

Income levels vary widely between and within regions

When considering regional disparities in living standards, the most widely-used measure is regional GDP (OECD, 2013). However, GDP is best understood as a measure of the economic production of each region, rather than of the income enjoyed by its residents. In addition, the regional economic production can be significantly higher than the income experienced by households in regions where the exploitation of natural resources constitutes a large share of GDP but the income generated is transferred elsewhere, or in metropolitan areas where the economic production is assured by workers living elsewhere. In general, regional disparities in GDP per capita are larger than those in household disposable income. Inter-regional disparities in household income are nevertheless large in many OECD countries, both in high- and medium-income countries such as the United States, Australia, Italy, Spain and Israel, and in low-income ones such as Chile, Mexico and Turkey (Figure 6.3). Large differences in household income are also observed between urban and rural areas. In Europe in 2011, for example, households living in densely populated areas had incomes about 10% higher than those living in sparsely populated areas (Eurostat, 2013). In half of the OECD countries, these inter-regional gaps in household income increased between 2000 and 2011 due to the weaker performance of disadvantaged regions. Regional differences are higher in terms of market incomes, since transfers and taxation reduce the gap between "rich" and "poor" regions. On the other hand, differences in household income might be biased by the fact that differences in living costs across regions in the same country are not taken into account.

Figure 6.3. **Regional disparities in GDP per capita, household market income and household disposable income**

Ratio between maximum and minimum regional value, 2013 or latest available year

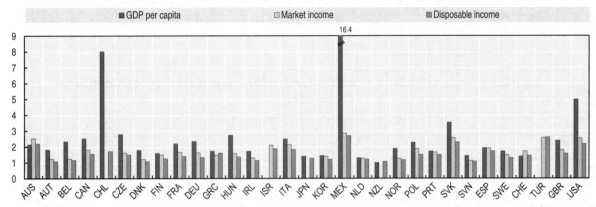

Notes: Data are based on regional national accounts information provided by the National Statistical Offices, except for Turkey and Switzerland where income data are OECD's calculations based on EU-SILC and Turkish SILC. Data refer to regions at TL2 level, except for Turkey for which the data are only available at a more aggregated level (NUTS1). Data refer to 2012 for Chile, Finland, Germany, Hungary, Ireland, Italy, Mexico, Norway, Poland, the Slovak Republic, Slovenia, Sweden and Switzerland; and to 2011 for Belgium, France, Israel, Japan, Portugal and Spain. The ratio between the maximum and minimum regional value is calculated over per capita USD in PPP adjusted values (2010=100).

Source: OECD Regional Well-Being (database), http://dx.doi.org/10.1787/region-data-en.

StatLink ᴹᔆ᠍᠍ http://dx.doi.org/10.1787/888933260031

In some regions income inequalities are much higher than in the country as a whole

Individual-level data at the sub-national level are needed to assess the relative importance of individual and place characteristics to people's well-being. In addition, the measurement of household income distribution at regional level can help to target social and redistributive policies. However, methodological constraints have hindered the development of comparable measures of income inequality within regions. Household surveys are rarely designed to be representative at the regional level; and differences in the regional population size and the cost of living between urban and rural regions may bias the assessment of income inequality, especially with respect to the identification of poverty lines. In this latter respect, recent studies show that accounting for price differences between urban and rural areas dramatically affects the estimations of regional poverty rates (Jolliffe, 2006; World Bank, 2015). The International Comparison Program (ICP) has initiated a data compilation to account for regional variations in prices through the use of Household Expenditure Surveys (HES). These can be integrated with the ICP classification to compute Purchasing Power Parities (PPPs) that can then be used as spatial deflators.[3]

In 2014, the OECD released estimates of income inequality and poverty within regions, whose features are discussed in Piacentini (2014).[4] While these estimates do not account directly for differences in price levels across regions, relative poverty rates are computed using both national and regional poverty lines, with regional poverty lines (set as a share of each region's median income) partly reflecting differences in the cost of living across regions.

The lack of available cost-of-living measures at the regional level does not necessarily affect the interpretation of regional income inequality indicators, such as the Gini Index. Regional differences in the distribution of household disposable income are, on average, higher in larger OECD countries than in smaller ones; they are also high in some small countries with large urban centres (e.g. Belgium and the United Kingdom). The difference in the Gini coefficients of household disposable income between the Mexican states of Tlaxcala (0.41) and Guerrero (0.53) is similar to the difference in Gini coefficients between national averages for Mexico and New Zealand. Similarly, income inequality in Iowa, the American State with the lowest Gini coefficient, is close to the national average for Canada and France, while the Gini coefficient of household disposable income in Washington, DC is close to that of Chile and Mexico (Figure 6.4).

Figure 6.4. **Regional values of the Gini Index for household disposable income**
Around 2010

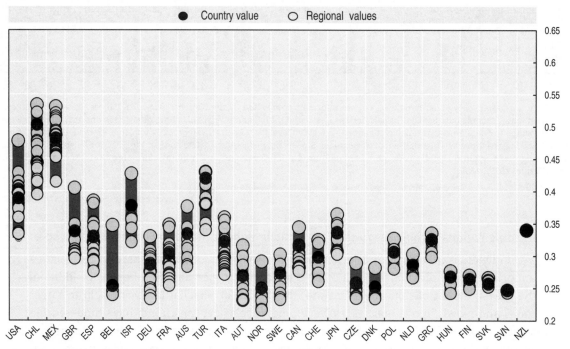

Note: Countries are ordered by the difference between maximum and minimum values of the Gini coefficient for the regional household disposable income. Each point in the panel represents a region. The Gini index is a measure of income concentration that ranges from zero, representing perfect equality, to 1, where all income flows to a single person.

Source: OECD Regional Well-Being (database), *http://dx.doi.org/10.1787/region-data-en.*

StatLink ⬛ᵐˢᵖ *http://dx.doi.org/10.1787/888933260046*

The level of income inequality within a country's regions varies widely across countries. While across regions in Japan and the Nordic countries, households with the highest 20% of disposable income earn between two and four times more than the poorest 20%, across the regions in Chile and Mexico, the income of the 20% richest people is at least ten times larger than that of the poorest 20%. In European countries, the largest differences within regions between the top 20% earners and the bottom 20% are recorded in Spain, Greece, Turkey and the South of Italy (Figure 6.5). Income inequality also depends on the urban structure of the region, and tends to be higher in larger cities (Kanbur and Zhuang, 2013; Royuela et al., 2014).

Empirical studies of the determinants of income inequality within regions have highlighted the importance of several characteristics of local labour markets such as employment density (Ciccone, 2002) and the proximity to highly populated centres (Rice et al., 2006). These factors translate into a higher income for people living in urban areas, driven by higher wage premia (Glaeser and Mare, 2001). Analysis across OECD regions highlights that income inequality has a strong positive correlation with both the unemployment rate

Figure 6.5. **Income inequality within regions**

Ratio between the household disposable income of the top and bottom quintiles of the distribution in each region, around 2010

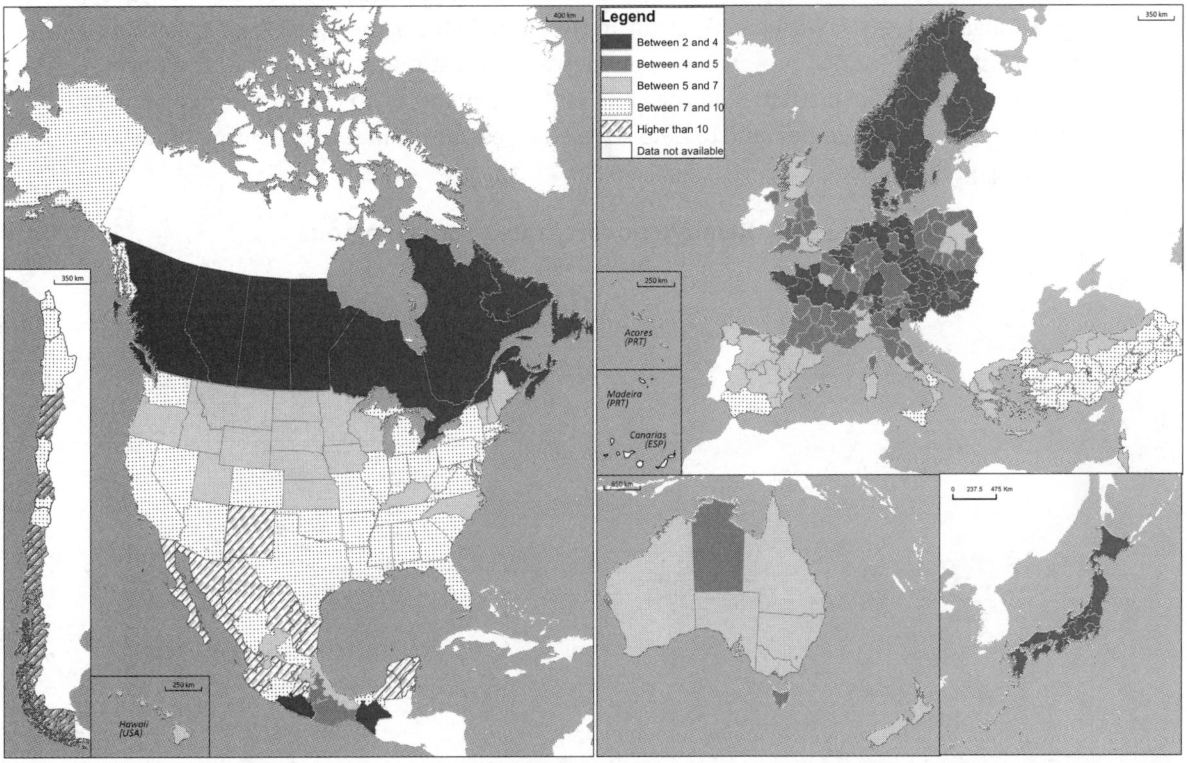

Legend
- Between 2 and 4
- Between 4 and 5
- Between 5 and 7
- Between 7 and 10
- Higher than 10
- Data not available

Note: This document and any map included herein are for illustrative purposes and without prejudice to the status of or sovereignty over any territory, to the delimitation of international frontiers and boundaries and to the name of any territory, city or area. Source of administrative boundaries: National Statistical Offices and FAO Global Administrative Unit Layers (GAUL).

Source: OECD (2014a), *How's Life in Your Region?*, OECD Publishing, Paris, *http://dx.doi.org/10.1787/9789264217416-en.*

StatLink ᴍᴸ᠍ᴀ᠍ *http://dx.doi.org/10.1787/888933260052*

and the share of the elderly population (over age 70), and a strong negative correlation with secondary educational attainment, the share of population in the age class 60-69 and the share of workers in manufacturing.

Income inequality is also strongly correlated with poverty rates, a relationship that is also confirmed at regional level. The OECD regional well-being database provides estimates of relative poverty rates, with poverty lines set at 60%, 50% and 40% of the national median income.[5] Regional variability in poverty rates can be very high within countries: for example, in 8 of the 27 countries considered, disparities in income poverty between regions (measured at 50% of the national median income) are larger than disparities between OECD countries themselves. In Mexico, income-poverty rates range from 5.4% in the Distrito Federal to 48.9% in Chiapas; in Turkey, they range from 4% in Istanbul to 50.4% in South-Eastern Anatolia (Figure 6.6).

The marked territorial dimension of poverty implies that policies to fight poverty would benefit from a more detailed geographical breakdown and a better understanding of its main determinants. In this context, several national and international initiatives have been undertaken in recent years to construct "poverty maps" with greater territorial detail. Poverty maps are usually estimated by linking census data with household survey data (or tax data) to monitor poverty in-between census years. In Mexico, the Ministry of Social

Development and the United Nations Development Programme have developed nutritional and income poverty maps at the municipal and state levels, to be used in programmes aimed at improving living standards in poor urban households (Székely Pardo et al., 2007; Lopez-Calva et al., 2007; World Bank, 2015). In the United States, the Small Area Income and Poverty Estimates (SAIPE) programme provides annual estimates of income and poverty statistics for all school districts, counties and states to support choices on the allocation of funds in federal programmes, and to help state and local authorities in allocating funds and managing programmes.

Figure 6.6. **Relative poverty rates across regions**
Around 2010

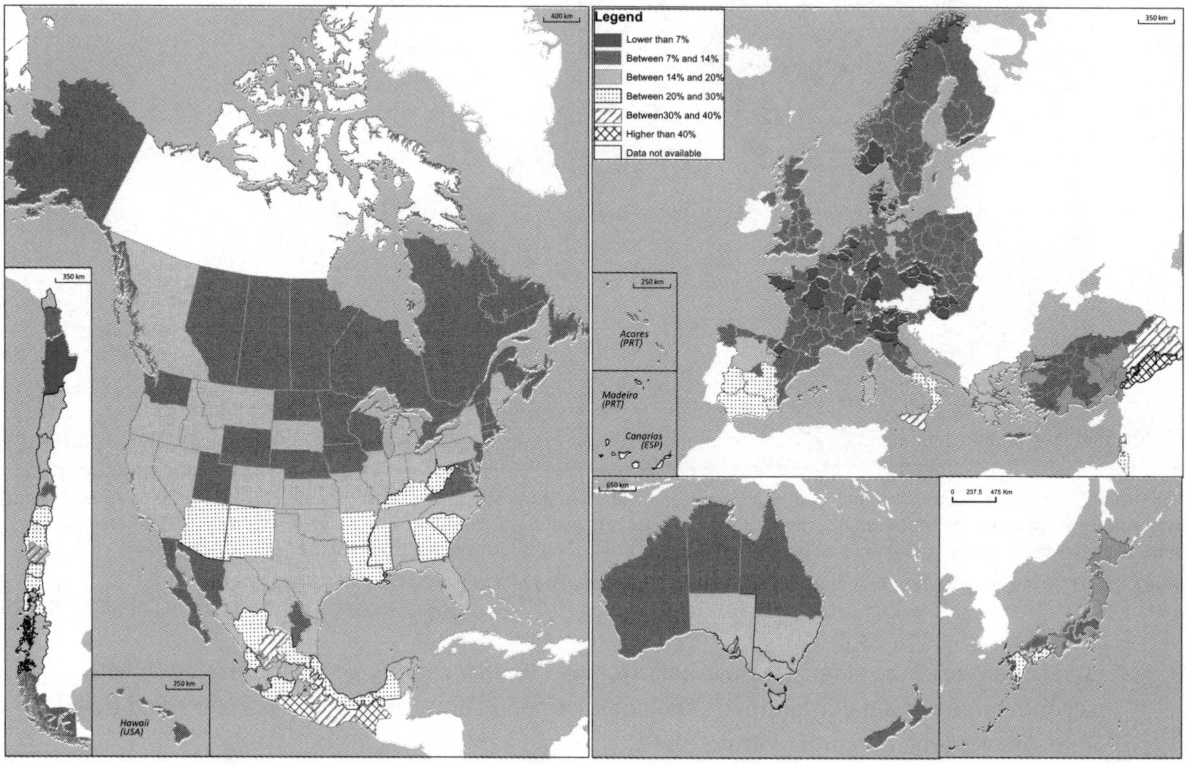

Note: Poverty headcounts, with the poverty line defined at 50% of the national median income. This document and any map included herein are for illustrative purposes and without prejudice to the status of or sovereignty over any territory, to the delimitation of international frontiers and boundaries and to the name of any territory, city or area. Source of administrative boundaries: National Statistical Offices and FAO Global Administrative Unit Layers (GAUL).

Source: OECD *Regional Well-Being* (database), *http://dx.doi.org/10.1787/region-data-en.*

StatLink ᵃᵢˢᵖ *http://dx.doi.org/10.1787/888933260069*

Regional disparities in unemployment remain large and have worsened since 2008

Over the last decade, job creation was disproportionately driven by a limited number of OECD regions that were more competitive and attractive thanks to their human capital and industrial mix: overall, 40% of the employment growth in OECD countries between 1999 and 2013 was accounted for by just 10% of OECD regions (OECD, 2013). In 2014, regional disparities in unemployment rates (33 percentage points in the OECD area between the regions with the highest and lowest unemployment rates) are significantly larger than disparities across OECD countries (23 percentage points). The largest regional differences in unemployment rates are found in Turkey, Spain, Italy, Belgium and the Slovak Republic (above 10 percentage points). In some cases, these disparities between regions are as large as disparities between all OECD countries: for example, the difference in the unemployment rate between the Italian regions of Campania and Trento (around 20 percentage points) is similar to that between the national averages for Spain and Switzerland (Figure 6.7).

Figure 6.7. **Regional variation in unemployment rates**

Percentage of the labour force, maximum and minimum regional values, 2014

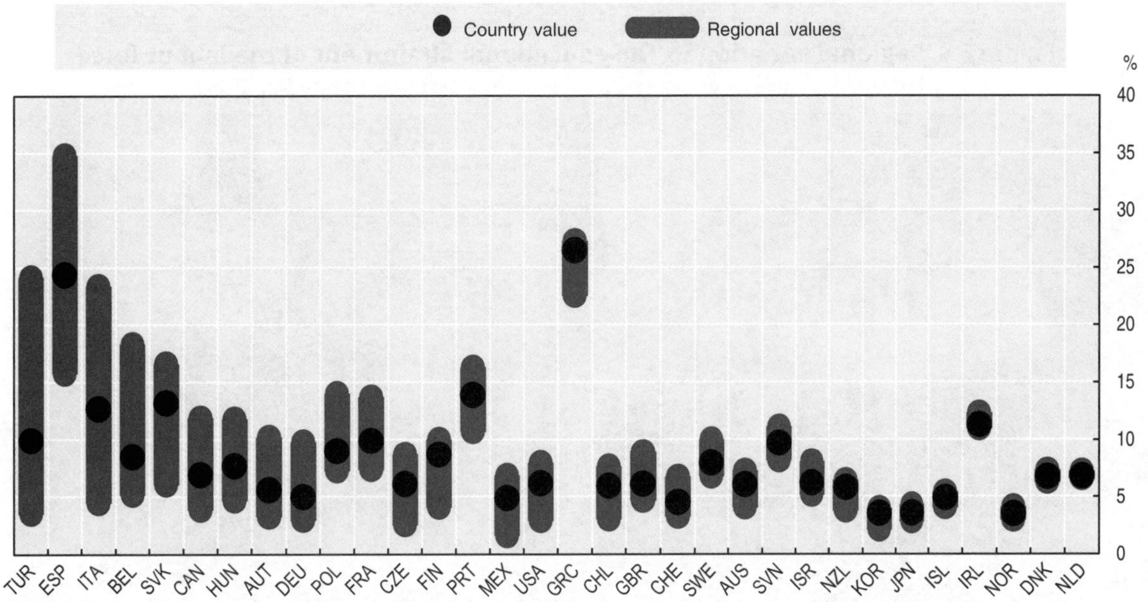

Note: Data refer to 2013 for Chile and Israel. Data refer to TL2 regions. Values for Canada exclude Yukon, Northwest Territories and Nunavut regions; values for Denmark exclude Åland.

Source: OECD Regional Well-Being (database), http://dx.doi.org/10.1787/region-data-en.

StatLink 🔢 http://dx.doi.org/10.1787/888933260073

Trends in unemployment across regions since the onset of the financial crisis have further amplified these differences: in 10 OECD countries, over 40% of the rise in national unemployment since 2008 was concentrated in just one region (OECD, 2013). Inter-regional differences in youth and long-term unemployment are even larger than for total unemployment, and have worsened since 2008. Spain has the highest inter-regional variation in youth unemployment rates, with a gap of 30 percentage points between the best and worst-performing regions. Andalusia and Catalonia alone accounted for over 40% of the increase in the number of unemployed youth in Spain over the period 2007-2012.

Large spatial disparities in educational outcomes

Among the non-material dimensions of well-being, education is especially important because of its relationship with many other outcomes, such as household income, employment, civic engagement and health. In the OECD regional well-being framework, educational outcomes are measured by the share of the workforce with at least an upper secondary education, an indicator that can be interpreted as a measure of regional skills endowments. Ideally, this measure should be complemented with outcome indicators that assess the competency of students or adults, as measured through the PISA and PIAAC OECD surveys: however, these data are currently available for only a small subset of OECD regions.

Regional differences in educational outcomes are as large as for the other well-being measures reviewed above. In 2013, in some regions in Spain, Portugal, Mexico and Turkey, less than half of the labour force had completed upper secondary education, while in regions in East European countries around 80% or more of the labour force had completed upper secondary education. In North American regions, the share of the labour force with at least an upper secondary education decreases as one moves from the "central" regions to more "peripheral areas" (Figure 6.8).

Figure 6.8. **Regional variation in the educational attainment of the labour force**

Percentage of the labour force with at least upper secondary education; 2013

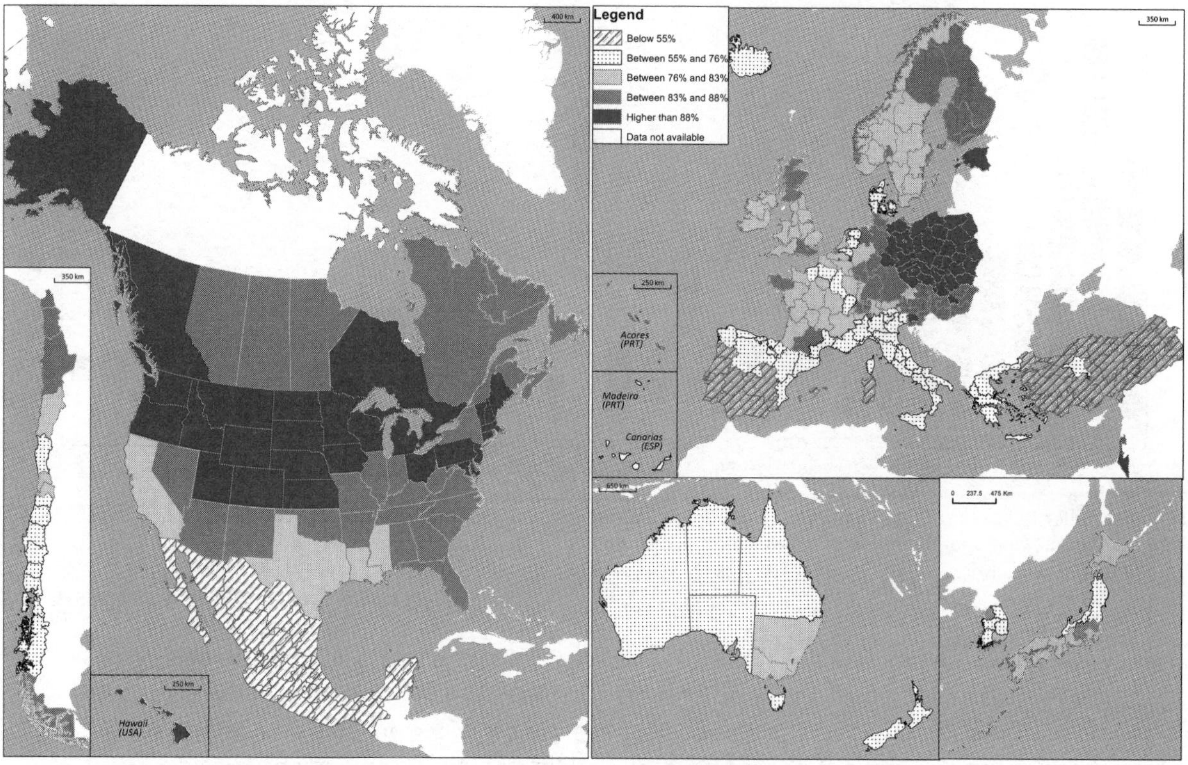

Note: This document and any map included herein are for illustrative purposes and without prejudice to the status of or sovereignty over any territory, to the delimitation of international frontiers and boundaries and to the name of any territory, city or area. Source of administrative boundaries: National Statistical Offices and FAO Global Administrative Unit Layers (GAUL).

Source: OECD *Regional Well-being* (database), *http://dx.doi.org/10.1787/region-data-en.*

StatLink 🔗 *http://dx.doi.org/10.1787/888933260086*

Air pollution exceeds recommended thresholds in half of OECD regions

Exposure to air pollution, and its causes, vary greatly depending on whether people live in cities or in rural areas, and in developed or in less developed countries. Besides being a public health concern, environmental quality is also an important determinant of individual well-being, life satisfaction and the choice of where to live (White et al., 2013; Ferreira, 2013). To provide consistent measures of the magnitude and spatial distribution of air pollution across and within countries, the OECD has developed a methodology that combines satellite data with the geographic information system (Box 6.3; Brezzi and Sanchez-Serra, 2014). This methodology allows measuring the average exposure of the population in each region to the concentration of fine particles in the air ($PM_{2.5}$).

Based on this measure, average exposure to air pollution ($PM_{2.5}$ levels) decreased in 31 out of 34 OECD countries between 2002 and 2011, with only the exceptions of Israel, New Zealand and Turkey. These estimates show wide variation in $PM_{2.5}$ exposure across regions, with the highest exposure recorded in Mexico, Italy, Chile and Turkey. According to 2011 estimates, in 58% of the OECD regions (accounting for 64% of the total OECD population), levels of air pollution were higher than the World Health Organisation's recommended maximum of 10 µg/m³. Very high values are found in some regions in Korea, Turkey, Mexico, Italy and Israel, as well as in China and India. For example, Chile shows a national average exposure to $PM_{2.5}$ of 6.4 µg/m³, which is comparatively low; however, in four out of fifteen regions, air pollution levels are higher than the recommended value of 10 µg/m³ (Figure 6.9).

Figure 6.9. **Regional disparities in average exposure to air pollution**

Regions with the lowest and highest exposure to $PM_{2.5}$ levels, 2011

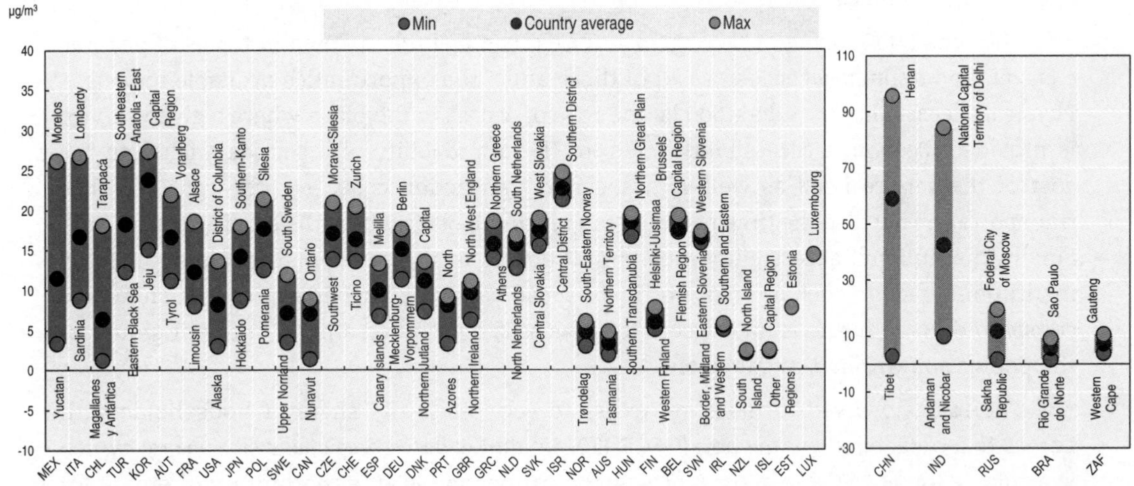

Note: Data refer to three-year average measures (2010-2012). The values provide the average level of air pollution in each region. The regional average is obtained by weighting the observed levels of $PM_{2.5}$ by the population in a 1 km² grid and summing the values within each region.

Source: OECD *Regional Well-being* (database), *http://dx.doi.org/10.1787/region-data-en.* Calculations based on Van Donkelaar et al. (2015).

StatLink ᴹˢᴸ *http://dx.doi.org/10.1787/888933260091*

Because of the geographical concentration of people, economic activities and emissions from different sources, cities usually record higher air pollution than the rest of the country. However, cities' differing characteristics (such as climate, altitude, density of population, geographical extension, transport network, economic activities, etc.) and local efforts to reduce air pollution (through regulations and policy on transport, energy and economic activities) lead to large differences in air quality across cities in the same country. For example, the average exposure to $PM_{2.5}$ in Cuernavaca (Mexico), Milan (Italy) and Kurnamoto (Japan) is three times higher than in other cities in the same country, while all the cities in Canada, Finland, Chile, Estonia, Norway and Ireland have relatively low levels of air pollution (Brezzi and Sanchez-Serra, 2014).

Currently, no environmental outcomes other than air pollution can be computed at sub-national level with a harmonised international method. Broadening the available environmental indicators is a priority for many OECD countries.

Access to services differs widely across space

Even within the same region, access to services can be remarkably different depending on the specific place where individuals live. The *access to services* dimension of the OECD regional well-being framework refers to the provision of both basic services (e.g. public utilities and health services) that contribute to a decent standard of living in terms of material conditions as well as services that improve the quality of life such as education, cultural and natural amenities, information and communication technologies, transport, etc. Better access to transport, including a broad choice of transportation modes, for example, helps individuals to reach places of employment and leisure, and to reduce their commuting time. As access to services varies depending on local conditions, this dimension has been added to the OECD regional well-being framework, even if it may be considered more as a driver of different aspects of individual well-being rather than a specific dimension *per se*.

The broad dimension of "access to services" can be broken down in terms of *physical*, *economic* and *institutional* access, as all of these affect the opportunities available to people. Physical accessibility is understood as the ease of access to the place where a given service is provided. Economic accessibility refers to the affordability of a service, including the cost of the service itself as well as associated transaction costs (e.g. the cost of public transportation but also the time necessary to reach the place where the service is provided). Finally, institutional accessibility means that access to the service is not constrained by institutional factors such as laws, norms or social values. A further aspect that should be considered in the future is how access to services is distributed among different groups of the population within a given region.

The indicator used to measure access to services is the share of households with access to a broadband connection (OECD (2014a) and *www.oecdregionalwellbeing.org*), which is available for all OECD regions. A broadband connection is an important requirement for having access to information and to other services that shape people's quality of life. While access to a broadband connection has been improving rapidly in all OECD countries, a rural-urban divide can still be seen in many of them, in particular when measured at a small geographical scale (OECD, 2014a). The indicator currently available captures the physical dimension of access to services, but it does not provide information on the actual use of broadband, e.g. on the share of households who have signed up to a broadband provider, or the quality of the services provided. Future efforts will be devoted to capturing the economic and institutional aspects of this indicator.

Access to health services varies between urban and rural areas

The OECD regional well-being framework measures regional inequalities in access to health services through two indicators that are available for a subsample of countries; both indicators capture aspects of physical, economic and institutional access to services.

The spatial distribution of physical resources like hospitals, clinics and primary care physicians influences physical access to health services. The OECD report *How's Life in Your Region?* provides evidence on the accessibility of hospitals in OECD TL3 regions in Germany, France and the United States. The indicator measures the distance to the closest hospital weighted by the population located in each square kilometre of the regional territory. This measure shows that, on average, regions with higher population density have greater physical access to a hospital (OECD, 2014a).

A second indicator relates to the characteristics of the population demanding the health service. The indicator measures the share of individuals who report one or more occasions when they needed medical treatment or an examination but failed to receive it. The indicator is collected through household surveys in which respondents indicate a list of reasons for foregoing a medical examination or treatment, such as cost, waiting lists, fear of doctors or transportation problems. Because of data sampling, the regional values cannot discriminate between the causes of foregoing a medical exam; however, the indicator can be viewed as a proxy for difficulty in accessing health services due to economic or other barriers.

Only a few national household surveys collect this type of information in ways that can be analysed at the regional level, due to small sample sizes. Moreover, the measure that is currently available has a limited capacity to discriminate between the causes (e.g. economic, knowledge, cultural, etc.) for not seeing a doctor (Koolman, 2007; Allin and Masseria, 2009). For those countries where data are available, a first descriptive analysis shows that regional differences in unmet medical needs differ significantly within countries, with Chile, Mexico and Italy displaying the largest gap between the best and worst performing regions (Figure 6.10). Empirical analysis based on regional data for six countries finds significant regional differences in unmet medical needs even after controlling for individual characteristics (Brezzi and Luongo, forthcoming *OECD Regional Development Working Paper*).

Figure 6.10. **Regional variations in the share of people reporting unmet medical needs**

2012

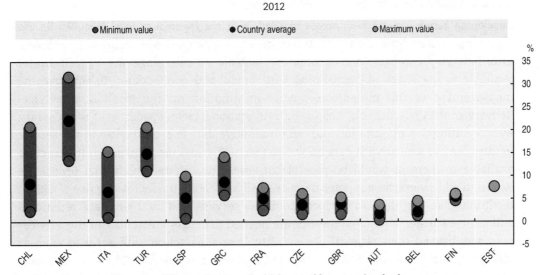

Note: Regions are ranked according to the difference between the highest and lowest regional value.

Source: OECD (2014a), *How's Life in Your Region?*, OECD Publishing, Paris, *http://dx.doi.org/10.1787/9789264217416-en*.

StatLink ᔥᔥᔥ *http://dx.doi.org/10.1787/888933260102*

The statistical agenda ahead for measuring regional well-being

Compared with other measurement exercises conducted at the national level, a regional or sub-national approach to measuring people's well-being confronts the challenge of finding reliable and comparable statistics to produce indicators at the desired spatial scale. Survey-based information for producing well-being indicators is often not available at the regional or local level, since surveys are usually designed to provide information that is population representative only at the national level. While there is scope for changing survey practices so that more information becomes available for the larger regions (ranging from changes in sample structure that give more weight to the smaller regions, to using multi-year averages and releasing those survey details that are necessary to compute standard errors), the future of the measurement of well-being at the sub-national and local levels rests largely on the possibility of mobilising a wide range of data sources and methods beyond those available through official statistics. These include greater reliance on administrative data and the use of other sources (e.g. big data to provide information on differences in rental costs across localities), including more extensive use of geographic information systems (GIS), together with the integration of these different sources. The design of specific surveys and the use of innovative tools such as small-area estimations techniques are also important areas for future research.

In light of the challenges faced when measuring regional well-being and of the budgetary pressures on statistical offices, it is paramount to set priorities in filling data gaps and to make the results more policy relevant. Five priorities can be stressed:

● *Updating more regularly the current set of OECD well-being indicators for large regions, and expanding the set to include additional well-being dimensions.* The set of well-being indicators identified in Table 6.2 for the OECD large regions could be updated annually with the support of National Statistical Offices, and efforts could be made to fill specific data gaps in certain countries and to develop similar indicators for non-OECD countries. The dataset should also be expanded in the future to include measures of subjective well-being[6], self-reports of people's victimisation, measures of the competency of students and adults, and measures of social connections.

● *Developing better indicators on access to services at the regional or local level.* While the access to services dimension is central to measuring people's well-being at local levels, internationally comparable measures are lacking. At this stage the only indicator available is the share of households with broadband connections. To improve the measurement of this dimension, spatial information on the location of service-delivery centres (e.g. schools, hospitals, train stations, green spaces, etc.) is necessary. By integrating this information with administrative data (e.g. on the use of the service in question), as well as with data on where people live and the transport infrastructure available to them, it would be possible to assess (at different territorial levels) the extent to which services are potentially accessible. Despite the increasing use of GIS for territorial planning, data on the location of key services and on their characteristics is still scarce. Further, additional metrics are needed to assess the quality of the services provided, beyond their physical accessibility. User satisfaction with services such as transport, healthcare and childcare would be particularly relevant. These are typically provided locally, with substantial differences in quality across space. While information on service availability and quality may be found in a variety of sources (administrative data, consumer-satisfaction surveys, etc.), common guidelines on how to produce and treat these data are necessary.

● *Advancing the measurement of well-being at more detailed geographical levels.* Much of the demand for better well-being metrics currently comes from city and municipal governments and communities. The OECD *Metropolitan Database*, which includes indicators on 275 metropolitan areas that have at least 500 000 inhabitants, offers a basis for the measurement of socio-economic conditions that could be extended to well-being indicators. At this spatial level, however, statistical information is particularly scarce since, unlike TL2 regions, metropolitan areas do not necessarily correspond to administrative regions, and much of the data produced by National Statistical Offices are not usable at such a scale. Identifying new data production methods and sources of information for these geographies is a necessary step.

● *Applying consistent definitions of urban and rural areas across all statistical sources*. A rural-urban divide exists for many well-being dimensions (education, access to services, health, etc.) in both developing countries and some OECD countries (OECD, 2011b). Even when it is not possible to provide credible data for various geographical units, a minimum requirement should be that all household surveys used to compile different types of well-being indicators (e.g. labour force surveys, general household surveys, victimisation surveys, etc.) apply consistent definitions in classifying whether respondents reside in rural or urban areas. Such consistent classifications would also contribute to monitoring the UN Sustainable Development Goals, which will include separate goals for cities and rural areas. In this respect, the OECD/EU definition of rural and urban regions could provide a base for such an international effort.

● *Measuring well-being inequalities within regions*. The evidence reviewed in this chapter shows that differences in well-being are important both across and within regions. The first data collection conducted by the OECD on income inequality and poverty at the regional level should be continued with regular updates in the future, and extended to other OECD countries. Steps should also be taken to estimate price levels across regions, so as to allow comparisons that reflect the purchasing power of people living in different places. Individual-level inequality measures across regions are also important for other aspects of well-being, such as household wealth or skills and competences, and steps should be taken to provide credible regional statistics in these fields. Such information, when based on the same definitions and data sources as the national level, would allow decomposing national measures into within- and across-region components, thereby providing critical insights on the relative importance of individual and area level characteristics.

The ultimate aim of improving the statistical information to measure well-being is to support countries' efforts to inform and shape the policy debate. To do this, many regions and cities have launched well-being initiatives aimed at improving the effectiveness and coherence of policies for regional competitiveness and quality of life. The OECD report *How's Life in Your Region?* (2014a) provides seven case studies to analyse how regional well-being indicators are actually used in policy making (Box 6.4). Three elements are common to the regional initiatives analysed. First, well-being metrics should be adapted to the local context, for example, by increasing the number of indicators and their accuracy, with linkages to indicators that measure policy outcomes. Second, the measurement should be connected with policy dialogues, identifying all the relevant stakeholders as well as possible regulatory and policy actions to coordinate policy making across sectors and among different levels of government. Finally, citizens should be encouraged to adapt well-being measurements to their needs. An open dialogue and the use of data are necessary conditions for mobilising citizens from the very outset.

Box 6.4. **Regional initiatives to use well-being indicators in policy making**

The OECD report *How's Life in Your Region?: Measuring Regional and Local Well-being for Policy Making* provides seven in-depth case studies on different methodological and political solutions for using well-being metrics in policy making. The different case studies provide good examples of how indicators can be used in different phases of the policy making process, such selecting regional well-being outcome indicators, monitoring progress in people's circumstances over time, and implementing a process of multi-stakeholder engagement to promote social change.

In the case of Rome, Italy, a comprehensive consultation process was used to prioritise the dimensions of well-being that matter most to citizens, through community surveys, a web tool, public meetings, workshops, etc. The region of Sardinia, Italy made concrete improvements in public service delivery (e.g. the amount of urban waste landfilled was halved and the share of recycled urban waste raised from 27% to 48% over five years) as a result of the effective engagement of public institutions, the private sector and civil society around clear and measurable well-being objectives. With its "Good Life" initiative, Southern Denmark included a comprehensive set of regional well-being indicators in its Regional Development Plan, combining objective and perception-based indicators to monitor social progress in the region. The North of the Netherlands developed a sophisticated set of regional well-being indicators by involving various stakeholders, such as the academic community (e.g. University of Groningen). Newcastle, UK is a good example of a city that built on national requirements (to establish local health and well-being boards per the 2012 Health and Social Care Act) in order to develop a wide-ranging local well-being strategy. The state of Morelos, Mexico designed its state development plan around a set of clear baselines and targets in different dimensions of well-being over a pre-determined time frame (corresponding to the state government mandate). Finally, the US Partnership for Sustainable Communities is a national initiative for jurisdictions of all sizes. It aims to align federal policies and funding in order to improve access to affordable housing, provide more transport options and reduce transport costs, and protect the environment. The initiative takes stock of existing indicators – identified with the help of focus groups and governmental agencies – and provides guidelines to local policy makers on their use.

Source: OECD (2014a), *How's Life in Your Region? Measuring Regional and Local Well-being for Policy Making*, OECD Publishing, Paris, *http://dx.doi.org/10.1787/9789264217416-en*.

Notes

1. Data on per capita income come from countries' regional household accounts, with the exception of Mexico, Turkey and Switzerland, for which the values are computed from national household surveys. Disposable income by region is collected in the current national currency and transformed into constant USD and constant Purchasing Power Parity (PPPs), for the reference year 2005. The transformation was done through the implicit price deflator of final consumption expenditure of households at national level. Disposable income values by region are then divided by the regional population to obtain income per capita. The disposable income at regional level derived from the regional household accounts has the advantage over household survey data of being generally available on a yearly basis.

2. The Pearson coefficients are 0.9 and 0.8, respectively, when all countries are considered and they maintain their statistical significance when the three countries are dropped.

3. For details, see *http://go.worldbank.org/OPQO6VS750* (accessed 29 May 2015).

4. The estimates reported in Piacentini (2014) are based on similar definitions and data sources as those underlying the national estimates released annually by the OECD in its Income Distribution Database. Regional estimates, which are available for 28 OECD countries for the year 2010, are based on the concept of equivalised household income (both market income,

i.e. income before taxes and transfers; and disposable income, i.e. income after taxes and transfers) expressed in nominal terms, i.e. they do not account for differences in price levels across regions.

5. The definition in the OECD Regional Well-being Database of disposable income used in poverty estimates may differ slightly from that used by Eurostat.

6. For example, since April 2011, the UK Office for National Statistics (ONS) has included a set of subjective well-being questions in its Annual Population Survey, which collects responses from around 165 000 individuals aged 16 and over every year, based on a set of four questions capturing respondent's life satisfaction, feelings about happiness and anxiety, and the extent to which they feel that the things they do in their lives are worthwhile. The ONS reports estimates for each of these four aspects of subjective well-being at the local authority and county level, at the regional (NUTS 1) level, and for England, Northern Ireland, Scotland and Wales. An interactive map enabling users to explore the results at the local authority level is available at: *www.neighbourhood.statistics.gov.uk/ HTMLDocs/dvc124/wrapper.html* (accessed 29 May 2015).

References

Allin, S. and C. Masseria (2009), "Unmet need as an indicator of health care access", *Eurohealth*, Vol. 15, No. 3, pp. 7-9.

Australian Bureau of Statistics (2011), "Socio-Economic Indexes for Areas", ABS, Canberra. *www.abs.gov. au/websitedbs/censushome.nsf/home/seifa* (accessed 29 May 2015).

Brezzi M., and P. Luongo (forthcoming), "Regional disparities in unmet medical needs: a multilevel analysis in selected OECD countries", *OECD Regional Development Working Papers*, OECD Publishing.

Brezzi, M. and D. Sanchez-Serra (2014), "Breathing the same air? Measuring air pollution in OECD cities and regions", *OECD Regional Development Working Papers*, OECD Publishing, Paris, *http://dx.doi. org/10.1787/5jxrb7rkxf21-en*.

Brezzi, M., L. Dijkstra and V. Ruiz (2011), "OECD Extended Regional Typology: The Economic Performance of Remote Rural Regions", *OECD Regional Development Working Papers*, 2011/06, OECD Publishing, Paris, *http://dx.doi.org/10.1787/5kg6z83tw7f4-en*.

Chetty, R., N. Hendren, P. Kline and E. Saez (2014), "Where is the land of opportunity? The geography of intergenerational mobility in the United States", *The Quarterly Journal of Economics* 129, No. 4, pp. 1553-1623.

Ciccone, A. (2002) "Agglomeration effects in Europe", *European Economic Review*, Vol. 46, No. 2, pp. 213-227.

Ferreira, S., A. Akay, F. Brereton, J. Cuñado, P. Martinsson, M. Moro and T.F. Ningal (2013), "Life satisfaction and air quality in Europe", *Ecological Economics*, Vol. 8(C), pp. 1-10.

Glaeser, E.L. and D.C. Mare (2001), "Cities and Skills", *Journal of Labor Economics*, Vol. 19, No. 2, pp. 316-342.

IEAG (2014), *A World That Counts: Mobilising The Data Revolution for Sustainable Development*, Independent Expert Advisory Group on a Data Revolution for Sustainable Development, United Nations Publishing.

Jolliffe, D. (2006), "Poverty, Prices, and Place: How Sensitive Is the Spatial Distribution of Poverty to Cost of Living Adjustments?", *Economic Inquiry*, Vol. 44, No. 2, pp. 296-310.

Kanbur, R. and J. Zhuang (2013), "Urbanization and inequality in Asia", *Asian Development Review*, Vol. 30, No. 1, pp. 131-147.

Koolman, X. (2007), "Unmet need for health care in Europe", in *Comparative EU statistics on income and living conditions: issues and challenges*, Proceedings of the EU-SILC Conference, Helsinki, Eurostat, pp. 181–191.

López-Calva, L.F., L. Rodriguez-Chamussy and M. Szekely (2007), "Poverty Maps and Public Policy: Lessons from Mexico", in T. Bedi, A. Coudouel and K. Simler (eds.) *More Than a Pretty Picture: Using Poverty Maps to Design Better Policies and Interventions*, World Bank, Washington, DC, Chap. 10, pp. 3–22, *http://ideas.repec.org/b/wbk/wbpubs/6800.html* (accessed 29 May 2015).

Moretti, E. (2004), "Estimating the social return to higher education: evidence from longitudinal and repeated cross-sectional data", *Journal of Econometrics*, 121, No. 1-2, pp. 175-212.

OECD (2014a), *How's Life in Your Region? Measuring regional and local well-being for policymaking*, OECD Publishing, Paris, *http://dx.doi.org/10.1787/9789264217416-en*.

OECD (2014b), *OECD Regional Outlook 2014: Regions and Cities: Where Policies and People Meet*, OECD Publishing, Paris, *http://dx.doi.org/10.1787/9789264201415-en*.

OECD (2014c), *How's Life in Your Region? Case study on the region of Southern Denmark*, OECD Publishing, Paris, *http://dx.doi.org/10.1787/9789264217416-en*.

OECD (2013), *OECD Regions at a Glance 2013*, OECD Publishing, Paris, *http://dx.doi.org/10.1787/reg_glance-2013-en*.

OECD (2012), *Redefining "Urban". A New Way to Measure Metropolitan Areas*. OECD Publishing, Paris, *http://dx.doi.org/10.1787/9789264174108-en*.

OECD (2011a), *How's Life?: Measuring Well-being*, OECD Publishing, Paris, *http://dx.doi.org/10.1787/9789264121164-en*.

OECD (2011b), *OECD Regions at a Glance 2011*, OECD Publishing, Paris, *http://dx.doi.org/10.1787/reg_glance-2011-en*.

ONS (2011), "Measure what matters. National Statistician's reflections on the national debate on measuring national well-being", Office for National Statistics Publishing, United Kingdom.

Piacentini, M. (2014), "Measuring income inequality and poverty at the regional level in OECD countries", *OECD Statistic Working Paper* 2014/03, OECD Publishing, Paris, *http://dx.doi.org/10.1787/5jxzf5khtg9t-en*.

Rice, P., A.J. Venables and E. Patacchini (2006), "Spatial determinants of productivity: Analysis for the regions of Great Britain", *Regional Science and Urban Economics*, Vol. 36, No. 6, pp. 727-752.

Rothwell, J.T. and D.S. Massey (2015), "Geographic Effects on Intergenerational Income Mobility", *Economic Geography*, Vol. 91, No. 1, pp. 83-106.

Royuela, V., P. Veneri and R. Ramos (2014), "Income inequality, urban size and economic growth in OECD regions", *OECD Regional Development Working Papers*, 2014/10, OECD Publishing, Paris, *http://dx.doi.org/10.1787/5jxrcmg88l8r-en*.

Sampson, R.J. (2008), "Moving to Inequality: Neighborhood Effects and Experiments Meet Social Structure", *American Journal of Sociology*, Vol. 114, No. 1, pp. 189-231.

Székely Pardo M., L.F. López-Calva, A. Meléndez Martínez, E.G. Rascón Ramírez and L. Rodríguez-Chamussy (2007), "Poniendo a la pobreza de ingresos y a la desigualdad en el mapa de México", *Economía Mexicana NUEVA ÉPOCA*, vol. XVI, 2.

Van Donkelaar, A., R.V. Martin, M. Brauer and B.L. Boys (2015) "Use of Satellite Observations for Long-Term Exposure Assessment of Global Concentrations of Fine Particulate Matter", *Environmental Health Perspectives*, Vol. 123, No. 2, pp. 135-143.

Wilson, W.J. (1987), *The Truly Disadvantaged: The Inner City, the Underclass, and Public Policy*, University of Chicago Press, Chicago, IL.

Wishlade, F. and D. Yuill (1997), "Measuring disparities for area designation purposes: Issues for the European Union", *Regional and Industrial Policy Research Paper*, N. 24, European Policies Research Centre.

White, M.P., I. Alcock, B.W. Wheeler and M.H. Depledge (2013), "Would you be happier living in a greener urban area? A fixed-effects analysis of panel data", *Psychological Science*, Vol. 24, No. 6, pp. 920-928.

World Bank (2014), "EU Accession Countries. Poverty Mapping of New Members in EU: Completion memo", World Bank Group, Washington, DC, *http://documents.worldbank.org/curated/en/2014/06/19764353/european-union-eu-accession-countries-poverty-mapping-new-members-eu-completion-memo* (accessed 29 May 2015).

World Bank (2015), "A Measured Approach to Ending Poverty and Boosting Shared Prosperity: Concepts, Data, and the Twin Goals", *Policy Research Report*, World Bank, Washington, DC, *http://elibrary.worldbank.org/doi/book/10.1596/978-1-4648-0361-1* (accessed 10 June 2015).

Database references

Eurostat (2013), "European Union Statistics on Income and Living Conditions (EU-SILC)", European Commission, Brussels, *http://ec.europa.eu/eurostat/web/income-and-living-conditions/overview* (last accessed 26 June 2015).

OECD Regional Statistics (database), *http://dx.doi.org/10.1787/region-data-en* (last accessed on 26 June 2015).

"Regional well-being", *OECD Regional Statistics* (database), *http://dx.doi.org/10.1787/data-00707-en* (last accessed on 11 June 2015).

"Metropolitan areas", *OECD Regional Statistics* (database), *http://dx.doi.org/10.1787/data-00531-en* (last accessed on 26 June 2015).

ORGANISATION FOR ECONOMIC CO-OPERATION AND DEVELOPMENT

The OECD is a unique forum where governments work together to address the economic, social and environmental challenges of globalisation. The OECD is also at the forefront of efforts to understand and to help governments respond to new developments and concerns, such as corporate governance, the information economy and the challenges of an ageing population. The Organisation provides a setting where governments can compare policy experiences, seek answers to common problems, identify good practice and work to co-ordinate domestic and international policies.

The OECD member countries are: Australia, Austria, Belgium, Canada, Chile, the Czech Republic, Denmark, Finland, France, Germany, Greece, Hungary, Iceland, Ireland, Israel, Italy, Japan, Korea, Luxembourg, Mexico, the Netherlands, New Zealand, Norway, Poland, Portugal, the Slovak Republic, Slovenia, Spain, Sweden, Switzerland, Turkey, the United Kingdom and the United States. The European Commission takes part in the work of the OECD.

OECD Publishing disseminates widely the results of the Organisation's statistics gathering and research on economic, social and environmental issues, as well as the conventions, guidelines and standards agreed by its members.

OECD PUBLISHING, 2, rue André-Pascal, 75775 PARIS CEDEX 16
(30 2014 02 1 P1) ISBN 978-92-64-21101-8 – 2015-02